AMERICANISM

Jürgen Gebhardt

AMERICANISM

Revolutionary Order and
Societal Self-Interpretation in the
American Republic

Translated by Ruth Hein

Louisiana State University Press

Baton Rouge and London

First printing

02 01 00 99 98 97 96 95 94 93   5 4 3 2 1

Designer: Barbara Werden
Typeface: Linotron Sabon
Typesetter: G&S Typesetters, Inc.
Printer and binder: Thomson-Shore, Inc.

Library of Congress Cataloging-in-Publication Data

Gebhardt, Jürgen.
  [Krise des Amerikanismus. English]
  Americanism : revolutionary order and societal self-interpretation
in the American Republic / Jürgen Gebhardt ; translated by Ruth
Hein.
    p.   cm.
  Translation of: Die Krise des Amerikanismus.
  Includes bibliographical references (p.   ) and index.
  ISBN 0-8071-1514-2 (alk. paper)
  1. Political science—United States—History.   2. Democracy—
United States—History.   3. Individualism—United States—History.
4. United States—Politics and government.   I. Title.
JA84.U5G3513   1992
320.5'12'0973—dc20   92-14094
                                                        CIP

Grateful acknowledgment is offered to the Earhart Foundation and to the Foundation for Faith in Search of Understanding for support provided at various stages in the preparation of this book for publication.

Contents

CONTENTS

Preface to the American Edition

In this study of Americanism, an outside observer attempts to make a historical and theoretical analysis of the symbolic form of order of the American republic.

The study was born during the "fourth Great Awakening and Revival" (McLoughlin) in the 1960s and 1970s, which once again were the result of a critical disjunction in American self-understanding. Many factors support the view not only that the interplay between "creedal passion" and "creedal apathy" (Huntington), which is characteristic of Americanism, still applies today, but also that it proves the vitality of the American creed. However, in view of the enormous demographic shifts and the far-reaching sociocultural structural changes connected to them, the question arises whether, in the long run, the symbolic world of Americanism is approaching an erosion that cannot be stopped any longer by the revitalizing effect of a new political and cultural revival alone.

Academic discourse in American historiography has produced an abundance of new data and insight since the German edition of this book was published. This new knowledge has introduced the quest for new interpretative frameworks and comprehensive syntheses, *i.e.*, taking into consideration the aspects of my specific question, in the original text. These recent findings were consulted for the sections on the Federalist Papers, which were not included in the German edition. Portions of the text new to the American edition were translated by Mrs. Virginia A. Schildhauer.

The American edition was shortened by several overly theoretical digressions. This does not, however, affect the theoretical intentions of the study. Since it is an empirical study of the historical and social phenomena of order, it follows, in terms of theory and method, a philosophy of politics, whose principles were described by Eric Voegelin: "A philosophy of politics is empirical in the pregnant sense of an investigation of experiences which penetrate the whole realm of ordered human existence. It requires . . . rigorous reciprocating examination of concrete phenomena of order and analysis of the consciousness, by which means alone the human order in society and history becomes understandable."

Preface to the
First Edition

The American Revolution brought to the stage of history a new and vital power: the young American Republic. This revolution created the political, social, and intellectual conditions that continue to govern the lives of Americans.

The revolutionary emergence of the American Republic created the social field for a specific form of consciousness and symbolism. The consciousness of order maintained by the Founding Fathers manifested itself in American society. The revolutionary aim of the *novus ordo seclorum*—the "new order of the ages"—is permanently enshrined in the Great Seal of the United States. Thus, historically, the act of founding proved to be the establishment of meaning: the political and economic institutions, the social behavior patterns, and their underlying psychological structures are felt by the citizens to be imbued with meaning. That same self-understanding of American society—traditionally consisting of the unbroken continuity of the world of conscousness and the symbolic world of its founders—is today more than ever called into question. The disintegration of the historical world of ideas under the pressures of an altered horizon of experience threatens the existence of the overall social order, since such decay would deprive the individual citizen of his status as *homo Americanus*.

The focal point of the present investigation is the relationship between founding and order in the self-understanding of the founders of the

American Republic. This focus leads us to the core of the symbolic self-interpretation of American society. John Adams, one of the Founding Fathers, marks the beginning of this analysis of the individuality and politics of the founders. We will investigate the occasion for and substance of all the experiences that became socially effective on the level of consciousness and power and ultimately shaped his self-awareness. In the course of our analysis it becomes clear that from the sociohistorical aspect, Adams' exemplary design for order grew out of the New England world of experience and came to represent the new Republic during the revolutionary process. Special emphasis must also be given to the analysis of the specific form of revolutionary consciousness in America, molded as it was by spiritual-political revivalism.

At the same time it proved necessary to place the problem of founding and order in the larger context of the spiritual-political evolution of the West. Furthermore, an attempt is made to develop a theory to account for the establishment of order in the act of founding a political society.

A subsequent chapter is devoted to a historical description of the process by which the design for living envisaged by the Founding Fathers—expressed in the concept of the "paradigmatic republic"—found its social field in the new society. The founders' experiences of order informed the Americans as they developed their particular patterns of political and economic institutions. Very soon this world of consciousness and symbol produced a form of American civil theology, which appeared with the claim of truth and was soon identified by the concept of Americanism. This Americanism functioned as the instrument of the national consensus and at the same time raised a universal claim: God, the world, humanity, society, and history all existed within the cosmos of American observances.

The American Civil War set off the first tremors in this symbolic universe. But in Abraham Lincoln, American society was granted a symbolic renewal of the "paradigmatic republic." It was thus possible for the nation's symbolic world to exercise its social function within the society well into the twentieth century, as will be amply documented.

The crisis of Americanism in the twentieth century is rooted in spiritual-political individualism—a threat to the American order recognized even by de Tocqueville—and in the consequences of modern industrialism. But it was precisely at this point that the integrative power of the nation's mental frame and symbolic self-expression was to prove itself; the Progressive Era and the New Deal were able to bring about a balance, though a precarious one, between the imperatives of an industrial society and the spiritual-political ethos of the Republic. Evidence for this statement will be offered through an analysis of American self-criticism, which shuttles between affirmation of the status quo and a search for lost traditions. In conclusion we will consider the contradictions of the American situation in which the political culture of Americanism continues to dominate while the attempt to break out of the American cosmos once more occurs in the form of spiritual-political revivalism.

AMERICANISM

One

Founding and Social Order

I. The Self-Understanding of a Founding Father: John Adams

"They called me venerable Father of New England, I resented that, because if there was any pretence for calling me Father of New England, there was equal pretence for calling me Father of Kentucky and Tennessee. I was therefore willing to be thought the Father of the Nation."[1] These self-confident words were written on May 24, 1809, by John Adams, a central figure in the creation of a new political society: the republic of the United States of America. From 1765 to 1801 he served it as publicist, statesman, and diplomat. "Father of the Nation" seemed to Adams the appropriate symbol to denote his role in the historical process that resulted in the American nation. This symbol expressed the self-assurance of a man determined to have all his public deeds understood as active participation in the ordering work of founding the *novus ordo seclorum*. "I must," he wrote his wife from Paris in 1780, "study politics and war that my sons may have liberty to study mathematics and philosophy. My sons ought to study mathematics and philosophy, geography, natural history and naval architecture, navigation, commerce and agriculture, in order to give their children a right to study painting, poetry, music, ar-

1. John Adams to William Cunningham, May 24, 1809, in *Correspondence Between the Hon. John Adams and the Late William Cunningham* (Boston, 1823), 116.

1

chitecture, statuary, tapestry, and porcelain."[2] Thus he had to deny himself occupation with the fascinating fruits of the mature culture of Old Europe because the "science of government" and the "arts of legislation, administration and negotiation" of necessity distanced him from all the other sciences and arts. Behind this concept—colored by the Enlightenment—of the civilizing process within a society stands the pathos of establishing order. Adams' understanding of the "science of government" was articulated in political action, the arts of legislation, administration, and negotiation; understood in this way, politics gives rise to a new society that subsequently passes through the corresponding stages of progressive civilization. The basic idea of the Platonic *politikos*—the statesman—underlies Adams' statement.

This conception of politics is displayed elsewhere as well. Adams' correspondence with Benjamin Rush raises the question of whether they should regret having entered politics. "I do not curse the day," writes Adams, "when I engaged in public affairs"; and he insists that he has never been a "politician."[3] He carefully distinguishes between the pejorative term *politician*—with the meaning of power-hungry intriguer, in use from the sixteenth century on—and his "public life." Adams follows this remark with a reflection on the day when he took his first step into politics, and he cites an important document from his youth. A letter of October 12, 1755, to his fellow student Nathan Webb concludes with the sentence "Be not surprised that I am turned politician." And what occasioned this turn to politics? A speculation about the *translatio imperii*: "the great seat of Empire" moved from Rome to America by way of England.[4] This "politician" is the classical *politikos*, as another passage from Adams' correspondence shows: "However, it is the Port of a great Politician to make the character of his People, to extinguish among them the Follies and Vices that he sees, and to create in them the Virtues and Abilities which he sees wanting."[5] Thus, to the end of his days Adams connected politics with the establishment of a new society; his last public act, on the eve of his death, consisted of choosing a toast for the celebra-

2. John Adams to Abigail Adams, 1780, in A. Adams, *Letters,* ed. C. F. Adams (Boston, 1841), II, 68.

3. John Adams to Benjamin Rush, May 1, 1807, in J. Adams, *Works,* ed. C. F. Adams (Boston, 1850–56), IX, 591–93.

4. John Adams to Nathan Webb, October 12, 1755, in J. Adams, *Old Family Letters: Copied from the Originals for Alexander Biddle* (Philadelphia, 1892), 35–36.

5. John Adams to Mercy Warren, January 8, 1776, *Adams-Warren Letters: Being Chiefly the Correspondence Among John Adams, Samuel Adams, and James Warren* (Boston, 1917–25), I, 202.

tion of the fiftieth anniversary of the Declaration of Independence on July 4, 1826—"Independence Forever."[6]

In this self-interpretation he consciously focused on his "public life" as a founder, insofar as he derived the meaning of his existence from his public actions. It is this interpretation of his political life that links Adams with most of the other Founding Fathers.

As early as 1778 Alexander Hamilton claimed this self-understanding for all the members of the Continental Congress: "The station of a member of C——ss, is the most illustrious and important of any I am able to conceive. He is to be regarded not only as a legislator, but as the founder of an empire. A man of virtue and ability, dignified with so precious a trust, would rejoice that fortune had given him birth at a time, and placed him in circumstances so favourable for promoting human happiness. He would esteem it not more the duty than the privilege and ornament of his office, to do good to mankind; from this commanding eminence, he would look down with contempt upon every mean or interested pursuit."[7]

The occasion for Hamilton's remark is significant; for the first time he was writing under the pen name of Publius (Publius Valerius Publicola was the savior of the Roman Republic; his biography is included in Plutarch's *Lives*) to inveigh against Samuel Chase, a delegate to the Congress from Maryland. Chase had shared with business acquaintances confidential information he had gleaned in Congress concerning the grain provisions for the French fleet; the purpose was to profit privately from the war. The *pathos* of creating order permeates the political-public existence of the founders; anyone who, in this position, allows his private life to corrupt him into espousing "selfish passion" banishes himself from this noble company. "It is time," Hamilton exhorted the evildoer, "you should cease to personate the fictitious character you have assumed, and appear what you really are—lay aside the mask of patriotism, and assert your station among the honorable tribe of speculators and projectors."[8] Hamilton unequivocally accepted the decision in favor of striving for private power and gain which, he believed, Chase had chosen; but he considered it in principle irreconcilable with the "public life" of a prospective founder.

Almost ten years later, James Madison identified himself and his fellow delegates to the Convention with the great lawgivers and founders of antiq-

---

6. G. Chinard, *Honest John Adams* (Boston, 1933), 375.

7. A. Hamilton, *Papers*, ed. H. C. Syrett and J. E. Cooke (New York, 1961ff.), I, 580–81.

8. *Ibid.*, 582.

uity—Lycurgus, Solon, and Romulus.[9] Thomas Jefferson perceived the Convention as "an assembly of demi-gods."[10] Himself he saw as founder and lawgiver of the Republic, in the learned tradition of a Francis Bacon, an Isaac Newton, or a John Locke, as Douglas Adair demonstrates by citing the epitaph Jefferson asked for: "Here was buried / Thomas Jefferson / Author of the Declaration of Independence, / Of the Statute of Virginia for Religious Freedom, / And Father of the University of Virginia."[11]

George Washington's self-understanding as a Founding Father is, according to Gerald Stourzh, brought to light by a characteristic event in the life of the first president. After he had settled at Mount Vernon, Washington sent to Europe for "busts of Alexander the Great, Charles XII of Sweden, Julius Caesar, Frederick of Prussia, Marlborough, and Prince Eugene" and gave them a place in his new home.[12]

The founders, however, derived this meaning of political life not only from the area of the *libido dominandi*. It is true that Hamilton's reference to "the love of fame, the ruling passion of the noblest minds, which would prompt a man to plan and undertake extensive and arduous enterprises for the public benefit" furnishes a key to the self-understanding of the leaders of the Revolution.[13] But without conscientious interpretation, analysis ends in a misleading psychological motivation, as happens to Adair. He notes that "Washington, Adams, Jefferson, and Madison were not entirely disinterested. The pursuit of fame, they had been taught, was a way of transforming egotism and self-aggrandizing impulses into public service." And Adair therefore concludes, "It is my argument that the lust for the psychic reward of fame, honor, glory, after 1776 becomes a key ingredient in the behavior of Washington and his great contemporaries."[14] Although not incorrect, Adair's argument falls short of the possible interpretations that Adair himself suggests in discussing the context of the founders' conceptions of fame and the idea of immortality. This view, however, provides access to the complementary component in the self-understanding of John Adams—that is, the consciousness that his function in the process of founding is in turn the expression of his experience of participating in an ordered reality greater than himself. This connection between the founders' consciousness of

9. *Federalist* No. 37.

10. Thomas Jefferson to John Adams, August 30, 1787, in *The Adams-Jefferson Letters,* ed. L. J. Cappon (Chapel Hill, N.C., 1959), I, 196.

11. D. Adair, "Fame and the Founding Fathers," in *Fame and the Founding Fathers: Essays,* ed. Trevor Colbourn (New York, 1974), 44.

12. G. Stourzh, *Alexander Hamilton and the Idea of Republican Government* (Stanford, Calif., 1970), 102.

13. *Federalist* No. 72.

14. Adair, "Fame and the Founding Fathers," 31.

order and the conscious founding of order will form the object of this study.

All his life Adams responded with anger to those numerous contemporaries who believed that his self-understanding as "Father of the Nation" and *politikos* grew out of his *amor sui* and so transformed the truth of his "public life" into the untruth of the private. He never disputed his creatural nature, but at all times he demanded a fair appraisal of his "public conduct" as a founder. "In vain will you soothe me," he confided in William Cunningham, "with the hopes of justice from posterity—from any future historian. Too many falsehoods are already transmitted to posterity that are irrevocable. Records themselves are often liars. No human being but myself can do me justice; and, I shall not be believed. All I can say will be imputed to vanity and selflove. Be it so. Job, Paul, and Tully shall be my exemplars."[15]

This passage may, of course, merely reflect the ill humor of an elder statesman, now retired from the political stage, who in the course of his career was forced to suffer many disappointments and accept many reverses. Insatiable ambition and boundless vanity were, after all, failings he had been accused of all his life. Adams knew his weaknesses in this direction, and we will bring a healthy skepticism to his protestations that *amor sui* was not what constituted his public existence. We are further aided by an *opinio communis*—one of the few in existence concerning Adams—that he was "Honest John Adams": "At all times he was himself and intensively honest . . . he was irrepressible and unguarded in his speech and writing."[16] This trait did not exactly increase his popularity, not even among his friends; that pragmatic and cunning favorite American of the Paris salons, Benjamin Franklin, rendered an evaluation of his unsociable colleague: "he . . . is always an honest man, often a wise one, but sometimes, and in some things, absolutely out of his senses."[17] His mind, both spirited and in certain ways extremely sensitive, inclined him in some respect to eccentricity; his thoughts agitated him ceaselessly and occasionally made him lose all sight of the effects of his behavior. "There have been very many times in my life," he confessed, "when I have been so agitated in my own mind as to have no consideration at all of the light in which my words, actions, and even writings, would be considered by others."[18] The preoccupations of this mind, the experiences that stimu-

15. John Adams to William Cunningham, April 24, 1809, in *Correspondence Between Adams and Cunningham,* 114.

16. Chinard, *Honest John Adams,* xi.

17. Benjamin Franklin to Robert R. Livingston, July 22, 1783, in Franklin, *Writings,* ed. A. H. Smyth (New York, 1905–1907), IX, 62.

18. John Adams to Benjamin Rush, July 23, 1806, in *Old Family Letters,* 106–107.

lated them, will be explored more fully. For Adams' reflections on political order are to a large extent an explication of his own existence—and it is precisely in this that their significance lies.

Before entering on an extensive analysis, which may still catch Adams in existential swindles, we will stay with the observation that the symbol "Father of the Nation" was Adams' attempt to construe his "public life," his actions as a founder of the Republic. Mercy Warren, a confidante and longtime family friend (though, true to her political convictions, she became a follower of Jefferson), wrote of Adams in her *History of the Rise, Progress, and Termination of the American Revolution* [19] that his enthusiasm and biases were at times stronger than his wisdom and judgment.[20] He did not deny the accusation; but he remonstrated with the author in emotional tones: "I am not conscious of having ever in my life taken one public step or performed one public act from passion or prejudice, or from any other motive than the public good." Had he done otherwise, he continued, the public affairs of his country would now be faring far worse, and John Adams' private ones far better.[21] He was, he reasoned in another letter, a mediocrity if judged on his talents. But he immediately moved on to the public sphere of his life: "I will open my whole soul to you on this subject. I have great satisfaction in believing that I have done more labor, run through more and greater dangers, and made greater sacrifices than any man among my contemporaries, living or dead, in the service of my country; and I should not hesitate to hazard all my reputation, if I did not convince the public of it too, if I should ever undertake it."[22] At the same time, however, he is capable of genuine humility: "I never could bring myself to consider that I was a great man, or of much importance or consideration in the world. The few traces that remain of me must . . . go down to posterity in much confusion and distraction, as my life has been passed."[23] Convinced of the limits imposed on all the heroes of the time by the *condicio humana*, he nevertheless always measured his own greatness against Washington's, Franklin's, and Jefferson's, with whose names on his lips he would die.

Thus he related to Francis Van der Kemp the following anecdote. To the statement that Washington was the greatest man in the world, Ed-

19. Mercy Warren, *The History of the Rise, Progress, and Termination of the American Revolution* (Boston, 1805).

20. *Ibid.*, III, 392.

21. John Adams to Mercy Warren, July 11, 1802, in "Correspondence Between John Adams and Mercy Warren," in *Collections of the Massachusetts Historical Society*, IV (1878), 322.

22. *Ibid.*, 470.

23. John Adams to Benjamin Rush, July 23, 1806, in *Old Family Letters*, 107.

mund Burke had replied, "I thought so too till I knew John Adams."[24] And Adams reminded Mrs. Warren that her brother, James Otis, leader of the colonists in the 1760s, had said even at the time "that John Adams would one day be the greatest man in North America."[25] In 1782, after Adams' successful diplomatic mission to the Netherlands, someone at the French court flattered Adams by calling him the "Washington of negotiations." Delighted, Adams noted the remark in his diary.[26] As the "Washington de la Negation," who with Franklin and John Jay concluded the Treaty of Paris with England, Adams saw to it that his diary—in which he described the negotiations from November 2 to December 13, 1782— fell into the hands of Robert R. Livingston, then United States secretary of Foreign Affairs. This "Peace Journal" was read to the Congress in March, 1783[27]; understandably, many delegates reacted with mixed feelings to the news that from now on they also had a "General Washington in politics" (in the words of Matthew Ridley[28]). Even two years later, in February, 1785, congressional delegates opposed Adams' nomination as ambassador to London by referring to the "Peace Journal," which had laid bare the weaknesses of the New Englander's character.[29] Informed of these occurrences by his compatriot Elbridge Gerry in May, 1785, Adams wrote Gerry a long letter about the "various kinds of vanity." He distinguished between a dangerous form, in which passion is the driving force of action, and the harmless sort, his own, which demands no more from the public than recognition commensurate with public achievement.[30]

This argument makes sense if we recall that Adams saw the substance of his political life not so much in his successful positions as a leader of the Revolution, diplomat, vice-president, and president. Rather, he considered it concretized in those "public acts" that were to his political disadvantage—the defense of Captain Thomas Preston, who commanded the English customhouse guards, after the Boston Massacre of 1770 and the peaceful resolution of the conflict with France in 1799. These actions were truly "public," since they were devoid of any "private" component.

Thus is revealed a further dimension of Adams' thought. His unquali-

24. John Adams to Francis Van der Kemp, July 5, 1814, in Adams Manuscripts, Historical Society of Pennsylvania, Philadelphia.

25. John Adams to Mercy Warren, July 27, 1807, in "Correspondence Between John Adams and Mercy Warren," 357.

26. Adams Papers (hereinafter cited as AP), *Diary and Autobiography*, ed. L. H. Butterfield (Cambridge, Mass., 1966), III, 50, 53.

27. See *ibid.*, 41*n*1.

28. *Ibid.*, 51*n*1.

29. *Ibid.*, 177*n*1.

30. John Adams to Elbridge Gerry, May 2, 1785, in John Adams Papers, Adams Family Microfilm (hereinafter cited as APM), Massachusetts Historical Society, Boston.

fied demand for an existential truth for himself and his life expresses an attitude that clearly sets him apart from other intellectuals and politicians of his time. Flirting with this demand, he remarked: "How is it, . . . that I, poor, ignorant I, must stand before posterity as differing from all the great men of the age? Priestley, Price, Franklin, Burke, Fox, Pitt, Mansfield, Camden, Jefferson, Madison. So it is. I shall be judged the most vain, conceited, impudent, arrogant creature in the world. I tremble when I think of it. I blush, I am ashamed."[31] And as his biographer Page Smith noted, he might have added, "convinced that I am right and they are wrong."[32] A dictum, formulated in response to Jefferson after the latter had expressed his displeasure at Adams' and Madison's policies, voices a similar conviction: "Whether you or I were right, Posterity must judge."[33]

The judgment about private "selfishness" and "public-mindedness" in the political life of the founder and lawgiver devolves, in the words of Adair, on an "audience of the wise and the good in the future—that part of posterity that can discriminate between virtue and vice—that audience that can recognize egotism transmuted gloriously into public service." However, Adair sees the motivating force exclusively in the "spur of fame." "The love of fame . . . can spur individuals to spend themselves to provide for the common defense, or to promote the general welfare, and even on occasion to establish justice in a world where justice is extremely rare."[34]

Adair worked out the specific significance of "fame," as distinct from "glory" and "honor," in English linguistic usage of the eighteenth century. Glory applies solely to God and the Elect, and honor is the guiding concept of a social code of conduct in the aristocratic society. Fame, on the other hand, "is more public, more inclusive, and looks to the largest possible human audience, horizontally in space and vertically in time." Adair goes on to say that fame is a demonic quality; "it must be won by a person who imposes his will, his ideas for good or ill, upon history in such a way that he will always be remembered."[35] In the final analysis, therefore, striving for fame means to strive for immortality. Fame as a form of immortality, Adair correctly observes, is in a tradition older than Christianity. "It is classical in its origin, and educated men of the Enlightenment were drilled and educated in it at college, not at church; from the

31. John Adams to Benjamin Rush, May 15, 1812, APM.

32. Page Smith, *John Adams* (Garden City, N.Y., 1962), II, 1102.

33. John Adams to Thomas Jefferson, May 1, 1812, in *Adams-Jefferson Letters,* ed. Cappon, II, 301.

34. Adair, "Fame and the Founding Fathers," 35.

35. *Ibid.*

Renaissance, with its 'revival' of classical values, it parallels and competes with the Christian tradition." [36]

Adair's analysis makes a considerable contribution to our understanding of the Founding Fathers, but it calls for corrective additions on three counts. First, it is too deeply imbued with the modern cult of the hero, the "event-making personality," as evidenced in the reference to a demonic quality; second, it takes its bearings too rigidly from the epigonic language of the eighteenth century, already distorted by the influence of instinctual psychology, to sufficiently emphasize the crucial position of the classical tradition in the concept of immortal fame; and third, here we are dealing with an archaic-compact understanding of the substantial creation and renewal of order through men acting paradigmatically within the medium of the political society. From this aspect in particular, undying fame had achieved a central social function in ancient Rome. The concept of fame prevailing in eighteenth-century England reflects the Roman concepts of *honos* and *gloria*.

In a persuasive examination, Ulrich Knoche works out the relevant elements of the Roman concept of fame. "Fame depends on the total citizenry's recognizing someone from among their midst as above average, as *vir magnus;* further, by giving visible expression to this recognition, the *societas* must confer on him honor and a kind of individual immortality." [37] This recognition can "descend only on such creatures . . . as are accessible to being judged by society" [38]—an army, a politically significant class, a people, but especially a single individual who, bound to the obligatory tradition of fame of the gentilitian society and the *res publica,* strives for personal fame. "These claims of a simple and clear ethic of fame lead to the demand that each perform a feat benefiting the totality of the state, a demand which increases from generation to generation. For the greater fame of the individual in each instance in turn benefits the fame of the *gens,* and thus also increases the demands made on the individual." [39]

The fame of the individual beyond his membership in *gens* and *respublica* consists of an individual immortality, not in remembrance, but in his effectiveness as a singular example shaping posterity even after his death. This sort of fame requires deeds that serve the *respublica*—extraordinary deeds in dangerous, critical situations. In the glorious deed

36. *Ibid.,* 36.
37. U. Knoche, "Der römische Ruhmesgedanke," in *Römische Wertbegriffe,* ed. H. Opperman (Darmstadt, 1967), 424.
38. *Ibid.,* 427.
39. *Ibid.,* 431.

the *virtus* of the individual unfolds in its unique political form; the ethical premise of fame resides in its link to the *salus publicus* of the *respublica*. *Virtus* here has the meaning of practical action for the welfare of the republic; according to Knoche, it requires "the ability and the willingness to perform some significant achievement for the totality of the state."[40] Not until Cicero does the deed come to transcend the republic; from that time on, what is done for fellow citizens and the fatherland is also done for all humanity. But in principle the striving for fame is limited by the laws and the *salus publicus*. The citizen attains fame in the exemplary actualization of the purported potential of order, not in recklessly exploiting demonic qualities in ways revealed by individual psychology. The *nimia cupiditatis gloriae*, the running amok of private passions, is diagnosed by Cicero as a "disease and disorder of the psyche."[41]

Only with the decline and fall of the republic does fame become separated from the *salus publicus;* only then is private striving for fame granted public status—a symptomatic phenomenon of a fundamental social crisis in Rome. The classical background stresses the eminently political significance of the "love of fame" and clarifies, at least provisionally, what is actually at the heart of the arguments concerning the founders' private "selfishness" and "public-mindedness." We will return to this problem in a different context. What matters here is merely the connection of immortal fame and political order in the consciousness of the founders.

They lived according to a tradition, Hans Jonas argues, that represents the oldest and most strongly empirical concept of immortality: "survive in undying fame." It was the reward for just deeds at the same time that it was the essential spur to noble actions. "The deeds must be visible—that is, public—in order to be noted and remembered as great. The dimension of this afterlife is the very dimension in which it is acquired: the political community. Accordingly, undying fame is public honor in perpetuity, just as the community itself is perpetual human life."[42] "Without this transcendence into a potential earthly immortality, no politics, strictly speaking, no common world and no public realm, is possible."

"Public realm" and "politics," according to Hannah Arendt, constitute the common world that outlasts the coming and going of generations. "Through many ages before us—but now not anymore—men entered the public realm because they wanted something of their own or something they had in common with others to be more permanent than

40. *Ibid.*, 434.
41. *Ibid.*, 432, 439.
42. H. Jonas, *Zwischen Nichts und Ewigkeit* (Göttingen, 1963), 45.

their earthly lives." At the same time, Arendt points out that "the almost total disappearance of authentic caring about immortality" may be the most telling "testimony to the loss of the public realm in the modern age." As proof of this assertion she notes "the current classification of striving for immortality with the private vice of vanity."[43]

It was precisely the accusation of vanity that wounded Adams so deeply, for the public-political sphere was the very arena he and the generation of his friends defended against a modern-privatist world of the passions. To its Founding Fathers the American Republic, seen from this aspect, resembled the *polis* of the Greeks and the *respublica* of the Romans in being "first of all their guarantee against the futility of individual life, the space protected against this futility and reserved for the relative permanence, if not immortality, of mortals."[44]

Although these remarks do not, of course, exhaust the problem of the founding of order and the Founding Fathers, they clarify an essential cause of the Founding Fathers' fear that their contemporaries and future generations would view them with suspicion. The negation of the elements of what is right and true in the life of the founders is not merely their personal affair; it also prevents their entering into the public order of the society that has been founded, which is thus deprived of its substance, its public dimension, and is threatened in perpetuity as human life—but this means nothing other than jeopardizing the meaning of the political life of the founders themselves.

This fear already foreshadows a specifically American problem: the latent dependence of the order of American society on the founders' experience of order (for which we will present extensive documentation below). The rhetoric of American leaders, from Washington's farewell address to the public statements of twentieth-century presidents, must be understood as an unvarying ritual in which, motivated by the fear of apostasy, they appeal for a renewal of the substance of order inherent in the beginnings.

A letter of 1811 from Benjamin Rush to the seventy-five-year-old Adams shows how conscious of these links the first political generation was. The time was approaching, Rush wrote, when this generation must join its forefathers. Adams, as an outstanding figure, invested with the highest honors the young Republic could bestow, would be able at his death to attract universal attention one last time. "Suppose you avail yourself . . . of the sensibility which awaits the public mind to your character soon after your death by leaving behind you a posthumous address

43. H. Arendt, *The Human Condition* (Chicago, 1950), 55–56.
44. *Ibid.*, 56.

to the citizens of the United States, in which shall be inculcated all those great national, social, domestic, and religious virtues which alone can make a people free, great, and happy."[45] Adams, so Rush believed, was especially qualified for this last public act *sub specie mortis,* for "you stand nearly alone in the history of our public men in never having had your *integrity* called in question or even suspected. Friends and enemies agree in believing you to be an honest man." The venerable patriots of 1776 would shed tears of gratitude and affection over such a last will and testament, "while their descendants, old and young, male and female, Federalists and Democrats, all unite in honouring and admiring their earl, their uniform, their upright, and their posthumous father and friend."[46]

Rush wanted the "Father of the Nation" to affect the social order even from beyond the grave; the founder's design for existing was to create for itself a social field in organized society. But now, because of his constant questioning of his own public existence, Adams seemed to have grown incapable of the task. "Your letter," he replied to Rush, "is the most serious and solemn one I ever received." He would gladly devote the rest of his life to the composition of such an address to his fellow citizens if only he could be certain that it would be to their advantage. But at the moment the difficulties seemed to him insurmountable, for his estimation of the "sensibility of the public mind" differed from Rush's.

Once again he would be accused of "selfishness and hypocrisy" as motives for such an act. For "I never could do anything but what was ascribed to sinister motives."[47] After these general remarks Adams dealt with the details of such an address. In his letter, Rush had indicated quite concretely what he imagined such a last will should contain. Once again it becomes clear that the subject at hand is the right order of man in society. The problems are formulated on the level of the prevailing *topoi* of the age. For Rush, religion is at the center, opening man to his *realissimum,* his ground of being. "In such a performance you may lay the foundation of national happiness *only* in religion, not by leaving it doubtful 'whether morals can exist without it,' but by asserting that without religion morals are the effects of causes as purely physical as pleasant breezes and fruitful seasons." Necessary to this aspect, Rush explained,

45. Benjamin Rush to John Adams, August 20, 1811, in Rush, *Letters,* ed. L. H. Butterfield (Princeton, 1951), II, 1095. Butterfield made a valiant attempt to disentangle the syntax in this confusing sentence. "He perhaps meant: 'the keen interest with which the public will await a posthumous statement by you.'"

46. *Ibid.,* 1096.

47. John Adams to Benjamin Rush, August 28, 1811, in J. Adams, *Works,* IX, 635–36.

are "public worship and the observance of the Sabbath, with which national prosperity has always intimately [been] connected." After all, natural man is just as much "a praying and worshipping animal as he is a social or domestic animal." The institutional details, the political order ("forms of government") take second place, in Rush's view, to the *ethos* of man in society. "It may be sufficient barely to declare that the virtues recommended are indispensably necessary to the existence of a REPUBLIC, and that the vices that are opposed to them necessarily lead to anarchy, monarchy, and despotism." [48]

Agreeing, Adams replied "that religion and virtue are the only foundations, not only of republicanism and of all free government, but of social felicity under all government and in all combinations of human society." But then he goes on to explain why he is unable to follow Rush's suggestions: "But if I should inculcate this doctrine in my will, I should be charged with hypocrisy and a desire to conciliate the good will of the clergy towards my family. . . . If I should inculcate those 'national, social, domestic, and religious virtues' you recommend, I should be suspected and charged with an hypocritical, Machiavellian, Jesuitical, Pharasaical attempt to promote a national establishment of Presbyterianism in America." (Digressing, we may note here, incidentally, a latent problem of modernity. The call to return to the ordering experiences of the transcendent ground of being is misunderstood as the attempt to establish an ecclesiastical organization and a dogmatic theology.)

Similar problems apply, Adams continued, to the peripheral points Rush suggested for such a testament. Adams' opponents would perceive any advocacy of the integrity of marriage as posthumous criticism of Hamilton, whose adultery was at the time turned into a political scandal. A warning against excessive consumption of alcohol would be ridiculed as New England "cant." The same would hold true for Adams' opposition to private commercial and credit banks and to paper money—after all, Washington, Hamilton, and Franklin had voted for this form of economic organization. In the face of such legitimation, the reservations of a John Adams would seem nothing but bigotry. [49] Adams the founder would therefore have to forgo any such "posthumous sermon, exhortation, advice, address, or whatever you may call it"; the traumatic experience of injustice to which his entire political life had been subject did not allow him to attain his full stature as "Father of the Nation." "Mau-

---

48. Benjamin Rush to John Adams, August 20, 1811, in Rush, *Letters*, ed. Butterfield, II, 1096–97.
49. *Ibid.*

soleums, statues, monuments will never be erected to me. . . . Panegyrical romances will never be written, nor flattering orations spoken to transmit me to posterity in brilliant colours."[50]

Greatness can be assigned to this lament only if it is implied that future disorder will be felt to be a decline from the founders' sense of order. To that extent Adams' fear was justified: "Adams is rarely admitted, except as an afterthought, to the inmost circle with Washington, Jefferson, Franklin, Hamilton, Marshall, Lincoln, and Lee; and even when admitted he is left standing by himself, shy and perplexing, over to one side."[51] It is consistent, however, that a society whose truth is embodied in the public existence of its founders and fathers would, in moments of crisis, remember these most particularly. At the present time, therefore, "honest John Adams" is becoming reestablished in the American consciousness.

It remains to be examined whether Adams' claim to a place among future generations was based on his services in conveying the ordering substance in society or was, instead, motivated by an inherent will to immortality in Comte's sense, so that, as the price for his achievements in the act of founding, he demanded immortality in human memory. The "Father of the Nation" recorded the truth of his political life in two autobiographical essays. "They are not generally read by any party and can not be expected to be so.—I am not anxious to have them read by the present age. I wish them to be preserved to posterity, that the truth may be known without panegyrics on one hand or reproaches on the other, which I have not deserved."[52] These are Adams' words concerning the detailed documentation of his diplomatic and political activities he published in the Boston *Patriot* from April 15, 1806, to May 16, 1812. He began to write his memoirs for posterity in 1802, and in 1806 he carried them to 1780. The event that occasioned this effort, however, was Alexander Hamilton's *Letter . . . Concerning the Public Conduct and Character of John Adams, Esqu.,* that biting attack of 1800 that jeopardized Adams' career and contributed significantly to his ruin as an American statesman.

But only Adams' letters—"my Life is already written in my Letter books . . . there I shall appear as I wish with all my imperfections on my head"[53]—and his diaries—"effusions of mind" John Quincy Adams called them—provide a guide to the intellectual center of his existence

---

50. John Adams to Benjamin Rush, March 23, 1809. *Old Family Letters*, 226.

51. C. L. Rossiter, "The Legacy of John Adams," *Yale Review*, XLVI (1957), 529.

52. John Adams to Ward, August 31, 1809, in Adams Manuscripts, Chicago Historical Society.

53. John Adams to Francis Van der Kemp, April 30, 1806, in Adams Manuscripts, Historical Society of Pennsylvania.

and demonstrate his consciousness during the continuing process of self-ordering. With the same intensity with which he attempted to clarify to himself and to the nation the phenomenon of the founding and his leading role in this endeavor, Adams campaigned against rival interpretations. He was determined to prevent the influx of mythic and revelatory elements into the symbolism used to explicate the founding process.

This attitude applied especially to the Founding Fathers themselves. Very early on, he began to be aware of real and presumptive beginnings of idolatry everywhere, Washington and other leaders of the Revolution being the objects of veneration. In 1777, after the successful defense of Forts Mifflin and Mercer on the Delaware, he gratefully welcomed a resolution of the Congress to observe a day of thanksgiving, since the decision made it clear that the glory of the victory was not due to the troops and their commanders. "If it had been, idolatrie and adulation would have been unbounded. . . . Now we can allow a certain citizen to be wise, virtuous, and good, without thinking him a Deity or a saviour."[54] In the same year Adams remarked to Benjamin Rush: "I have been distressed to see some of our members disposed to idolize an image which their own hands have molten. I speak of the superstitious veneration which is paid to General Washington."[55] When, after his death, Washington was increasingly transformed into a mythical figure, Adams spoke of the "hypocritical cult" and appended the malicious observation: "divus Washington, sancte Washington, ora pro nobis!"[56] What was true for Washington was, of course, all the more true for Adams: "Do not however, I pray you, call me 'the godlike Adams,' 'the sainted Adams,' 'Our Saviour Adams,' 'Our Redeemer Adams' . . . "[57]

Alongside efforts to mythologize the founders, Adams noted, the history of the Revolution was being transformed into a "fable plot." "The essence of the whole will be that Dr. Franklin's electrical rod smote the earth and out sprung General Washington. That Franklin electrified him with his rod—and thence forward these two concluded the policy, negotiations, and war." Although the language of his parody legend of the founding is based on Newtonian physics, the form is a typical myth. But Adams understood very clearly the function of the "fable plot" as the instrument of the self-interpretation of a new national society. The Netherlands, he continued, saw in William of Orange the symbol of their revo-

54. John Adams to Abigail Adams, October 26, 1777, in AP, *Adams Family Correspondence,* ed. L. H. Butterfield (Cambridge, Mass., 1963), II, 361.
55. Quoted in J. Adams, *Letters,* ed. C. F. Adams (Boston, 1841), II, 15.
56. John Adams to Benjamin Rush, February 25, 1808, in *Old Family Letters,* 178.
57. John Adams to Waterhouse, August 16, 1812, in APM.

lution and forgot the deeds of all the other actors, since the nation now had to concentrate its veneration on a single person as "Saviour, Deliverer and Founder."[58]

In the foreword to his *Defence of the Constitutions of Government of the United States of America* (to be discussed below in detail) Adams defined his concern. The nations of antiquity were unanimously of the opinion "that Divinity alone was adequate to the important office of giving laws to men." In the American case, however, "it will never be pretended that any persons employed in that service (s. c. of the formation of American governments!) had interviews with the gods, or were in any degree under the inspirations of Heaven, more than those at work upon ships or houses, or laboring in merchandise or agriculture."[59]

Adams' position requires some clarification. For him, mythic and apocalyptic symbols lost their intellectual transparency, becoming concretized into tales of world-immanent events, in the sense of *res gestae*. Separated from the events that motivated them, rationalist critique revealed whole classes of traditional symbols to be fictive creations of the human imagination. In this fundamentalism Adams was a victim of the great intellectual crisis at the beginning of modernism. In the light of his rationalist sentiments, the symbols became untrue; they were, in short, a "fable plot."

Behind Adams stand the problems of David Hume's *Natural History of Religion* (1757). Hume retreated from the enigma and mystery of all religiousness to the calm if distant regions of a philosophy that proclaimed a Newtonian theism. Hume's investigation is an outstanding example of a broadly applied attempt to bring order to the disparate symbolic material of religious origin produced by the widening of spatial and temporal horizons. To this purpose the category of religion was transformed in the seventeenth century into a system of reified dogmas and behaviors that could be described in phenomenological terms and classified by geography and history.[60] From a preexisting universal consensus concerning an invisible, intelligent power in the world, Hume deduced two modes of religious articulation: polytheism and theism. Polytheism, or idolatry, he considers the first and oldest of human religions.[61] In principle the godhead is organized hierarchically and encompasses a multi-

---

58. John Adams to Benjamin Rush, April 4, 1790, in *Old Family Letters*, 55–56.

59. Adams, *Works*, IV, 292.

60. For this development, see W. C. Smith, *The Meaning and End of Religion* (New York, 1965), 25–50.

61. D. Hume, *Philosophical Works*, ed. T. H. Green and T. H. Grose (Aalen, 1964), IV, 310, 320.

tude of gods, demigods, and deified beings. Wherever the supreme being is not radically dissociated from the world, the religion is polytheistic. In this way are created the various *kosmoi* filled with gods, angels, nature demons, demigods, and heroes characteristic of all idolatrous nations.[62] Polytheism is rooted in a pernicious trait of human nature. It owes its existence to an interpretation of the divine analogous to the "course of human events," during which man finds himself exposed to a wealth of "unknown Causes." The sphere of human existence is defined by the passions, by disorder. This disorder is reflected in the polytheistic interpretation of the deity.[63]

Protagonists of this world of disorder are the priests, mythologues, and poets who manipulate and preserve for their own profit the "fabulous history and mythical tradition."[64] According to a "natural progress of human thought,"[65] not further specified, men arrive at faith in a supreme being "by reasoning from the frame of nature." The principles of reason and true philosophy unfold in reflection on the order of the universe, the regular and uniform "course of nature."[66] Hume conceptualized a kind of axial time of such theistic eruptions. They occur at the end of a process during which polytheistic deities gradually attain monotheistic status. But for Hume the "events of human life" constitute a polytheistic constant in human history. He speaks of the "flux and reflux of Polytheism and Theism."[67] From the apex of theism, which evolved its finest expression in the post-Reformation Christianity of Protestantism and was always espoused by only the few, a steady decline takes place to the polytheism of the *vulgus;* but this group, inextricably enmeshed in the passions and appetites of the social world, is unable to escape to the remote serenity of a Humean philosophizing aristocracy. It is a decline in the existential sense: "As the good, the great, the sublime, the ravishing are found eminently in the genuine principles of theism; it may be expected, from the analogy of nature, that the base, the absurd, the mean, the terrifying will be equally discovered in religious fictions and chimeras."[68] Such a decline—and this is what lends the essay an authentic religiopolitical tone—is said to be Roman Catholicism. Hume interprets this faith to be like any other idolatrous trend, which interposes some

62. *Ibid.*, 320, 325ff.
63. *Ibid.*, 315ff., 327–28, and *passim.*
64. *Ibid.*, 327.
65. *Ibid.*, 311.
66. *Ibid.*, 312–13, 318, 330.
67. *Ibid.*, 334ff.
68. *Ibid.*, 362.

deified authorities between men and the "Supreme Being," and sees in it the return of the tyranny of "sick men's dreams" and "playsome whimsies of monckeys in human shapes" over human existence.[69]

Such a denunciation of Roman Catholicism—which had its origins in the literature of the Reformation, though the arguments then had different motives—was empirically confirmed some years before Hume by Conyers Middleton in his *Letter from Rome* (1729). Middleton originally went to Rome to take up classical studies. But soon ancient and modern Rome, paganism and Catholicism, merged for him into the single phenomenon of idolatry. In one comparative description of pagan and Roman Catholic cults, he believed himself justified in proving Catholicism to be a variant of ancient polytheism.[70]

Of course Middleton and Hume were less interested in anti-Catholic polemics than in the general problems of religion and theology. They were writing in reaction to a petrified and spiritually diluted orthodoxy on one hand and the expansion of the horizon of human experience on the other.

The works of both had a place in the libraries of the American colonists. The new land was particularly receptive to the religiopolitical arguments offered in this literature. After all, the Anglican Church had made some modest attempts to consolidate its position in the colonies as imperial policies intensified during the 1760s; and these attempts aroused the gravest fears of Papist corruption and tyranny in America. The colonists' abhorrence of Anglicanism before and around 1776 saw at the very least the High Church party in suspicious proximity to the Papists, making it suspect of idolatry. Very much in Hume's sense, this concept stood for a *parekbasis,* a derailment, of the true religion and topically delineated a syndrome of intellectual-religious and political corruption.

Of course opinions differed on what was idolatrous. In his sermon "The United States Elevated to Glory and Honour" (1783), Ezra Stiles, president of Yale and an outstanding theologian of the Revolutionary period, named three types of spiritual order in the "civil polity." Referring to Middleton, he classified just about everything from Brahmanism through Lamaism to Catholicism as idolatrous religions. To these decadent forms Stiles added the type of deism represented by Confucius, Shaftesbury, and Matthew Tindal. Man can find the fulfillment of the "good life," however, only in the "Christian Republic" of nonidolatrous Apostolic Christianity, which is best expressed in New England Congre-

69. *Ibid.*
70. C. Middleton, *Miscellaneous Works* (2nd ed.; London, 1755), V, 91–127 and *passim.*

gationalism.[71] But Stiles, a Trinitarian, clings to the divine inspiration of the Bible; he is a Monophysite rather than an Arian. The boundaries he sets for idolatry are therefore narrower than Adams'.

Adams had read Hume and Middleton and had diligently provided them with annotations.[72] Principally he tended to accept not only the explicit elimination of mythic elements, but also the implicit rejection of revelatory symbols found in Hume and Middleton. There is no doubt that Adams' vehement attacks on "fictive," idolatrous interpretations of the founding can be understood only in the context of Hume. He considered the furthering of handed-down idolatries and the formation of new ones eminently threatening phenomena of disorder, jeopardizing the quality of the American order as well. Surely the biographical facts of his self-tormenting vanity and excessive sensitivity to his own successes and failures served to sharpen Adams' critical sense for the speculative interpretation of social processes and the people acting within them. But precisely this vanity and sensitivity were the product of his lifelong impetus to come to intellectual terms with the reality of men in society and history.

But even Adams is unable to arrive at a theory of the founding entirely free from mythic and apocalyptic elements. When he spoke of the genesis of the American Republic, he protested against all images objectified into stories of divine or supernatural intervention. He pointed out that in the Continental Congress and in the Massachusetts Constitutional Convention he had spoken with Richard Henry Lee and Benjamin Rush and Patrick Henry, with James Bowdoin, Sam Adams, and John Hancock, but never with any gods—let alone with God Himself. Thus he is also on firm ground in vehemently refuting any "Legend of the Founding Fathers," all founding myths of the traditional sort. In noting this, we must for the moment leave aside considerations of why these protests remained largely ineffective.

In his protest, however, the legislative divinity of antiquity and the divine inspiration of revelation have become merely the interpretation of an experience that has its real content in the existential tension between humanity and its *realissimum* and that creates a center of order in human consciousness. This center in turn, spreading outward into society, becomes socially effective. That is why, much as he was opposed to symbols grown obsolete, Adams had to shift to other forms of symbolization for this very situation—forms he considered legitimate. The Anglo-Saxon

71. W. J. Thornton, ed. *The Pulpit of the American Revolution* (Boston, 1860), 495–99.

72. See Swift, *Catalogue of the John Adams Library;* Z. Haraszti, *John Adams and the Prophets of Progress* (Cambridge, Mass., 1952), 291ff.

variant of modern speculations on the hero from Bacon to Smith and Hume seemed, of course, eminently suitable to this purpose, since they represented an antiapocalyptic and antimythically motivated adaptation of the classical tradition. "Of all men that distinguish themselves by memorable achievements, the first place of honor seems due to legislators and founders of states who transmit a system of laws and institutions to secure the peace, happiness, and liberty of future generations."[73]

In *Discourses on Davila,* Adams, referring to Smith, distinguishes among three kinds of fame. "Glory" applies to "Great actions of heroes and lawgivers" and "management of the Great Commands and first offices of State"; "reputation" is the attribute of any "Gentleman"; and "credit" is granted to merchants and tradesmen.[74]

II. The Work of Founding

A Defence of the Constitution of Government of the United States of America was the only attempt at a far-ranging *political theory* produced by the American Revolution. According to its principal intention, *Defence* was written as an exegesis of the founding: "As the writer was personally acquainted with most of the gentlemen in each of the states, who had the principal share in the first draughts, the following work was really written to lay before the public a specimen of that kind of reading and reasoning which produced the American constitutions."[75] Adams was anxious to display to public view the founders' contents of consciousness as institutionalized in organized society. But surely it does no injustice to our author's intention to note that his pen is informed primarily by his own experiences.

Toward the close of the Stamp Act crisis, in 1766, Adams investigated the nature of the British constitution and found himself faced with the question of defining government and its purposes. The justification he cited for avoiding a more detailed discussion of this problem is characteristic: "The public good, the salus populus is the professed end of all government, the most despotic as well as the most free. I shall enter into no examination which kind of government . . . is best calculated for this end. This is the proper inquiry of the founders of empires."[76] Adams still respected rule under the British constitution; it furnished him with the outward frame for his reflections on man and society. Paradigms of right

---

73. Hume, "Of Parties in General," in Hume, *Philosophical Works.* See also Adam Smith, "Theory of Moral Sentiments," in Smith, *Works* (Aalen, 1963).

74. J. Adams, *Works,* VI, 241.

75. *Ibid.,* IV, 293–94.

76. AP, *Diary and Autobiography,* I, 298.

order could be developed only by a founder. Adams never abandoned these correlations. When he became conscious of the disintegration of British rule in New England, Adams saw himself as the "founder of empire," for whom the quest for right order became thematic. At the same time he tried to realize himself as an actor in the power process. Let us call to mind briefly the occasion and content of the experiences that affected the levels both of consciousness and power, culminating ultimately in the founder's self-understanding.

The Massachusetts Government Act of May 20, 1774, effectively revoked the Massachusetts Charter of 1691 and, together with other parliamentary regulations, formed the so-called Coercive Acts. These, in combination with the instructions of the new governor, General Thomas Gage, established a de facto military dictatorship. On October 5, 1774, Gage dissolved the General Court; this body, calling itself Provincial Congress, rallied on October 7 in Concord as the revolutionary representative of the colony. Each of the two organizations exercised sovereign rights and organized a rudimentary government apparatus, even if the sphere of influence of the Provincial Congress considerably outshone that of Governor Gage. However, the situation was quite generally characterized by a political and constitutional stalemate. "Government is dissolved," was Patrick Henry's interpretation of the situation in the Continental Congress. He came from Virginia, where the view that the Coercive Acts were directed against all the colonies was gaining ground.

But the majority of delegates to the Continental Congress were reluctant to agree with Henry. Adams regretted this attitude: "You see by this, what they are for; namely, that you stand stock still, and live without government of law, at least for the present, and as long as you can."[77] What did he mean by "want of law and government"? What prevailed was "a total stagnation of law and commerce almost."[78] "We have no house, no council, no legislative, no courts."[79] For Adams the situation had become untenable. "I have represented them the utter impossibility of four hundred thousand people existing long without a legislature, or courts of justice."[80]

"Life without government" is Adams' formula for the experience of disorder. From the aspect of the Continental Congress, he felt compelled as late as September, 1774, to caution against the creation of a revolutionary Provincial Congress and the return to the old charter; it was questionable, he held, "whether they will ever be prevailed on to think it

77. John Adams to Tudor, September 20, 1774, in J. Adams, *Works,* IX, 347.
78. John Adams to Alexander Biddle, December 12, 1774, in J. Adams, *Works,* IX, 349.
79. John Adams to Burgh, December 28, 1774, in Adams, *Works,* IX, 351.
80. John Adams to Tudor, September 20, 1774, in Adams, *Works,* IX, 347.

necessary for you to set up another form of government."[81] Although he spoke of the great and dangerous crisis "when the British empire seems ripe for destruction,"[82] he still clung to the early modern concept, typical for the American colonies, of a relationship of loyalty to George III, agreed to in perpetuity. Only the onset of hostilities in April, 1775, altered this view.

With this the crisis of the British Empire had reached its apogee for Adams, and a new "American Empire" gradually took shape. The hour of the "Founder" was at hand. The establishment of a new political order, the search for a new political authority to legitimate this order, and finally the details of an adequate government were, in late April, the frequent object of conversations Adams carried on in Massachusetts with John Winthrop, Cooper, James Otis, the Warrens, Joseph Hawley, and his colleagues in the Continental Congress.[83]

In Massachusetts the Provincial Congress deposed Governor Gage and on May 16, 1775, formally requested the body in Philadelphia, which was no less unconstitutional, to advise them concerning the establishment of a "Civil Government, which we think absolutely necessary for the salvation of our country." They hoped for a nationwide resolution in the form of "a general plan as congress might direct for the colonies"; after all, the problem concerned all the colonies. The request therefore closed with the promise "to establish such a form of government here, as shall not only promote our advantage but the union and interest of all America."[84]

On June 2, 1775, the Congress discussed the request. For the first time Adams formulated his concept of a new American order. His diary preserves that recommendation. It was for a confederation of sovereign states, to whose populations the Congress must recommend "to call such conventions immediately and set up governments of their own under their own authority. . . . We must realize the theories of the wisest writers and invite the people to erect the whole building with their own hands upon the broadest foundations."[85] But the Congress hesitated and acted as the English Parliament had in 1688 when it declared the throne vacant after James II's flight. It recommended close adherence to the spirit and substance of the charter of 1691—that is, a modified charter government—

81. John Adams to Warren, September 25, 1774, in APM.

82. John Adams to Burgh, December 28, 1774, in Adams, Works, IX, 351.

83. AP, Diary and Autobiography, III, 351.

84. R. J. Taylor, ed., Massachusetts, Colony to Commonwealth (Chapel Hill, N.C., 1961), 6.

85. AP, Diary and Autobiography, III, 352.

and declared the offices of the governor and his deputies vacant. According to this proposal, the affairs of state were assumed in June, 1775, by the council, the lower chamber of which had been elected by the General Court according to the old charter.

In the debates over similar inquiries from New Hampshire and South Carolina in October, 1775, Adams specified his and his friends' "desire of revolutionizing all the governments"[86]: "I embraced with joy the opportunity of haranguing on the subject at large, and of urging Congress to resolve on a general recommendation to all the States to call Conventions and institute regular governments." "Here it would have been the most natural to have made a Motion that Congress should appoint a Committee to prepare a plan of government, to be reported to Congress and there discussed paragraph by paragraph, and that which should be adopted should be recommended to all the States."[87] There was to be no more talk of "Colony," "Province," and "Mother Country"; instead, the terms were to be *State* and *America*.[88] But in this effort the English Crown would need to be replaced by a source of authority to legitimate the government: the people of America. To this extent the "subject of Independence" and the "institutions of government" were "always the same thing."[89] The Congress had been elected to legislate the new order, but it had shirked this monumental duty. Therefore Adams assumed the burden. His speeches before the whole and in committee elicited one question from all sides: "What plan of government would you recommend." "These questions I answered by sporting off hand, a variety of short Sketches of plans, which might be adopted by the conventions." In the winter of 1775 to 1776, the detailed discussions resulted in "a plan as nearly resembling the governments under which we were born and have lived as the circumstances of the country will admit."[90]

This first paradigm of a republic and variants on it were captured in several letters and collected in *Thoughts on Government*. W. P. Adams interpreted the *Thoughts*—to my mind incorrectly—principally as a reaction to Thomas Paine's *Common Sense*.[91] He pointed out that the con-

---

86. *Ibid.*, III, 357. This quotation, like the ones that follow, are taken from the autobiography, which is not very reliable as far as historical details are concerned. But it reflects Adams' self-understanding without distortion, as can be documented by the letters and by statements from others who knew him during the same time.

87. *Ibid.*, 358.

88. *Ibid.*, 357.

89. *Ibid.*, 366.

90. *Ibid.*, 356, 358.

91. W. P. Adams, "Republikanismus und die ersten amerikanischen Einzelstaatsverfassungen" (Ph.D. dissertation, Berlin, 1968), 177.

cepts *republic* and *republicanism* "played no part" in the discussions at the Continental Congress.[92] For up until the colonies' break with the mother country, the concept of republicanism in the English colonies of North America also had the negative connotation of subversive and constitutionally hostile attitudes attached to it, which dated back to the liquidation of the Cromwellian Republic during the Restoration of 1660. Whereas the colonists, in their conflict with the Crown and Parliament, always viewed themselves as the actual upholders of the British Constitution, the representatives of the mother country believed to have discovered "republican" practices in the activities of the colonists. Only much later did the American colonists find their own common point of reference with regard to patterns of thought and action in the idea of the republic. Because of their conflict with the Crown and Parliament, the colonists discovered the "republican" character of their own colonial world, and they consciously took recourse to the political-intellectual tradition of the Commonwealth because it offered the critical instruments necessary for a principle-guided opposition against the ruling order of the Empire. As in the seventeenth century, the radical Protestant republicanism of "God's new chosen people" could easily be combined with the classic republicanism of civic self-government in order to achieve a concept of order suitable for the American experiential reality. By breaking off their loyalty as subjects of Her British Majesty, the alternative of 1649—the republic—was given in the logic of historical development.

W. P. Adams notes that long before 1776, a majority "concluded from the efficiency of colonial self-government that government without a king and nobles would do for them."[93] And J. R. Pole comments on the rapid adoption of the terms *republic, republican,* and *republicanism* as key concepts of the revolutionary order: "The American colonies developed the characteristics of what would later be known as 'republican form of government' many years before they were to claim to be republican in principle."[94] But what is more decisive for the self-understanding of John Adams the founder is another observation by Gordon S. Wood: "Republicanism meant more for Americans than simply the elimination of a king and the institution of an elective system. It added a moral dimension, a utopian depth, to the political separation from England—a depth that involved the very character of their society."[95]

92. *Ibid.,* 50.

93. W. P. Adams, "Republicanism in Political Rhetoric Before 1776," *Political Science Quarterly,* LXXXV (1970), 420–21.

94. See J. R. Pole, *The Seventeenth Century* (Charlottesville, Va., 1969), 69, for documentation of Adams' social relations. See also Jonathan Trumbull to John Adams, November 14, 1775, and Joseph Hawley to John Adams, December 16, 1775, in APM.

95. G. S. Wood, *The Creation of the American Republic, 1776–1787* (Chapel Hill,

John Adams conceptualized this in-depth dimension in his *Thoughts on Government*. Under this title Richard Henry Lee published a version in 1776, "to mark out a path, and put men upon thinking."[96] In Adams' letter to John Penn of North Carolina, the solemnity of the founding narrows all reality of history and society to the instantaneous point of new beginning:

> It has been the will of Heaven that we should be thrown into existence at a period when the greatest philosophers and lawgivers of antiquity would have wished to live. A period when a coincidence of circumstances without example has afforded to thirteen colonies, at once, an opportunity of beginning government anew from the foundation, and building as they chose. How few of the human race have ever had any opportunity of choosing a system of government for themselves and their children! How few have ever had any thing more of choice in government than in climate! These colonies have now their election; and it is much to be wished that it may not prove to be like a prize in the hands of a man who has no heart to improve it.[97]

Here the reflection is on historical parallels with the classical world; freed of its sociopolitical context, antiquity appears as a mythic whole that is structured entirely by a succession of order-giving philosopher-statesmen. This view becomes the common property of the American Revolution.

But Adams' letter to Penn, demonstrating the founder's self-understanding in its purest, richest form, suggests the precarious balance between a solemnity based on the awareness that a social order of one's choice is at hand and the fear that this great moment would pass unused, that the social process would once again revert to a state of nature to which mankind would finally be subject in the age-old way. Adams was only too aware that even the enthusiasm of 1776 did not allow for existential reductions to an apocalyptic zero point that by closing off consciousness from the reality, produces the violent revolutionary in the metaphysical sense. This insight is surely rooted less in speculative considerations than in the daily encounters with the American reality, the divergent views, interests, and actions on the local, state, and congressional levels. The various struggles—from the wrangles about militia commandos, to the political strivings for autarky and the jealousies of the counties and towns, to the major conflicts concerning nonexporta-

---

N.C., 1969), 47. Besides Wood, I base my argument primarily on P. Maier, "The Beginnings of American Republicanism, 1763–1776," and Greene, "The Preconditions for American Republicanism," both in *The Development of Revolutionary Mentality* (Washington, D.C., 1972), 99–124.

96. Quoted in Page Smith, *John Adams*, I, 245.

97. J. Adams, *Works*, IV, 203.

tion, nonimportation, and nonconsumption in Congress, in which the fundamentals of the American economy were at stake—furnished ample experiences to warn against the transformation of the founders' solemnity into metastatic revolutionary faith. "A mind as vast as an ocean or atmosphere is necessary to penetrate and comprehend all the intricate and complicated interests which compose the machine of the confederate colonies." The legislative impetus is safeguarded by the existential construction: "that serenity of mind and steadiness of heart which is necessary to watch the motions of friends and enemies, of the violent and the timid, the credulous and the dull, as well as the wicked. But if I can ever contribute ever so little towards preserving the principles of virtue and freedom in the world my time and life will not be ill spent. A man must have a wider expansion of genius than has fallen to my share to see to the end of these great commotions. But on such a full sea are we now afloat that we must be content to trust to winds and currents with the best skill we have under a kind Providence to land us in a port of peace, liberty and safety."[98]

In April, 1776, Franklin reported that "there is a rapid increase of the formerly small party, who were for an independent government."[99] And on May 8, 1776, Adams wrote to Warren, "We are certainly ripe here for the grand resolution."[100] On May 6 the Congress had constituted itself into a committee of the whole to discuss "the state of the United Colonies"; on May 10 it approved the following resolution: "Resolved, that it be recommended to the respective assemblies and conventions of the United Colonies . . . to adopt such government as shall, in the opinions of the representatives of the people, best conduce to the happiness and safety of their constituents in particular, and America in general." Adams seconded the resolution, which constitutionally operated under the fiction of 1688. Subsequently he saw to it that he was elected, along with Richard Henry Lee and John Rutledge, to the committee to develop a preamble to the resolution and used this opportunity to bring about, through ingenious parliamentary tactics, a *fait accompli*. That is, he wrote into the preamble a condition that had not been part of the resolution: "whereas, it appears absolutely irreconcilable to reason and good conscience for the people of these colonies now to take the oath and affirmations necessary for the support of any government under the Crown of Great Britain, and it is necessary that every kind of authority under the

---

98. John Adams to James Warren, April 20, 1776, in *Warren-Adams Letters*, I, 230ff.
99. Benjamin Franklin to Quincy, April 15, 1776; J. Adams, *Works*, IV, 12.
100. John Adams to James Warren, May 8, 1776, in APM.

said Crown should be totally suppressed, and all the powers of government exerted, under the authority of the people of these colonies." [101]

James Wilson of Pennsylvania made clear the implication of this preamble: "In this Province . . . there will be an immediate dissolution of every kind of authority. The people will be instantly in a state of nature." He argued against Congress as the legislator of the new order in the name of the "Maxim, that all government originates from the people, we are the servants of the people sent here to act under a delegated authority." [102]

But the reference to delegated authority made no impression. Adams correctly understood the resolution to be the decisive break with the old order. In his richly documented investigation of the genesis of the earliest state constitutions of the individual colonies, W. P. Adams has shown that by virtue of their authoritative nature the recommendations of the Continental Congress of May 10 and 15 had triggered the discussion and effort on behalf of a constitution throughout the colonies. [103]

I cite the details of the debate only because Wilson's objection, regardless of his specific role in the congressional debate, points out a dilemma that Adams and many others who felt as he did tacitly agreed to bury. This premise assumes a central function in Adams' self-understanding as a founder. He always took his bearings from the circumstance that he, together with the growing number of supporters of independence in Congress, acted according to a substantial solidarity with the people. This communality he considered expressed in the formal delegations to the Congress. The events of 1774 to 1776—when the expanding political participation of the New England population was converted into the spontaneous creation of extralegal political bodies—seemed to him to warrant this assumption. This new situation first enabled Adams to become a leader of superregional significance, at the same time providing his political activities with a certain revolutionary legitimation. This solid popular backing allowed him to understand his own design of a paradigmatic republic as the result of the collective strivings for a new order. The private determination of July, 1775, that "we ought immediately to . . . set up governments of our own" [104] was thus for him identical with its public version, "that Congress ought now to recommend to the people in the several colonies to . . . set up governments of their own, under their own authority." Accordingly, the individual members of society acting on behalf of the people participated in the procedure of founding, insofar as

---

101. E. C. Burnett, *The Continental Congress* (New York, 1964), 156ff.
102. AP, *Diary and Autobiography*, II, 239.
103. See Adams, "Republikanismus," 49, 51–127.
104. John Adams to James Warren, July 6, 1775, in *Warren-Adams Letters*, I, 74.

"this could be done only by conventions of representatives chosen by the people in the several colonies, in the most exact proportions."[105]

Impressed by the congruence of the popular mood and his personal political convictions, Adams identified his own consciousness of order with that of the people under whose authority the American Republic was established. This mediation, however, springs from the common experience of the unseen measure of right judgment as evidenced by the reason, virtue, and piety of the people and their representatives. In its order-legitimating function, the people were, for Adams, not simply the human substratum of a political society, but a group of human beings, for the most part existentially rightly ordered, settled not by accident in the American colonies, predominantly in New England. The social dominance of the practice of dianoetic and ethical existential virtues—praised from Adams' era until well into the 1790s as the character of American existence—safeguarded the harmonious accord of the authority of the people with the authority of the "Father of the Nation." The source of the authority, however, resides not in the realm of power politics but in the transcending sphere of "reason" and "virtue." From this it follows that Adams' self-understanding was in serious difficulties as soon as the views and demands of the popular authority were contrasted with the founder's concept of order. In the course of the political events, the authority of the people increasingly dissociated itself from that of the *pater patriae*, Adams. He, however, could understand such a situation only as a decline in the shared ethos rooted in the obligating unseen measure of a substantially right order.

This insight furnishes us with a key to Adams' attitude in the years after 1780. Certain events during the Revolutionary period foreshadowed the dilemma. In late 1775 various towns in Massachusetts expressed their alarm at the current state of the constitution and of politics under the modified charter government, with its salvational clause. The cessation of all governmental activity while a de facto state of war with Great Britain existed was metaphorically expressed: "since the Dissolution of the power of Great Britain over these Colonies they have fallen into a state of Nature."[106] The Resolves of the Stockbridge Convention of December 15, 1775, and the Petitions of Pittsfield of December 26, 1775, and May, 1776, begin with the voters' specific demand to select the local, military, judicial, and administrative officeholders through direct elections. In 1776 they further called for democratic approval of the constitution by the people. Open conflict broke out when local leaders in

---

105. AP, *Diary and Autobiography*, III, 352.
106. Taylor, ed., *Massachusetts: Colony to Commonwealth*, 27.

Berkshire and Hampshire prevented the courts staffed by the Boston government from exercising their offices.[107]

Although this concretization of popular authority on the lowest political level did not vary substantially from the content of his design for order, Adams came to believe early on that these expressions of the popular will were anarchic interference with the founding process. This attitude is shown in the Proclamation of the General Court of January 23, 1776, which he helped to write. In its introduction the proclamation established a nexus among the "happiness of the people" as the purpose of the political order, the "consent of the people" as its basis of political order and the expression of a "supreme, sovereign, absolute and uncontrollable power" ever present "in the body of the people," and the grounding of all these in "reason, morality, and the natural fitness of things."[108] This is followed by the description of the constitutional status quo, along with a defense of the present regime: "The present generation, therefore, may be congratulated on the acquisition of a form of Government more immediately, in all its branches, under the influence and control of the people, and, therefore, more free and happy than was enjoyed by their ancestors." But such a popular government must be based on qualities of "universal knowledge . . . , virtue . . . true religion, purity of manners, and integrity of life." Thus the proclamation ends by exhorting spiritual and secular leaders and the people to introduce reforms. But such action also calls for the popular government to extend "support," "assistance," and "obedience" to the General Court. Anarchic protest on the part of restless and dissatisfied county conventions is understood as a punishable disturbance of the colony's peace; "riotous and tumultous proceedings" are worked up into a catalogue of "vice and immorality"—"debauchery, profaneness, corruption, venality"—including all possible deviations from the substantial order of the people.[109]

Besides specifying the very solid political and economic interests of the ruling majority of the colonial elite in the General Court, the proclamation allows us to see Adams' ambivalent nexus between the founder's authority and the authority of the people. It is characteristic that he abjures the metaphor of the "state of nature," with its implications of an arbitrarily granted political reality. In April, 1776, he felt it necessary "to contrive some method . . . to glide insensibly, from under the old govern-

107. *Ibid.*, 16–19; E. P. Douglass, *Rebels and Democrats* (Chapel Hill, N.C., 1955), 136–61; R. E. Brown, *Middle-Class Democracy and the Revolution in Massachusetts, 1691–1780* (Ithaca, N.Y., 1955), 328–400.

108. Taylor, ed., *Massachusetts: Colony to Commonwealth*, 20; see also J. Adams, *Works*, I, 192ff.

109. *Ibid.*, 21–22.

ment, into a peaceable and contented submission to new ones." He feared that these measures would have to end in a "compleate Revolution," though "there is danger of convulsions, but I hope, not great ones."[110] He took up the principal theme of the proclamation once more: "There must be a decency, and respect, and veneration, introduced for persons in authority, of every rank, or we are undone."[111] The "persons in authority" are, of course, the founders, who form a new order under the tacit premise of the harmony of the two authorities. As soon as conflict threatened, Adams charged the divergent tendencies with the stigma of disorder: "I am grieved to hear . . . of that rage of innovation, which appears in so many wild shapes in our province. . . . Many of these projects that I heard of are not repairing the building that is on fire. They are pulling the building down, instead of laboring to extinguish the flames. The project of country assemblies, town registers, and town probates of wills, are founded in narrow, contracted notions, sordid stinginess, and profound ignorance, and tend directly to barbarism."[112]

Such deviations have clearly escaped the authority of the people. They can exercise it only in "religion, morality, . . . true virtue"—that is, existentially rightly ordered and thus in accord with the consciousness of order of the "Father of the Nation," John Adams. But such an accord still seemed to him a given, and the process of founding remained solidly in place. "I suppose you will have a Constitution this year," he wrote his wife from Philadelphia in 1777. "Who will be the Moses, the Lycurgus, the Solon? . . . Whoever they may be and what ever form may be adapted, I am persuaded there is among the Mass of our people a fund of wisdom, integrity and humanity which will preserve their happiness, in a tolerable measure."[113]

This is the clearest possible expression of the belief that the founder's knowledge of order must coincide with that of his people in the act of founding; and behind this, in turn, stands an anticipatory hope that a Moses-Adams will confer on his wise people the right order. Thus, for Adams the work on the constitution of Massachusetts became the high point and conclusion of the creation of order. This aspect, however, goes beyond this disgression on the problematic tensions between the founder's consciousness and popular authority.

110. John Adams to Mercy Warren, April 16, 1776, in *Warren-Adams Letters*, I, 223.

111. John Adams to James Warren, April 22, 1776, in *Warren-Adams Letters*, I, 234.

112. John Adams to John Winthrop, June 22, 1776, in J. Adams, *Works*, IX, 410; see also T. H. Breen, "John Adams' Fight Against Innovation in the New England Constitution, 1776," *New England Quarterly*, XL (1967), 301–20. However, Breen discusses 1776 only.

113. John Adams to Abigail Adams, June 2, 1777, in AP, *Adams Family Correspondence*, II, 253.

In the meantime, in Philadelpha, Adams—as the "Atlas of American Independence"[114]—put all his efforts into replacing the interim solution of 1688 with the decision of 1649. On June 7, 1776, Richard Henry Lee, seconded by Adams, proposed "Resolutions respecting Independence." The first stated "that these colonies are, and of right ought to be, free and independent states."[115] Adams commented, "Objects of the most stupendous magnitude, and measures in which the lives and liberties of millions yet unborn are intimately interested, are now before us. We are in the very midst of a revolution, the most complete, unexpected, and remarkable, of any in the history of nations."[116] He saw in the completion of this work the *telos* of his public existence: "When these things are once completed, I shall think I have answered the end of my creation, and sing my *nunc dimittis,* return to my farm, family, ride circuits, plead law, or judge causes."[117] To his mind, founding, public life, and fulfilling his existence were one and the same.

On June 11 a committee was formed under Jefferson's chairmanship "to prepare a declaration to the effect of the said first resolution"; committee members were Adams, Benjamin Franklin, Roger Sherman, and Robert R. Livingston. On July 2 Congress declared independence, and on July 4 it issued the formal justification for the act as formulated by Jefferson. The statement followed the accusation and judgment against Charles I. In 1776, however, the High Court of Justice of 1649 was replaced by "the opinion of mankind."[118]

"The second day of July 1776," Adams informed his wife, "will be the most memorable epocha, in the history of America. I am apt to believe that it will be celebrated, by succeeding generations, as the great anniversary festival. It ought to be commemorated, as the day of deliverance by solemn Acts of devotion to God Almighty. . . . I can see the Rays of ravishing light and glory. I can see that the end is more than worth the means. And that posterity will triumph in that day's transaction, even altho we should rue it, which I trust in God we shall not."[119]

In the midst of urgent political affairs in Congress, of warfare and the

114. So called by Richard Stockton, a delegate from New Jersey; quoted in Page Smith, *John Adams,* I, 268.

115. Burnett, *Continental Congress,* 171–72.

116. John Adams to Cushing, June 9, 1776, in J. Adams, *Works,* IX, 391.

117. *Ibid.*

118. Burnett, *Continental Congress,* 172ff; see also E. Angerman, "Ständische Rechtstraditionen in der amerikanischen Unabhängigkeitserklärung," *Historische Zeitschrift,* CC (1965), 65–91; W. Blackstone, *Commentaries on the Laws of England* (Oxford, 1770), and various works by G. Stourzh.

119. John Adams to Abigail Adams, July 3, 1776, in AP, *Adams Family Correspondence,* II, 30–31.

first tentative steps on the slippery tiles of foreign policy, the new order became consolidated as various state constitutions were enacted and the Articles of Confederation were drafted to unite the states. The founding was completed in the elevenfold experiment of the creation of order: "We live in the age of political experiments. Among many that will fail some, I hope will succeed." Adams critically measured the experiments against the design of his paradigmatic republic. "Best Pennsylvania will be divided and weakened, and rendered much less vigorous in the cause, by the wretched ideas of government which prevail, in the minds of many people in it." This prediction would come true.[120]

During Adams' first short stay in France, the jeremiads of his friends from home made him fear the increasing corruption of his countrymen. The attitude the majority of the congressional delegates displayed toward him seemed to him symptomatic; the situation eventually led to his being in Paris without office or mission, so that, as he believed, he was forced to return home deeply humiliated.[121]

But he believed that the principle of agreement between the people and the founder continued to operate: "I have hitherto had the happiness to find that my pulse beat in exact union with those of my Countrymen."[122] This faith was confirmed in 1779, after his return from Europe, when Massachusetts chose him to legislate for it. His *Thoughts on Government* were realized in a political order. Elected as a delegate from his hometown of Braintree to the constitutional convention, he was charged by the constitution committee to draft a constitution. The ensuing document was ratified by the convention with very few changes. For Adams this event was "a phenomenon in the political world that is new and singular" and an "epoch in the history of the progress of society."[123] The Massachusetts Constitution was the result of the substantial community, in the sense of *philia politike,* of their fathers: "I never spent six weeks in a manner that I shall ever reflect upon with more pleasure than with that society of wise men who composed that convention. So much caution, moderation, sagacity and integrity has not often been together in the world." The constitution "is Sidney, Locke, Rousseau and Mably reduced to practice in the first instance."[124] This last sentence is to be understood metaphorically, insofar as it explicates the infusion of rational

120. John Adams to Abigail Adams, October 4, 1776, *ibid.,* II, 137–38.

121. See also J. R. Howe, *The Changing Political Thought of John Adams* (Princeton, 1966), 108ff.

122. John Adams to James Warren, August 4, 1778, in *Warren-Adams Letters,* II, 39.

123. John Adams to Gordon, May 26, 1780, in APM.

124. John Adams to Wilson, June 24, 1780, in APM.

ordering processes into the process of power; it does not in fact accurately reflect the traditional material that has been incorporated: James Harrington, the great supplier of ideas for this constitution, is not mentioned, while Jean-Jacques Rousseau and Gabriel Bonnot de Mably left few if any marks on the document.

We have now paced off the experiential horizon under which Adams' self-understanding as a Founding Father took shape. "I had read," he summarized this process in one section of his autobiography, "Harrington, Sydney, Hobbes, Nedham and Locke, but with very little application to any particular views: till these debates in Congress, and these interrogations in public and private, turned my thoughts to those researches, which produced the Thoughts on Government, the constitution of Massachusetts, and at length the Defence of the Constitution of the United States and the Discourses on Davila." Out of the intellectual and political tradition of order, under the pressure of the experiences of the crisis of the colonial order, grew Adams' paradigmatic republic in speech and writing. This conception of order created for itself a social field in the institutional framework of the American Republic, as Adams, reflecting on his writings, claimed: "Writings which have never done any good to me though some of them have undoubtedly contributed to produce the constitution of New York, the constitution of the United States, and the last constitutions of Pennyslvania and Georgia. They undoubtedly also contributed to the writings of Publius, called the Federalist, which were all written after the publication of my work. . . . I have done all in my power, according to what I thought my duty, I can do no more."[125] Another remark, written down at a moment of strong existential emotion, brings us a step closer to the person-centered sphere and makes clear the intensity of the experience of founding. After the congressional resolution of May, 1776—which Adams saw as "an epocha, a decisive event" and for which he had to fight for a whole year "through a scene and a series of anxiety, labour, study, argument, and obloquy"[126]—he confided in his wife: "Is it not a saying of Moses, who am I, that I should go in and out before this great people? When I consider the great events which are passed and those greater which are rapidly advancing, and that I may have been instrumental of touching some springs, and turning some small wheels, which have had and will have such effects, I feel an awe upon my mind, which is not easily described." These sentences follow on a reflection on a sermon in which "the case of Israel and that of America" are

125. AP, *Diary and Autobiography,* III, 358–59.
126. *Ibid.,* 383.

compared and the separation from Great Britain is interpreted as an act of Providence.[127] Awe seized his spirit and made him shudder. Thus inspired, he experienced his action as a participatory propulsion through the numinous.

III. The Founder as Nomothetes

We classify *Defence* as a report on the founding that deliberately renounces mythic and revelatory symbols. Adams, so deeply impressed with the possibility of creating a social order, describes the new society as the result of a process of production, as product of the *techne*—that is, as an artifact, like the work of an architect—and he is fascinated by the know-how that brings about the correct order. This attitude is wholly congruent with his own involvement in the process of shaping the will of the American people. "It will for ever be acknowledged that these governments were contrived merely by the use of reason and the senses. . . . Neither the people, nor their conventions, committees, or sub-committees, considered legislation in any other light than as ordinary arts and sciences, only more important."[128] This last addition provides the interpretation of the act of founding as a production with a vague *differentia specifica;* but of course this interpretation is applied to the picture of the process of production from the outside rather than resulting from the *paradigma* itself. "Called without expectation, and compelled without previous inclination, though undoubtedly at the best period of time, both for England and America, suddenly to erect new systems of laws for their future government, they adopted the method of a wise architect, in erecting a new palace for the residence of his sovereign. They determined to consult Vitruvius, Palladio, and all other writers of reputation in the art." The people, according to Adams, determined further "to examine the most celebrated buildings, whether they remain entire or in ruins; to compare these with the principles of writers, and inquire how far both the theories and models were founded in nature, or created by fancy; and when this was done, so far as their circumstances would allow, to adopt the advantages and reject the inconveniences of all. Unembarrassed by attachments to noble families, hereditary lines and successions, or any considerations of royal blood, even the pious mystery of holy oil had no more influence than that other one of holy water." The analogy of eliminating all symbolism of spiritual observances felt to be obsolete (that is what "holy

127. John Adams to Abigail Adams, May 17, 1776, in AP, *Family Correspondence,* I, 410.
128. J. Adams, *Works,* IV, 293.

water" stands for) now extends to the fate of all those elements of the medieval-temporal understanding of order that were transmitted to the Christian-Germanic civilization, particularly in Central and Western Europe, by its archaic-Germanic substratum.[129] Adams noted as a social fact for America what James Harrington in the preliminaries to his *Commonwealth of Oceana* had speculatively anticipated: all modes of social order, from the migration of nations to Charles I, figure only under the collective designation of "modern prudence" and are part of a concluded period, a *corso* of history with, in the sense of "ancient prudence," a defective character.

Adams justified this rejection: "The people were universally too enlightened to be imposed on by artifice; and their leaders, or more properly followers, were men of too much honour to attempt it." This decision leaves "thirteen governments thus founded on the natural authority of the people alone, without a pretence of miracle or mystery. . . . The experiment is made, and has completely succeeded; it can no longer be called in question, whether authority in magistrates and obedience of citizens can be grounded on reason, morality, and the Christian religion, without the monkery of priests, or the knavery of politicians."[130]

The concept of an experiment assigns the founding to the producing sector, but such symbols as "nature," "reason," "morality," and "Christian religion" stress an actual context transcending the process of producing, which in turn becomes transparent in the production of order. An additional remark brings us to the point at which we can begin to grasp the nature of Adams' symbolism of the founding: "The Systems of legislators are experiments made on human life, and manners, society and government, Zoroaster, Confucius, Mithras, Odin, Thor, Mahomet, Lycurgus, Solon, Romulus, and a thousand others, may be compared to philosophers making experiments on the elements. Unhappily, political experiments cannot be made in a laboratory, nor determined in a few hours. The operation, once begun, runs over the whole quarters of the globe and is not finished in many thousand years."[131]

These sentences interpret the field of history as a structure patterned by the epochal establishment of order; notwithstanding the technical language, they understand the individual founding to be the nomothetic practice of the knowledge of order as contained in Aristotle's *episteme politike*. Adams calls this nomothetic function the "divine science of poli-

---

129. See also Bosl, "Die germanische Kontinuität im deutschen Mittelalter," in *Fruhformen der Gesellschaft im Mittelalterlichen Europa* (Munich, 1964).

130. J. Adams, *Works*, IV, 293.

131. *Ibid.*, 297.

tics." In Europe it was reduced to the technique of asserting the small passions and private interests of the failed sons of the fallen Adam; in America it was restored to its greatness in the "independent statesman . . . who will worship nothing as a divinity but truth, virtue, and his country."[132]

The renunciation of mythic and revelatory symbols returns Adams to the surviving tradition of a Whiggishly curtailed Aristotelian politics. This thesis requires considerable elucidation. The noetic interpretation of reality by Plato and Aristotle became incorporated in an extensive literary *corpus* that, unsystematic in itself, encompasses a wealth of theoretical complexes—that is, it examines man's realm of being in history and society by theoretically analyzing problems and sets of problems. But the political science constructed from this noetic knowledge of order became formally restricted, specifically by Aristotle, to a nomothetic science of the polis, with a tendency to become an independent tool for the design of institutions that guarantee a good order, appropriate to the given circumstances, and minimize the threat of revolution. The nomothetes blends with the architect. In this form Cicero allied it with the Roman tradition, making a connection that stamped Western civilization.

This legislative concept of political science was crucial to the political ideas of Whig constitutionalism espoused by the English commonwealth's-men of the seventeenth and eighteenth centuries, as it was for the Continental variants. The latter eventually dropped the classical content, and the *sciences morales et politiques* were replaced by the *science des idées*, or ideology.[133] The nomothetic element informed the overall political thought of the American Revolutionaries. In the founding, the "Whig science of politics" was made concrete, and under the pressure of experience it became transformed into the American science of politics that, in David Ramsay's opinion, came to occupy the same plane as the other sciences.[134]

Adams is backed by Book X of the *Nichomachean Ethics* and Books IV and V of the *Politics*, as well as Cicero's *De Republica*. In Book VI of the *Nichomachean Ethics*, Aristotle describes political science as the permanent shaping of *phronesis*, insofar as it is directed at the polis. The statesman (*politikos*), as the architect of the good polis, realizes it as *architektonike nomothetike;* the craftsman of politics, dealing with concrete events, turns it into a political science in his daily activities in the context

---

132. John Adams to James Warren, June 17, 1782, in Adams, *Works*, IX, 512.

133. See also H. Barth, *Wahrheit und Ideologie* (Erlenbach, 1961).

134. In G. S. Wood, *Creation of the American Republic*, 613. Wood begins his comprehensive study with the chapter "The Whig Science of Politics" and concludes with the chapter "The American Science of Politics."

of the existing society of the polis. This differentiation is largely blurred in Adams and survives only in the vague notion of the epochal significance of nomothetic activity in contrast to everyday political action.

The last book of the *Nichomachean Ethics* begins with the problem posed by the circumstance that it would be easy to order societies if ethical treatises alone were able to lead mankind to virtue. But apart from some individuals whose innate nobility of character and love for the good make them open to virtue, ethical instruction will not lead the masses to moral excellence. Not shame but fear compels them to obey; they are deterred from evil not by the baseness of evil but by fear of punishment. They live through their passions, look for happiness in pleasure, the corresponding joys, without ever having experienced noble joy. Arguments can hardly change such habits, rooted deeply in human nature. Passions seem to respond less to reason than to force. From the outset, therefore, it becomes a matter of creating in man an affinity for virtue. Accordingly, the education of the individual in society must be supplemented by coercion. Personal influence and moral exemplars are to be supported by the supraindividual pressure of the law: "the law has compulsive power, while it is at the same time a rule [*logos*] proceeding from a sort of practical wisdom [*phronesis*] and reason [*nous*]."[135] A correct system of laws and its corresponding institutions provide the necessary nurture for youth, wield the corresponding punishments over adults, and thus make possible a stable public order in the interdependence of authority and obedience. The actions of legislators give concrete form to knowledge of order by designing institutions that result in the social dominance of human existence in society—an existence developed paradigmatically in the *spoudaios*. The study of traditional speculations on order, the comparison of historical ruling organizations, and the knowledge of political everyday affairs allows the nomothetes who has arrived at the truth of his existence to approximate the model of the *ariste politeia* under the given social conditions.

IV. Founding and Constitution Making: The Nomothetical Aspects of the *Federalist* Papers

John Adams was not alone in viewing the founders as nomothetai within the meaning of ancient tradition. Their self-understanding, which had been formed by the spirit of classic politics, found a common point of reference for their ordering action in the figure of the legislator. The au-

---

135. Aristotle, *The Nichomachean Ethics*, ed. R. McKeon (New York, 1947), X, 1180a12.

thors of the *Federalist* papers are excellent proof of this. The pseudonym they chose, Publius, already professes their opinion that the nomothetical work of the founders of 1776 will be brought to perfection in the draft of the Constitution of 1786. In the wake of a new concept of a constitution, the *Federalist* Americanizes the idea of the nomothetes, who had won increasing universal validity in the political thought and political practice of the Americans through the large constitutional debates held since 1776. Now the work of the makers of the Constitution could be identified with the ordering done on the part of the legislator, taking into account the numerous constitution-making processes since 1776, as Adams had already claimed for himself as the author of the constitution of Massachusetts in 1780.

In the eyes of the authors of the constitution, transforming the confederation into a union under a national constitution merely brought to perfection the world-historical experiment of reestablishing the political order on the North American continent. Consequently, Publius viewed himself as a reformer and legislator, completely in accordance with the great legislators of ancient times, as the choice of the pseudonym, which Hamilton had already used in 1778 for a series of articles, clearly illustrates. In Plutarch's *Parallel Lives,* the legislators Solon and Publius Valerius are the third pair of great founders of order of the Graeco-Roman world, following the founders Theseus and Romulus and the renovators Lycurgus and Numa. Alexander Hamilton, John Jay, and James Madison considered the American work of establishing a political order in the period of 1776 to 1787 to be the great world-historical analogy to ancient times, where "government has been established with deliberation and consent" alone.[136] Also in Publius' opinion the ethics of the American people and their leaders proved its worth in the ordering act of founding the republican regime. The concept of humanity implied in these ethics, as varied as it may be in detail, determines—in normative terms—the tectonics of the new institutional structure. Only insofar as the founding of a new political body was the conscious institutional arrangement of the condensed experience of order through a selective process on the part of those involved could the founding act as such be termed the source of social-political authority. Thus Hamilton describes his self-understanding, as mentioned before, in the following way: "The station of a member of Congress is the most illustrious and important of any I am able to conceive. He is to be regarded not only as a legislator, but as the founder of empire. A man of virtue and ability, dignified with so precious trust, would rejoice that fortune had given him birth at a

136. *Federalist* No. 38.

time, and placed him in circumstances so favorable for promoting human happiness."[137] In his study *Alexander Hamilton and the Idea of Republican Government,* Gerald Stourzh points out that one of the last great debates between the classicists and the modernists took place "in the context of the role of the great individual in founding political institutions." In fact, Hamilton's choice in favor of the classical position was a contradiction in principle of a different, modern view of the decisive influence of anonymous historical movements on the process of creating social orders, such as Jefferson advocated.[138] Like Douglas Adair, Stourzh also includes the authors of the *Federalist* papers in the historical tradition of the legislator, which was the central concept in the political thought of classical antiquity. In the civic humanism of early modern times, the concept of the legislator once again became important with respect to the civic order: "The image of the Legislator who could establish the perfect constitution, haunted the minds of leading political thinkers from the time of Machiavelli to Hume. Harrington, Bolingbroke, Montesquieu, Rousseau, all specifically associate their writings with the idea of the perfect commonwealth created by great lawgivers. And it is obvious if one notes the pseudonym signed to the Federalist Papers, and reads carefully Madison's Federalist 38, that in 1787 Hamilton and Madison self-consciously identify their labors with the role of classical Lawgivers and Legislators."[139]

Plutarch's Graeco-Roman double model of the founders as well as reforming legislators and statemen systematized, as it were, the paradigmatic experience gained in classical antiquity of the historical eruption of a strictly political type of order, that is, a free type of order based on human action, so as to prove the equality of the two political cultures on the basis of this assumption. It needs to be pointed out, however, that Plutarch wrote *Parallel Lives* in the face of the end of the civic constitutions of Rome and Athens. In his writings, he follows a critical intention by explaining their contents of order with examples of representative leaders of great nomothetic potency. Thus, *Parallel Lives* is a late echo of Cicero's crisis program for the Roman republic, which was a synthesis of Greek and Roman thought: "For there is really no occupation in which human virtue approaches more closely the august function of the gods than that of founding new States or preserving those already in existence" (*De Republica I,* 7). Cicero combines the Roman conception of history with Greek political theory, the *auctoritas maiorum* with the idea of the

137. Hamilton, *Papers,* I, 580.
138. Stourzh, *Alexander Hamilton,* 177ff.
139. Adair, "Fame and the Founding Fathers," 46.

nomothetes. He outlines the figure of the reformer, who recognizes the corruption inherent in the process of transforming the commonwealth and knows that it can be contained by restoring the conventional mixed constitution of the *Res Publica:* It is the concern of wise men to recognize such processes of transformation, "but it is the concern of a great citizen and almost divine man to anticipate the threat of such processes of transformation, to dominate in the government of the commonwealth, and to keep it in his power." This symbolic recourse to the ordering acts of powerful historical figures of representative humanity linked the content of order of the commonwealth with the original morals of the political elite. In addition, Cicero also provides a model of the social regeneration of political ethics that can continuously be updated by imitating moral-political examples.

At the time that the political world of early epochs underwent a critical transformation, this ancient paradigm of the founder and renovator of order gained new significance. Machiavelli's intricate presentation of the *ordinatore* in *Il Principe* and the *Discorsi* is excellent proof of this. Although Machiavelli's ambivalent paradigm could be applied to each experience and program of a specifically modern political heroism, the particular republican association between the virtue of founders and the civic legal and constitutional order described in the *Discorsi* continued to be effective in the neoclassical republican tradition prevalent in the Atlantic region. When political theory and practice consciously referred to the Graeco-Roman ideas of community and man as regards civic politics, mixing them with Christian notions of equality and making them the motives behind the establishment of political order, the greatness and immortal fame of the founders and reformers were dependent on the normative component of the legislative performance. Publius definitely follows the tradition of neoclassical politics as it was formulated by David Hume, who was held in high esteem by the authors of the *Federalist* papers: "Of all men that distinguish themselves by memorable achievements, the first place of honour seems due to legislators and founders of states who transmit a system of laws and institutions to secure the peace, happiness, and liberty of future generations."[140]

However, the Constitutional Convention, and together with it Publius, acts as a reforming legislator with respect to the founding initiated by the leaders of the Revolution, which is experiencing a critical period and whose existence is threatened: "Happily for America, happily, we trust for the whole human race, they [the leaders of the revolution] pursued a new and more noble course. They accomplished a revolution which has

---

140. Hume, *Political Essays,* 77.

no parallel in the annals of human society. They reared the fabrics of governments which have no model on the face of the globe. They formed the design of a great Confederacy, which is incumbent on their successors to improve and perpetuate." Only in the structure of the Union does the originally created order prove to be defective, requiring a new draft, which is now under discussion and needs to be decided.[141] Although the reform is played down—by means of substantial tactical skill—as a structural improvement, the overall line of reasoning in the essays shows that the draft of the constitution is supposed to renovate and bring to perfection the republican order starting from its principles. By having recourse to the principles underlying the great experiment of self-government, the constitutional reform can prove to be a renovator and improvement of the republican forms of order. "Recurring to principles"[142] is Machiavelli's tenet for a regular renovator, which alone can ensure the permanent existence of a commonwealth. This concept will be studied in more detail below. The idea of a continuous renewal of the political body by resorting to the founding ethics and the content of order agreed upon therein was common to classical and neoclassical political thought. It was Publius, though, who gave the figure of the legislator, as well as the idea of returning the Republic to its fundamental order on the basis of its own historical experience, an appearance that was unmistakably typical of the times.

As early as 1777, Hamilton had already taken into account the remarkable Anglo-American experience of the collective ability of organized "citizens" to act. At that time, Madison had seen the "founders of empire" assembled at the Continental Congress; now he was already emphasizing "the improvement made by America on the ancient mode of preparing and establishing regular plans of government." Not the individual citizen "of pre-eminent wisdom and approved integrity," but an "assembly of men," a "select body of citizens," whose common deliberations were expected to be guided by a higher measure of wisdom, was commissioned to design the work of reform.[143] This convention is purposely represented as a new version of the "memorable congress of 1774" of the Founding Fathers. These prominent figures of the Revolution made the convention an assembly characterized by patriotism, virtue, wisdom, power of judgment, and experience. Borne by the trust of the people, unaffected by passion and self-interest, and obligated only to the public good, the convention formulated with one voice its plan for a free and democratic and a good regime and unanimously passed its draft of the

141. *Federalist* No. 15.
142. *Federalist* No. 39.
143. *Federalist* No. 38.

Constitution. Publius continually lets the convention appear as a collective legislator, bearing all traits of representative humanity, an "assembly of half gods," as Jefferson puts it later. This collective legislator, however, does not stand outside of the people; rather, it forms and guides, as Adams had already described, the people's legislative work of reform on the basis of its ethical-political authority. The republican order finds its roots in the consensus of the people, "that pure, original fountain of all legitimate authority."[144] Publius notes that the famous legislators of classical antiquity were to a large extent "clothed with the legitimate authority of the people" and, therefore, their methods of proceeding were "strictly regular."[145] However, the Americans combined the new idea of the collective legislator with another new process of legitimation, namely, ratification by the people. Publius repudiates the reproach that the convention had acted in an irregular manner by going beyond its original task of revising the Articles of Confederation and adopting a new national constitution. The right of the people to abolish or modify its form of government if such an action is required for the safety and happiness of the people, which is set down in the Declaration of Independence, is undisputed; but "it is impossible for the people spontaneously and universally to move in concert toward their objects." That is why such a change requires several "informal and unauthorized propositions, made by some patriotic and respectable citizens or number of citizens."

Finally, the revolutionary new order of 1776 also developed from unauthorized committees and congresses. Then, as today, it was necessary to defer formal rules of conduct in the face of substantial problems of order. The advice and recommendations given by prominent citizens had to be oriented along this question alone so as to fulfill their duty toward the people, who would then make the final decision: "They must have borne in mind that as the plan to be framed and proposed was to be submitted to *the people themselves,* the disapprobation of this supreme authority would destroy it forever; its approbation would blot out antecedent errors and irregularities."[146] Thus the people are the only legitimate source of government, but not every conflict as to the misuse of the power of government justifies appealing to the people: "[A] constitutional road to the decision of the people ought to be marked out and kept open, for certain great and extraordinary occasions."[147] It is only in times of serious crisis that passions that endanger order and unity are put

144. *Federalist* No. 21.
145. *Federalist* No. 38.
146. *Federalist* No. 40.
147. *Federalist* No. 49.

aside, letting an overall trust in patriotic leaders and universal enthusiasm for new forms of government dominate. In all other political situations, however, general social decisions are clouded by the spirit of faction and conflict between factions: "The passions therefore, not the reason, of the public would sit judgment. But it is reason, alone, of the public, that ought to control and regulate the government. The passion ought to be controlled and regulated by the government."[148]

The event of founding order by means of the collective action of the entire society cannot be repeated any number of times and presupposes that the society is in full possession of reasoning abilities at the moment of acting. Thus, insofar as the republican order, as such, reflects the reasonable nature of man and is standardized as a *paramount law* or *supreme law* in the form of a written constitution, the act of newly establishing the political order springs from the principle of self-government. The interaction of the collective legislator and the consensus of the people, as well as of the substantial republican content of order and formal process of legitimation, can only be defined by means of the new concept of the constitution developed by the Americans. The starting point is the important distinction "between a Constitution established by the people and unalterable by the government, and a law established by the government and alterable by the government."[149] In the course of their dispute with Great Britain about the British constitution, the Americans had developed a concept of the constitution that differed considerably from the British understanding of a constitution in the eighteenth century: "a notion of a constitution that has come to characterize the very distinctiveness of American political thought." The term *constitution* now implied "a written superior law set above the entire government against which all other law is to be measured."[150] The significant difference can be found in the "exclusive documentation" of the principles of order and in the "identification of a good order of the state—in other words that which was the *eunomia* for the antique polis and *iustitia* for the medieval empires—based on a fundamental legal document."[151]

By making the basic decision on the constitution, the politically organized people, acting as a representative of themselves, exert their au-

---

148. *Ibid.*
149. *Federalist* No. 53.
150. G. S. Wood, *Creation of the American Republic*, 260.
151. H. Hofmann, *Recht-Politik-Verfassung* (Frankfurt, 1986), 264ff.; see also G. Stourzh, "Staatsformenlehre und Fundamentalgesetze in England und Nordamerika im 17. und 18. Jahrhundert," in *Herrschaftsverträge, Wahlkapitulationen, Fundamentalgesetze*, ed. R. Vierhaus (Göttingen, 1977), 294–327.

thority. Politically organized refers, not to the people as the sum of all individuals, but to the people as a legally constituted body of free and independent citizens (white and male) of common understanding. However, the discovery that the constitution could be used as an instrument to achieve political self-order of the citizenry immediately led to the institutionalization of new decision-making processes that included the people: the institution of the *convention,* the Constitutional Convention, and popular ratification, both of which, significantly enough, had their origins in New England's revolutionary politics. "The convention in American thinking . . . has become an extraordinary constitution-making body that was considered to be something very different from and even superior to the ordinary legislature." "It was an extraordinary invention, the most distinctive institutional contribution, it has been said, the American revolutionaries made to Western politics." [152] The convention in Philadelphia drew the necessary conclusions from the past constitution-making processes in the individual states. The majority of the delegates voted against having the new constitution passed by the state parliaments because, as Madison explained, this was no longer a treaty among the states as the Articles of Confederation had been: "He considered the difference between a system founded on the Legislatures (of the individual states) only, and one founded on the people, to be the true difference between a *league* or *treaty* and a *Constitution.*" The present case, however, concerned "a union of people under one Constitution." And the delegate Rufus King made the issue clear: he would prefer "a reference to the people expressly delegated to Conventions, as the most certain means of obviating all disputes and doubts concerning the Legitimacy of the new Constitution; as well as the most likely means of drawing forth the best men in the States to decide on it." [153]

The prominent role that the nomothetic concept of political science played in the consciousness of the political elite of the new Republic can be proven in an exemplary manner by the self-understanding of John Adams and Publius. It dominates the thoughts of all those leaders of the Revolution who were under the spell of the Graeco-Roman ideology. Since Adams, Publius, and many other statesmen identified with the classical figure of the nomothetes, they not only purposely imitated the antique model, but established the *auctoritas maiorum,* which, in the minds of the Founding Fathers, was to allow continual recourse to the ordering power of the founders in accordance with Roman tradition.

152. G. S. Wood, *Creation of the American Republic,* 318, 342; W. P. Adams, "Republikanismus," 522–35.

153. M. Farrand, *The Records of the Federal Convention* (New Haven, Conn., 1937), II, 92.

V. The Symbol of the Father in the American Tradition

The symbol of the father, which the founders tried to use to present themselves, was by no means new or unique; it carried a dual meaning in American society.

A. The terms *fathers* and *forefathers* had a precisely defined meaning in the New England consciousness and, radiating outward, in all the colonies. It originated in New England historiography, which arose out of the consciousness of crisis held by the Puritan orthodoxy of the second and third generations. It understood itself as a jeremiad on the decline of the original order of the City Upon the Hill and aimed at the reformation of society by returning to the beginnings of Plymouth and Massachusetts Bay. The most monumental effort of this sort was Cotton Mather's *Magnalia Christi Americana* (1702). Citing the careers of such representative figures as a John Winthrop or a John Cotton, Mather deduced a model order from which New England had fallen away and which could be restored by the method of *imitatio*.[154] In the course of the eighteenth century "Our Fathers" are recalled as *topoi* whenever questions arise concerning the order of collective and individual existence, no matter how much the social, political, and mental structures may have changed over the course of time. This tendency became reinforced during the crisis following the end of the Seven Years War. The Founding Fathers were elevated to the central symbol of the understanding of order, which had its outward manifestation in an intensification of the corresponding cults and rites even beyond the borders of New England.[155] On the other hand, the cluster of complaints, opinions, ideas, sentiments, and traditions that during the confrontation with Great Britain solidified into coherent concepts of political order was rigorously made part of the content of all the fathers had stood for.[156]

In *A Dissertation on the Canon and Feudal Law* (1765), John Adams identified "the views and ends of our own more immediate forefathers" with the political demands of the day. He kept to the traditional pattern of ideas: The British machinations indicate decline, resistance is spiritually rooted in the *imitatio* of the fathers and is aimed at the restoration of an original existence under God.[157] In this context we may end the

154. See P. Miller and T. Johnson, eds., *The Puritans* (New York, 1963), II, 162–79; P. Miller, *The New England Mind* (Boston, 1961), II, 135, 189–90, and *passim*; W. F. Craven, *The Legend of the Founding Fathers* (New York, 1956), 9–22 and *passim*.

155. Miller and Johnson, eds., *The Puritans*, 33–52.

156. *Ibid.*, 27–32; Dixon Wecter, *The Hero in America: A Chronicle of Hero Worship* (New York, 1942), 34–43.

157. John Adams, *The Political Writings*, ed. G. A. Peek (New York, 1946), 19; Craven, *Legend of the Founding Fathers*, 27ff.; see also the analysis offered in subsequent chapters.

discussion by noting that as far as content goes, the continuity from the "first founding" to the "second founding" of the Revolution of 1776, which indisputably exists, did not consist of the "principles of civil and religious liberty," as Adams understood them, and their endangerment by British tyranny.

Subsequently the *Pilgrim Fathers*—an expression that brought about the unification of Plymouth and Massachusetts even on the symbolic plane—were combined with the *Fathers of the Republic* into a collectivity of fathers. This pantheon functioned as a source of authority for the national, self-understanding of society, and since its composition was so heterogeneous, the divergent forces within society were given ample scope for interpretative resort to the tradition. Consequently the canon of the fathers of the first period (Winthrop or Williams) and of the second (Hamilton or Jefferson) in the United States also varies to respond to the needs of time and place. Washington alone never slipped from his position as first among the Founding Fathers. The introductory sentence of Lincoln's Gettysburg Address is a representative example of the meaning- and authority-conferring role of the fathers: "Fourscore and seven years ago our fathers brought forth on this continent a new nation, conceived in liberty, and dedicated to the proposition that all men are created equal."[158] "Our Fathers," "the Fathers of the Republic," and the twentieth-century phrasing "the Founding Fathers" are key symbols for the specifically American nexus of founding and self-understanding. "America is the only country in the world which pretends to listen to the teachings of its founders as if they were still alive," a French observer noted as recently as 1930.[159]

B. In 1776, the end of the English Crown's function as the legitimator of government left the traditional appellation of *pater patriae* available as a welcome attribute for the political leader and statesman. Its advantage was that it would not conflict with the new legitimation of rule through the authority of the people.

Several examples suffice to show the prehistory of this Roman honorary title. The *pater patriae* and the related concept of *parens patriae* seem, with one exception, to have aroused little interest among researchers to date.[160] Audrás Alföldi describes the "affective father trope" entering "the political life of the republic in various ways"—"a concomitant phe-

---

158. A. Lincoln, *Collected Works,* ed. R. P. Basler (New Brunswick, N.J., 1953–55), VII, 15.

159. Quoted in Wector, *Hero in America,* 81; see also the analyses in Chapter 3.

160. In their *Realenzyklopädie des klassischen Altertums,* Pauly and Wissowa do not include any article on *pater patriae.* For the continuity of the *pater patriae* from Rome to America, see G. Highet, *The Classical Tradition* (New York, 1964), 399.

nomenon of the political reorganization" of Rome after the Second Punic War. "The intellectual content of the idea of the father of the country" was rooted "in the ancient Roman military tradition . . . in the binding singularity and in the relationship of filial love contained in the pure Roman idea of the savior, which during the final centuries of the republic was elevated from reference to the saved individual to the sphere of state existence; the idea of the *servator* was strengthened by adding political content. As the monarchy developed, the new meaning grew into a sort of description of the benevolent savior of the state and the people. From Augustus on, the awarding of the title was considered the republican legalization of sovereignty through the Senate."[161]

Thus the symbolism gained increasing acceptance in politics in the context of the crisis of authority of the Roman republic. For one, it prevailed in literary references to the beginnings of Rome in the Romulus and Camillus legends; these references hoped to reestablish the consolidation of an order that had grown fragile by recalling the great figures of founder and savior and the legitimacy they had brought about. For another, the conferring of this honorific title on particular persons seemed to promise a restoration of order; bearers of the name were Marius, Cicero, Caesar, and finally, Augustus.[162] It makes sense, therefore, that in the late period, not least under Greek influence, the trait of *conditor,* founder, also accreted to the *pater patriae.* Just as the origin of order is referred back to the mythical primal founder, so the renewal or reconstruction of order is revealed to be a "new act of founding."[163]

But the title was apparently ignored by Western rulers when they adopted the rest of the cult of the ruler (conception of the ruler, symbolism, nomenclature, insignias, and rituals of sovereignty) from antiquity. It appeared only in the Ottonian Renaissance, once again in connection with a particular problem of legitimation. The historian of the Saxons, Widukind von Korvey, used the designation *pater patriae* in a "learned construction on an ancient model" to support the idea of a non-Roman empire legitimated by Saxon military proclamation. Thus, writing of Henry the Fowler after the defeat of the Magyars in 933 and of Otto I after the Battle of the Lechfeld in 955, Widukind proclaimed both men as emperor and *pater patriae.*[164] Subsequently the appellation *pater pa-*

161. A. Alföldi, *Der Vater des Vaterlandes im römischen Denken* (Darmstadt, 1971), 46, 96.

162. T. Mommsen, *Römisches Staatsrecht* (Darmstadt, 1971), II, Pt. 2, p. 755; F. Taeger, *Charisma* (Stuttgart, 1957–60), II, 35, 66–67, 104, 124, 134, 191.

163. Alföldi, *Vater des Vaterlandes,* 115–18.

164. Widukind von Corvey, *Rerum gestarum soxonicarum* (Hannoverae, 1882), I, 39; ibid., III, 49; see P. E. Schramm, *Kaiser, Rom und Renovatio* (Darmstadt, 1957), 80–81;

triae remained a subordinate component of the symbolism of royal and imperial sovereignty, the unquestionably dominant motif of founder and savior found in Widukind being combined with the welfare motif, which is primarily grounded in the *parens patriae*.[165] James I furnished a later example: "The king is truly *pater patriae,* the political father of his country."[166]

During the crises of authority of the early modern age, the title in turn became detached from the dynastic context and became independent as the symbol of a legitimacy that could not be derived from the Germanic right of sacred lineage and of the Lord's anointment establishing the sacred kingship in its specific Western form of hereditary monarchy. This was especially true once again for all the illegitimate Italian rulers since the thirteenth century (illegitimate in the sense of the given principles of legitimacy). The triad of founding, salvation, and welfare is evident in Petrarch's dedication to Francesco Carrara, ruler of Padua,[167] and in Machiavelli's report on the public tribute paid to Cosimo de' Medici by the inscription "Padre Della Patria" on his tombstone.[168] Whenever someone with leadership qualities rose to become the existential representative of a particular society, and when the legitimacy of his rule was based exclusively on this fact but was to be distinguished from tyranny, we find the honorary title *pater patriae.* Cromwell[169] as well as Washington thought of himself as "father of his country."

Furthermore, the Roman connotations suited the image of Cincinnatus to an extraordinary degree; and the figure of the man whom the people had called away from his plow to rule them and who, after he had set things right, returned to his peaceful existence as a farmer was dear to Americans. In his election sermon of 1783, cited above, Ezra Stiles called Governor Jonathan Trumbull of Connecticut *pater patriae,* and he referred to the delegates as "nursing fathers of our spiritual Israel"—a form of the phrase that must be unique.[170] The *epitheton ornans* "father

---

C. Erdmann, *Forschungen zur politischen Ideengeschichte des Frühmittelalters* (Berlin, 1951), 44–45.

165. See also the Arenga of a document of Frederick I of 1152, quoted in F. Kern, *Gottesgnadentum und Widerstandsrecht im frühen Mittelalter* (Darmstadt, 1973), 123.

166. In J. P. Kenyon, ed., *The Stuart Constitution* (Cambridge, Mass., 1966), 12–13.

167. Patrarca, *De republica optime administrada,* quoted in J. C. Burckhardt, *Kultur der Renaissance,* Vol. III of *Gesammelte Werke* (Berlin, 1955–57), 5; see *ibid.,* 10ff., on political illegitimacy in the Italian states.

168. N. Machiavelli, *Istorie florentine, Opere,* VII, 463.

169. C. Blitzer, ed., *The Commonwealth of England, 1641–1660* (New York, 1963), 104–105.

170. W. J. Thornton, ed., *The Pulpit of the American Revolution* (Boston, 1860), 508, 512.

of his country" was first conferred on Washington in Francis Bailey Lancaster's *Almanac* for 1778; in the case of Jefferson, the first instance of this designation can be found in 1804.[171] But at no time did *pater patriae* or any of its variants become a formal appellation of officeholders. If for no other reason, such a move was precluded by republican opposition in Congress, which knew how to prevent the adoption of every kind of ceremony and titular form of address. Characteristically, this republican fervor was most vigorously directed at Vice-President Adams; his conviction that social structures could not be repealed and his experience of court ceremony in Europe persuaded him to believe in the "efficacy of pageantry." The Senate, under the expert leadership of its presiding officer, discussed such forms of address as "Excellency," "Highness," "Elective Highness," and "His Most Benign Highness," and the sovereign title "Protector of the Rights of the United States"; but thanks to the obstinacy of Senator William Maclay of Pennsylvania, the form "Mr. President" won out.[172]

Thus "father of the nation" and "father of the country" remained symbols by which the members of society expressed the specific authority of their leaders, especially Washington and Jefferson and to a much lesser degree Adams, and they in turn expressed their relationship to the society they had shaped. In the national tradition, however, the *patres patriae* of 1776, as Founding Fathers, remained the spiritual patriarchs of the *novus ordo seclorum*.

VI. On the Theory of the Founding

In his report on the founding, Adams insisted that none of the architects of the new Republic "had interviews with the gods, or were in any degree under the inspiration of Heaven."[173] This praise of man as the founder of order, which has already been discussed in another context, was echoed by Publius' comment that it was up to the American people to prove "whether societies of men are really capable or not of establishing good government from reflection and choice."[174] Hannah Arendt, who significantly enough has been the only one to try giving a theoretic interpretation of the problem of the founding of the American Republic, rightly refers to the self-understanding of the Founding Fathers with the following comment: "The foundation which now, for the first time, had oc-

171. Wector, *Hero in America*, 112, 157.
172. Page Smith, *John Adams*, II, 752–56; L. G. DePauw, ed., *Documentary History of the First Federal Congress of the United States of America* (Baltimore, 1972), I, 24–45.
173. J. Adams, *Works*, IV, 292.
174. *Federalist* No. 1.

cured in broad daylight to be witnessed by all who were present had been, for thousands of years, the object of foundation legends in which imagination tried to reach out into the past and to an event which memory could not reach." She points out that the historical significance of such founding myths are shown by "how the human mind attempted to solve the problem of the beginning, of an unconnected, new event breaking into the continuous sequence of historical time."[175] She maintains that the leaders of the Revolution were so conscious of the "absolute novelty in their enterprise" that no historical or legendary truth belonging to their own tradition could have symbolically interpreted the radical new beginning—the beginning of American national history, as it were. Irrespective of her own interpretation of the classic Christian traditional base of the American founding, Arendt wants to trace the content of order of the foundation to the founding act itself: "No doubt the American founders had donned the clothes of the Roman maiores, those ancestors who by definition were 'the greater ones,' even before they were recognized as such by the people. But the spirit in this claim was not arrogance; it sprang from the simple recognition that either they were founders and, consequently, would become ancestors, or they had failed. What counted was neither wisdom nor virtue, but solely the act itself, which was indisputable."[176]

In my opinion, the one does not exclude the other but brings it about. This also applies to another comparison made by Arendt, namely, her assertion that their self-understanding as founders shows "the extent to which they must have known that it would be the act of foundation itself, rather than an Immortal Legislator or self-evident truth or any other transcendent, trans-mundane source, which eventually would become the fountain of authority in the new body politic."[177] In opposition to this it can be said that at least in the consciousness of the Founding Fathers, the act of creating order cannot be separated from their experience of order. In the historical reality of the Americans, the founding experience and the experience of order are one and the same. Only through this coincidence of the principle of order and the founding of institutions does society in an organized form receive its *raison d'être* as a representative of a metahistorical, transpersonal reality. As a matter of fact, the idea of the radical new beginning contained in the act of foundation has its origins in the classic Christian content of the experience of order that the founders and their people had undergone. After all, the founders took over the

175. H. Arendt, *On Revolution* (New York, 1963), 205ff.
176. *Ibid.*, 204.
177. *Ibid.*, 200.

stoic attitude reflected in the fourth eclogue of *The Aeneid* by Vergil—
Magnus ab integro saeclorum nascitur ordo—so as to be able to extend
the Christian-apocalyptic *novus* to *novus ordo seclorum,* expressing the
specific content of order of their foundation. The symbolism peculiar to
the American founding myth proceeded from this concept of the establishment of a *novus ordo seclorum* by the Founding Fathers.

The concluding theoretical comments by Arendt herself better illustrate the convergence of the founding experience and the experience of
order in the act of founding than her own interpretations would let the
reader suppose. She asks herself whether there is a solution to the problem of origin that does not start out from the concept of the absolute,
without being subjected to the arbitrariness that is inevitably involved in
each beginning. The following comments take up Arendt's thought, but
develop it further in another direction, because Arendt's recourse to the
nativity of man alone does not seem plausible to me. In connection with
this point, Arendt states: "The absolute from which the beginning is to
derive its own validity and which must save it, as it were, from its inherent arbitrariness is the principle which, together with it, makes its appearance in the world. The way the beginner starts whatever he intends
to do lays down the law of action for those who have joined him in order
to partake in the enterprise and to bring about its accomplishments. As
such, the principle inspires the deeds that are to follow and remains apparent as long as the action lasts." Arendt's insight is informed by the
language of antiquity on the threshold between myth and philosophy:
"beginning and principle, *principium* and principle, are not only related
to each other but are coeval. . . . The Greek language . . . tells the same
story: For the Greek word for beginning is *arche,* and *arche* means both
beginning and principle." [178]

This is again the language of classical politics, of Machiavelli, and of
Anglo-Saxon Whiggery. In the *Discorsi,* Machiavelli explains that the
permanence of social order in a republic necessitates "ritirarla spesso
verso il su principio"—"bring them back to their original principles." [179]
For renewal always means bringing republics back "to their original principles." Beginning and principle are identical in that at the moment of its
founding every society contains a *bontà* "by means of which they obtain
their first growth and reputation." Return to the beginning means regain-
ing a primary *bontà,* the original content of order within the founding
principles. Frequently these principles are not simply external, formal,
and institutional; rather, they are principles of civic virtue underlying the

178. *Ibid.,* 214.
179. N. Machiavelli, *Discourses* (New York, 1940), 367–68.

institutions. Such a return to the original principles and beginnings serves the rehabilitation of the *virtù e bontà* of an outstanding man or of the law, which, however, lives only in the *virtù* of the citizens. Only the courage of excellent citizens allows the law to assert itself against the power of those who habitually transgress it and must learn to fear it.[180] Recourse to the original institutions of the social order is inseparable from determining the substance inherent in the founding generation. This is true for the Whigs, who relied on Machiavelli, and for the Founding Fathers, who included the formulaic "frequent recurrence to fundamental principles" in the Declaration of Rights of Virginia (George Mason), the Declaration of Rights of Massachussets (Adams), and the equivalent declarations of North Carolina and Pennsylvania.[181] W. P. Adams misunderstands the formula when he writes that all that matters to a polity is to find its way back to the "prevailing conditions that led to its founding." John Adams and Mason are far more knowledgeable about the theoretical implications.[182] Article 15 of the Virginia Bill of Rights states "that no free government, or the blessings of liberty, can be preserved to any people, but by a firm adherence to justice, moderation, temperance, frugality, and virtue, and by frequent recurrence to fundamental principles."[183] Article 19 of the Massachusetts Constitution reads, "A frequent recurrence to the fundamental principles of the constitution, and a constant adherence to those of piety, justice, moderation, temperance, industry, and frugality, are absolutely necessary to preserve the advantages of liberty, and to maintain a free government. The people ought, consequently, to have a particular attention to all those principles, in the choice of their officers and representatives, and they have a right to require of their lawgivers and magistrates an exact and constant observation of them, in the formation and execution of the laws necessary for the good administration of the commonwealth."[184] Recurrence to fundamental principles is not, as W. P. Adams believes, in any way to be equated with the "frequent recourse to the will of the majority by means of an effective system of representatives."[185] The provision of limited terms of office makes sense only on the presumption that the civic ethos in the Republic is constantly renewed; frequent elections were intended to remove corrupt elements

---

180. *Ibid.*, 369.

181. See Adams, "Republikanismus," 422–32.

182. See also Stourzh, *Alexander Hamilton*, 10, 35.

183. F. N. Thorpe, *The Federal and State Constitutions, Colonial Charters* (Washington, D.C., 1909), 3814.

184. J. Adams, *Works*, IV, 227–28.

185. Adams, "Republikanismus," 431.

from politics.[186] The continuity of the symbolism lends plausibility to Arendt's interpretation. Furthermore, the identity of beginning and principle also underlies Maurice Hauriou's theory of institution and founding, developed on the model of the French state. Hauriou sums up the problem in the "vitalist principle": of the *idée directrice,* the guiding idea of the enterprise: "An institution is an idea of the work or of the enterprise that finds realization and justification in a social milieu. To translate this idea into the actual world, a power develops that provides it with organs. Among the members of the social groups who share in establishing the idea, there result declarations of solidarity under the overall direction of the organs, and these declarations follow certain rules."[187] A founding begins with an "action and enterprise principle," which takes hold of the consciousness of certain individuals and eventually solidifies into the social reality of institutions. But of greater theoretical importance is the question, Precisely what is the *idée directrice?* It clearly goes beyond the intellectual or sociohistorical description. In his reply, Hauriou availed himself of the anthropological principle that human nature exists in the human spirit, which, as it were, emits the guiding idea of the psychosomatic organism called man. The guiding idea of a communal institution precisely typifies the human spirit; that attribution not only reflects the shaping principle "but also the ethical nature of this principle." In this way the human spirit appears as an objective given, "which has as much positive validity as does the idea of the work to be performed in a communal institution."[188]

Therefore the founding allowed a creative impetus to materialize in a sudden spurt; this was the *élan vital* of the human mind. The phenomenal objectivity of ideas was the result; but whether it "also corresponds to a substantial mental reality" is another question Hauriou chooses to beg. "It would surely be important to know, for it might turn out that some ideas will exhibit more reality than others, they might also come closer to the truth."[189] Hauriou thus avoids the theoretical question concerning not only the factual content of order, implied by the "ethical nature" of an *idée directrice,* but also the experiential substratum that, as a guiding

186. See also Lüthy's comments; he considers Jefferson the author. "What Jefferson established . . . as a newly discovered constitutional law of life was nothing more than the teaching, adopted since Plato and Aristotle by all state philosophies . . . , that the republic could exist only through the virtue of its citizens" (Lüthy, "Tugend und Menschenrechte," *Merkur,* XXVIII [1974], 35).

187. M. Hauriou, *Die Theorie der Institution* (Berlin, 1965), 34.

188. *Ibid.,* 46.

189. *Ibid.,* 66.

idea, becomes realized in the concrete consciousness of founders to the extent that it expresses participation in the "substantial reality," the investigation of which Hauriou unfortunately assigns to philosophers, though it surely belongs at the center of a political science in the classical sense.

The same problem arises in connection with Bernard de Jouvenel's *vis politica,* "the driving force of all social forms." Jouvenel considers the examination of this "starting power" an essential aspect of political science as such. The *vis politica* is expressed in the justification of any sort of human aggregates and their maintenance; it describes the actual situation of the eruption of social entities. Ahead of all social aggregates ranks "the pure political form": the *cité,* the *état.* The analysis of the separate aspects of the *vis politica* remains functional: "This power can be analyzed from three aspects, though these are not often found united in one agency: the ability to settle on a direction, the ability to channel action, the ability to regularize, institutionalize this cooperation." According to Jouvenel, what is crucial to the emergence of social forms is always the founder, the creator. He is endowed with *autorité;* it is a property at the same time that it is the "efficient cause of voluntarily coming together"—voluntarily to the extent that every founding achieves its existence through the conscious actions of persons. Thus the creator is the father of actions undertaken freely, "having their origin in him." But for Jouvenel the creator–founding father remains strangely indeterminate, rather like a functionist variant of the mythical founder-legislator. The first to become comprehensible is the *dux,* the leader, to whom Jouvenel assigns the role of achiever and completer in the collective action of founding. The process from creator to *dux* is left obscure, understandable only as a differentiated but mutually referrent explication of the *vis politica.*[190] Creator and leader, initiator and promoter of collective social objectives in the social aggregates, though merely catalysts in the social process, can also in the end be described merely as agents of the *vis politica.* This is not a quality of the founders but an anonymous force, which can be represented only functionally. "It should be thought of as a relationship in which suggestion and response are part of a global process. . . . [W]e can say, by definition, that the quantity of movement in a society will be a function of the vis politica at work." Freedom within a society is then determined by the freedom "to create a gathering, to create generate [*sic*] a group, and thereby introduce in society a new power, a source of movement and change."[191]

190. B. de Jouvenel, *De la Souveraineté* (Paris, 1955), 37, 44–45.
191. B. de Jouvenel, *Sovereignty* (Chicago, 1957), 299. This summary is found only in the English edition.

But Arendt, also, is too cautious in her observation on the convergence of beginning and principle. She concludes with a paraphrase of an incidental statement from Plato's *Laws,* which—against the background of the *Statesman,* the *Timaeus,* and the *Crito*—contains the solution of the problem in a nutshell. Aristotle discourses on the statement at length, unlocking it insofar as philosophical meditation without the aid of mythic symbolization is able to do. Arendt renders "arche gar kai theos en anthropois idroumene sozei panta" as follows: "For the beginning, because it contains its own principle, is also a god, who as long as he dwells among men, as long as he inspires their deeds, saves everything." [192] A less interpretative translation reads as follows: "For a beginning established by man gives existence to all as would a god." In a passage that Arendt did not quote, the connection between order and founding in the concept of the beginning is explained more clearly: "We perceive (do we not?) that for *poleis* that are thus founded for the first time some persons there must necessarily be; but who can they be before any offices (archai) exist, it is impossible to see. Yet somehow or other they must be there—and men, too of no mean quality, but of the highest quality possible. For as the saying goes 'the beginning is the half of every work'; and every man always commends a good beginning; but it is truly . . . something more than the half, and no man has ever yet commended as it serves a beginning that is well made." In a typically Greek manner, Plato takes recourse to the *protos nomos* of the ordering legislator, who provides the beginning of the polis with its principle, insofar as the order content of the law expresses the encounter of human and divine reason. [193]

Stating a structural principle of the historical process—that is, that founding involves creating order—of necessity, therefore, includes the observation that the content of order has something to do with the question of its genesis in the consciousness of the founder himself as presented paradigmatically in Plato's *Politeia.* The "validity" of the absolute, which is evident in the "beginning," to use Arendt's vocabulary, can formally raise the claim to truth only by reason of the fact that in every "beginning," human beings respond to their experience of the tension between eternal being and temporal being in terms of creating an image of man and reality that is supposed to serve as an ordering principle for political action. This process of the constitution of order involves psychic processes that are explicated analogously in symbols reflecting the ordering experiences of the persons concerned, not to be misread as exercises in the ontological reification of the human condition, as so many a modern

192. Arendt, *On Revolution,* 214.
193. Plato, Nomoi, 753e.

interpreter is inclined to impute to the Hellenic philosophers. On the contrary, we are informed by them that the ordering experiences emerge from the consciousness of concrete human beings engaged in the search for their humanity and its order.

By Aristotle's elimination of the mythic dimension, existentially ordered man perceives *arche,* beginning and principle, in the dianoetic virtue of *nous,* through which participation in the divine is habitually revealed. Recognition of the *archai,* the first principles, stands for the concrete experience of letting oneself be permeated by eternal and temporal being, from which results the *ratio* as the conscious structure of things, which affects the spatial-temporal area of human existence and which brings about the quality that is concretized in habitually correct behavior in typical situations.[194] It is only the oneness of *arche* and principle, anthropologically applied, that allows political science to view itself as the soul's attitude in which the dianoetic virtue of prudence (*phronesis*) becomes the conferrer and conveyer of public virtues and justice in the conduct of correctly acting persons, constituting the *zoon politikon.*

The self-understanding of the Founding Fathers and the theory of founding thus converge at the point on which our further reflections must focus and which is also the precondition for any analysis of American self-understanding that seeks to go beyond the self-evident correlation of founding and order in the American consciousness. That focus is the consciousness of the men who, in the revolutionary act of founding anew, make themselves into the representatives of this society and create for their experience of order a social field that represents the dominant pattern of thought and action in the new society over long periods of time.

---

194. See Aristotle, *Nichomachean Ethics,* VI, 1139b18–1142a10; on the *nous* as the site of the *archai,* see also especially Aristotle, *The Categories, On Interpretation, Prior Analytics,* ed. H. P. Cook and H. Tredennih (London, 1962), I, 71b9–72b4.

Two

John Adams: Genesis of One Man's Common Sense

I. The New England Heritage

John Adams was a farmer and lawyer from the Boston hinterlands, the outermost periphery of the inhabited Western world of the eighteenth century; it took the historical process to move him, one step at a time, by way of Boston (1759),[1] New York (1774),[2] and Paris (1778)[3] into the center of this civilization. But the stirring experience in these cities more deeply drenched in civilization did not essentially affect his original personality structure. He merely reflected all the harder on the standards he had brought with him when the expansion of his geographical and historical horizons brought new materials and previously unknown situations to his consciousness.

The social world of Massachusetts was the matrix that shaped his personality. No doubt Adams was thinking of himself as well when he never tired of declaring, "The meetinghouse, the schoolhouse and training field are the scenes where New England men were formed." He had always, he noted, listed the "towns, militia, schools and churches" as "the four causes of the growth and defence of New England. The virtues and talents of the people are there formed."[4] And he had his hometown of

---

1. AP, *Diary and Autobiography*, I, 80–81.
2. *Ibid.*, II, 103.
3. John Adams to Abigail Adams, April 12, 1778, in A. Adams, *Letters*, II, 21.
4. AP, *Diary and Autobiography*, II, 195; see also J. Adams, *Works*, V, 494–95.

Braintree, a typical country community, in mind when he remarked elsewhere, "There is no country where the common people, I mean the tradesmen, the husband, and the laboring people, have such advantages of education as in that; and it may be truely said, that their education, their understanding, and their knowledge are as nearly equal as their birth, fortune, dignities, and titles."[5] He was fully aware of the interdependence of educational opportunity and social structure. He insisted that the difference between "gentlemen" and "common people" was slight. And he was surely correct for vast areas of agrarian New England, with its minimal economic and social and class differences and a middle class of independent landowners making up as much as 50 percent of the white population, which also included artisans, small entrepreneurs, wage earners, and professionals. Here, too, the social pyramid had a bottom of wage earners, uncontracted temporary labor, freed and bound Africans (3 percent in New England), and a peak of well-to-do landowners and merchants, who for generations formed a political class of their own.[6] But of course what was crucial to Adams was not the social hierarchy of colonial society, with its relatively active horizontal and vertical mobility, but the absence of a stratified corporative society along the old European lines. After all, he instructed the Europeans, in the colonies there were no kings, princes, aristocrats, or church hierarchy, no inherited offices and titles, no entailed estates, no primogeniture. "We are all equal in America, in a political view."[7]

This experience correctly measures equality against the inequality of the old European corporative societies and singles out a principal difference. Adams, Jefferson, and others in this context wrote of "artificial inequalities." This definition did not dispose of the problem of "natural inequalities" among individuals or groups from the socioeconomic aspect; much less did it address the question of the differential actualization of individual reasonableness in wisdom and virtue.[8]

Scholarship has not spoken the last word on the extent and manifes-

5. J. Adams, *Works*, VII, 283.
6. See the detailed account in J. T. Main, *The Social Structure of Revolutionary America* (Princeton, 1965).
7. J. Adams, *Works*, VII, 279.
8. John Adams to Elbridge Gerry, April 25, 1785, in APM; Thomas Jefferson to John Adams, October 28, 1813, in J. Adams, *Adams-Jefferson Letters*, II, 387–89; John Adams to Thomas Jefferson, November 15, 1813, *ibid.*, II, 397–402 (This letter expresses the expectation of an involution to a corporative society.); Adams treats the problem of "natural inequalities" in detail in *Defence of the Constitutions of Government of the United States of America*, in *Works*, IV, 393–401. In general, see also G. S. Wood, *Creation of the American Republic*, 70–75; W. P. Adams, *Republikanische Verfassung und bürgerliche Freiheit* (Darmstadt, 1973), 163–89.

tations of "natural inequalities" in the American colonies of the eighteenth century. Adams' opinion, however, is valid even when we accept the sociohistorical hypothesis of a tendency to Europeanization in New England society, such as Kenneth Lockridge has formulated. He believes in a development toward overpopulation, reduction in the average size of farms, an increasingly differentiated social hierarchy, and an increase in the number of "poor." But these tendencies—emphatically so called—by no means result in an "old world society," as Lockridge claims. Although it is true that the New England society of the eighteenth century was changing, the transformation cannot be defined in the categories of early modern European corporative society.[9] Therefore I do not believe that even this sociohistorical finding contradicts Adams' experience of the nature of New England society, precisely because he, too, thought that he could detect increasing Europeanization, which he saw as a corruption of the society.

Adams' intellectual biography reveals a psyche that reflected traditional structures of consciousness and social order without thereby sacrificing a certain meditative energy and an uncommon openness to all reality. His understanding of reality was, of course, first woven into the forms of thought and life of New England, notwithstanding Adams' intense individual process of acculturation. From the age of twenty, Adams appropriated vast complexes of the intellectual culture of Europe, which he turned, often quite forcefully, to his own intellectual use.[10] Although Adams understood himself as the product of an unbroken New England tradition, there are striking signs of the ruptures in the most recent past of the New England colonies, the most violent of which was the Great Awakening of the 1740s, in which an irresistible process of spiritual restructuring resulted in a series of revivals, the last of which Perry Miller, not entirely without justification, took to be the Revolution.[11]

The institutionalization of the concept of the "visible saint" in apoca-

---

9. K. A. Lockridge, "Land, Population, and the Evolution of New England Society, 1630–1790," in *Class and Society in Early America*, ed. G. B. Nash (Englewood Cliffs, N.J., 1970), especially 165–66. This volume is informative on the various research results. See also R. N. Dunn, "Social History of Early New England," *American Quarterly*, XXIV (1972), 661–79; J. P. Greene, "The Social Origins of the American Revolution," *Political Science Quarterly*, LXXXVIII (1973), 1–22; J. M. Murrin, Review Essay, in *History and Theory*, XI (1972), 226–75; K. A. Lockridge, "Social Change and the Meaning of the American Revolution," *Journal of Social History*, VI (1973), 403–39.

10. This aspect of Adams' intellectual biography has been thoroughly explored in A. Iacuzzi, *John Adams: Scholar* (New York, 1952); Haraszti, *Adams and the Prophets of Progress;* H. T. Colbourn, *The Lamp of Experience* (Chapel Hill, N.C., 1965), 83–106.

11. P. Miller, "From Covenant to Revival," in *Religion in American Life*, ed. J. W. Smith and A. L. Jameson (Princeton, 1961), 353 and *passim*.

lyptic respect to the civilization-historical *tabula rasa* of the wilderness could succeed provisionally, given the conditions of an uncomplicated agrarian society. But with the departure of the leader and the erosion of the original spiritual substance, the irrationality of reifying God's grace in the "visible saint" became only too quickly apparent, to the advantage of the liberated energies of the civilizing work of colonization. Territorial expansion, rapid population growth, the beginning of urbanization along the coast, the division of land into many subsistence farms along with a few prospering large commercial enterprises, and the incorporation of the colonies into the mercantile economic system of the British Empire, all accelerated the emancipation of the temporal sphere from the "visible church," by now a Calvinist orthodoxy, which in alliance with a provincial gentry was more and more overtaken by the inherent laws of human existence in society.

The civilizing process, which ran counter to the Puritan consciousness, thrust New England into a permanent crisis, which found its literary expression in the jeremiad concerning the decline of the people and its temporal, emotional reflection in the witch hunts of the 1690s. The clerical-political controversies from the Halfway Covenant through Stoddardianism to the separatism of the Great Awakening gradually blurred the identification of community and polity.[12] This specific crisis of Puritan consciousness ran its further course in an overall American context.[13] The reciprocal relations of France's military pressure and the political counterpressure of imperial policies beginning in the late seventeenth century; independent social conflicts and power conflicts within the colonies; the formation and new independence of traditional English political institutions as functioning organs of collective political action; and the rise of a political class which, especially in New England, penetrated to the broad level of midsize landowners—all these developments made it possible for Massachusetts to rediscover the old truth of Richard Hooker, who had once pointed out to the Puritans that "church" and "common-

---

12. See, among others, T. J. Wertenbaker, *The Puritan Oligarchy: The Founding of American Civilization* (New York, 1947); P. Miller, *The New England Mind* and *Errand into the Wilderness* (Cambridge, Mass., 1956); A. Simpson, *Puritanism in Old and New England* (Chicago, 1955); E. S. Morgan, *Visible Saints* (Ithaca, N.Y., 1965).

13. Compare the standard works in historiography: H. L. Osgood, *The American Colonies in the Seventeenth Century* (New York, 1930), and *The American Colonies in the Eighteenth Century* (New York, 1924); C. M. Andrews, *The Colonial Period of American History* (New Haven, Conn., 1934–38); L. H. Gipson, *The British Empire Before the American Revolution* (New York, 1936–67). C. L. Rossiter, *Seedtime of the Republic* (New York, 1953), offers an excellent overview but remains mired in American self-understanding and therefore seems superficial; D. J. Boorstin, *The Americans* (New York, 1958–73), I, is preferable.

wealth" were not two completely independent societies, with mutually exclusive membership. This conception, along with the delay of the apocalyptic millennium, led to a de facto oligarchy of "saints," since the problems of social order had not, as expected, vanished into thin air. Church and polity, as Hooker's argument ran, each deal with the same members of a society: "which society being termed a commonwealth as it lives under whatsoever form of secular law and regiment, a church as it has the spiritual law of Jesus Christ. . . ."[14] When we oppose the church therefore and the commonwealth in a Christian society, we mean by the commonwealth that society with relation unto all the public affairs thereof, only the matter of true religion excepted; by the church, the same society with only reference unto the matter of true religion, without any other affairs besides."[15] This did not, of course, mean a return to the church-state solution of the Anglican Richard Hooker nor an abrupt change in the positions of Congregationalism in the society; but the road was paved for recognition of a pluralism of Christian churches and a majority of nondenominational Christians. The Lockean idea of the complete privatization of the spiritual sphere only gradually asserted itself in New England and became a constitutional norm in Massachusetts only in 1820.

The altered situation was embodied in the new charter of 1691,[16] which separated civil rights from church membership; in John Wise's *A Vindication of the Government of New England Churches* (1717),[17] which separated the church and the civil government by organization and content; and in Jeremiah Dummer's *A Defense of the New England Charters* (1721),[18] which interpreted New England existence in the categories of the English constitution and of mercantilism: "Here, at long last was the secular measurement, here the ground upon which Americanized Puritans must learn to stand if they were to stand at all."[19] The process of history set the temporal sphere back in its rightful place; but bound to ingrained mental structures, it began in the eighteenth century to wrest from the church the privilege of caring for man's *euzen*. For the original spiritual solidarity continued in the new understanding of contracted society as a people under God—"fraternity under the Gospel" is what

---

14. R. Hooker, *Of the Laws of Ecclesiastical Polity*, ed. J. Keble (Oxford, 1888), VIII, 334.
15. *Ibid.*, 336—37.
16. M. G. Hall *et al.*, *The Glorious Revolution in America* (Chapel Hill, N.C., 1964), 54—79.
17. On this point, see G. A. Cook, *John Wise* (New York, 1952).
18. P. Miller, *New England Mind*, II, 386—92 and *passim*.
19. *Ibid.*, 386.

John Wise called it—with a pervasive apocalyptic undertone. But Puritan "spiritualizing daily" conveyed standards of intellectual and ethical excellence and engendered a continuous alertness of consciousness, in which the persons so affected were worried by the question of "why came we here," an answer to which could be found only beyond ecclesiastic orthodoxy in the individual experience of the Great Awakening and its revivalist eruptions and in a restitution of order in politics.

After the cessation of external political pressure following the Peace of Paris of 1763, the logic of developments, of which Massachusetts formed the center, could not help but place the affected colonies in conflict with the national policy, directed along mercantilist and privilegist lines, of the mother country. Under the influences of civil war in the seventeenth century, England immediately responded to every spiritual and ethical impetus with reserve, lack of understanding, and suspicion; it might be said to follow Hume, the theoretician of this attitude, in considering such impulses as no more than instances of pleonexia, the rationalization of regulatable interests.[20]

Consequently in the eighteenth century the intellectual culture of New England also achieved new dimensions of symbolization; the conventional idea constructs became detached from their previous positions and entered on new connections; and the exponential value of the various strands of tradition were considerably raised. Genetically this culture was a fragment of English seventeenth-century culture that, transplanted across the Atlantic, developed a dynamic of its own.[21] The Anglo-Saxon variant of Calvinism, primarily of the Congregationalist and Presbyterian sort, predominated, and the other shadings of reformatory Christianity, from latitudinarian Anglicanism to radical Antinomianism, were clustered around it. The most essential elements of these movements are Scripture, the Fathers, and the Reformers, as well as all of classical culture.[22] Further important elements were the common law and the cluster of ideas, doctrines, conventions, attitudes, and practices called the constitution by the parliamentary opposition of the English Civil War; finally there was the literary body of that specifically English humanism espoused by the commonwealth's-men, who, during the crisis of Crom-

20. Compare the analysis of English politics by L. B. Namier in *The Structure of Politics at the Accession of George III* (London, 1957) and *England in the Age of the American Revolution* (London, 1961).

21. Compare S. E. Morison, *The Intellectual Life of Colonial New England* (Ithaca, N.Y., 1960); K. B. Murdock, *Literature and Theology in Colonial New England* (New York, 1963); T. J. Wertenbaker, *The Golden Age of Colonial Culture* (Ithaca, N.Y., 1959); L. B. Wright, *The Cultural Life of the American Colonies, 1607–1763* (New York, 1957).

22. R. M. Gummere, *The American Colonial Mind and the Classical Tradition* (Cambridge, Mass., 1963).

well's government, opposed their alternative of a paradigmatic republic to an exhausted Puritanism and an opposition greedy for power and wealth. This paradigmatic republic was enriched in the most fortunate way by classical politics and the outcome of the Italian Renaissance.[23] J. G. A. Pocock describes this "neo-Harringtonian civic humanism" as the "Machiavellian moment" of the Atlantic republican tradition. "Civic humanism denotes a style of thought . . . in which it is contended that the development of the individual towards self-fulfillment is possible only when the individual acts as a citizen, that is as a conscious and autonomous participant in an autonomous decision-taking political community, the polis or republic."[24]

Pocock's *Machiavellian Moment* is no history of ideas; rather, the study views the republic-oriented politics of the Renaissance as a symbol for mastering post-Christian experiences of contingency within the context of Italian urban culture. The existence of man in society and history is interpreted within the framework of this republicanism, or civic humanism, which found a universal criterion in the political life-style of the well-ordered civil psyche as well as the *telos* of an action in an otherwise contingent historical-social world. In Pocock's opinion, this concept reveals a specific reading of Aristotelian politics: "it may also be read as the originator of a body of thought about the citizen and his relation to the republic, and about the republic (or polis) as a community of values, and this is the approach which reveals its importance to humanists and Italian thinkers in search of means of vindicating the universality and stability of the *vivere civile*."[25] Machiavelli and Guicciardini are the most prominent representatives of a school of thought and language that articulated the concepts of civic humanism under the pressure of the critical situation in Florence from 1494 to 1530. Machiavelli's republican revisionism as well as the excessive praise of the Aristotelian-Polybian theory of a mixed constitution through the quasi-eschatological myth of the timeless permanence of Venice, to which Contarini and Giannotti contributed, has its origins in the failure of the republican city of Florence. According to Pocock, the final product of the Florentine experience is an impressive sociology of liberty, which was adopted by the European En-

23. Z. S. Fink, *The Classical Republicans* (Evanston, Ill., 1945); C. Robbins, *The Eighteenth Century Commonwealth Man: Studies in the Transmission, Development, and Circumstance of English Liberal Thought from the Restoration of Charles II Until the War with the Thirteen Colonies* (Cambridge, Mass., 1959); in general, here and the following, also B. Bailyn, *The Ideological Origins of the American Revolution* (Cambridge, Mass., 1967).

24. J. G. A. Pocock, *Politics, Language and Time* (New York, 1971), 85, and Pocock, *The Machiavellian Moment* (Princeton, 1975).

25. Pocock, *Machiavellian Moment*, 67.

lightenment as well as the English and the American Revolution as the answer to the challenge "posed by the republics' commitment to existence in secular history." [26] Pocock uses Harrington as a key figure in his line of argumentation "that the English-speaking political tradition has been a bearer of republican and Machiavellian as well as constitutionalist, Lockean and Burkean concepts and values" [27] because of Harrington's synthesis of civic humanism and English political and social consciousness.

Thus Pocock works out a theory of neoclassical politics that is in complete opposition, as it were, to the party factions of the Whigs and Tories, whose metamorphoses in the eighteenth century manifested themselves in a form of neo-Harringtonianism. Neo-Harringtonianism articulated the political position of the country party, integrated the traditional complex of the ancient constitution in the neoclassical concept of order, and, last but not least, tried to find a theoretical explanation for the transformation of the economic structures. The Florentine legacy increasingly enriched this "Anglo-Atlantic equivalent of the Machiavellian Moment" with general European religious and political ideas prevailing in the early stages of the Enlightenment. In this way, the manifold neoclassical forms of republicanism from western, northern, and central Europe, which Pocock hardly takes into consideration, met to form a general European synthesis, which altogether constitutes the Atlantic republican tradition of the early modern period and which, in the opinion of Pocock, finds new expression in the eighteenth century in the works of Montesquieu: "the Aristotelian, Polybian, Machiavellian, and now Harringtonian 'science of virtue,' or sociology of civic ethics, had to be restated with paradigmatic force for the eighteenth century West at large. Montesquieu, seen from this angle, is the greatest practitioner of that science." [28] The self-understanding of the American colonists and their leaders arose from this tradition: "The Whig canon and the Neo-Harringtonians, Milton, Harrington and Sidney, Trenchard, Gordon and Bolingbroke, together with the Greek, Roman, and Renaissance masters of the tradition as far as Montesquieu, formed the authoritative literature of this culture. A neoclassical politics provided both the ethos of the elites and the rhetoric of the upwardly mobile, and accounts for the singular cultural and intellectual homogeneity of the Founding Fathers and their generation. Not all Americans were schooled in this tradition, but there was . . . no alternative tradition in which to be schooled." [29] Yet this self-perception of the

26. *Ibid.*, 85.
27. *Ibid.*, viii.
28. *Ibid.*, 484.
29. *Ibid.*, 507.

colonists in the light of a neoclassical realistic view of the world still contained the original experience of a common radical Protestant tradition of a people confederated with God. In New England, however, radical Protestant spirituality and the symbols of order central to it remained a vital ferment for authentic American self-understanding and, not least, a decisive factor in the political mobilization of the common man. He found a plausible interpretation of his revolutionary aspirations in biblical republicanism. Because of this apocalyptic dimension in the language of the American Revolution, Pocock speaks about an "apocalyptic Machiavellism,"[30] which, however, does not sufficiently describe the blend of radical Protestant and classical elements in the idea of a free republic that was peculiar, above all, to the revolutionary colonists from New England.

In a certain sense, Pocock considers the American Revolution and the Constitution to be "the last act of the civic Renaissance,"[31] which, even if its American metamorphosis often changed the original beyond any resemblance, provided the criteria and guiding principles for the civic culture of the United States of America up to the present time: "the unique conditions of the continental virtue and commerce, the Puritan tension between election and apostasy, the Machiavellian tension between virtue and extension, and in general the humanist tension between the active civic life and the secular time continuum in which it must be lived."[32] Civic humanism provided a framework which, in the course of the eighteenth century, allowed everything that had been offered in England and on the European continent in the way of speculations on man in society, from Locke to the Scottish moral philosophers and from Pufendorf and Grotius to Montesquieu, to be selectively included. Secondary, at least in the consciousness of those involved, was the transformation of the medieval cosmos into the Newtonian universe. Its consequences did not frighten even Calvinist orthodoxy, to which nature continued to be the spatial-temporal indicator of God and which saw that the application of the new physics brought valuable technical assistance in the civilizing work in the wilderness.[33]

The genesis of this republican realm of ideas and consciousness, as well as its diverse forms within the tension of ideological conflicts prevalent in the early history of the American republic, has been the object of almost unsurveyable and in itself often controversial historiographical

---

30. *Ibid.*, 513.
31. *Ibid.*, 461.
32. *Ibid.*, 549.
33. P. Miller, *New England Mind*, II, *passim*.

research. The most prominent supporters, besides Pocock, were Bernard Bailyn's studies *The Ideological Origins of the American Revolution* (1967) and *The Origins of American Politics* (1968) as well as Gordon S. Wood's *The Creation of the American Republic* (1969). Here the paradigm of a republic based on the ideas of civic humanism develops into the leitmotif for a sociocultural consensus of the American revolution. Since that time the idea of a "republican synthesis"[34] as the common denominator in the interpretations of the intellectual-political world of the Founding Fathers has been developing its own dynamics.[35] Thus Joyce Appleby writes: "Exuberance over classical republicanism has engendered both opportunities and confusions."[36] The reaction of historians to the discovery that republicanism was the predominant social theory in America during the eighteenth century can be compared to the reaction of chemists upon discovering a new element: "Once having been identified, it can be found everywhere."[37] This may be a lame comparison, but as a matter of fact, republican revisionism thoroughly threw over the traditional methods of interpretation, particularly the role of John Locke as the primogenitor of the American republic. However, especially the liberal and individualistic aspects of Locke's philosophy in antebellum America are returning to the fore in research endeavors, posing special problems for the republican synthesis. This is particularly obvious in the controversy, as Wood already postulated, whether the end of the Revolution also signaled the end of the "classical conception of politics" and the birth of a distinct "American science of politics," or, as Pocock claims, whether the "language of practice" merely lost its classical connotations, whose historical form, however, is guaranteed in the language of myths and the metahistory of the *res publica*. The question as to the intellectual and cultural formative power of civic humanism with regard to the political culture of the United States is the focal point of most recent discussions. The answer is not of academic interest for the United States.[38] The concept of republicanism as a "cultural system" based on

34. R. E. Shalope, "Toward a Republican Synthesis," *William and Mary Quarterly,* XXIX (1972), 49–80.

35. R. E. Shalope, "Republicanism and Early American Historiography," *William and Mary Quarterly,* XXXIX (1982), 334–56.

36. J. O. Appleby, "Republicanism and Ideology," *American Quarterly,* XXXVII (1985), 471.

37. *Ibid.,* 461.

38. See L. Banning, *The Jeffersonian Persuasion: Evolution of a Party Ideology* (Ithaca, N.Y., 1978); D. R. McCoy, *The Elusive Republic: Political Economy in Jeffersonian America* (Chapel Hill, N.C., 1980); J. O. Appleby, *Capitalism and a New Social Order* (New York, 1984).

the dynamic interaction of life and language[39]—in short, an intellectual-cultural form of life, as already proposed by de Tocqueville—has proven helpful in studying this new question. Robert Kelley's *The Cultural Pattern in American Politics* (1979) argues in this direction. Yet Kelley also proceeds on the assumption that republicanism was a form of consciousness peculiar to the revolutionary generation. However, this notion constitutes more a "universe of discourse" than a "prescriptive faith." "It stated a framework of argument; certain agreed-upon fundamentals provided the boundaries, and particular goals and a kind of language shared. However, the meaning of those goals and the devices for reaching them remained quite unsettled."[40] From this the sociocultural and region-related discernible modes of republicanism resulted: New England's *moralistic* republicanism; the *libertarian* republicanism of the South; and both types of republicanism prevalent in the center states, the agrarian *egalitarian* republicanism of the Irish-Scots, and the urban *nationalistic* republicanism of the mercantile elites. In Kelley's opinion, this pluralistic form of republicanism is representative of the interaction between consensus and conflict in the political life of the United States up to the present time: "the essential cultural pattern of our politics is still that of the nation's beginnings."[41]

This history of the development of republican convictions in the American colonies is intricately interwoven with the processes of change that American Protestantism underwent. The transformation of the Puritan into the Yankee and of the Reformation into the Enlightenment was reflected particularly in the moralistic republicanism of New England, and the intellectual biography of John Adams is an excellent example of this. The decisive impulse for the development of an overall American Christian-republican worldview with all the features peculiar to it came from New England's Great Awakening, the American version of a religious movement of awakening that spread throughout the entire Western civilization. "Historians have variously pointed out that the decade of the Awakening, 1740–50, is a watershed in American development. They have difficulty in putting their fingers on just what precisely the transformation was, since there were no revolutionary changes in political institutions. . . . The social scene in 1750 seems fairly much what it was in 1740. And yet you feel, the moment you get to the sources, that after 1750 we are in a 'modern period,' whereas before that, and down to the

---

39. Shalope, "Republicanism and Early American Historiography," 356.
40. R. Kelley, *The Cultural Pattern in American Politics* (New York, 1979), 83.
41. *Ibid.*, 288.

very outburst, the intellectual world is still medieval, scholastic, static, authoritarian."[42]

As an all-colonial phenomenon, the movement integrated the colonies into a unified field of consciousness and substantially advanced the New England tendencies toward mental-political assimilation with the middle and southern colonies. It further created a sounding board for conceptions of a political unification of North America in the framework of a new understanding of empire as it was first formulated in Benjamin Franklin's plan of union at the Albany Congress of 1754.[43] More important than the effects on religion, then, are the new interpolations in consciousness left behind by the Great Awakening, which indicate the motivating forces that restructured social reality.

On the level of Calvinist doctrine, the intended renewal fails, as is clearly evident in Jonathan Edwards' spiritual biography. Here the representatives of Arminianism—that is, an urbane gentlemen's Christianity with a minimal dogmatic program—held their ground in the long run; what was strengthened was merely the position of doctrinaire scripturalism that, aside from the episode of Samuel Hopkins' *New Divinity*, eventually found a suitable home among the Baptists.[44]

The Christian symbolism that was undogmatically cut to size was conditionally based on the needs of a worldly minded upper level and the great mass of nonaffiliated Bible-inspired Christians; but neither this fact nor any inherent logic of the symbols themselves can explain its dominance. For in the consciousness of believers, their sterility was so firmly linked to the crisis of New England that they became the occasion of the spiritual revolt called the Great Awakening. It released emotional, intellectual, and spiritual energies to the point of hysteria, in such measure that at the conclusion of the movement, Arminian Christianity had found a completely adequate substratum of experience. This paradox resulted from the separation of dogmatic religious faith and mysticism, a process

42. P. Miller, "The Great Awakening from 1740–1750," *Encounter* (1956), 5ff.

43. R. Koebner, *Empire* (Cambridge, 1961), 85–118; G. Stourzh, *Benjamin Franklin* (Chicago, 1954).

44. On the Great Awakening and on religion in the eighteenth-century colonies, compare J. Harountunian, *Piety versus Moralism: The Passing of the New England Theology* (New York, 1932); E. S. Gaustad, *The Great Awakening in New England* (New York, 1957); P. Miller, *Errand into the Wilderness;* C. Bridenbaugh, *Mitre and Sceptre: Transatlantic Faiths, Ideas, Personalities, and Politics, 1689–1775* (New York, 1962); C. C. Goen, *Revivalism and Separatism in New England, 1740–1800* (New Haven, Conn., 1962); A. Heimert, *Religion and the American Mind* (Cambridge, Mass., 1966); A. Heimert and P. Miller, eds., *The Great Awakening* (Indianapolis, 1967); C. B. Cowing, *The Great Awakening and the American Revolution: Colonial Thought in the Eighteenth Century* (Chicago, 1971).

carried out in an exemplary way by Edwards. "Mysticism, which was a partial phenomenon in the total structure of Calvinist theology, became separated from this context and turned into the origin of a new religiosity independent of the European forms."[45] Edwards once again dissolved the reality of "being in general," which had become rigidified in the doctrinal system. Starting from the experience of opening oneself to and allowing oneself to be permeated by the divine, he reconstructed participation in reality: "benevolence to being in general" constituted "true virtue," the mental stance of conscious man.[46] The conversion "was attended by a change in man's entire personality (the center of which Edwards called 'heart' and was expressed in the holiest of religious affections, 'love'). And such holiness of heart must and would manifest itself in a holy 'will,' as benevolence, not of thought merely, but of deed."[47] Although Edwards began with the dogmatic problem of predestination, the doubt of whether one was among the elect, the flow of speculation carried him beyond dogma. The crisis of predestination was, after all, the crisis of the Puritan God, whose reification had left merely an angry Jehovah as unmerciful party to the contract, a *deus absconditus* no longer able to be revealed by any *amor dei*. Beyond a chosenness mediated by Christ, mystical experience allows an immediate transcendence reference, which can then find its dogmatic form of expression in Arminian or even deist symbolism. The empirical findings of the disturbance and transformation of the personality structure required from Edwards a reformulation of traditional psychology that owed its modernity to the study of Locke and its quality to Edwards' consciousness of man's total existence.

But the new spirituality that the awakening amply produced—though on a sliding scale, with Edwards' mysticism as the highest value and Davenport's emotional excitement as its null point—revolutionized the newly won dimension of social existence. This tendency, too, is prefigured in Edwards in an exemplary way in the existential aspect of conversion that he formulated in the concept of "experimental religion." "The principal evidence of this power of godliness, is in those exercises of holy affections that are practical and in their being practical."[48] As Perry

---

45. E. Voegelin, *Über die Form des amerikanischen Geistes* (Tübingen, 1928), 111.

46. Of particular pertinence are the early works, the experience analyses, and the late works "Concerning the End for which God Created the World" and "The Nature of True Virtue." Of particular importance to his psychology is "Concerning Religious Affections"; compare Perry Miller, *Jonathan Edwards* (New York, 1949); J. Opie, ed., *Jonathan Edwards and the Enlightenment* (Lexington, Ky., 1969).

47. Heimert and Miller, eds., *Great Awakening*, lii.

48. J. Edwards, "Religious Affections," in *Representative Selections,* ed. C. F. Faust and T. H. Johnson (New York, 1935), 252.

Miller shows in his analysis of the eulogy for Colonel Stoddard,[49] Edwards renewed the standard for Puritan *eupraxia,* the life of correct action in the world, which in the altered social situation neither the abstraction of Calvinist doctrine nor the Arminians' moralistic banalities was able to clarify. "'Experimental religion,' as defined by Edwards . . . was not designed to allow men existential solace in the midst of a troubled world, but demanded of them strenuous exertions bent on setting the world aright."[50] But—and this is what links the Great Awakening and Edwards with the Puritan tradition—the setting aright of the world was anticipated as an apocalyptic event. Following the revitalization of the apocalypse of history, however, it once more came to occupy the temporal sphere. Released from identification with the "holy," the "visible church," the people-of-God symbol became attached to all of American society, claiming the privilege of electedness for all its members. The indubitable spiritualization of the common man in a religious mass movement with pronouncedly anti-establishment affect legitimated the apocalyptic self-understanding of the "fraternity under the gospel."

This new addition to consciousness gave rise to the idea of the *translatio imperii* to the North American colonies; it allowed young John Adams to discover politics. But Adams' was not an isolated instance. Ernest L. Tuveson quotes the report of Andrew Burnaby, an English clergyman who traveled, in 1759 to 1760, through the middle colonies. "He reports, with distaste, that 'an idea as strange as it is visionary' has entered into the minds of the generality of mankind, that empire is traveling westward; and everyone is looking forward with eager and impatient expectation to the destined moment, when America is to give law to the rest of the world."[51] By its content, however, this American law could mean for the world only the regeneration of concrete political order, and so the demand for an incorporation of the newly won standard in a model. On this point the newly awakened "sense of heart" inexorably coincided with the classical *ratio* in a design for existence of the *zoon politikon* of the paradigmatic republic as the guarantor of "true virtue" in society.[52] New England played a crucial role in this blending of awakening and classicism.

The New England crisis, according to one sum of our study, brought consciousness, not to a radical destruction of its original structure, but to recourse to the immediate reality of knowledge, under whose impact

49. P. Miller, *Errand into the Wilderness,* 163ff., and P. Miller, ed., "Jonathan Edwards' Sociology of the Great Awakening," *New England Quarterly,* XXI (1948), 50–77.

50. Heimert and Miller, eds., *Great Awakening,* liii.

51. E. L. Tuveson, *Redeemer Nation* (Chicago, 1968), 101.

52. Pocock, *Machiavellian Moment,* 506–52.

the reality complexes of God, man, world, society, and history were placed in new relations to each other and selective traditional symbolic forms were preferred to explicate the new image of reality. But two remarks must be noted concerning the social relevance of the process just described.

A. The spiritual vitality of New England, the familiarity with essential material complexes of the intellectual culture of Western civilization, the sensitivity to the existential problems of order and disorder, none of these came about arbitrarily; they were conveyed socially to a largely literate population through a system of public education. After Harvard was founded in 1636, the Massachusetts Act of 1647, which established a network of compulsory public elementary and secondary schools, completed a system of public education that was supplemented by numerous private schools. With the exception of Rhode Island, all the New England colonies had followed the Massachusetts example by 1672. Instruction in the public schools took place entirely in the medium of Calvinist Christianity. Reading and writing, in that order, were the declared aim of instruction. The curriculum of the grammar schools and of Harvard were shaped by the classical program of the *septem artes liberales,* which linked antiquity and Christianity and which had been opened to successive European influences.[53]

B. The power of the educational system to impress, however, also had a retarding effect in that it integrated the civilizing substance in the life of reason as an effective ferment. Our summary of the transformation of New England stressed trends that did not, in fact, always influence all of society with the same intensity. An accelerated social differentiation in the mercantile centers—actually no more than provincial villages with a population of a few tens of thousands—was opposed by static elements in the hinterlands, where tradition prevailed when it came to managing affairs, praying, and making decisions; where town and church made up a small, intelligible cosmos; where warfare, currency devaluation, the burden of taxes, or a small revival satisfied the occasional restlessness. Only in the second half of the century did the social relevance of the restructuring of the New England consciousness become evident in the altered patterns of thought and behavior. These new ways grew into a massive reaction, which made itself felt throughout the colonies in the form of controversy with the mother country. This was the American Revolution.

53. Compare Morison, *Intellectual Life of Colonial New England,* 27–112; R. Hofstadter and W. Smith, eds., *American Higher Education: A Documentary History* (Chicago, 1961); R. Middlekauff, *Ancients and Axioms: Secondary Education in Eighteenth Century New England* (New Haven, Conn., 1963).

John Adams understood the situation very clearly. Since 1759, he noted, a "great intellectual, moral, and political change"[54] was evident, and it had gradually taken hold of the people's minds. "The revolution was in the minds of the people."[55] The "real American revolution," so he recalled, was "this radical change in the principles, opinions, sentiments, and affections of the people." Since the Revolution brought about a change in the "religious, moral, political and social character of the people," the "revolution was effected before the war commenced."[56]

II. Meditationes Imperfectae

Braintree, a typical New England town, experienced itself, regardless of its nearness to Boston, as a social cosmos in its own right; a farming community with rich acreage, its life rhythm was determined by the cycle of the seasons, with the hot summers and cold winters of the New England inland climate. The singular social organization of the towns reproduced English exemplars adapted to the conditions of colonial existence, the Puritan consciousness molding all social relations down to the family, the basic social element of the town. Thus was created a collective of heads of families who were empowered to take political action; the group was supported by the self-consciousness of a "covenanted community."[57] The town had entered on an existential engagement, "the terms of which were set by its theology." This resulted in a life "led, within the confines of the rural village, on the highest plateau of self-consciousness and led, moreover, with an intensity that modern man cannot imagine."[58] "Protestant Christianity, Calvinist in its temper, if increasingly relaxed in its dogma, dominated the town's life, shaped it, directed it, made it, in its own view at least, an important arena in the universal drama of salvation." This consciousness integrated the world of work, intellectual culture, and politics in a mode of existence that guaranteed a high actualization of human potential. "To spend one's boyhood," explained Adams' biographer, Page Smith, "in such a community meant to bear its imprint for life on the conscious and subconscious levels of one's existence."[59]

---

54. John Adams to Thomas McKean, November 26, 1815, in J. Adams, *Works*, X, 180.
55. John Adams to Morse, November 29, 1815, in J. Adams, *Works*, X, 182.
56. John Adams to Niles, February 13, 1818, in J. Adams, *Works*, X, 282–83.
57. Page Smith, *City Upon a Hill* (New York, 1966), 6; compare especially M. Zuckerman, "The Social Context of Democracy in Massachusetts," *William and Mary Quarterly*, XXV (1968), 523–44; R. E. Brown, *Revolutionary Politics in Massachusetts* (Cambridge, Mass., 1970), 2–14; J. R. Pole, *Political Representation in England and the Origins of the American Republic* (New York, 1966), 38–75.
58. P. Smith, *John Adams*, I, 3.
59. *Ibid.*, 5.

The Adams family lived in Braintree from the town's founding and boasted that its ancestors had been persecuted by Archbishop Laud (though no historical proof has yet been found to support this claim).[60] John Adams, Sr., improved his social station—which began considerably below that of Colonel Quincy, the acknowledged political leader of the area—by marrying into the Boylston family. Both farmer and artisan, councilman, officer of the militia, and church deacon, the older John Adams was a typical example of New England versatility: "almost all the business of the town being managed by him . . . for twenty years together," recalled his son, "a man of strict piety, and great integrity; much esteemed and beloved, where ever he was known, which was not far, his sphere of life being not very extensive."[61] The son of this man, with his "admiration of learning," found his path laid out for him: "a liberal education," which was to lead him past village school and Latin school to Harvard and from there directly into the ranks of the clergy, whose primary duty it was, according to the idea of one devout deacon, to fulfill the spiritual calling of man.

For the meetinghouse of the congregation was still the hub of the town's social and spiritual existence: "the clergy, who continued to be the principal exponents of political ideas and the most influential members of the community, devoted their creative intellectual efforts to theology, and their congregation continued to search for goals." Every Sunday morning or afternoon the entire town gathered in the meetinghouse for several hours of prayer, sermons, and hymns. "Then they went home to write in their diaries and measure their lives against what they had learned in the sermons. Daily they read their bibles and prayed, in private and with their families."[62] Thus for generations a habit of meditation was inculcated that put individual consciousness in touch with reality. Outstanding documents of such meditative efforts are the diaries of the New England intelligentsia. Notes made by John Winthrop, Increase Mather, Cotton Mather, Samuel Sewall, John Hull, Michael Wigglesworth, Jonathan Edwards, and finally John Adams document the continuity of the existential engagement of a self-ordering psyche in the process of ordering itself in the Christian-classical context.[63] A comparative reading of

60. John Adams to Benjamin Rush, July 19, 1812, in J. Adams, *Old Family Letters*, 411.

61. AP, *Diary and Autobiography*, III, 256.

62. E. S. Morgan, "American Revolution Considered as an Intellectual Movement," in *Paths of American Thought*, ed. A. M. Schlesinger and M. White (Boston, 1963), 147; see also P. Smith, *John Adams*, I, 5.

63. On the literature about Puritanism mentioned above, see R. Middlekauff, "Piety and Intellect in Puritanism," *William and Mary Quarterly*, XXII (1965), 435–56; on the continuity of self-reflection, see E. S. Morgan, "John Adams and the Puritan Tradition," *William and Mary Quarterly*, XXXIV (1961), 236–42.

this material allows us to determine a pervasive pattern of self-reflection, whose aim and content were precisely defined by Thomas Hooker: "Meditation is a serious intention of the mind whereby we come to search out the truth, and settle it effectually upon the heart."[64]

Adams' diaries for the years 1755 to 1766 provide an insight into the development process of consciousness and existential attitude in which his personality structure was largely fixed. "The tormented tossings and turnings and the corrosive self-examination . . . dominate completely the first 250 pages . . . of the Diary, which brings Adams to the age of thirty. But then, suddenly, there is a change—a rapid growth; a sudden emergence into maturity."[65] Subsequently only occasional passages testify to self-examinations. His psychological maturation coincides with his marriage. From that time on, his wife, Abigail, was the congenial partner of his meditations, as their correspondence shows. Furthermore, his public life after 1766 called for practical documentation of his meditative experience. But one aspect is crucial: "Though John Adams changed, around his thirtieth year, he was not transformed. The earlier characteristics were transmuted, not eliminated; and they continued to shape his, and in part the nation's history."[66]

Our attempt at an existential analysis, using materials from Adams' diaries and correspondence, is followed by an examination of the categories in which Adams grasped the reality of man in the world, in society, and in history. He made generous use of both traditional and newly developed symbolic material; but no clear-cut literary filiations can be read into his writing, nor does Adams engage in systemic speculation.

Released from the closed world of Harvard, Adams became a schoolmaster in Worcester, where for the first time he found himself alone with himself and the world. He reflects a Pascalian consciousness of human lostness in an infinite universe[67] and inner abandonment to the drives and compulsions of his ego[68] in the periodic experience of an existential paralysis: "I can easily still the fierce tempests or stop the rapid thunderbolt, as commend the motions and operations of my own mind. I am dull, and inactive, and all my resolution, all the spirits I can muster, are insufficient to rouse me from this senseless torpitude. My brain seems constantly in as great confusion, and wild disorder, as Milton's chaos. They are numb

---

64. Thomas Hooker, "The Application of Redemption," in *The Puritans,* ed. P. Miller and T. Johnson (New York, 1963), I, 301.

65. B. Bailyn, "Butterfield's Adams: Notes for a Sketch," *William and Mary Quarterly,* XIX (1962), 249.

66. *Ibid.,* 250.

67. AP, *Diary and Autobiography,* I, 22.

68. *Ibid.,* 7.

and dead. . . . Every thing appears in my mind dim and obscure like objects seen thro a dirty glass or roiled water."[69] Saint Thomas Aquinas described this experience in the concept of *acedia,* which is a "reluctance to set oneself against the heavy weight of earthly being and pull oneself upward to the divine"[70] and which allows refuge in *filiae acedia,* substitute attitudes, extending from spiritual apathy through restless diversions in the world to rebellion against God. A modern analysis was given to this experience by Pascal, who used the expression *ennui,* introduced by the French psychologists; he added *ennui* to the *condition de l'homme.* Without passions, without business, without distraction, without activity, man finds himself in an unbearable situation of absolute calm. "'Tis then he feels his nothingness, his foolishness, his insufficiency, his dependence, his emptiness. Forthwith there will issue from the depth of his soul ennui, blackness, gloom, chagrin, vexation, despair."[71] Adams carefully describes this psychological state: "I had an aching void within my breast, this night. I feel anxious, eager after something. What is it? I feel my own ignorance. I feel concern for knowledge, and fame."[72] In order to escape the emptiness of ennui, according to Pascal, man thinks of diversion to free himself of reflecting on his true situation. "The only good thing for men, therefore, is to be diverted from thinking of what they are, either by some occupation which takes their mind off it, or by some novel and agreeable passion which keeps them busy, like gambling, hunting, some absorbing show, in short by what is called diversion."[73] But according to Pascal, it is not a problem that in their excitement men seek diversion, so long as they consider it merely a distraction; the problem lies in the fact that they want it "as though, once they had the things they seek, they could not fail to be truly happy."[74]

Walter Rehm places Pascal's analysis in the context of the existential crisis of the seventeenth century and comments on this development in a "genealogy of boredom in Europe": "Ennui and divertissement descend as pain and torment, as it were, step by step from the ruler and the court, from the 'grand seigneur' down into bourgeois society, to which they were at first strange in this form. Then they describe their destructive and draining circles there as well, dashing almost every attempt at achieving

69. *Ibid.,* 21.

70. Compare K. Stenzel, "Pascals Theorie des Divertissement" (Ph.D. dissertation, Munich, 1966), 66.

71. B. Pascal, *Pensées,* Classiques Garnier (Paris, n.d.), frag. 131, p. 108 (English from B. Pascal, *Pensées,* trans. Turnell, frag. 111, pp. 56–57).

72. See AP, *Diary and Autobiography,* 100.

73. Pascal, *Pensées,* ed. Chevalier (Paris, n.d.), frag. 205, p. 1139n1 (English from B. Pascal, *Pensées,* trans. A. J. Krailsheimer [Middlesex, 1966], frag. 136, pp. 67–68).

74. *Ibid.,* frag. 139, p. 111; *ibid.,* frag. 139, p. 69.

an inner balance in the household of spiritual forces."[75] Adams' reflections reveal a conscious attempt at such a balance, and at the same time they document the intimate relationship between psychological processes and the political order of a society. He experienced the whole spectrum of diversion, from momentary distraction all the way to the existential consolidation that allows man to seek his happiness in the infinite progress of inward activities and still only turns the disorder of existence into the norm from which social corruption spreads.

"What is the cause of procrastination," Adams complained. "To day my stomack is disordered, and my thoughts of consequence, unsteady and confused. I can't study today but will begin to morrow. Tomorrow comes. Well, I feel pretty well, my head is pretty clear, but company comes in"[76]; "my resolutions are like bubbles," he graphically described his condition, "they are perpetually rising to the surface of the stream and then are [broke] and vanish by every puff of wind."[77] "I have got a restless habit. . . . I find my thoughts ruminating the idle chat and banter."[78] They wander from girls to friends, from Worcester to Newbury, from poetry to jurisprudence, without satisfying him: "What is to be acquired by this wavering life . . . ?"[79] "Where is my soul, where are my thoughts?"[80] Distracting oneself by hedonistic devotion to the stimulants of the impulse mechanism merely intensifies—in spite of an "amorous disposition,"[81] in spite of pleasure in social life—the occasional attacks of existential nausea. The banal hedonism of an existence of leisure and luxury, with alcohol, promiscuity, cockfights, hunting trips, and card games could never appear meaningful to a New Englander, since from childhood the system of the secondary virtues of industry, simplicity, moderation, and a sense of duty had been instilled in him.

"Each individual must and will have some employment for his thought, some amusement, business, study, pleasure or diversion, virtuous or vicious, laudable or contemptible, to consume his time."[82] But what, he asked himself, was the motivating force that drove him to occupations beyond pure diversion? "The desire of fame, fortune and personal pleasure." For "I never shall shine till some animating occasion calls forth all

---

75. W. Rehm, *Experimentum Medietatis* (Munich, 1947), 103–104.
76. AP, *The Earliest Diary*, ed. L. H. Butterfield (Cambridge, Mass., 1966), 72.
77. *Ibid.*, 67.
78. AP, *Diary and Autobiography*, I, 104.
79. *Ibid.*, 86.
80. *Ibid.*, 95.
81. *Ibid.*, III, 260.
82. AP, *Earliest Diary*, 70.

my powers. I find that the mind must be agitated with some passion, either love, fear, hope etc. before she will do her best."[83] He became aware of "concern for fame" as the driving motivation of his own thought and acting. "When shall I start some new thought, make some new discovery, that shall surprise the world with its novelty and grandeur? . . . that may rise me at once to fame."[84] Popularity and reputation steadily emerge as criteria for correct behavior. Reason, knowledge, and wisdom, the complete cluster of the ethical virtues, it seems, became the instrument for the self-assertion of an ego thirsty for fame in the world. As it seemed to one scholar, Adams made "the Protestant ethic the way to fame."[85] And at times Adams toyed with a radical immanentist psychology that revealed man to be a bundle of libidinous compulsions.

> Men of the most exalted genius and active minds are generally perfect slaves to the love of fame. They sometimes descend to as mean tricks and artifices in pursuit of honour and reputation, as the miser descends to, in pursuit of gold. The greatest men have been the most envious, malicious and revengeful. The miser toils by night and day, fasts and watches till he emaciates his body to fatten his purse and increase his coffers. The ambitious man rolls and tumbles in his bed, a stranger to refreshing sleep and repose thro anxiety about a preferment he has in view. The philosopher sweats and labours at his book, and ruminates in his closet till his bearded and grim countenance exhibits the effigies of pale want and care and death in quest of hard work, solemn nonsense, and ridiculous grimace. The gay gentleman rambles over half the globe, buys one thing and steals another, and gets his own limbs and head broke for a few transitory flashes of happiness.[86]

Adams came to realize that the *movens* of the man seeking diversion as well as the objects for which he strives are both products of his power of imagination:

> I am conscious . . . that this faculty is very active and stirring. It is constantly in action unless interrupted by the presence of external objects, by reading or restrained by attention. It hates restraint, it runs backward to past scenes and or forward to the future . . . . This prospect of futurity which imagination gilds and brightens is the greatest spur to industry and

83. AP, *Diary and Autobiography*, I, 133.

84. *Ibid.*, 95.

85. S. E. Morison, "John Adams and the Puritan Tradition," *New England Quarterly*, XXXIV (1961), 526.

86. AP, *Diary and Autobiography*, I, 8.

application. The scholars spur to study. The commanders spur to activity and courage. The statesmen spur to invention and execution of plans of politics . . . . Men are aspiring and ambitious in their souls (and hearts?) as their imaginations are vivid.[87]

But immediately Adams began to doubt the possibility of happiness from diversion, from the constant anticipation of fame, power, and possessions. He ended his reflection with the question, "Is it perfection or downright madness and distraction?"[88] His sensitive mind was first made uncertain by the experience that the search for immortality and fame repeatedly brought him into conflict with the world around him, that his personality structure was apparently not at all suited to such obsessions. "The love of fame naturally betrays a man into several weaknesses and fopperies that tend very much to diminish his reputation, and so defeat itself. Vanity I am sensible, is my cardinal vice and cardinal folly."[89]

Adams' use of the word *vanity* provides a link with our analysis of self-understanding, clearly indicating a complex of determinants in his consciousness that allowed him to imagine inward happiness from social success. Adams confirms Pascal's statement that man's *vanité*, the state of being pleased with oneself, is realized in *divertissement*. This is a manifestation of *orgueil*, pride, which has its origin in *amour-propre*. "The nature of self-love and of this human ego is to love self alone and think of self alone."[90] After reading the English and French moralists, Adams had recourse to this same expression. "Self-love" describes the field of tension of psychological forces in that area called the ego by modern motivational psychology.[91] But Adams' "self-love" reaches deep into the id, including "self-preservation," the physical and mental characteristics of man's animal existence. "Self-love" insulates this world of the passions through its attendant principle of self-deception, which presents impulses of passion as a dictate of conscience.[92] Unlike Pascal, who was forced to set himself against an established psychology of *amour-propre*, Adams'

---

87. *Ibid.*, 98ff. Compare "Imagination" in T. Hobbes, *Leviathan*, ed. M. Oakeshott (Oxford, 1960), I, 2, and Pascal, *Pensées*, frag. 82, pp. 95ff.

88. AP, *Diary and Autobiography*, I, 8.

89. *Ibid.*, 25.

90. Pascal, *Pensées*, Classiques Garnier, frag. 100, pp. 101–102 (English from Turnell, frag. 145, pp. 73–74).

91. Compare S. Freud, *Civilization and its Discontents*, trans. J. Riviere (New York, 1958). Here he defines libido as "the whole available energy of Eros" (23). But Freud himself and especially the neo-Freudians unequivocally located the instinct apparatus in the ego that Pascal summarized in the phenomenon of *amour-propre* and for which I use the encompassing term *libido*.

92. J. Adams, *Works*, III, 433–34.

thoughts were worked out in an intellectual climate in which *amour-propre* could not be the last word of a meditation on man, especially when the meditating person was himself aware of the problem of *vanitas*.

The act of becoming conscious of one's being pleased with oneself may even have conferred a dynamic momentum to the meditation in the self-centeredness of the still-unformed young man. That would be the impetus of the vanity of which Thomas Mann claims that "it can be a profound preoccupation, serious and contemplative absorption in the self, passion for autobiography, compelling curiosity about the why and wherefore of one's physical and moral being, nature's devious ways, the hidden secrets of her dark laboratory, that produced this being which is you, to the wonder and admiration of the world."[93] It is not therefore surprising that a lifelong concern with his own complacency made Adams sensitive to the function of the libido in himself and in his fellows. For, so he noted in old age: "Vanity is really what the French call it, *amour-propre*, and it is an universal passion. All men have it in an equal degree."[94] But when Bolingbroke, whom Adams much admired, claimed that self-love was the core of all social being, Adams quoted the source for the statement, one of his favorite passages in Pope:

> Self-love but serves the virtuous mind to wake,
> As the small pebble stirs the peaceful lake;
> The centre mov'd, a circle strait succeeds,
> Another still, and still another spreads.

And he commented: "But this is not correct in the verse or prose. Self-Love is not the mover."[95] He returned to the question of the moving center in another commentary on the same lines from Pope. "To what object are my views directed? What is the end and purpose of my studies, journeys, labours of all kinds of body and mind, of tongue and pen? Am I grasping at money, or scheming for power? Am I planning the illustration of my family or the welfare of my country? These are great questions. In truth, I am tossed about so much from post to pillar, that I have not leisure and tranquillity enough to consider distinctly my own views, objects and feelings." He feels his daily life to be "a life of here and everywhere . . . a rambling, roving, vagrant, vagabond life."[96] This diary entry was from the year 1768, proving that time and again Adams was brought back to the question of how to order his existence.

93. T. Mann, *Lotte in Weimar* (1940; rpr. Frankfurt, 1959), 262 (English from H. T. Lowe-Porter, translated under the title *The Beloved Returns* [New York, 1948], 323).
94. John Adams to Benjamin Rush, May 21, 1807, in J. Adams, *Works*, IX, 598.
95. Quoted in Haraszti, *Adams and the Prophets of Progress*, 72.
96. AP, *Diary and Autobiography*, I, 337.

Aimlessly wandering thoughts, a life without a center, signaled to the Puritan consciousness, in the spirit of Ephesians 4:17–18, alienation from a life in God. "When our thoughts start aside from under the government of God's wisdom, the rule of truth and stability, they wander up and down in the ways of error and vanity, and find no end or measure, follow vanity, and become vain, nor can they attain any stability before they return thither," Hooker wrote. "Further than they are under the eye of God, and awed with his presence, it's not possible to stop them from the pursuit of vanity, or confine them to settled consideration of that which concerns our duty and comfort."[97] Adams' meditation clings to the Christian paradigm of meditative effort, as it was practiced in Puritan New England: "the Diary and Autobiography . . . may be read as the culminating volumes of the history of vanity in New England. . . . Keeping a diary was itself a duty in the war against vanity." For "the very act of self-assessment helped to control vanity and induce humility."[98] "Oh that I could wear out of my mind every mean and base affection," Adams complained, "conquer my natural pride and self-conceit."[99] And elsewhere:

> We shall find that we have been through the greatest part of our lives pursuing shadows, and empty but glittering phantoms rather than substances. We shall find that we have applied our whole vigour, all our faculties, in the pursuit of honour, or wealth, or learning, or some other such delusive trifle, instead of the real and everlasting excellences of piety and virtue. Habits of contemplating the deity and his transcendent excellences, and correspondent habits of complacency in and dependence of him, habits of reverence and gratitude to God, and habits of love and compassion to our fellow men and habits of temperance, recollection and self-government will afford us a real and substantial pleasure. We many then exult in a consciousness of the favor of God, and the prospect of everlasting felicity.[100]

Here Adams completed the countermovement to diversion, which, according to Pascal, moves man toward the "ordre de la charité": "This order consists mainly in digressions upon each point which relates to the end, so that this shall be kept always in sight."[101] "He was young . . . when he wrote these words," commented Bernard Bailyn on Adams' di-

---

97. Hooker, "Application of Redemption," in *The Puritans,* ed. Miller and Johnson, I, 308.

98. E. S. Morgan, "Adams and the Puritan Tradition," 523.

99. AP, *Diary and Autobiography,* I, 7.

100. *Ibid.,* 31.

101. Pascal, *Pensées,* Classiques Garnier, frag. 283, p. 148 (English from Pascal, *Pensées,* trans. Krailsheimer, frag. 298, p. 122).

gression in which he pondered the *telos* of his existence, "but he meant them, and continued to mean them, and he loathed himself for violating his spirit."[102] "If I could but conform my life and my conversation to my speculations, I should be happy," he exclaimed elsewhere.[103] Meditation proved to him the "love of god," *amor dei,* as man's center of order beyond *amor sui,* which reveals itself to meditation as the "woof and web of wickedness" (Hooker), which had its roots in the deficiency of the contemporary human condition and was accepted as an integral part of reality but which conscience must provide with order. "Vice and folly are so interwoven in all human affairs that they could not possibly be wholly separated from them without tearing and rending the whole system of human nature and state."[104]

But Adams' meditation no longer moved in the medium of Hooker's "law of God"—that is, of Calvinist dogmatics, which had already grown meaningless for him. Nor did he undergo a mystical union with God, like Pascal and Edwards. To that extent his meditations were incomplete. Some of the material from his later years may help us to clarify the nature of his religiosity, for the real content of his digression in Pascal's sense will not allow for the label of deism, leaving it open whether, as already indicated, the deists' God is not quite simply the subsequent dogmatization of the God of the mystics. Freed from all dogma, Adams' God— the God of Pope's *Universal Prayer*—remains a *deus absconditus,* divine ground of all being and *realissimum* behind every symbolization.[105] Himself a "church-going animal"[106] all his life, he was convinced that "Man is constitutionally, essentially, and inchangeably a religious animal,"[107] and he asked himself a few not entirely fictive questions concerning the consequences of the radically immanent credo "that men are but fireflies, and that this all is without a father." "Is this the way to make man, as man, an object of respect? Or is it to make murder itself as indifferent as shooting a plover, and the extermination of the Rohilla nation as innocent as the swallowing of mites on a morsel of cheese?"[108] He never ceased to insist that "I am a Christian,"[109] and he was certain that

---

102. Bailyn, "Butterfield's Adams," 244.

103. AP, *Diary and Autobiography,* I, 42.

104. *Ibid.,* 184.

105. That is why, as he grew older, Adams was increasingly fascinated with the study of religions; compare the correspondence with that of Jefferson, Rush, and Van der Kemp.

106. John Adams to Benjamin Rush, August 28, 1811, in J. Adams, *Works,* IX, 636.

107. John Adams to Francis Van der Kemp, October 2, 1818, in Adams Manuscripts, Historical Society of Pennsylvania.

108. J. Adams, *Works,* IV, 281.

109. John Adams to Francis Van der Kemp, January 23, 1818, in Adams Manuscripts, Historical Society of Pennsylvania.

"Christian religion, as I understand it, is the brightness of the glory and the express portrait of the character of the eternal, self-existent, independent, benevolent, all-powerful and all-merciful Creator, preserver, and father of the universe; the first good, first perfect, and first fair."[110] Another phrase leads back from the speculation on being to the meditative core of experience: "The love of God and his creation; delight, joy, triumph, exultation in my own existence ... are my religion."[111] It is, as he wrote Van der Kemp, "founded on the love of God and my neighbour."[112] Adams' *amor dei* is not the result of pneumatic spirituality; it must be understood theoretically as resembling a variant of Aristotelian *philautia*.[113] In this version man lives in harmony with his true self, the *nous*. In ordering himself toward his *nous*, the *theotaton* within himself, he transcends his humanness. In the actualization of the *nous*, however, is also born solidarity (*homonoia*) with other human beings in the substantial form of friendship; as *philia politike*, it becomes the core of every social organization, which acquires the necessary measure of humanity only through the socialization of virtue in *eupraxia*.[114] On one crucial point the Christian dimension skips over this civic humanism with its classical-Greek limitation: faced with the task "to improve ourselves in habits of society and virtue," Adams concluded, "the meanest mechanic who endeavors in proportion to his ability to promote the happiness of his fellowmen deserves better of society and should be held in higher esteem than the greatest magistrate who uses his power for his own pleasures or avarice or ambition."[115] In Adams' discovery of the truth of his existence, an experience of reality comes to light that clarifies the true meaning of the idea of man and of human nature embodied in the repub-

110. John Adams to Benjamin Rush, January 21, 1810, in John Adams, *The Spur of Fame: Dialogues of John Adams and Benjamin Rush*, ed. J. A. Schutz and Douglas Adair (San Marino, Calif., 1956), 160.

111. John Adams to Thomas Jefferson, September 14, 1812, in J. Adams, *Adams-Jefferson Letters*, II, 374.

112. John Adams to Francis Van der Kemp, July 13, 1815, in Adams Manuscripts, Historical Society of Pennsylvania.

113. Compare Aristotle, *Nichomachean Ethics*, 1161a15–1169a20. D. M. Robathan, "John Adams and the Classics," *New England Quarterly*, XIX (1946), 91–98; Iacuzzi, *John Adams: Scholar;* R. M. Gummere, "The Classical Politics of John Adams," *Boston Public Library Quarterly*, X (1958), 203–12, all merely supply material documenting Adams' intense preoccupation with classical politics; they do not discuss their theoretical relevance for Adams' thought.

114. Compare the quotation concerning the function of virtue in society, which Adams copied out of Joseph Butler, *Analogy of Religion* (1740), and recorded in his Literary Commonplace Book, APM. See also the essay by Friedrich, Germino, and Taubes in C. J. Friedrich, ed., *Community* (New York, 1959).

115. AP, *Diary and Autobiography*, I, 23.

lican paradigm. Cut off from the constituent experiences, the symbols, reified into the term *tradition* by dogmatic historiography, are usually explained by the modern observer in terms of motivational psychology or social history.[116] But if the person-centered experience of self-ordering as the self-educative effort at governing one's own person by one's true, rational self is negated, the crucial psychosocial condition for "self-government" will no longer be able to be comprehended as the structural principle of public order. "Virtue" and "vice" lose their sense as existential categories of eminent political significance.[117] Only the dynamics of experiencing the potential of personal reason and the difficulties of its existential actualization justify the institutions of education and voting as a "recurrence to first principles" of the existential virtues of self-ordering man. Education conveys by means of reenactment the constituent experiences of the rational self, and in voting the citizen uses his reason to the extent of entrusting public government to reasonable persons for a time and, if need be, to take this trust back again.[118]

Assuming that the meditative process has a predominantly noetic character (to put it cautiously in philosophical language), although the language used mixes Christian, classical, and Enlightenment elements, it nevertheless gives some pointers to the significant nuances of the concept of "reason" as used by Adams, without ignoring the vagueness of the term that Adams shared with his contemporaries. For one, reason is the *differentia specifica* of man in general, distinguishing him from inorganic, organic, and animal being. Further, it has a noetic function through which man finds the truth of his existence.[119] But occasionally it is also, in the Lockean sense, merely the organizational principle of consciousness—though again it includes the classical *episteme*, the faculty of deductive reasoning from first principles. But reason is also generally identical with *techne*, knowledge about the making of objects, of "engines

116. An example of such a misinterpretation on the level of motivational history as it applies to Adams' diaries is furnished by S. Kagle, "Instrument for Ambition: The Diaries of John Adams" (Ph.D. dissertation, Michigan State University, 1968).

117. Compare R. Maurer, *Platons "Staat" und die Demokratie* (Berlin, 1970), especially 91–98.

118. Compare Thomas Jefferson to John Adams, October 28, 1813: "to leave to the citizens the free election and separation of the aristoi from the pseudo-aristoi" (in J. Adams, *Adams-Jefferson Letters*, II, 388). This context of experience becomes immediately clear as well in the writings of the English Christian radicals such as Richard Price and Joseph Priestley; compare S. Lynd, *Intellectual Origins of American Radicalism* (New York, 1968), 28–29, 56.

119. AP, *Diary and Autobiography*, I, 26; John Adams to Cranch, August 29, 1765, APM.

and instruments, to take advantage of the powers of nature,"[120] and *phronesis,* which conveys the habit of right action, which in Adams coincides with "virtue" as the content of the order of social existence.

Noetic meditation in a Christian setting, however, of necessity also implies the tension between the world-immanent *eudaimonia* of the "good life" and eternal otherworldly *beautitudo;* in Adams it unconsciously becomes thematic. He always insisted "that this life was designed to be an education for a future one."[121] Given his strong distaste for any kind of dogma, it seems unlikely that Adams "retained" the "future state" out of consideration for his surroundings, or out of fear of social repressions; nor is he a cynic who believes that his fellow man must be forced to adopt good behavior through sanctions in the hereafter, though he did deal with this aspect of the matter. But some formulations seem to point more readily to a reality of experience expressed in the symbol of the "future state": Should there be at some later time a revelation or proof "that there is no future state, and my advice to every man, woman and child would be, as our existence would be in our own power, to take opium. For I am certain there is nothing in this world worth living for but hope, and every hope will fail us, if the last hope, the hope of a future state, is extinguished."[122] We cannot help but recall Marx's famous dictum that turns the metaphor around, for in Adams it is only the loss of the existential tension, which he calls hope, toward eternity that calls for intoxication with opium; Marx, on the other hand, assigns the stupefying effect of opium to the tension, which can be relieved by criticism of a religion that gives immanence to eternity.[123]

Opposed to all Christian doctrines about the hereafter, since institutionalized religion misuses them purely to manipulate man, Adams, faced with the "future state," made use of the Socratic openness Plato spoke of in the *Apology.* Logically Adams also reflected on "eternal felicity," not in the category of the *visio beatifica,* but in terms of friendship: "I know not how to prove physically that we shall meet and know each other in a future state; nor does revelation as I can find give us any positive assurance of such a felicity. My reasons for believing it, as I do, most undoubtingly are all moral and divine.... Why should the Almighty dissolve

120. AP, *Diary and Autobiography,* I, 133.

121. *Ibid.,* 25.

122. John Adams to Francis Van der Kemp, December 27, 1816, in Adams Manuscripts, Historical Society of Pennsylvania; compare John Adams to Francis Van der Kemp, July 13, 1815, *ibid.;* and John Adams to Thomas Jefferson, May 3, 1816, in J. Adams, *Adams-Jefferson Letters,* II, 470.

123. K. Marx, *Kritik der Hegelschen Rechtsphilosophie,* in *Werke,* ed. H. J. Leber (Darmstadt, 1962–), I, 488.

forever all the tender ties which unite us so delightfully in the world and forbid us to see each other in the next?"[124]

"This world," he concludes, "was not designed for a lasting and happy state, but rather for a state of moral discipline that we might have a fair opportunity and continual excitements to labour after a cheerful resignation to all the events of Providence after habits of virtue, self-government, and piety. . . . A World in flames, and a whole system tumbling in ruins to the center has nothing terrifying in it to a man whose security is built on the adamantine basis of good conscience and confirmed piety."[125] For Adams, having experienced finite existence in an infinite universe and the emptiness of self-love, meditation returned consciousness to reality. An extraordinarily intense capacity for perception activated the experience of reality in conscious experiences of participation: "Experience is the only source of human knowledge. It is the crutch men hopple on in the course of reasoning."[126] Bernard Bailyn speaks of a "sensuous apprehension of experience. For all his mental efforts and intellectual accomplishments, his knowledge and ideas, he responded first and fundamentally to the physical—the tangible, audible, visual—qualities of life. He felt the world directly and sensitively, before he thought about it; and he expressed his feelings with a vividness and an accuracy of phrasing, that make his prose the most alive and readable of any written in eighteenth-century America."[127]

That attitude reflects a form of perception that maintained the tradition of an extreme sensitivity to states of being in America, as held from Edwards to Pierce and to William James. It links the immediate apperception of reality to the world of men and things, thus elucidating the presence of "being in general" in a world of particulars. "Being in general" is Edwards' symbol for a primary experience, behind which it was not possible to go. It involves the experimental notion of "love of being," whose meditative component utilized Locke's tools without being taken in by his sensualism. The same is true for Adams' thinking: it was "Puritan before it was Lockean," and therefore "Puritanism recast in the idiom of empirical psychology."[128] In Adams, the drama of the psyche was ex-

---

124. John Adams to Thomas Jefferson, December 8, 1818, in J. Adams, *Adams-Jefferson Letters*, II, 530; similarly, John Adams to Abigail Adams, May 12, 1796, in J. Adams, *Letters*, II, 208.

125. AP, *Diary and Autobiography*, I, 41–42.

126. J. Adams, Literary Commonplace Book, APM.

127. Bailyn, "Butterfield's Adams," 246.

128. P. Miller, *Jonathan Edwards*, 62; compare especially Heimert, *Religion and the American Mind*, 109ff.; Haroutunian, *Piety versus Moralism*, 78ff; Jonathan Edwards' early "Of Being" and "Notes on the Mind."

tended to the drama of the New England farmers, clergymen, and colonels, until it became finally absorbed in the drama of being. "The nature and essence of the material world is not less concealed from our knowledge than the nature and essence of God," Adams wrote.

> We see ourselves surrounded on all sides with vast expanse of heavens, and we feel ourselves astonished at the grandeur, the blazing pomp of those stars with which it is adorned. The birds fly over our heads and our fellow animals labour and sport around us, the trees wave and murmur in the winds, and clouds float and shine on high, the surging billows rise in the sea, and ships break through the tempest. Here rises a spacious city, and yonder is spread out an extensive plain. These objects are so common and familiar, that we think ourselves fully acquainted with them; but these are only effects and properties, the substance from whence they flow is hid from us in impenetrable obscurity.

In animate as in inanimate creation, an astonishing diversity as well as a surprising uniformity exists. But "there is from the highest species of animal upon this globe, which is generally thought to be man, a regular and uniform subordination of one tribe to another down to the apparently insignificant animalcules in pepper water, and the same subordination continues quite through the vegetable kingdom." [129]

Subsequently Adams speculatively transformed these reflections into the concept of an order encompassing all realms of being: "Nature, which has established in the universe a chain of being and universal order, descending from archangels to microscopic animalcules, has ordained that no two objects shall be perfectly alike, and no creatures perfectly equal." [130] Adams expressed the reality grasped by meditation in a speculation on being that presents immanence and transcendence in the form of the great chain of being. Such a speculative compromise, which was offered in the seventeenth and eighteenth centuries, recoiled from the obvious consequences of the radicality of Christian transcendence and gradually grasped the universe of the new physics, being forced to call upon the mediation of the philosophical *ratio*.[131] But under Adams' horizon of experience, this speculation was given thoroughly original touches

129. AP, *Diary and Autobiography*, I, 38–39.

130. J. Adams, *Works*, VI, 285.

131. Compare the comprehensive account of this type of speculation in A. O. Lovejoy, *The Great Chain of Being* (New York, 1960). This speculation was widespread among the New England clergy of the eighteenth century, but Adams may have been stimulated just as easily by Alexander Pope, Henry St. John Bolingbroke, and Joseph Addison to arrive at this construction.

in order to combine Aristotelian nomothetics, the Puritan heritage, and a cosmic hierarchy of being, as shall be seen below.

III. "Calling" and Politics

Meditation could do more than search for truth; beyond this, "it settles it effectually upon the heart." Properly organized reflection brings with it the correct reformation. "A settled and serious meditation of any thing, is as the setting open the flood-gates, which carries the soul with a kind of force and violence, to the performance of what he bestows his mind upon."[132] The meditative act of self-ordering implies a *eupraxia* in which the *conversio* is verified. To this extent, meditation disclosed to the Puritan his calling, which determined his place in the world. This existential engagement also underlay the reflections of John Adams, Harvard graduate and schoolmaster: What had he been called to do, and how was he to follow this calling appropriately? "Upon the stage of life, we have each of us a part, laborious and difficult part, to act, but we are all capable of acting our parts, however difficult, to the best advantage." While in the theater the applause of the audience is more important than self-approbation, "upon the stage of life" conscience is what counts. "We have indeed the liberty of choosing what character we shall sustain in this great and important drama. But to choose rightly we should consider in what character we can do the most service to our fellow men, as well as to ourselves. The man who lives wholly to himself is of less worth than the cattle in his barn."[133] Only in *eupraxia* does knowledge take on an existential dimension. "Now to what higher object, to what greater character can any mortal aspire than to be possessed of all this knowledge, well digested and ready at command, to assist the feeble and friendless, to discountenance the haughty and lawless, to procure redress of wrongs, the advancement of right, to assert and maintain liberty and virtue, to discourage and abolish tyranny and vice."[134] In 1756 Adams was still prepared, in accord with his father's wishes, to accept the poverty, suspicion of heresy, and theological dogmatics of a minister in exchange for "an opportunity of diffusing truth and virtue among the people," since the clergyman "will be able to do more good to his fellow men, and make

132. Hooker, "Application of Redemption," in *The Puritans*, ed. Miller and Johnson, I, 304–305.
133. John Adams to Cushing, May 1, 1765, in *Proceedings of the Massachusetts Historical Society*, XLVI, 411.
134. John Adams to Sewall, October, 1759, in AP, *Diary and Autobiography*, I, 224.

better provisions for his own future happiness in this profession than in any other."[135] On the theological plane he was already an Arminian with antidogmatic leanings; the dogma of predestination, the divinity of Jesus, eternal damnation, and the like had ceased to mean anything to him.[136] A long-standing bitter controversy concerning details of dogmatics and church policy in his home community had taught him "that the study of theology and the pursuit of it as a profession would involve me in endless altercations and make my life miserable without any prospect of doing any good to my fellow men."[137] Medicine was out of the question, since a good doctor would not find a place and a bad doctor did no more than put people underground. Of course in these reflections the mingling of "calling" with opportunity cannot be overlooked. But Adams' choice of the law clearly shows that original patterns of consciousness could be successfully adapted to altered social conditions. Various family members, Adams noted, were "full of the most illiberal prejudices against the law."[138] At the time, Adams fully shared these views. "Let us look upon a lawyer: In the beginning of life we see him fumbling and raking amidst the rubbish of writs, indightments, pleas, ejectments, enfiefed, illatebration and a 1000 other lignum vitae words that have neither harmonie nor meaning. When he gets into business he often foments more quarrels than he composes, and inriches himself at the expense of impoverishing others more honest and deserving than himself."[139] Far from being an idiosyncrasy of the Adams family, this negative image of the lawyer was an integral element of Puritan thinking. Since the rise of the legal profession in the High Middle Ages, Christian enthusiasm saw it as one of its archenemies. This was particularly true for seventeenth-century England. Exorbitant to the masses, the lawyers, the monopolistic administrators of the common law in an increasingly complicated social world, legitimated acts of the privileged classes that were felt to be unjust. Clarity, simplicity, and the written form of the law were therefore part of the fundamental achievements of the City Upon the Hill; and Article 26 of the Body of Liberties prohibited legal representation for pay. Although an elaborately

135. John Adams to Cushing, May 1, 1765, in *Proceedings of the Massachusetts Historical Society*, XLVI, 411–12.

136. Compare *ibid.*, 412; John Adams to Nathan Webb, September 1, 1755, in APM; John Adams to Quincy, May 22, 1761, in J. Adams, *Works*, I, 645; AP, *Diary and Autobiography*, I, 6, 8, 15; on Adams' minimal Christian dogma, see AP, *Diary and Autobiography*, II, 31.

137. AP, *Diary and Autobiography*, III, 262.

138. *Ibid.*, 263.

139. John Adams to Cushing, May 1, 1765, in *Proceedings of the Massachusetts Historical Society*, XLVI, 411.

stratified legal hierarchy splendidly survived the Civil War in England, the attempt to transplant this machinery to the colonies was not successful. Although in America the process of civilization also produced a body of positive law, the merchants and large landowners acted on their own behalf, and the educated local elites were happy to take on the petty legal aspects of the farmers' everyday problems. So it was that not until the eighteenth century did a legal profession develop on a low organizational level and with a highly informal system of training in the form of private tutoring relationships. The level of education and experience of the individual lawyers took the place of technical specialization and social hierarchy, and well into the nineteenth century, laymen, the beneficiaries of political appointments, often occupied the judicial benches; they were apt to be guided more by common sense and the commonly accepted standards of justice than by precedents and the established works of Anglo-Saxon jurisprudence.

In this situation the systematization of the common law in William Blackstone's *Commentaries on the Laws of England* was extremely welcome, furnishing a broad level of self-taught lawyers with a collection of laws that they could easily adapt to American conditions. The increase in foreign trade and intermediate trade most particularly allowed young, ambitious men to rise in the legal profession.[140] In Massachusetts at the outbreak of the Revolution, more than sixty judges and lawyers practiced at the superior court (barrister since 1762), and in a certain sense they made up a legal profession.[141]

The whole complex of "law and justice," however, acquired increasing importance from the structural changes taking place in the order of consciousness and society. The "law"—that is, the aggregate of common law, statutes, and precedents (colonial and English), traditional privileges, liberties, and conventions—became the dominant symbolism in America's self-understanding. The symbolism of the law existentially explicated the substance of public order. The "fusion of law and politics" (Boorstin) meant the identification of essential lawfulness with the positive law and the institutions of colonial society, the paradigmatic republic on American soil. The dominance of "lawyers" in the movement for independence, in the Constitutional Convention, and in the representative

---

140. Compare the account in Boorstin, *The Americans*, I, 195–205.

141. The legal order and the conditions of attorneys in Massachusetts in Adams' time are treated in the introduction to AP, *Legal Papers*, ed. L. K. Wroth and H. B. Zobel (Cambridge, Mass., 1965), xxxviii–cxiv, and in J. M. Murrin, "The Legal Transformation: The Bench and Bar of Eighteenth Century Massachusetts," in *Colonial America*, ed. S. N. Katz (Boston, 1971).

bodies therefore attests, not to the predominance of jurisprudence in the technical sense, but merely to the alliance of legal tradition and nomothetics, which was reflected in the compact formula of a "government of laws and not of men."

Adams is the best example of this alliance. Even when he was still caught up in Puritan prejudice, he declared, "The study of law is indeed an avenue to the more important offices of the state, and the happiness of human society is an object worth the pursuit of any man."[142] Shortly thereafter he was already persuaded: "The study and praxis of law, I am sure, does not dissolve the obligations of morality or of religion."[143] As time went on, Adams, already excited by the predominantly historical basis of the common law, discovered the great source of all knowledge of order in *law*. He found satisfaction "in tracing to their original sources in morality, in the constitution of human nature, and the connection and relations of human life, the laws which the wisdom of perhaps fifty centuries has established for the government of human kind."[144] Here the tendencies of a later development are already manifest—the anamnestic recourse to the history of mankind to illuminate its problems of order: "How is the nature of man, and of society, and of government to be studied or known, but in the history and by experience of human nature in its terrestrial existence."[145]

Adams hoped that the legal profession would furnish a balance of the three clusters of motives that, in combination, made up the continuum of his existence. His *amour-propre* motivated *divertissement* in his social success as a lawyer: encompassing general and legal knowledge "will draw upon me the esteem and perhaps the admiration . . . of the judges of both courts, of the lawyers, and of the juries, who will spread my fame thro the province, will draw around me a swarm of clients who will furnish me with a plentiful provision for my own support, and for the increase of my fortune." But at once his "calling" asserted its claim to *eupraxia*: "By means of this authority and consideration with judges, lawyers, juries and clients, I shall be able to defend innocence, to punish guilt, and to promote truth and justice among mankind." But this *telos* was inspired by a different sort of knowledge, and leisure was required to acquire it: "More leisure to inform his mind, to subdue his passions" had already attracted him to the pulpit. Leisure for contemplation, that is, the therapeutic process to correct compulsive drives to diversion, was

142. John Adams to Cushing, May 1, 1765, in *Proceedings of the Massachusetts Historical Society*, XLVI, 411.
143. AP, *Diary and Autobiography*, I, 43.
144. AP, *Earliest Diary*, 66.
145. J. Adams, *Works*, VI, 481; compare also 479 and 483.

the other strong motive for his choice of profession. "I should moderate my passions, regulate my desires, increase my veneration for virtue, and resolution to pursue it, here I should range the whole material and intellectual world, as far as human powers can comprehend it, in silent contemplation." [146] For "learn to conquer your appetites and passions! Know thyself, came down from Heaven and the government of one's own soul requires greater parts and virtues than the management of kingdoms, and the conquest of the disorderly rebellious principles in our own nature is more glorious than the acquisition of universal dominion." [147] Adams consciously lived through this permanent process of self-ordering in which knowledge and action are resolved in the existential conduct of the *spoudaios,* the mature human being—of course under the social condition of the "covenanted community" in which, according to Adams, "knowledge and dexterity at public affairs" are "common." [148]

These contemplations upon calling and politics reveal also how closely Adams thought the happiness of the individual, that is, private happiness, was tied to the public happiness of the political actor and to the happiness of society to be brought forth by political action.

> My opinion of the duties of religion and morality comprehends a very extensive connection with society at large, and the great interest of the public. Does not natural morality, and much more Christian benevolence, make it our indispensable duty to lay ourselves out, to serve our fellow creatures to the utmost of our power in promoting and supporting those great political systems and general regulations upon which the happiness of multitudes depends. The benevolence, charity, capacity and industry which exerted in private life would make a family, a parish, or a town happy, employed upon a larger scale in the support of the great principles of virtue and freedom of political regulations might secure whole nations and generations from misery, want, and contempt. Public virtues and political qualities therefore should be incessantly cherished in our children. [149]

Talking about the American notion of "public happiness," Arendt explains that "the American knew that public freedom consisted in having a share in public business, and that the activities connected with this business by no means constituted a burden but gave who discharges them in public a feeling of happiness they could acquire nowhere else." [150]

146. AP, *Earliest Diary,* 77.

147. John Adams to Abigail Smith, May 20, 1763, in AP, *Adams Family Correspondence,* I, 5.

148. John Adams to Abigail Adams, October 29, 1775, *ibid.,* 317.

149. John Adams to Abigail Adams, October 29, 1775, *ibid.,* 316.

150. Arendt, *On Revolution,* 115. A. M. Schlesinger, Jr., "The Lost Meaning of the

These words clearly apply to the concrete experiential content of a "Participator in the government of affairs"[151] in the institutional context of colonial society.

But participation demands of the participant in public affairs that he have "public virtue," that he be shaped by the existential virtue of prudence, and that his political action be *eupraxia*.[152] Only then can the individual's "feeling of happiness" be assigned the nature of "public happiness." The citizen's political action, however, should not be played off, as Arendt has done, against man's contemplativeness.[153] It is true that in his problem-oriented method, Aristotle occasionally arrived at the point at which there is danger of a separation between theory and politics. The Aristotelian concept of *eupraxia* reconciles theory and action as modes of actualization of human potential in society, insofar as both necessarily collaborate to achieve the eudaemonia of the polis, while each independently represents a possibility of personal eudaemonia. This linkage of contemplation and action has been preserved in the Puritan concept of a calling in the world. *Public happiness* is the central symbol for the specific republican dimension of the "public realm," in which the members of the society meet in a solidarity transcending the sphere of self-love. Corresponding symbols are *public* liberty, *public* justice, *public* rights, and *public* good.[154] Adams shows that public happiness is grounded in the contemplative act of becoming conscious of one's rational self. Political participation without this premise is private in the existential sense. It was precisely the massive appearance of this type of existentially not-public political action in the new republic that inclined Adams to resignation all his life. Distinct from this is an attitude that combines social and existential privacy in withdrawal into "private, social and domestic

---

'Pursuit of Happiness,'" *William and Mary Quarterly,* XXI (1964), 325–27, emphasizes that here "pursuit" means "the practicing rather than the quest of happiness" (325). Compare the richly documented studies on American self-understanding: H. M. Jones, *Pursuit of Happiness* (Cambridge, Mass., 1953); U. M. von Eckhardt, *The Pursuit of Happiness in the Democratic Creed* (New York, 1959). An analysis directed to modern-day problems is A. Heckscher, *The Public Happiness* (New York, 1962).

151. Thomas Jefferson to Cabell, February 2, 1816, in T. Jefferson, *Writings,* ed. P. L. Ford (New York, 1892–99), XIV, 422.

152. John Adams to Benjamin Rush, May 12, 1807, in J. Adams, *Old Family Letters,* 131; John Adams to Benjamin Rush, September 1, 1807, *ibid.,* 158.

153. H. Arendt, "Action and the 'Pursuit of Happiness,'" in *Politische Ordnung und Menschliche Existenz,* ed. A. Dempf *et al.* (Munich, 1962), 9.

154. Compare G. S. Wood, *Creation of the American Republic,* 55–65. Adams, *Republikanische Verfassung und bürgerliche Freiheit,* largely overlooks this dimension; see especially 229.

life."[155] Adams also felt this temptation of self-love on occasion, but conditioned as his conscience was, he could not give in to it.[156] For even in the social privacy of old age, the contemplatively active "Father of the Nation" led an existentially public life.

155. John Adams to Abigail Adams, January 29, 1775, in AP, *Adams Family Correspondence*, I, 316.

156. None of Adams' biographers surveys his financial situation. According to his own account, his public life was carried out at the cost of potential private prosperity. The heroes of the Revolution in Massachusetts, he declared in 1812, died in poverty or at best in modest comfort. But only those grew rich who devoted themselves to their private affairs during this time. Whereas John Lowell, who took over Adams' practice in 1776–77, left $100,000 at his death in 1812, Adams estimated his own estate in 1812 at $50,000, which returned an interest of less than 2 percent. The estate consisted of two farms in Quincy, worth from $10,000 to $20,000; land valued at $500; and investments (for example, participation in the Middlesex Canal) that brought in no interest. He owed his holdings entirely to his activities as a lawyer in the period 1758–75, as well as to three inheritances: from his father in 1761, from his father-in-law in 1783, and from his wife's uncle in 1803; furthermore, he lost a part of his cash fortune in the economic crisis of the postwar period. John Adams to Benjamin Rush, August 25, 1812, in J. Adams, *Old Family Letters*, 348; John Adams to Benjamin Rush, September 12, 1811, *ibid.*, 362.

Three

Revolutionary Statesmanship

I. Between Reformation and Revolution

"Let me search for the clue which led great Shakespeare into the labyrinth of human nature! Let me examine how men think! Shakespeare had never seen in real life persons under the influence of all those scenes of pleasure and distress, which he has described in his works, but he imagined how a person of such a character would behave in such circumstances, by analogy from the behavior of others that were most like that character in nearly similar circumstances which he had seen."[1] The Puritanical fervor in discovering overt and hidden manifestations of vice within oneself and in one's fellow man, still extensively practiced during the Great Awakening, in Adams turned into an attitude of fascination with everything human, without losing its original impetus to reformation. For the method, which he ascribed to Shakespeare, was his own: concrete experiences with others revealed to him the structures of the social process, as one of the schoolmaster's diary entries shows:

> I sometimes . . . consider myself in my great chair at school as some dictator at the head of a commonwealth. In this little state I can discover all the great genius', all the surprizing actions and revolutions of the great world in miniature. I have several renowned generals but 3 feet high, and several deep-projecting politicians in peticoats. I have others catching and dissect-

[1]. AP, *Diary and Autobiography,* I, 61.

ing flies, accumulating remarkable pebbles, cockle shells etc., with as ardent curiosity as any virtuoso in the royal society. Some rattle and thunder out A, B, C, with as much fire and impetuosity as Alexander fought, and very often sit down and cry as heartily upon being outspelt, as Cesar did, when at Alexanders sepulchre he recollected that the Macedonian hero had conquered the world before his age. At one table sits Mr. Insipid foppling and fluttering, spinning his whirligig, or playing with his fingers as gaily and wittingly as any frenchified coxcomb brandishes his cane or rattles his snuffbox. At another sits the polemical divine plodding and wrangling in his mind about Adam's fall in which we sinned all as his primer has it. In short my little school like the great world is made up of kings, politicians, divines, L. D., fops, buffoons, fidlers, sychophants, fools, coxcombs, chimneysweepers, and every other character drawn in history or seen in the world.[2]

Similarly, a legal dispute becomes the model of social conflict. Looking back he recalled, "In all these cases it seemed to have wrought an entire metamorphosis of the human character. It destroyed all sense and understanding, all equity and humanity, all memory and regard to truth, all virtue, honor, decorum, and veracity. Never in my life was I so griefed and disgusted with my species."[3]

In his role of "critical spy,"[4] he was not only interested in the psychological background of such metamorphoses in the human character; he also made a connection between these phenomena and long-range cycles of order and disorder, of corruption and reform in the social arena, revealing a kind of cosmic justice. "The government of the supreme and all-perfect mind over all his intellectual creation is by proportioning rewards to piety and virtue, and punishment to disobedience and vice." This mechanism of sanctions is guaranteed by the restoration of order, the completion of the "moral government of the universe." From this Adams developed a criterion for social order, which correlated public life and cosmic justice:

Human government is more or less perfect as it approaches nearer or diverges farther from the imitation of this perfect plan of divine and moral government. In times of simplicity and innocence ability and integrity will be the principal recommendations to the public service, and the sole title to those honours and emoluments which are in the power of the public to bestow. But when elegance, luxury and effiminacy begin to be established,

2. *Ibid.*, 14.
3. *Ibid.*, III, 255; compare I, 333–34.
4. *Ibid.*, I, 59.

these rewards will begin to be distributed to vanity and folly. But when a government becomes totally corrupted, the system of God the Almighty in the government of the world and the rules of all good government upon earth will be reversed, and virtue, integrity, and ability will become the objects of the malice, hatred and revenge of the men in power and folly, vice and villany will be cherished and supported.[5]

In his speculation on being, Adams added a few new elements to the great chain of being in order to escape its conservative consequences. For the fairly low position assigned to man in this cosmic hierarchy condemned mankind to an "ethics of prudent mediocrity"[6] and inevitably gave rise to doubts "that a creature so limited and so near to the other animals . . . must necessarily be incapable of attaining any very high level of political wisdom or virtue, and that consequently no great improvement in men's political behavior or in the organization of society could be hoped for."[7] This position could serve as an apologia for any status quo. Furthermore, any materialization of the chain of being had to claim "that the specific and defining defect of man consists precisely in his being the creature whose destiny it is to have visions of perfections which he can not possess and of virtues which he is nevertheless constitutionally incapable of attaining."[8] In this way a correct statement of man's ontic status threatened to become erroneously extended to man's existence, depriving him of his opportunity to sensibly shape his life here and now according to his wealth of experience.

Adams did not flee the static consequence of his speculation by embracing the solution of the European Enlightenment. This view, to which he always objected, temporalized the great chain of being into a progressive historical process and thus arrived at an immanent condition of perfection.[9] The empirical results of his meditations kept him from positing any apocalyptic emergence from the *condicio humana*.[10] Since "all magistrates and all civil officers and all civil government is founded and maintained by the sins of the people,"[11] the state of the millennium would obviate all problems of political order; as he wrote at a later date, "all civil government is then to cease and the Messiah is to reign. That happy

5. *Ibid.*, 365.

6. A. O. Lovejoy, *Great Chain of Being*, 200.

7. *Ibid.*, 203.

8. *Ibid.*, 205.

9. *Ibid.*, 242–87.

10. AP, *Diary and Autobiography*, I, 9; *ibid.*, III, 265. Haraszti, *Adams and the Prophets of Progress*, deals in detail with Adams' relation to the *philosophes*.

11. AP, *Diary and Autobiography*, I, 184.

and holy state is therefore wholly out of the question."[12] In a discussion of man's "perfectibility," Adams described the mode of existence that allows for maximal activation of the experience of human perfection without deviating into apocalypse. He accepted the ontological situation of the chain of being: "The human mind is made capable of conceiving something more perfect than any created being that exists." In the arts as in ethics, what matters is "to aim at a greater perfection than has ever been attained and, perhaps, than ever can be attained." Although he had to rely on the language of philosophical and theological dogmatics, he managed the central theoretical problem quite effectively: he referred to the origin of the debate on perfectibility among philosophers and Christians. Plato's imitation of God, the sage of the Stoics, and the Christian maxim "Be ye perfect, even as your Father in heaven is perfect," all signified the existential tension between the human and the divine: "The external, omniscient, omnipotent, and allbenevolent model of perfection is placed before men for their perpetual meditation and imitation. By this, however, it is not intended that every man can ever become eternal and allmighty, and allwise." Christianity "and . . . all believers in the immortality of the soul" understand this to be a transcendental movement of the intellect, he claimed, characteristically misunderstanding Christian eschatology in the Platonic sense: "the intellectual part of man is capable of progressive improvement for ever." But what did the *philosophes* mean when they spoke of perfectibility? "Do they mean that human body can be made immortal on earth and incorruptible, free from pains and diseases, by human reason? . . . Do they mean that the strength of the human body can be increased so, as to remove mountains, to shake the earth and stop the planets? . . . Do they mean that the human intellect can be enlarged, here in the body, to comprehend the whole constitution and course of nature? . . . I consider the perfectibility of man as used by the modern philosophers to be mere words without a meaning, that is mere nonsense." This was written in the face of the Promethean hopes of Condorcet's apocalypse of history. Adams denied neither the technological consequences of the process of civilization nor the practice of man's self-actualization in society and history. "The continual amelioration of the condition of man in this world, moral, physical, political, civil, and economical, is a very intelligible idea and no doubt is to be desired, mediated, labored, and promoted by all men, and those who do most for it ought to be most esteemed."[13]

12. John Adams to Samuel Adams, October 18, 1790, in J. Adams, *Works*, VI, 416.
13. John Adams to Benjamin Rush, September 19, 1806, in J. Adams, *Old Family Letters*, 111–12.

But in Adams too the nomothetic impetus originally had certain apocalyptic undertones, for in 1765 he, too, saw in the American people the "theopolis Americana" (Cotton Mather). "I always consider the settlement of America with reverence and wonder as the opening of a grand scene and design in Providence for the illumination of the ignorant, and the emancipation of the slavish part of mankind all over the earth." [14] That, too, is why Adams expressed the social phenomena of order and disorder in the traditional category of the jeremiad. Disorder is the falling away from the *paradigma* of the fathers, but he identified this paradigm with the entire body of the common law and the "British Constitution"; "British laws and government" are grounded "in the frame of nature, in the constitution of the intellectual and moral world." [15] He believed, he noted elsewhere, "that the liberty, the unalienable, indefeasible rights of men, the honour and dignity of human nature, the grandeur and glory of the public, and the universal happiness of the individuals, were never so skillfully and successfully consulted as in the most excellent monument of human art, the common law." [16] The concept of *constitution* implies both the political and the existential composition of a society: therefore, decay and corruption have always been phenomena of the whole society. The dysfunction of political institutions signaled spiritual-ethical corruption and demanded self-examination and spiritual reformation, called for by a biblical "remnant."

Adams is a good illustration of the continuity of the jeremiad as the structural determinant of the New Englander's consciousness of crisis. As a consequence of the Great Awakening, the jeremiad increasingly became an all-American manifestation. With its help, social changes were interpreted critically. "In the eyes of many Americans, whether southern planters or New England clergymen, the society was far from virtuous and in fact seemed to be approaching some kind of crisis in its development." [17] In 1760 and 1761, Adams, like many of his contemporaries, was deeply troubled by the symptoms of decline. Politics, he claimed, was rotten, the voters corrupted; the rulers ruled according to their own pockets; justice was incompetent—in short, public affairs had become the plaything of private interests; vice and injustice were spreading. "Many things are

14. J. Adams, *Works*, III, 452. For the American form of the apocalypse during this period, see Tuveson, *Redeemer Nation*, and G. S. Wood, *Creation of the American Republic*.

15. J. Adams, *Works*, III, 463. What is important is that Adams always kept in mind the Constitution in its 1688 form and measured it against the reality of the Constitution of 1760.

16. *Ibid.*, 444; see also 477–78.

17. G. S. Wood, *Creation of the American Republic*, 107.

running wild. Many symptoms begin to appear, that threaten their happiness, their morals, health, properties and liberties, in a very melancholy manner." The source of the evil is Boston: "But even these symptoms are produced in great measure by the inconsiderate politics of this town."[18]

Adams' jeremiad was still bound by the anticivilizational traces of Puritan dogmatics; the blame for the rapid increase in sinfulness was borne by the taverns, which Adams never tired of describing, in words appropriate to any clergyman, as true dens of iniquity. "These houses, like so many boxes of Pandora, are sending forth every day innumerable plagues of every kind, natural, moral and political, that increase and multiply fast enough to lay waste in a little while the whole world."[19] The licensing of countless public houses was a result of corrupt politics, and these in turn were the products of the resulting social milieu: taverns attracted the people, and there they gradually lost the "natural dignity and freedom of English minds," bestowing the offices "which belong by nature and the spirit of all government to probity and honesty" on the "meanest, and weakest, and worst of human characters."[20] Numerous drafts on this topic show that in the spring of 1761—when, after the death of his father, Adams had become a freeholder and was beginning to be politically active—Adams was anxious to exhort his fellow citizens to turn back to first principles by launching a publicity campaign against the taverns.[21] He also persuaded the town to pass an ordinance to limit the licensing of taverns. But during these months he must have realized that the superficial vices promoted in the taverns were not the cause of "the present prevailing depravity of manners through the land in general and in this town in particular and the shameful neglect of religious and civil duties, so highly offensive in the sight of God, and so injurious to the peace and welfare of society," as the minutes of the town meeting on the resolution read.[22] The extent of the crisis forbade assigning the corruption of the American character to the frequenting of taverns, whereas it pointed to a general process of decadence that originated in the malaise of the mother country. "As the colonists were drawn more fully into imperial affairs after 1750, the provincial view of corruption expanded in meaning. . . . As experience with parliament made that idea a reality for Americans, the word 'corruption' attained the fullness of meaning in colonial politics that it had long had among English radicals. It grew from simple greed to include corruption of the legislature through patronage and elec-

18. AP, *Diary and Autobiography,* I, 214.
19. *Ibid.,* 191.
20. *Ibid.,* 214.
21. *Ibid.,* 128–29, 204–205, 212ff.
22. Quoted from *ibid.,* 129–30.

toral influence and thus came to threaten the entire destruction of the constitution."[23]

The impetus for this development was furnished by the case of the Writs of Assistance, which excited the minds of the local political class in Massachusetts in 1761, not least because of their local implications. The historical-legal problems of the case are not at issue here; I must restrict myself to a few remarks.[24] To relieve England's desperate financial situation, a preliminary measure intended to tighten the organization of the empire was the vigorous enforcement of the existing Acts of Trade and Navigation. Since a lively trade in smuggled molasses cheerfully violated the Sugar Act of 1733, in 1760 the customs authorities applied to the superior court for writs of assistance allowing them to search any premises where the contraband goods were supposedly stored. The death of George II necessitated a renewal of the authorization, but this procedure, in itself far from revolutionary in a legal sense, not only ran counter to the interests of a merchant class grown self-confident but also affected an internal power constellation to such an extent that it could furnish a consciousness grown sensitive to crises with the desired explanation for the influx of evil into society. The oligarchic colonial politics allowed family and interest alliances—a junto, as the opposition was in the habit of calling such things—with good connections to England to assume a dominant position, to the disadvantage of other segments of the political class and of energetic *homines novi,* of whom John Adams was definitely one.[25]

Shortly before the first debate at the superior court bar, the chief justice died. The man Governor Francis Bernard appointed to succeed him was not James Otis, Sr., the king's advocate general, but Thomas Hutchinson, the head of a prominent Boston family. Hutchinson was already lieutenant governor, constable, member of the governor's council, and judge of the Suffolk probate court; he had helped his brother-in-law, his

23. R. L. Bushman, "Corruption and Power in Provincial America," in *The Development of a Revolutionary Mentality* (Washington, D.C., 1972), 83.

24. Compare the detailed account by Wroth and Zobel in AP, *Legal Papers,* II, 106–23. On the domestic aspect of the affair, see E. E. Brennan, *Plural Office-Holding in Massachusetts, 1760–1780* (Chapel Hill, N.C., 1945); J. J. Waters and J. A. Schutz, "Patterns of Massachusetts Colonial Politics," *William and Mary Quarterly,* XXIV (1967), 543–67. Generally, see Brown, *Revolutionary Politics in Massachusetts,* 17–37.

25. This state of affairs is nicely brought out by a 1772 anecdote: Provoked by the opposition offered in the colonial House of Representatives, Governor Shirley asked for the names of the delegates from Boston. "Mr. Cushing, Mr. Hancock, Mr. Adams, and Mr. Adams," he was told. "Mr. Cushing I know," Shirley responded; "and Mr. Hancock I know, but where the devil this brace of Adams' came from, I can't conceive" (AP, *Diary and Autobiography,* II, 54–55).

son, his half-brother, and two relatives by marriage to handsome positions. James Otis, Jr., was the attorney representing the interests of those opposed to granting the writs of assistance. He lost the case, but the present combination of growing accumulation of governmental power and plain corruption caused the opposition to agree on the political jeremiad as the instrument of criticism and agent of reform.

This process lasted nearly ten years, but it is precisely Adams' reaction to the writs of assistance that reveals with great clarity the pattern of thought and symbolism of the American Revolution in its genesis. Retrospectively he claimed that American independence was born in that February debate.[26] He saw the controversy as the first confrontation between America and England. For the Americans, to submit would have meant the "entire devastation of the country and a general destruction of their lives. . . . There was no alternative left but to take the side, which appeared to be just, to march intrepidly forward in the right paths, to trust in providence for the protection of truth and right, and to die with a good conscience and a decent grace, if that trial should become indispensable."[27] Adams' original diary entry, after attending the court sessions, betrays no particular excitement. But in the spring—perhaps in elaborating his notes on the proceedings—he realized the connection between social disorder and the writs of assistance. They are, he quoted Otis, "instruments of slavery . . . and villainy . . . the most destructive of English liberty and the fundamental principles of the constitution."[28] In this way the law becomes separated from what is right. "An act against the Constitution is void," for "reason and the constitution are both against the writ." Coke furnished Otis with the constitutional doctrine by which existential justice can deprive legality of the appearance of justice. It is therefore "the business of this court to demolish this monster of oppression." Not without justification Adams later called Otis one of the great movers of the Revolution, for Otis initiated "the experiences that touch and transform; these are the moments in which truth seems to have descended from heaven in the inspired word."[29] But the insight that unconstitutional acts were symptoms of the decline of order and therefore null and void and that opposition of necessity included reform does not yet grow into principled criticism of the "king in parliament" as repre-

26. J. Adams to Benjamin Waterhouse, March 19, 1817, in J. Adams, *Statesman and Friend: Correspondence of John Adams with Benjamin Waterhouse*, ed. W. C. Ford (Boston, 1927), 124; compare J. Adams to Tudor, March 29, 1817, in J. Adams, *Works*, X, 244–49.
27. AP, *Diary and Autobiography*, III, 276.
28. AP, *Legal Papers*, II, 140.
29. P. Smith, *John Adams*, I, 56.

sentatives of the higher law, of the transcendent truth incorporated in the "British Constitution." Only the existential shock of the Stamp Act crisis of 1765 to 1766 attuned Adams' consciousness to the realization that the authority of the "true constitution" was grounded solely in himself and his fellow New Englanders, since the authority of the "king in parliament" had ceased to exist. The occasion was not the Stamp Act itself, though he called it unconstitutional in the *Instructions of the Town of Boston to Their Representatives*. He was moved by one of its consequences: the closing of the Massachusetts courts.[30] Since the proposed stamp tax required documents of every sort, the colony's resistance, beginning on November 1, 1765, also paralyzed the courts. Adams had just established his own family, his legal practice was beginning to be lucrative, he was able to expand his farmlands, and he was looking forward to enjoying prosperity. Thus the general suspension of business and legal affairs first affected his self-love, proving to him anew the illusory nature of diversion in private existence. He lamented:

> So sudden an interruption of my career is very unfortunate for me. I was but just getting into my geers, just getting under sail, and an embargo is upon the ship. Thirty years of my life are passed in preparation for business. I have had poverty to struggle with—envy and jealousy and malice of enemies to encounter—no friends or but few to assist me, so that I have groped in dark obscurity, till of late, and had but just become known, and gained a small degree of reputation, when this execrable project was set on foot for my ruin as well as that of America in general.[31]

He found comfort, when the question of reopening the courts arose, in the request that along with his illustrious colleagues Jeremiah Gridley and James Otis he appear before the governor as legal adviser and spokesman for the town of Boston. Naturally such access to the political leadership of the capital's opposition first of all flattered his ambition; but though Adams, along with his colleagues and the politicians, was looking for a legal way out, recommending that the judges in the various courts be left free to decide on the legality of their actions without the required tax stamp, he began to doubt the legitimacy of the existing order as such. "What are the consequences of the supposition that the courts are shut up? The king is the fountain of justice by the constitution—and

30. See, among others, E. S. Morgan, ed., *Prologue to Revolution: Sources and Documents on the Stamp Act Crises, 1764 to 1766* (Chapel Hill, N.C., 1959); E. S. Morgan and H. M. Morgan, *The Stamp Act Crisis: Prologue to Revolution* (Chapel Hill, N.C., 1953); L. H. Gipson, *The Coming of the Revolution, 1763–1775* (New York, 1954); B. Knollenberg, *Origins of the American Revolution, 1759–1766* (New York, 1960).

31. AP, *Diary and Autobiography*, I, 265.

it is a maxim of the law that the king never dies. Are not protection and allegiance reciprocal? And if we are out of the king's protection, are we not discharged from our allegiance? Are not all the ligaments of government dissolved? Is it not . . . an abdication of the throne? In short where will such an horrid doctrine terminate? It would run us into treason."[32]

He still felt horror at this alternative. But his existential engagement made him aware that the people and their leaders, reduced to a "state of nature," must renew the "true constitution" on the authority of their own knowledge of order. An event of 1768, after a time of peace that had allowed Adams to become a successful and influential attorney in the colony, documents this decision. His old schoolmate Jonathan Sewall, now attorney general acting in the governor's behalf, offered him the post of advocate general at the admiralty court. It was the last and most prestigious of a number of offers, and accepting any one would have made Adams an influential member of the colonial establishment, allowed him access to the distribution system of patronage, and brought the most lucrative clients from the ruling oligarchy. True to the conception prevalent at that time in English political thinking, that political conviction was a minor detail, he was assured of absolute freedom of opinion. Adams tried to explain to Sewall that it was a matter of different existential positions: "I answered that he knew very well my political principles, the system I had adopted and the connections and friendships I had formed in consequence of them; he also knew that the British government, including the king, his ministers and parliament, apparently supported by a great majority of the nation, were persevering in a system wholly inconsistent with all my ideas of right, justice and policy, and therefore I could not place myself in a situation in which my duty and my inclination would be so much in variance." This statement appears to me reliable, since it accords precisely with Adams' development. But the interpretation of the event by the other side, which Hutchinson later took over in London from the Loyalists, seems equally reasonable: Sewall had offered Adams a position, and when Governor Bernard took too long to think about the matter, Adams' disappointment made him join the opposition.[33]

The episode clearly illustrates the contrast between the political attitudes in Georgian England, which began to prevail in the colonies as well, and the New England political consciousness, to which such a mere cyni-

---

32. *Ibid.,* 270; similarly, 291, in a draft for an article, "Clarendon to Pym," which characteristically he never published. But on January 6, 1766, this line of thought appeared under the pseudonym Hampden (probably Otis) in the Boston *Gazette;* compare *ibid.,* 282–83.

33. *Ibid.,* III, 287.

cal stance must seem deficient. The dilemma informed a resistance resulting from the concrete interest position of the colonies with a revolutionary dynamic—mystifying to the British—insofar as *eupraxia* could only
be possible in terms of the restoration of a lost order, as Adams' transformation into a leader of the Revolution shows.

His road from representative from Braintree to delegate to the House
of Representatives and to the Continental Congress and the details of his
varying political positions between 1768 and 1774 have been amply discussed.[34] Using the materials at hand, we shall merely point out the specific form that he gave to his revolutionary consciousness in the crucial
years and that underlies his self-understanding as a Founding Father.

A. The source of all vice in the colonies, beginning in the 1760s, is
the "political innovations" of British policy.[35] In the Novangelus essays
(1774), Adams described the process in drastic terms. "The nature of the
encroachment upon the American constitution is such, as to grow every
day more and more encroaching. Like a cancer, it eats faster and faster
every hour. The revenue creates pensioners, and the pensioners urge for
more revenue. The people grow less steady, spirited, and virtuous, the
seekers more numerous and corrupt, and every day increases the circle of
their dependents and expectants, until virtue, public spirit, simplicity,
and frugality become the object of ridicule and scorn, and vanity, luxury,
foppery, selfishness, meanness, and downright venality swallow up the
whole society."[36] The various manifestations of the civilizing process in
the colonies in general, as well as the effects of English national policy on
the Americans' political style, political consciousness, and political behavior in particular, are interpreted by the crisis-shaken consciousness of
different persons and groups as *one* continuous process of corruption
emanating from England. "The cancerous corruption of Europe," G. S.
Wood quotes from a speech by David Rittenhouse, "had spanned the
Atlantic and had secured a hold in the New World."[37] But again and
again corruption meant loss of qualitative order, surrender of the members of society to the conduct of existential disorder. "This prevalence of

34. See, among others, Chinard, *Honest John Adams*, 44–72; P. Smith, *John Adams*, I,
93–157; R. G. Adams, *Political Ideas of the American Revolution* (Durham, N.C., 1922),
107–27; J. R. Howe, *Changing Political Thought of John Adams*, 3–58. The course of
events in Massachusetts is treated in Brown, *Revolutionary Politics in Massachusetts*.

35. J. Adams to Abigail Adams, June 5, 1774, in AP, *Adams Family Correspondence*, I,
125.

36. J. Adams, *Works*, III, 43; AP, *Diary and Autobiography*, II, 75.

37. G.. S. Wood, *Creation of the American Republic*, 110; compare the account of
"American Corruption," *ibid.*, 107–14.

vice and corruption in their midst . . . became in fact a stimulus, perhaps in the end the most important stimulus, to revolution."[38]

B. Adams, however, also regarded the general decline as an affliction from God, punishment for the sins of the English and of the powerful in America. Echoing Jugurtha, Adams declared England, an empire at the height of its power, as "a venal city, ripe for destruction if it can only find a purchaser."[39] The consciousness of the uncorrupted, the "real constitution," had ceased to exist anywhere but in America. Opposed to the English constitution, which had made corruption a necessary instrument of politics, stands the "American constitution," in which knowledge of order and *eupraxia* still merged. But even the American ethos was endangered, though, Adams hoped, "perhaps the punishment that is inflicted may work medicinally and cure the disease."[40] The therapeutic effect consists, in the literary sense of the revival, in the advancement of the existential habit of virtue and the curbing of vice. This symbolism fuses the Whig science of politics and Protestant theology. Clerical and secular writers agreed: British tyranny is God's punishment for general sinfulness. "Yet the Americans were still a peculiarly blessed and covenanted people; if they would but mend their ways and humbly acknowledge their God, good might come out of all this suffering."[41] Yet the crisis also presented a worldwide historical opportunity—offered by a benevolent Providence—"for a reformation in principles and practices, involving 'a change of mind, and our entertaining different thoughts of past conduct.'" Wood correctly points out that the clergy's call for a return to moderation and the virtue of the forefathers was fully consonant with the political science of the time: *regeneration* was the central event in the process of the self-ordering psyche; only the collective act of such a regeneration held the hope that the disorder of political society could be overcome.[42]

C. "Independence thus became not only political but moral. Revolution, Republicanism, and Regeneration all blended in American thinking."[43] Resistance to British tyranny is to that extent revolt against a

---

38. *Ibid.*, 107. See also Bushman, "Corruption and Power in Provincial America"; and Morgan, "Royal and Republican Corruption," in *Development of Revolutionary Mentality* (Washington, D.C., 1972).

39. J. Adams, *Works*, III, 55.

40. J. Adams to Abigail Adams, July 5, 1774, in AP, *Adams Family Correspondence*, I, 125.

41. G. S. Wood, *Creation of the American Republic*, 117.

42. *Ibid.*, 118.

43. *Ibid.*, 117.

deficient mode of existence, restoration of the constitution, spiritual regeneration of individual existence, "work of the Lord"[44]: "The furnace
of affliction produces refinement in states as well as in individuals. And
the new governments we are assuming . . . will require a purification from
our vices and an augmentation of our virtues or they will be no blessings."[45] Thus in 1777 Benjamin Rush could also write his friend Adams,
in Europe at the time, that he hoped the war with England would last
long enough to purge all monarchic impurities, to cleanse the American
soul, and to lead back to "the same temperance in pleasure, the same
modesty in dress, the same justice in business, and the same veneration
for the name of the Deity which distinguished our ancestors."[46] Adams
also assigned apocalyptic meaning to this work of the Lord: the Americans carried it out "as much for the benefit of the generality of mankind
in Europe as for their own."[47] "The Progress of society will be accelerated by centuries by this revolution. . . . Light spreads from the dayspring
in the west, and may it shine more and more until the perfect day."[48]

Recent studies furnish proof of this radical Protestant dimension of
revolutionary republicanism together with all its apocalyptic undertones,
in particular the convergence of millennialism and republicanism, for
wide social strata: "if millennialism cannot explain the grievances against
the Stamp Act or the structure of the United States Constitution, it can
illuminate how many Americans understood the ultimate meaning of the
revolutionary crisis and the birth of the American nation."[49] However,
as a rule, these radical Christian exaltations of the American spirit took
place under the horizon of biblical promise, even insofar as the concept
of millennialism was concerned. This can be illustrated particularly well
by using the Christian apocalyptist Rush as an example. Contrary to the
radical revolutionary ideology of Europe, in which the revolutionary
wanted to create his paradise by his own efforts, God's work of redemption was never questioned. The revolution as military, political, and
social event was understood to be cathartic. At the beginning stood a
general and fundamental experience of social order, combined with collective social unrest. It was only under this horizon that the social status
quo proved to be unbearable and the "invisible measure" of right order

44. John Adams to Samuel Chase, June 24, 1776, in J. Adams, *Works*, IX, 413.
45. John Adams to Abigail Adams, July 3, 1776, in AP, *Adams Family Correspondence*,
II, 28.
46. Benjamin Rush to John Adams, August 8, 1777, in B. Rush, *Letters*, I, 152.
47. John Adams to Digges, May 13, 1780, in J. Adams, *Works*, VII, 168.
48. John Adams to Abigail Adams, December 18, 1881, in A. Adams, *Letters*, II, 82.
49. R. N. Bloch, *Visionary Republic: Millennial Themes in American Thought, 1775–
1800* (Cambridge, Mass., 1985), xiii.

could be discovered and formulated in an immediate and, despite all differences, common experience of Christian-philosophical transcendence. Revolution meant the reformation of human existence in society through the collective regeneration of the individual psyche and the formation of a new political order of the republic. This new republic, an exemplar to all mankind, restores order in the qualitative sense.

Such a structuring of revolutionary consciousness was not limited to Adams, nor to the strong "black regiment" of the New England clergy; it was, as pointed out, typical of many political leaders, and especially of the middle and lower levels of the population.[50] "When the ideas of the Americans are examined comprehensively, when all of the Whig rhetoric irrational as well as rational, is taken into account, one cannot but be struck by the predominant characteristics of fear and frenzy, the exaggeration and the enthusiasm, the general sense of social corruption and disorder out of which would be born a new world of benevolence and harmony."[51] These somewhat baffled remarks come from a modern historian. The ideas, though not always "factually true," were always "psychologically true." "In this sense their rhetoric was never detached from the social and political reality. Their repeated overstatements of reality, their incessant talk of 'tyranny' when there seems to have been no real oppression, their obsession with 'virtue,' 'luxury,' and 'corruption,' their devotion to 'liberty' and 'equality'—all these notions . . . were . . . ideas with real personal and social significance for those who used them." According to Wood, they show that "something profoundly unsettling was going on in the society." But then he becomes perplexed and refers to Arthur F. Bentley's urging "to search carefully to find out what it really is they stand for, what the factors of the social life are that are expressing themselves through the ideas."[52] Wood is aware that any study of the experiences engendering the symbols should explain their function in the dynamics of the historical process; but he can do no more than reject an interpretation solely in terms of intellectual history and falls back on Bentley and his positivism, since he lacks the theoretical tools for an existential-analytical inquiry into the engendering reality of the psyche in question.

50. Compare, among others, the documentation in Thornton, *Pulpit of the American Revolution;* A. M. Baldwin, *The New England Clergy and the American Revolution* (Durham, N.C., 1928); P. Miller, "From Covenant to the Revival"; Heimert, *Religion and the American Mind;* Tuveson, *Redeemer Nation;* J. W. Davidson, *The Logic of Millennial Thought* (New Haven, Conn., 1977); Hatch, *Sacred Thought of Liberty.*

51. G. S. Wood, "Rhetoric and Reality in the American Revolution," *William and Mary Quarterly,* XXIII (1966), 31.

52. *Ibid.,* 32.

Herein too lies the explanation for Edward Handler's misjudgment: "There was no counterpart in the American experience to revolutions aiming not merely at removal of political tyranny but at conscious re-ordering of society."[53] This statement results from an unreflected acceptance of the Continental-European category of the social revolutionary, linked to the civil-theological axiom of English tyranny. "The truth is that if Adams was a revolutionary, he was so in a sense very different than that produced by the great modern revolutions." It is true that Adams "exhibited little of the political messianism or apocalyptic fervor of the French or Russian revolution,"[54] but he certainly intended a deliberate reordering of society, though not in the sense of apocalyptic dreams. Perhaps that requires, one might say, a more differentiated consciousness and sense for reality than the metaphysical revolution is ready to grant.

D. For Adams, however, renewal is no longer exclusively a collective revival of Puritan spirituality; it has turned nomothetic. This statement requires further elucidation. We may begin with another formulation of reformation: "Calamities are the caustics and cathartics of the body politic," Adams wrote in 1767; "they arouse the soul. They restore original virtues. They reduce a constitution back to its first principles." The looming threat of tyranny "terrified the inhabitants into a resolution and an ardor for the noble foundations of their ancestors."[55] The cathartic motion of the soul aims at the formation of a public character of the citizens. "It is the part of the great politician to make the Character of his people, to extinguish among them the follies and vices, and to create in them the virtues and abilities which he sees wanting."[56] "Public virtue can not exist in a nation without private, and public virtue is the only foundation of republics."[57]

The paradigm of the nomothetes becomes apparent. "As politics is the science of human happiness and human happiness is clearly best promoted by virtue, what thorough politician can hesitate who has a new government to build whether to prefer a commonwealth or a monarchy?"[58] But conversely, the success of the revolutionary founding was

---

53. E. Handler, *America and Europe in the Political Thought of John Adams* (Cambridge, Mass., 1964), 20.

54. *Ibid.*, 101.

55. J. Adams, *Works*, III, 485.

56. John Adams to James Warren, January 8, 1776, in J. Adams, *Warren-Adams Letters*, I, 202.

57. John Adams to James Warren, April 16, 1776, *ibid.*, I, 223.

58. John Adams to James Warren, January 8, 1776, *ibid.*, I, 202. Evidence of Adams' cheerful way of making use of the available symbolic material is furnished by his acceptance of Montesquieu; at this time Adams still identified Montesquieu's psychic prerequisite for a republic, the *vertu politique,* with his own concept of the existential virtues without

proof of the people's quality. "A revolution of government successfully conducted and compleated is the strongest proof that can be given by a people of their virtue and good sense. An enterprise of so much difficulty can never be planned and carried on without abilities, and a people without principle cannot have confidence enough in each other."[59] This nexus, however, inevitably made the American experiment seem under renewed threat from every social disorder.

E. Though Adams had little use for the "astrological and mystical whimsies" of Plato, he nevertheless accepted Plato's anthropological principle of society: the paradigmatic commonwealth or the republic required an organization of law and education "to produce the virtues of fortitude, temperance, wisdom and justice in the whole city and in all the individual citizens."[60] The model therefore postulates an ordering of consciousness, that of the nomothetes, as the precondition of the behavioral model suited to the particular and concrete circumstances; but it also in essence reproduced the existing political and social structures of the New England way of life. Adams' definition of the republic as an "Empire of Laws" includes all these meanings. Since the commonwealth's-men, especially Harrington, had returned Aristotelian politics to Anglo-Saxon consciousness, this formula was included in the *topoi* of political discussion.[61] For Adams this symbolism signifies the following cluster of ideas.

1. It stands for the influx of what is right by nature, the "higher law," in the concrete-historical society, signifying the presence of Solon's "invisible measure" as the counterpole to a legal order from the ruler's *amor sui*.[62] This means, as it does in Aristotle, that the rule of law is identical with the rule of the intellect (*nous*), which is not affected by the libido of whatever ruler happens to be in power.[63] The reference, however, is not to Aristotle's immediate experience; the argument continues from Cicero's symbolic explication, in which he elaborated the reality content of experience under the pressure of Rome's national crisis and arrived at an aggregate of propositional truths concerning the proper order of man in society. "True law is right reason in agreement with nature; it is of uni-

---

further examination. Only later did he realize that the classical-Christian cardinal virtues as the shaping principle of the soul were significantly different from Montesquieu's other-directed "sentiment" of the "vertu politique." See J. Adams, *Works,* VI, 206 ff.; G. Stourzh, "Die tugendhafte Republik," in *Österreich und Europa,* ed. H. Hantsch (Gray, 1965), 247–67.

59. AP, *Diary and Autobiography,* III, 194.

60. J. Adams, *Works,* IV, 448.

61. J. Gebhardt, "James Harrington," in *Zwischen Revolution und Restauration,* ed. E. Voegelin (Munich, 1968), 103 ff.

62. J. Adams, *Works,* VI, 56.

63. Aristotle, *Politics,* III, 1287a25–1287b5 (English translation by C. W. Keyes).

versal application, unchanging and everlasting; it summons to duty by its commands, and averts from wrongdoing by its prohibitions. And it does not lay its commands or prohibitions upon good men in vain, though neither have any effect on the wicked. It is a sin to try to alter this law, nor is it allowable to attempt to repeal any part of it, and it is impossible to abolish it entirely."[64] The Americans operated in the medium of Ciceronian symbolization.

The American conception of the "higher law" was, according to Edward Samuel Corwin in his classic study on the topic, structured on a theory of law that states:

> There are . . . certain principles of right and justice which are entitled to prevail of their own intrinsic excellence, altogether regardless of the attitude of those who wield the physical resources of the community. Such principles were made by no human hands; indeed, if they did not antedate deity itself, they still so express its nature as to bind and control it. They are eternal and immutable. In relation to such principles, human laws are, when entitled to obedience save as to matters indifferent, merely a record or transcript, and their enactment not an act of will or power but one of discovery and declaration.[65]

2. It is not a matter of an irrevocable, uniform, reified natural right— an everpresent misunderstanding, thanks to the obviously imperishable human need to objectify symbols. What is right by nature has its being in man's concrete experience of a justice that is everywhere the same and yet in its actualization is changeable and different everywhere. Thus justice is realized according to the historical conditions in the right action of the specific human being motivated by *philautia,* the love of his rational self, and at the same time discovering his fellow citizen in the *philia politike,* political friendship.

Only through this act is a *people* in the substantial sense brought about: "Haec ipse populus jam populus est si sit injustus quoniam non est multitude juris consensu, et utilitatis communione societa sicut populus fuerat definitus," Adams quotes from Cicero's *De Republica.*[66] Our analyses so far have made it clear that Adams must include in the repub-

---

64. Cicero, *De Republica* (Zurich, 1960), III, 33 (English translation by C. W. Keyes); compare also *De Legibus,* I, 42–43.

65. E. S. Corwin, *The "Higher Law" Background of American Constitutional Law* (Ithaca, N.Y., 1957), 5. Compare also D. J. Boorstin, *The Mysterious Science of the Law* (Boston, 1958); C. Manion, "The Natural Law Philosophy on the Founding Fathers"; B. F. Wright, *American Interpretations of Natural Law* (Cambridge, Mass., 1931); C. J. Friedrich, *Christliche Gerechtigkeit und Verfassungsstaat* (Cologne, 1967).

66. J. Adams, *Works,* IV, 296.

lican people the peasants, merchants, and workers whom Aristotle had excluded from the polity;[67] but Adams had experienced as a living reality the model of the Aristotelian-Ciceronian republic in the spiritual-political consensus of the New England town. Michael Zuckerman describes this specific consensus of New England politics, which Adams always saw as an endangered norm: "governance by concord and concurrence required inclusiveness. In communities in which effective enforcement depended on the moral binding of decisions upon men who made them, it was essential that most men be parties to such decisions," for there was no structured pluralism of divergent norms, in which pure majority decisions held sway.[68] Adams was eager to preserve in the paradigmatic republic the quality of public life in the township. Habitual right action in public and private affairs, so to speak, was turned into a norm of behavior upon which positive law and the political institutions were to be modeled and which was to be brought forth through the education of the members of society. "Reformation must begin with the body of the people which can be done only to effect in their education."[69]

> The instruction of the people, in every kind of knowledge that can be of use to them in the practice of their moral duties, as men, citizens and Christians, and of their political and civil duties, as members of society and freemen, ought to be the care of the public, and of all who have any share in the conduct of its affairs, in a manner that never yet has been practiced in any age or nation. The education here intended is not merely that of the children of the rich and noble, but of every rank and class of people, down to the lowest and the poorest.[70]

Adams had already incorporated public education in Chapter V of the Massachusetts Constitution.[71] Only under such a condition can the concept of self-government in the republican paradigm be meaningful—a matter that cannot be stressed enough: "If you want it to be a meritorious polity, you have to care about what kind of people govern it. Indeed, it puts the matter more strongly and declares that if you want self-government, you are only entitled to it if that 'self' is worthy of governing. There is no inherent right to self-government if it means that such government is vicious, mean, squalid, and debased." Irving Kristol introduces the anthropological justification of civil government, today almost forgotten, with all the required clarity and continues: "Because the desir-

---

67. *Ibid.*, V, 457.
68. Zuckerman, "Social Context of Democracy in Massachusetts," 527–28.
69. John Adams to Jebb, September 10, 1785, in APM.
70. J. Adams, *Works*, VI, 108.
71. J. Adams, *Works*, IV, 257 ff.

ability of self-government depends on the character of the people who govern, the older idea of democracy was very solicitous of the condition of this character. It was solicitous of the individual self, and felt an obligation to educate it into what used to be called 'republican virtue.' And it was solicitous of that collective self which we call public opinion and which, in a democracy, governs us collectively."[72]

3. "Men should endevor," Adams concluded from the anthropological principle of political order, "at a balance of affections and appetites, under the monarchy of reason and conscience, within, as well as at a balance of power without."[73] "The passions and appetites are parts of human nature as well as reason and the moral sense. In the institution of government, it must be remembered that, although reason ought always to govern individuals, it never did since the Fall, and never will till the Millennium; and human nature must be taken as it is, and as it has been, and will be." Institutional consequence is, for Adams, the principle of the *archein kai archesthai*—to govern and be governed. "Each man must be content with his share of empire; and if the nature and reason of mankind, the nobleness of his qualities and affections, and his natural desires prove his right to a share in the government, they cannot surely prove more than the constitutions of the United States have allowed."[74]

The irrevocable and at times overriding forces of *amour-propre* obtain by force a sociopolitical constitution of government in which the needs resulting from its members' life processes are fairly satisfied, in which the space of public happiness is shielded from private interests, and in which the citizens are assured of a minimum of *eupraxia* (man being considered "an end in himself," as Kant says). In his *Thoughts on Government,* the constitution of Massachusetts, and the *Defence of the Constitutions of Government of the United States of America,* Adams developed in exemplary fashion the institutional arrangement that, under the premise of political equality, enables the citizen both to participate in public affairs and to have access to government. At the same time the arrangement creates authorities that promise to resolve all conflicts originating in the libidinous self while they are ordered in such a way as to accommodate the multiplicity and actual inequality of people as to their mental, social,

---

72. I. Kristol, *On the Democratic Idea in America* (New York, 1972), 42.
73. J. Adams, *Works,* IV, 407.
74. J. Adams, *Works,* VI, 114–15. For the institutional details we can refer to the detailed accounts of C. M. Walsh, *The Political Science of John Adams* (New York, 1915); C. Warren, "John Adams and the American Constitutions," *George Washington University Bulletin,* XXVI (1926); A. Koch, *Power, Morals, and the Founding Fathers* (Ithaca, N.Y., 1961); Haraszti, *Adams and the Prophets of Progress;* Handler, *America and Europe;* J. R. Howe, *Changing Political Thought of John Adams.*

economic, and physical being. To this end Adams provided a mixed constitution, based on representation of the autarchic individual and the
most important social interests, resulting from direct, preferably yearly
elections, with a complicated system of checks and balances and a division among the three powers and a separation of the legislative branch
into three organs, as well as a strong executive with a long term of office.

4. The paradigmatic republic, however, reaches down into the private
area of the organization of living processes, the economy, for it postulates
the citizens' power of disposing over their material existence. "The property of every citizen is a part of public property, as each citizen is a part
of the public, people or community. The property, therefore, of every man
has a share in government, and is more powerful than any citizen, or any
party of citizens, it is governed only by law." [75] Thus, the safeguarding of
property does not sanction every excess of the acquisitive enterprise;
rather, it asserts autarchic "life" as the guarantor of the citizen's "good
life." William Appleton Williams tried to sum up the dilemma of the
republican economy within his too widely stretched concept of mercantilism. "As the mercantilists knew the construction of a successful economic system and the acquisition of personal fortunes was not the greater
part of their conception of the world. Beyond those goals they were concerned with the public welfare and the spirit of a true corporate commonwealth. Hence the mercantilists were caught in their own argument:
if property was essential to the individual's sense of identity, then it was
by the same logic the basis of any public identity; the sense of ours was
as vital as the sense of mine." [76] "To resolve the mercantilist's dilemma,
how to use private property to achieve the corporate welfare and yet prevent interest and faction from running roughshod over the common good,
Adams stressed the importance of a firm and active sense of justice." [77]
However, Williams fails to make clear the historical continuity of this
"mercantilism," a term that misses the specifics of a "republican" economy. Nor does Williams see that there is no dilemma whatever from the
aspect of the design for living of the *vivere civile;* a dilemma arises only
under the pragmatic pressure of modern economic society. The economics
of the paradigmatic republic was thoroughly imbued with the "Machia-

75. J. Adams, *Works,* V, 454. Compare the excellent treatment by M. J. Dauer, "The
Political Economy of John Adams," *Political Science Quarterly,* LVI (1941), 545–72; fur-
ther, the one-sided analysis in the spirit of progressivist historiography in C. A. Beard,
Economic Origins of Jeffersonian Democracy (New York, 1915), 299–321; V. L. Parring-
ton, *Main Currents in American Thought* (New York, 1954), I, 312–25; J. Dorfman, *The
Economic Mind in the American Civilization* (New York, 1946–59), I, 417–33.

76. W. A. Williams, *The Contours of American History* (Cleveland, 1961), 233.

77. *Ibid.,* 156.

vellian moment" of the Anglo-American version of neo-Harringtonism. This was already true for the concrete social order of New England, of which Zuckerman writes: "Participation in community decisions was the prerogative of independent men, of all of the town's independent men, but ideally, only of those. Indeed, it was precisely because of their independence that they had to be accorded a vote, since only by their participation did they bind themselves to concur in the community's chosen course of action." Zuckerman stresses the fact that it is not the principle of individual property that determines the right to vote but the capacity for independent participation in common affairs within the framework of spiritual-political consensus.[78] True to the Aristotelian-Machiavellian tradition, Anglo-American Harringtonism insisted that

> the individual citizen might be known by the autonomy of his participation in politics, but it was peculiarly concerned with the material basis of that autonomy. The function of property was to render the individual independent, and the ideal paradigm—though by no means the only form—of the property which did this was an inheritable freehold of land. . . . The point about freehold in this context is that it involves its proprietor as little as possible in dependence upon, or even in relations with other people, and so leaves him free for the full austerity of citizenship in the classical sense. . . . If the end of property was independence, the end of independence was citizenship and moral personality.[79]

For Adams, this connection was self-evident. "At present a husbandman, merchant, or artificer, provided he has any small property, by which he may be supposed to have a judgment and will of his own, instead of depending for his daily bread on some patron or master, is a sufficient judge of the qualifications of a person to represent him in the legislature."[80] Therefore, "friendship or political community" depends—quite in the spirit of Aristotle—on the equality of a "middle state" with "moderate and convenient fortune"; it admits as few rich and poor as possible.[81] What is noteworthy is that Adams still starts from the socioeconomic presumption of an agrarian society, in which the majority is occupied with securing a bare subsistence. "The great question will for ever remain, who shall work? Our species cannot all be idle. Leisure for

---

78. Zuckerman, "Social Context of Democracy in Massachusetts," 532 ff.

79. J. G. A. Pocock, *Politics, Language and Time* (New York, 1971), 91–92. Compare J. Gebhardt, "Die Republik eines Humanisten," in *James Harrington: Politische Schriften,* ed. J. Gebhardt (Munich, 1973).

80. J. Adams, *Works,* V, 456.

81. *Ibid.,* 458–59.

study must ever be the portion of the few. The number employed in government must forever be very small. Food, raiment, and habitation, the indispensable wants of all, are not to be obtained without the continual toil of ninety-nine in a hundred of mankind."[82] "The natural, necessary, and unavoidable consequence of all this is, that the multiplication of the means of subsistence, that the constant labor of nine tenths of our species will forever be necessary to prevent all of them from starving with hunger, cold, and pestilence."[83]

So Adams concludes: Of necessity, this condition of scarcity gives rise to a structural class conflict between rich and poor, privileged and underprivileged, which is aggravated by the psychological disposition of the passion for private property, a passion that causes man to amass wealth exceeding the satisfaction of basic needs—that is, that makes men dissatisfied with their existence as farmers, craftsmen, or workers.[84] The paradigmatic republic must minimize such conflicts by an equal distribution of land, combined with universal public education, including especially the poor, in order to provide them with the knowledge essential to independence and autonomy. In America, Adams always insisted, socioeconomic conditions favor the republican order: "The agrarian in America is divided among the common people, in such a manner, that nineteen twentieth of the property would be in the hands of the commons."[85] Adams, the New England farmer and lawyer, is fully persuaded that Harrington's agrarian law was a social reality; in this, Adams is completely the New England farmer and completely under Harrington's influence. He imagined that free access to land would create an agrarian society of midlevel landowners, with a narrow layer of rich private capitalists, a trade bourgeoisie, and small entrepreneurs and their employees—a society in which all the poor were made up of people unable or unwilling to work; he had come to know this last group when dealing with poor relief in Braintree. Since he hoped that the increase in the white work force would soon make slavery economically inefficient, he believed in an integration of African-Americans into this social pyramid.[86] It was a class

82. J. Adams, *Works*, VI, 279–80.
83. *Ibid.*, 516; compare 520.
84. *Ibid.*, 512, 237 ff.
85. J. Adams, *Works*, IV, 359.
86. J. Adams, *Works*, VI, 511; John Adams to Belknap, October 22, 1795, in Belknap Papers, II, *Collections of the Massachusetts Historical Society*, III, 416; John Adams to Evans, June 8, 1819, in APM. Of course Adams did not yet realize the consequences of the mechanization of cotton production, but his principled opposition to the enslavement of Africans was never in doubt. Compare also his prophetic statement to Jefferson: "Slavery in this country I have seen hanging over it like a black cloud for half a century. If I were as

society with only moderate social differentiations; its conflicts could be contained by its sociopolitical constitution.

The formula "Empire of Laws and not Men" describes the "free republic," it expresses the substantive order of the *novus ordo seclorum:* the correct existence of man in society under the concrete conditions of the American "wilderness."

II. Reform Versus Institutionalism

"Statesmen . . . may plan and speculate for liberty," Adams reflected in 1776, "but it is religion and morality alone which can establish the principles upon which freedom can securely stand. . . . The only foundation of a free constitution is pure virtue, and if this can not be inspired into our people in a greater measure than it have now they may change their rulers and the forms of government but they will not obtain a lasting liberty."[87] This was the extent to which the experiment of the founding was linked to a type of psyche that was to undergo a permanent spiritual revival. But Adams was not the only one who, unconsciously, harbored a fear of failure—a fear grounded in the concrete experience of personal sinfulness and the sinfulness of fellow citizens, all beyond redemption. The everyday conditions of domestic and foreign affairs in the confederation and under the Constitution of 1789–1800; his own experiences as diplomat, vice-president and president; the rapid socioeconomic differentiation in America; and not least the course of the French Revolution—all these caused Adams to doubt, not his own design for existence, but the collective regeneration of American society.[88] Such a doubt presupposed that the apocalyptic hope of the chosenness of the American people, on which the concept of restoration was essentially based, had been shaken. "There is no special providence for us. We are not a chosen people that I know of. . . . We must and we shall go the way of all the earth."[89] The consequences of this insight can already be felt in the *Defence,* and they wholly inform the *Discourses on Davila.* They can easily be understood from the unchanged basic structure of his conscious-

---

drunk with enthusiasm as Swedenborg or Wesley, I might probably say I had seen armies of negroes marching and countermarching in the air shining in armour" (John Adams to Thomas Jefferson, February 3, 1821, in *Adams-Jefferson Letters,* II, 571).

87. John Adams to Zabdiel Adams, June 21, 1776, in AP, *Adams Family Correspondence,* II, 21.

88. On this and the following, compare especially Handler, *America and Europe;* J. R. Howe, *Changing Political Thought of John Adams.*

89. John Adams to Rush, October 22, 1812, in J. Adams, *Old Family Letters,* 311; similarly, John Adams to Rush, July 28, 1789, *ibid.,* 48.

ness, and they involve two complexes dovetailed by the anthropological principle.

A. The societal function of *amour-propre* is considered in a new way. The theoretical stipulation does not change, but now Adams sees in it the unvarying theme of social-dominant behavior in society. *Divertissement* found in the infinite striving after immanent immortality—like Adam Smith, Adams called it the "passion for distinction"—is "the great spring of social activity."[90] At times overwhelmed by the dynamics of *amour-propre,* he reduced all social processes to a permanent antagonism within man's passionate nature.

B. This view of matters makes Adams fear an involution of America to the old European corporative society, with an inherited aristocracy and absolute monarchy. For beyond the apocalyptic hope, he is thrown back on the traditional pattern of a cyclical theory of history.[91] The American republic will inevitably run through the same stages of the forms of order as any other republic in human history. Only the comparative study of the historical material allows a prognosis for America. This is the explanation for the accumulation of massive quantities of material for the history of classical, medieval, and modern republics in the *Defence.*[92]

C. But what is crucial is that the consciousness of the nomothetes is willing to despair neither at the preponderance of *amour-propre* nor at the irreversibility of a cyclical historical process. Under the presumption that the passionate nature of man and the internal processes of society underlie an inherent mechanism whose laws, like Newton's, can be examined by the nomothetes, law and institutions can be substituted as repositories of the ordering substance for the spiritual regeneration of society. "Neither philosophy, nor religion, nor morality, nor wisdom, nor interest will ever govern nations or parties against their vanity, their pride, their resentment or revenge, or their avarice or ambition but force and power and strength can restrain them."[93] But Adams means, not the power of a despot, but the force of law and political institutions: "If a majority are capable of preferring their own private interest . . . to that of the nation collectively, some provision must be made in the constitution in favor of justice to compell all to respect the common right, the

90. J. Adams, *Works,* VI, 245.

91. S. Persons, "The Cyclical Theory of History in Eighteenth Century America," *American Quarterly,* VI (1954), 147–63; Colbourn, *Lamp of Experience.*

92. For the origin of the material, see Iacuzzi, *John Adams: Scholar;* Haraszti, *Adams and the Prophets of Progress.*

93. John Adams to Thomas Jefferson, October 9, 1789, in J. Adams, *Adams-Jefferson Letters,* I, 202.

public good, the universal law on preference to all private and partial considerations."[94] Thus, society neither is a self-regulating system nor does it transform itself into a Leviathan; rather, the *Defence* and *Davila* objectify the knowledge of order of Adams the nomothetes within prescriptions for a constitution, and adhering to them sets society to rights again. "Americans! Rejoice that from experience you have learned wisdom; instead of whimsical and fantastical projects you have adopted a promising essay toward a well ordered government. . . . In a well balanced government reason, conscience, truth and virtue must be respected by all parties and exerted for the public good."[95]

But Adams was given to this extreme form of institutionalism only during times of deep depression, sensing the return of the chosen people into the circle of all the other peoples. It remains, as it were, a private Thermidorean experience. It was the fear of failure of the paradigm of order, which gripped not Adams alone but also Hamilton, Jefferson, Madison, Webster, Rush, and many others. "The most cursory reading of speeches, sermons, newspapers, and letters originating during the time that Adams, Jefferson, and Madison were president reveals a general unease over the citizen's innate selfishness and an acclaim for individual will's capitulation to national achievement. Such an outcome was usually said to require God's encouragement."[96] Adams' *Davila* did no more than summarize these fears in a penetrating study of the calculating self-interest of an acquisitive society in the manner of Adam Smith. Not only did his own spirituality balk at a radical turning to institutionalism, which views problems of order exclusively in terms of a political mechanism of interest regulation, but his public position as vice-president and president also committed him to the original form of revolutionary consciousness. From the Continental Congress to the time of the presidency of John Adams, it was incumbent upon the political representative of the "people under God" to reenact the revolutionary awakening and carry out the spiritual-moral reformation of society by means of the traditional ritual of public days of mortification, confession of sins, contrition, atonement, and a change of ways, followed by thanksgiving. Thus on June 12, 1775, the Continental Congress recommended a "day of public humiliation, fasting, and prayer . . . that we may with united hearts and voices unfeignedly confess and deplore our many sins, and offer up our joint supplications to the allwise, omnipotent, and merciful disposer of

94. J. Adams, *Works*, VI, 8.

95. *Ibid.*, 277.

96. P. C. Nagel, *The Sacred Trust: American Nationality, 1798–1898* (New York, 1971), 13–14; G. S. Wood, *Creation of the American Republic*, 413–29.

all events; humbly beseeching him to forgive our iniquities, to remove our present calamities, to avert those desolating judgments with which we are threatened."[97] This pattern of public meditation during times of crisis was also adopted by Washington (1789 and 1795) and Adams (1798 and 1799).[98] The end of this institution of public days of prayer and repentance—there was only one more attempt, under Madison (1812)—until the time of Lincoln (1861 and 1863) coincides with the depolitization of the revival during the Second Awakening of 1801 to 1802 (which was, once again, an affair of the churches and sects) and the creation of new temporal sacred forms. The necessary turning away from unreason and vice could no longer occur in the form of massive experience of awakening but had to assume the form of educating the citizens. "The Almighty was often given an agent, education, for directing stewardship. Society needed aid and education was the means of enhancing civic worth."[99]

Adams always tended to replace revival with education, in order to communicate to the society his republican design as a kind of "republican religion" (Koch). The experiential substratum of this symbolism, to which Adams assigns the designation "Christian," has been discussed at length. It is grounded not in any Christian theology but in man's rational self, the sole source of all true Christianity and of all true religion in general.

> One great advantage of the Christian religion is that it brings the great principle of the law of nature and nations, love your neighbour as yourself, and do to others as you would that others should do to you, to the knowledge, belief, and veneration of the whole people. Children, servants, women and men are all professors in the science of public and private morality. No other institution for education, no kind of political discipline could diffuse this kind of necessary information so universally among all ranks and descriptions of citizens. The duties and rights of men and the citizens are thus taught from early infancy to every creature. The sanctions of a future life are thus added to the observance of civil and political as well as domestic, and private duties. Prudence, Justice, Temperance and fortitude are thus taught to be the means and conditions of future as well as present happiness.[100]

The specific political element of this spirituality comes into view in Adams' evaluation of Zaleucus' preamble to the Locrian code, which he

97. Quoted in P. Miller, "From Covenant to Revival," 322.
98. J. Adams, *Works*, VIII, 169ff.
99. Nagel, *Sacred Trust*, 14.
100. AP, *Diary and Autobiography*, III, 204–41.

considered one of antiquity's major contributions to the progress of civilization.

> He declares that all those who shall inhabit the city ought, above all things, to be persuaded that there is a God . . . that . . . they ought to adore the gods, as the authors of all which life presents us of good and beautiful; that they should hold their souls pure from every vice, because the gods accept neither the prayers, offerings, or sacrifices of the wicked, and are pleased only with the just and beneficent actions of virtuous men. Having thus . . . fixed the attention of his fellow-citizens upon piety and wisdom, he ordains . . . that there should never be among them any irreconcilable enmity. . . . The chiefs of his republic ought not to govern with arrogance or pride; nor should the magistrates be guided in their judgment by hatred nor by friendship.

"This preamble," Adams commented, "places religion, morals, and government upon a basis of philosophy which is rational, intelligible, and eternal, for the real happiness of man in society."[101]

In G. S. Wood's opinion, Adams' *Defence* articulates the position of all those Federalists who were still in the grip of the neoclassical politics of the eighteenth century and did not understand the significance of the new American political science expounded in the *Federalist* papers. "By defending more comprehensively and stridently than anyone else the traditional conception of Eighteenth Century politics at the very moment of its disintegration, Adams steadily and perversely moved in a direction that eventually left him isolated from the main line of American intellectual development."[102] This is certainly correct as far as Adams' unswerving neo-Harringtonian interpretation of American society as well as his increasing interest in the classical cyclic theory of political forms of order are concerned. However, Pocock shows that the conflict between traditional republicans and their critics was not merely a dispute between republicanism and post-classical liberalism, but that it arose from the ideopolitical logic of development of the republican paradigm itself.[103] In a certain sense, John Adams deserves a special position in the republican discourse of his time: Not only is he familiar with the ancient and modern traditions of republicanism to an incomparable extent, but, beyond that, he discovers for himself, as described in detail, the historical-social world in a continuous meditative effort, the Puritan roots of which are unmistakable. It is in his reflective search for the reason of humanity, of

---

101. J. Adams, *Works*, IV, 519; compare 556.
102. G. S. Wood, *Creation of the American Republic*, 569.
103. Pocock, *Machiavellian Moment*, 451.

which Adams conceived republicanism to be the historically appropriate reflection, that I see the intellectual performance characteristic of Adams, the most important classic republican among the Founding Fathers. As shown above, Adams, from early youth, considered self-reflection to be contemplation on the essence of man and the way he appears in the course of history. Adams' response to John Taylor's criticism that he followed the "Analysis of Antiquity" is characteristic of this attitude. Why, he asks, when conflicts regarding domestic policy arise, cannot the eternal and unchanging truth of the role of one, of a few, and of many just as well be the "Analysis of Modernity." "An ancient might say to a modern, as Nathan said unto David, thou art the man."[104] In his intellectual encounter with classicism, Adams not only increasingly found his own political experience with politics confirmed, but also deepened his fears that the world-historical republican experiment of the United States would meet the same destiny of all past free republics unless the "divine science of politics" kept in mind the strict application of the Harringtonian formula of stability, which prescribes rule by law, a mixed constitution, property laws, and civic education, as Adams himself put into practice in the constitution for Massachusetts.

The forced belief that a well-planned institutional structure would have the power to preserve order, which becomes evident in Adams' late works, is not far removed from the republican institutionalism propounded in the *Federalist* papers. Yet Adams did not want to renounce neoclassical conceptuality and, consistent with this attitude, the solutions it offered. The thoughts of the neoclassicist Adams were also in harmony with the basic ideopolitical flow of thought manifested in the *Federalist* papers on another point: thus, in the republican theory expounded in the *Defence*, there is no longer any room for the radical Puritan motifs that his republican mode of thought contained during the 1760s and 1770s. This shift of opinion in John Adams, which was noted by many authors,[105] lets him tread a special path, since he wanted to develop a consistently neoclassical form of political science under the horizon of modern experience. Wood is correct in stating that Adams tried "to translate what he thought he and other Americans had learned about themselves and their politics into basic principles of social and political science that were applicable to all peoples at all times."[106] If one bears this intention in mind when

104. J. Adams, *Works*, VI, 293–94; compare 2 Samuel 12.
105. J. R. Howe, *Changing Political Thought of John Adams*, 147; P. Shaw, *The Character of John Adams* (Chapel Hill, N.C., 1976), 214; J. O. Appleby, "The New Republican Synthesis and the Changing Political Ideas of John Adams," *American Quarterly*, XXV (1973), 578–95.
106. G. S. Wood, *Creation of the American Republic*, 458.

studying Adams' *Defence,* it becomes clear that this work is not merely an intellectual relic of the declining era of classical politics. On the contrary, it is only in this republican *summa* that Adams develops into a pure exponent of classic civic humanism, because he wants to give it a universal form. For Adams the characteristics peculiar to American republicanism, which the members of the Constitutional Convention in Philadelphia took as the basis for drafting the constitution and its theoretical explanation, could not be the point of departure from which to develop a universal theory. Adams' universalism considered an American science of politics to be a *contradictio in adjecto.* He agreed with Madison, Hamilton, and Jay that the American people and their leaders had to thank the general progress of civilization, as well as the progress made in the theory and practice of politics, for the success of their republican experiment. A scientific theory on the principles of politics alone can protect the republican order against the ubiquitous threat of internal decay. Whereas the authors of the *Federalist* papers wanted to develop their principles on the theory and practice of the republic completely within the American context and with the help of the epistemology expounded by the Scottish commonsense philosophy, Adams wanted to grasp the basic principles of the American constitutional order from a critical viewpoint that encompassed the entire republican tradition, from its beginnings in classical antiquity up to its current protagonists in Europe. Basically, Adams' intention is more ambitious: he wants to prove that the constitutions of the American states are virtually a quintessence of the republican view of the history of mankind.

In a certain way, the *Defence* can indeed be viewed as "the last major work of political theory written within the unmodified tradition of classical republicanism," [107] even though the numerous volumes comprising this work and the subsequent work, *Discourses on Davila,* were by no means to be the last words that Adams, the republican, spoke on politics. His untypical reception of Machiavelli supports the thesis that in the *Defence* Adams proves to be the most resolute representative of classical civic humanism. Only in the course of his studies of republican literature and historiography did Adams discover the "Machiavellian moment" in the classical tradition. As far as I know, he is the only Founding Father who studied Machiavelli at length and considered him to be of crucial importance to modern republicanism. Of course, his relationship to Machiavelli was not completely free of a certain conflicting nature; for example, in 1813 he writes: "I have been somewhat of a student of Machiavelli but he has always been disagreeable to me, because I never could

---

107. Pocock, *Machiavellian Moment,* 526.

know whether he was in jest or in earnest. I cannot discern one Trait of Sincerety in all his writings."[108] Several years earlier, he had written to the same person: "I know not that your time could have been better employed than in reading Machiavel, whose writings contain a good deal of wisdom, though it is unfortunately mixed with too much wickedness."[109] In the *Defence,* he defines Machiavelli's role: "Machiavel was the first who revived the ancient politics. The best part of his writings he translated almost literally from Plato and Aristotle, without acknowledging his obligation; and the worst of the sentiments, even in his *Prince,* he translated from Aristotle, without throwing upon him the reproach. Montesquieu borrowed the best part of his book from Machiavel, without acknowledging the quotation. Milton, Harrington, Sidney were intimately acquainted with the ancients and with Machiavel. They were followed by Locke, Hoadly etc."[110] In the *Defence,* Adams discusses the *Discorsi* (I, 2), the *Istorie Florentine* (II—VII), and the *Discursus Florentinarum Rerum.* However, the material is selected and interpreted according to Adams' specific epistemological interests, namely, to furnish proof that only a free republic that is socially balanced and organized on the principle of separation of powers will be able to force the tremendous passionate nature of man into the mold of the law.

Adams refuses to give up the credo of civic humanism that a republic requires virtue. However, the highly esteemed Christian virtues of the radical Protestants, the moralistic virtue of the classicists, and the political virtue of the modern republicans are all insufficient for this; the ethical basis of the republic is the ordering of all individual virtues into the common standard of public reason: namely, the law. "That form of government which unites all the virtue, honour, and fear of the citizens, in reverence and obedience to the laws, is the only one in which liberty can be secure, and all orders, and ranks, and parties compelled to prefer the public good before their own;—that is the government for which we plead." The love of law as the political existential virtue—it is in this way that John Adams' civic humanism once again proves the significant influence of the Roman Stoic, Cicero:

> The law alone can be trusted with the unlimited confidence:—Those laws, which alone can secure equity between all and everyone; which are the bond of that dignity which we enjoy in the commonwealth; the foundation of liberty, and the fountain of equity; the mind, the soul, the counsel, and judgement of the city, whose ministers are the magistrates, whose interpret-

108. John Adams to Francis Van der Kemp, August 9, 1813.
109. John Adams to Francis Van der Kemp, March 19, 1813.
110. J. Adams, *Works,* IV, 559.

ers of judges, whose servants are all men who mean to be free: Those laws which are right reason, derived from the Divinity, commanding honesty and forbidding iniquity; which are silent magistrates, where the magistrates are only speaking laws; which, as they are founded in eternal morals, are emanations of the Divine mind. [111]

The language of the classic republican tradition may sound strange to our modern ears, but the spirit of civic humanism has taken shape in the civic culture; not to understand it means to do without the knowledge of the content of order of the constitutional state. Thus, it appears inadmissible to me to play the Whig science of politics of 1776 off against the American science of politics of 1787. By comparison, L. Banning makes the following statement: "Most of the inherited structure of eighteenth-century political thought persisted in America for years after 1789. And this persistence was not a matter of a shadowy halfline of fragmentary ideas. A structured universe of classical thought continued to serve as the intellectual medium through which Americans perceived the political world, and an inherited political language was the primary vehicle for the expression of their hopes and discontents." Banning not only disputes that the Constitution was the expression of a new American science of politics; he also turns Wood's argument around: "The world of classical politics assured the quick apotheosis of the constitution of the United States." [112] The design for existence of the generation of 1776 and its interpretation in the concept of the paradigmatic republic took hold so speedily of the souls and minds of the American people that a "social field of consciousness" (Eric Voegelin) expressing itself in common meanings came into existence. From this common reference world that integrated the web of intersubjective meanings into the whole of community emerged the institutional framework of the politically organized society under the national Constitution. Once the concept of the paradigmatic republic had become "self-evident" to the majority, the struggle for the institutional implementation of the republican project brought the antagonistic moment of social and economic conflicts to light as the framers of the federal Constitution knew very well. But even the *Federalist* papers do not design a model that rests exclusively on a pluralist system of mutually balancing interests. For the establishment of public order is, according to Publius, grounded in human reason after all.

---

111. J. Adams, *Works*, VI, 208, 56.

112. L. Banning, "Republican Ideology and the Triumph of the Constitution, 1789 to 1793," *William and Mary Quarterly*, XXXI (1974), 173, 188.

III. The Paradigmatic Republic and the American Science of Politics in the *Federalist* Papers

In the *Federalist* papers and in the constitutional debate, an American science of politics was to a large extent formulated under the horizon of the republican tradition, as illustrated by the fact that the writers of the Constitution viewed themselves as founders and reformers. Thus, only recently Russell L. Hanson also found that the constitutional debate viewed all differences as to the nature and purpose of a republican regime within the framework handed down by tradition. "All important factions of this period in American politics claimed to be republican, in principle, if not in name; all used republican terminology to justify their own positions, and to criticize others; and all appealed to revolutionary republicanism as the inspirational exemplar." Interpreted differently, republicanism defined the normative universe of discourse.[113] The decisive moment of continuity can be found in the constitutive principles of classical political science applied to the ordering designs as well as the questions and methods of research based on these principles. From this point of view, the republican theory is marked by the classical understanding that the political order and its institutions are basically derived from the nature and destiny of man. This principle of classical political science is a theme of the constitutional debate; it is explored and varied.

In this respect, the constitutional debate of 1786 to 1787 was determined by the spirit of republican tradition, and this is true also for the discussions on the new experiences of the American society. According to Herbert J. Storing, the differences in opinion between the Federalists and the anti-Federalists "were not based on different premises about the nature of man or the ends of political life. They were not the deep cleavages of contending regimes." It is true, however, that there was considerable controversy about the organization of the republican order under the given social and historical conditions, and that the various positions were reflected in the political language.[114]

The prominent position that the *Federalist* papers occupied in the constitutional debate can be attributed not least to the way these papers represented the new constitution as a manifestation of an innovative and revised republicanism, thereby doing justice to the authors' self-understanding as classical legislators, who, according to Aristotle, not only have in mind the best constitution for a small autarkic community

---

113. R. L. Hanson, *The Democratic Imagination in America* (Princeton, 1985), 90.
114. H. J. Storing, *What the Antifederalists Were For* (Chicago, 1981), 5–6.

of virtuous citizens (as many an American republican hoped to achieve), but who try to find the best possible constitution for the majority of the people, taking into consideration that under certain circumstances it may be better to decide in favor of a less perfect constitution for reasons of practicability (*Politics*, 1288b). Publius states that the precarious situation does not allow "successive experiments in the chimerical pursuit of a perfect plan." Thus, the result of the discussions necessarily was a blend of errors and prejudices as well as of good sense and wisdom: "I never expect to see a perfect work from imperfect men." A treaty able to bind the thirteen states by means of common bonds of friendship and unity can only be a compromise between diverse interests and inclinations. "How can perfection spring from such materials?"[115] Thus, it is futile to hope for a "happy empire of perfect wisdom and perfect virtue."[116] This statement refers both to the being of man, in other words his nature, and to the special historical circumstances of the American people. The voice of enlightened reason alone would move an entire nation of philosophers to have the necessary respect for the law. "But a nation of philosophers is as little to be expected as the philosophical race of kings wished for by Plato."[117] Another passage states: "If men were angels, no government would be necessary. If angels were to govern men, neither external nor internal controls on government would be necessary."[118] This leads back to the major reason for institutions as such: the human state of being. And the key phrase of the study is, "But what is government itself but the greatest of all reflections on human nature."[119] "Why has government been instituted at all? Because the passions of men will not conform to the dictates of reason and justice without constraint."[120] In accordance with the classical view of the two-sided nature of man as a reasonable and passionate being, which will be addressed in more detail below, Publius also recognized the necessity of political institutions. Moreover, their purpose was to use reason to mold the passionate nature of man. Therefore they are oriented along the standards of industrious and wise citizens and men, as discussed above. Thus, Publius does not reduce man to his passionate nature, his private greed for power and property, only to later identify reason with the dictates put forth in *Leviathan*: "As there is a degree of depravity in mankind which requires a certain degree of circumspection and distrust, so there are other qualities in human nature

115. *Federalist* No. 85.
116. *Federalist* No. 6.
117. *Federalist* No. 49.
118. *Federalist* No. 51.
119. *Ibid.*
120. *Federalist* No. 15.

which justify a certain portion of esteem and confidence. Republican Government presupposes the existence of these qualities in a higher degree than any other form." If, however, the descriptions of human character inspired by the political suspicions of several contemporaries were fitting, then "the inference would be that there is not sufficient virtue among men for self-government; and that nothing less than the changes of despotism can restrain them from destroying and devouring one another."[121]

The following is an attempt to explain the intellectual-historical origins and the theoretical form of the philosophically oriented anthropology developed by Publius. Publius is convinced that, in the constitutional debate, the question of incorporating the principle of self-government in the Constitution will prove to be the only real and correct principle of order for the American people, insofar as the power of judgment and common sense of each individual citizen will cause him to agree to the Constitution, if he does not let himself be guided by prejudice, passion, or selfish interests. Viewed from this angle, the structure of the arguments in the essays proves throughout to be a rational discourse with competent citizens, aimed at reaching reasonable agreement on the Constitution. This reasonable agreement is based on the claim to truth that is incorporated in the Constitution as well as on the principles and maxims of the revised republican politics put forth in the *Federalist* papers. This evidence in favor of the ordering principles, which is obvious to all reasonable persons, is proven by specifically epistemological means, especially because it concerns those principles of ethical-political science that are readily accessible to the human power of judgment. The fact that the constitutional order is based on the knowledge of order of a political-moral civic science indicates the core of the classical concept of politics. For this purpose, Publius, contrary to Adams, falls back on the renewed republican science of the Scottish Enlightenment, which was indebted to English Whiggism. The significant role that the Scottish Enlightenment played in shaping American republicanism has been disputed in recent research, even if the role of the Scots is weighed differently.[122] The "science of man" developed in the reformed Scottish universities was a determining educational experience for many colonists, among them Madison, particularly because it contained a "modern" restitution of the classical-Christian republican tradition without its theological and

---

121. *Federalist* No. 56.

122. G. Wills, *Inventing America: Jefferson's Declaration of Independence* (n.p., 1980); Adair, "Fame and the Founding Fathers"; D. W. Howe, "The Political Psychology of 'The Federalist,'" *William and Mary Quarterly*, XLIV (1987), 485–509.

corporate implications. This can be attributed to the peculiar combination of neo-Stoical thought as well as the new worldview offered by the mathematical and physical sciences. In particular, however, the concept of civilized progress in a dynamic commercial and mercantile society was combined to such an extent with republican tradition that it was not only possible to refute numerous dogmatic assumptions as to the sociocultural prerequisites for a free republic but also to reevaluate the American situation in the light of historical experience and to integrate immediately the institutional innovations in a revised paradigm of the republic. If this standpoint is taken, Publius referred to David Hume in many aspects. However, regarding the theoretical basis of the anthropological premise of self-government, Publius refuses to accept Hume's skeptical psychology of perception, turning to the commonsense philosophy of Thomas Reid, an opponent of David Hume, which vouched for truth and reality. According to Reid, the predogmatic reality of human existence is derived from the intuitive apperception of initial principles or primary truths by taking recourse to the primary experience of humanity's common sense. The common sense of competent persons is the common source of knowing and distinguishing truth and falseness, good and evil, beauty and ugliness, which, in turn, ensure the rational modality of individual and collective existence.

In contrast to Hume, who combined empiricism and subjectivism, Reid's philosophy of the human spirit is an antiskeptical response to the philosophy of subjectivity that had been accepted since Descartes and Locke. Reid includes man in a comprehensive, theonomously structured order of existence, which is reflected in the fabric of human nature and which is based on the mutuality of the human world. To what extent the *Federalist* papers are influenced by Reid's philosophy was made clear recently by Daniel W. Howe. Howe points out that Reid "was followed by a large and distinguished school" in North America; therefore, Reid's influence upon Hamilton and Madison has "not to be traced through personal connections" (although these can be proven, too), because this form of faculty psychology "was common intellectual property in the Eighteenth century." "At the time Madison and Hamilton were writing the *Federalist,*" Howe states, "the last volume of the definitive redaction of Reid's lectures . . . was just being published." Howe was not able to determine "whether either of them had access to it, but the faculty psychology they drew on was a pattern of thought with which they and their readers were well familiar, not a paraphrase or transcription of any single book."[123]

123. *Ibid.*, 489–90.

The following are only a few significant factors that will probably prove to be important for the restitution of a theory of the republic:

1. Reid provided the republican design of existence with a realistic metaphysics of the self-responsible citizenry from the point of view of a "modern" empirical interpretation of the ancient Christian theory on human nature.

2. Reid developed an egalitarian theory of knowledge: the original truths and first principles are "dictates of common sense and reason" that are accessible to *all* people, irrespective of their social standing. They are the guiding motif for leading a right life that is common to *all* people.

3. Reid consistently considers all knowledge to be based on empirical knowledge that is directly connected to the constitution of human nature and that, however, is understandable to the citizen of common understanding.

4. Thus, the communal order of the social existence of man is a direct result of the common rational nature of man given by common sense. "This inward light or sense is given by heaven to different persons in different degrees. There is a certain degree of it which is necessary to our being subjects of law and government, capable of managing our own affairs, and answerable for our conduct to others: this is called common sense, because it is common to all men with whom we can transact business, or call to account for their conduct." Insofar as common sense enables man to judge self-evident primary principles, it can be equated "with reason in its whole extent." [124] In a more restricted sense, reason is the ability to draw rational conclusions from self-evident principles of common sense. "Rational principles" understood in such a way make it possible to lead a wise and virtuous life, whose purpose is "the happiness upon the whole of the good man." It is the "rational principles of action" alone that make "political" and "moral government" possible.

Political government describes that sphere of human perfection of power within which "a subordinate dominion or government" befits man, and that is why it can be said of him that he was created "after the image of God, the supreme Governeur. But, as his dominion is subordinate, he is under a moral obligation to make a right use of it, as far as the reason which God has given him can direct him." Thus the "moral government" of the divine legislator arches over the "political government" of man,

124. T. Reid, *Works,* ed. W. Hamilton (Edinburgh, 1985), I, 425.

who is created in the likeness of God.[125] The law of the one is the imperfect image of the other.

In complete accordance with an undogmatic restored ancient theory of ethics, Reid raises man's ability to achieve rational political solidarity, which has its origins in the common sense of man and has been put to the test by everyday life, to the anthropological premise of the political organization of society, without, however, developing the theory of republican politics. Publius adopts Reid's anthropology, using it as a basis for his republic-centered political science.

In the *Federalist* this is done by means of the classical analogy between an individual's frame of mind and the political society. "For Publius the art of governing was a decision-making process analogous to that of an individual; the institutions of government were analogous to the individual's faculty of the mind."[126] Just as Reid defines the control of reason over passion as "the happiness of the good man," Publius determines that the control of reason over the public mind is the public happiness of a well-ordered society. Thus the political concept of self-government is formed analogously to the ethical concept of self-government or self-command. As unsystematic and partial as this adoption of Reid may be, Publius, in the strategically significant points of the argument, does have recourse to Reid's epistemologically substantiated anthropological argumentation for his model of republican institutions.

D. W. Howe points out that Reid's "faculty psychology" "influenced both his substantive arguments (his political science) and his techniques of persuasion (his rhetoric)." "Publius made use of the paradigm to present his case for guarding political liberty with social order. In both systems, parts were subordinated to the welfare of the whole, balances were struck between conflicting motives and order was based on a rational hierarchy."[127] Right at the beginning of his discourse, Publius urges his fellow citizens to let themselves be guided only by the "evidence of truth" when making a decision.[128] He elaborates on Reid, explaining that all types of research are based on certain original truths (primary truths) or primary principles, on which all further conclusions depend. "These contain an internal evidence which, antecedent to all reflection or combination, commands the assent of the mind. Where it produces not this effect, it must proceed either from some disorder in the organs of perception, or from the influence of some strong interest, or passion, or prejudice."[129]

125. *Ibid.*, II, 613–15.
126. D. W. Howe, "Political Psychology of 'The Federalist,'" 499.
127. *Ibid.*, 486.
128. *Federalist* No. 1.
129. *Federalist* No. 31.

This also applies to the truths of ethics and politics. If they are derived from original nature or from original truths, they are so obviously complete in themselves "and so agreeable to the natural and unsophisticated dictates of common sense that they challenge the assent of a sound and unbiased mind with a degree of force and conviction almost equally irresistible." The principles of moral and political knowledge cannot be compared with those of mathematics as regards certainty, "yet they have much better claims in this respect than to judge from the conduct of men in particular situations we should be disposed to allow them." If there is a lack of clarity, then this can more likely than not be attributed to the passions and prejudices of the individual who is thinking than to the object. "Men, upon too many occasions, do not give their own understanding fair play." [130]

Not only in his epistemological excursus but throughout his line of argumentation does Publius refer back to the self-evidence of the primary principles (or axioms) given directly by common sense so as to obtain the structure of the republican order through deduction (line of reasoning), the (secondary) principles or maxims. [131] In this epistemological context, the *Federalist* papers, on behalf of epistemological common sense and its reason, try to master apperceptive refusal due to passion, prejudice, and self-interest. Whenever a statement is to be particularly persuasive, Publius appeals to common sense or "good sense," [132] the "general sense of mankind," [133] or "judgment." [134]

And in another passage Publius once again yields to epistemological reflection: "the institutions of man" constitute a field of objects the description of which leaves much to be desired, because the indefiniteness as regards the definition, delimitation, and classification of the object is not only based on the imperfection of the perceptive organ as it is found in nature, but can be attributed to the indefiniteness of the object itself. Not only the complexity of the object, the imperfection of human epistemological abilities, but language itself is the reason why complex and new objects are not accurately defined in the science of government. [135] These considerations tell us a great deal about the authors' objectives: the new teachings of the "institutions of man" that are laid down in the Constitution are not only based on the self-evidence of original truths,

---

130. *Ibid.*
131. Compare *Federalist* No. 6, *Federalist* No. 23, *Federalist* No. 46, *Federalist* No. 47, *Federalist* No. 51.
132. *Federalist* No. 5; *Federalist* No. 83; *Federalist* No. 84.
133. *Federalist* No. 6; *Federalist* No. 81.
134. *Federalist* No. 1; *Federalist* No. 27.
135. *Federalist* No. 37.

but undergo a hitherto unknown conceptual and theoretical definition by Publius. Precisely this idea of the epistemological progress of science—the *opinio communis* of the Founding Fathers and their Scottish teachers— together with the epistemological teachings of the commonsense philoso- phy enabled Publius to make the alterations in the Constitution, which were plausibly introduced because of a revision of republicanism, in such a manner that not only the objections of the opponents were defeated, but the Constitution had to be understood as the implementation of the latest knowledge, which reflected the progress made in political science. The past history of the republics was indeed marked by a constant alter- nation between anarchy and tyranny, and it would have been difficult to defend the cause of the free republic had it not been possible to develop a model "of a more perfect structure." Like other sciences, political sci- ence also underwent great improvements: "the efficacy of various prin- ciples is now well understood, which were either not known at all, or imperfectly known to the ancients."[136] Separation of powers, the intro- duction of a legislature that is equipped with reciprocal checks and bal- ances, the independence and irremovability of the judges, the represen- tation of the people in the parliament by means of representatives elected by the people, and finally, the extension of the effectiveness of the "popu- lar system of civil government" in an individual state or a federation of states by means of a "judicious modification and mixture of the federal principles":[137] "these are wholly new discoveries, or have made their principal progress toward perfection in modern times." These princi- ples—rational deductions of political science based on the self-evident truths of the *sensus communis*—form the basis for the special modern institutional instruments that are aimed at maintaining the advantages and eliminating the traditional defects of the republican regime.[138] Pub- lius then goes one step further in his attempts to arrive at a clearer lin- guistic definition of the concepts, letting only the term *republic* apply to the institutional complex determined in the Constitution by raising the concept of representation to the leading principle of the republican order. By means of these radical redefinitions Publius wants to overcome the traditional terminology of classical republicanism, which also governed the American constitutional debate because of the impression Montes- quieu had made on all the Founding Fathers and which found its most prominent representative in John Adams. Publius opposed Adams, and on behalf of his revised theory of the republic he challenged the republi-

136. *Federalist* No. 9.
137. *Federalist* No. 51.
138. *Federalist* No. 9.

can character of the Dutch, Polish, or Venetian politics and last but not least, the English mixed constitution. Contrary to the English neoclassical republicans, Publius maintained that any traditional corporate order was incompatible with the principle of the republic. A "genuine republic" is only that political order "which derives all its powers directly or indirectly from the great body of the people, and is administered by persons holding their offices during pleasure for a limited period, or during good behavior. It is *essential* to such a government that it be derived from the great body of society." In view of this definition, an aristocratic or a monarchical republic, in which a social minority rules, cannot claim the "honorable title of republic"; rather, it is the rule of a "handful of tyrannical nobles." The political thrust of this line of argumentation is aimed against all those who, like Adams, were suspected of being in favor of a constitution resembling that of England. At the same time, Publius makes clear that his revised concept of republicanism is above any suspicion of being aristocratic.[139] Conversely, however, this break with the neoclassical teachings of political forms of order further showed that the old concept of the democratic republic had been declared obsolete. A republic must not be confused with the classical concept of a small state with a landed citizenry: the difference is "that in a democracy the people meet and exercise the government in person; in a republic they assemble and administer it by their representatives and agents. A democracy, consequently, must be confined to a small spot. A republic may be extended over a large region." Any inferences made on the basis of the concept of democracy cannot be applied to the republic, and once again he puts forward the increased knowledge gained in political science. It was the discovery of the principle of representation that provided the foundation for an "unmixed and extensive republic," which now had to be developed within the political system of the new Constitution.[140] It is on this point that Publius seriously breaks with the neo-Harringtonism propounded by John Adams. However, the concept of democracy could not be eliminated in the constitutional debate as consistently as in the *Federalist* papers. Thus, in his speech before the ratifying convention of New York on July 12, 1787, Hamilton defined the republic as a representative democracy,[141] a neologism that met with the approval of all political views. Jefferson, the antipode of Hamilton, wrote: "The introduction of this new principle of representative democracy has rendered useless almost everything written before on the structure of government." In Jef-

139. *Federalist* No. 39.
140. *Federalist* No. 14.
141. A. Hamilton, *Papers*, V, 150–51.

ferson's opinion, city-state democracy was still the "pure republic," but the representative democracy represented a republican regime "of second grade of purity" that was suitable for spatial extension.[142]

According to Publius, this new concept of the republic alone reflects the content of order of American constitutional practice and the notion of the constitution developed on the basis of it. Within this theoretical framework, however, Publius attempts to solve the classical problems of order exhibited by civic humanistic politics in such a way that the authority of reason, truth, and justice over the public mind is also maintained in a dynamic society based on property and commerce, with its individualistic acquisitive attitudes,[143] since "it is reason, alone, of the public, that ought to control and regulate the government. The passions ought to be controlled and regulated by the government."[144]

This objective, however, presupposes that the institutional arrangement provided by the new Constitution, which is based on principles, is in a position to overcome the greatest evil of all republican orders: "to break and control the violence of faction. The friend of popular governments never finds himself so much alarmed for their character and fate as when he contemplates their propensity to this dangerous vice." Faction leads to the mortal diseases, "under which popular governments have everywhere perished."[145] Faction or party divides the citizenry, destroys communal political life, the basis of self-government, and finally, results in tyranny or anarchy, thereby threatening the continued existence of society itself. In accordance with the prevailing republican doctrine, Publius defines faction as any number of citizens, irrespective of whether it is a minority or a majority, "who are united and actuated by some common impulse of passion, or of interest, adverse to the rights of other citizens, or to the permanent and aggregate interests of community."[146] In another passage, Publius (Madison) asserts that if a faction becomes the majority, then "the fundamental principle of republican government," which states "that the majority who rule in such Governments are the safest guardians both of the public Good and of private rights," is jeopardized.[147] Thus, faction is a question, not of the numerical strength of the citizens involved, but of the quality of the motives behind the action: "The interest of the majority is the political standard of right and

---

142. T. Jefferson, *Political Writings*, ed. E. Dumbauld (New York, 1955), 87.
143. *Federalist* No. 63.
144. *Federalist* No. 49.
145. *Federalist* No. 10.
146. *Ibid.*
147. Madison, *Papers,* IX, 354.

wrong"—if the term *interest* is understood to be synonymous with *ultimate happiness*—"in which sense it is qualified with every necessary moral ingredient." With respect to the popular meaning of "immediate augmentation of property and wealth," the interest of the majority is nothing other than the exploitation and enslavement of a minority of individuals.[148] The latter definition of interest as "private interest" can well be regarded as the motive guiding the formation of factions. The notion of passion, which the *Federalist* papers considered to be the decisive motive for political misconduct, can be tentatively deciphered with the help of Reid's philosophy: "The passions are blind desires of some particular object, without any judgement, or consideration, whether it be good for us upon the whole or ill."[149] The significant point seems to be that passion and interest are impulses of action aimed at particular objects, which were caused by the practice of faction and which stand in contrast to moral action based on the principles of reason common to all men. As long as the "spirit of faction" activates only political or even religious *minorities,* the "republican principle" of majority vote can be used as a remedial measure because minorities, as disturbing as they may be to society, can never give constitutional power to their demands. Yet, whenever the majority is grasped by the "spirit of faction," the form of popular rule itself makes it possible "to sacrifice to its ruling passion or interest both the public good and the rights of other citizens."[150] If passion or interest becomes the common motive of the majority, then the republican institutions turn against the principle of order of the republican regime.

On the other hand, the objectives of the republic that guide all action are identical to the objectives of political institutions as such: "the good of the whole" is the "supreme object to be pursued," "the public good, the real welfare of the great body of the people," "private rights and public happiness," "common interest," as Publius describes the decisive criteria of civic politics in a classical manner.[151] Thus, "a coalition of the majority of the whole" on the basis of the principles of "justice and the general good"[152] corresponds to the republican principle. If the constitutional reform is to be successful, then republican reform will have to prove itself by solving the problem of faction: "To secure the public good and private rights against the danger of such a faction, and at the same

148. *Ibid.,* 141.
149. Reid, *Works,* II, 581.
150. *Federalist* No. 10.
151. *Ibid.; Federalist* No. 43; *Federalist* No. 45.
152. *Federalist* No. 51.

time to preserve the spirit and the form of popular government, is then the great object to which our inquiries are directed." [153] In their clear-sighted and realistic analysis of the tremendous problems posed by the task of integrating the former colonies in a large political nation with the capacity to act on domestic and foreign issues, the authors started out from the ubiquity of complex political, religious, and socioeconomic patterns of conflict in a republican civil policy. The contradictory nature of consensus and conflict cannot be set aside, but it can be regulated. According to classical politics, Publius sought to solve the problem from its roots, namely, human nature: "The latent causes of faction are thus sown in the nature of man." Under the premise of republican freedom, the tension between fallible reason and self-love necessarily gives rise to the incongruity between political equality and personal as well as social inequality. For this reason, dogmatic republicanism errs in its assumption "that by reducing mankind to a perfect equality in their political rights, they would at the same time be perfectly equalized and assimilated in their possessions, their opinions, and their passions." [154] This statement, which is aimed at the neo-Harringtonian idea of an egalitarian structure of property, corresponds truly to the logic of Aristotelian politics and takes into account the American reality of a socially and economically stratified "civilized nation" on the basis of the right to property. Publius essentially seems to attribute "private interests" in the sense described above to the various ways of acquiring property or the diverse forms of property holding; they are the expression of a complex socioeconomic stratification with reciprocal and overlapping patterns of conflict: class conflicts, conflicts between the large branches of industry, as well as re-gional and sectional conflicts. The formation of factions caused by such a diversity of interests in a society of proprietors can, in the final analysis, be ascribed to the manifold abilities of human nature, in which the rights to property find their roots. Protecting these abilities (and not the prop-erty as such) is the principal task of government. Thus, the interests can-not be made uniform by equalizing the property.

Although it is often combined with private interests, the impulse of passion, which seems to be the actual political ingredient of any faction, has been determined the sole disturbing factor. As we have seen, passion provides the motive for political action on the part of individuals and groups against the public good. According to Publius, passion, as a rule, is a more or less temporary outburst, which virtually neutralizes the fac-ulties of judgment of the citizenry, placing them under the "tyranny of

153. *Federalist* No. 10.
154. *Ibid.*

their passions," which interfere with the "cool and deliberate sense of community"[155] and the "public tranquillity" by introducing a tendency toward violent particularity.[156] In Publius' opinion, this appearance of passion in the public domain can, as a rule, be ascribed to the effectiveness of demagogic popular leaders: "an attachment to different leaders ambitiously contending for preeminence and power, or to persons of other prescriptions whose fortunes have been interesting to the human passions, have, in turn, divided mankind into parties, inflamed them with mutual animosity, and rendered them much more disposed to vex and oppress each other than to cooperate for their common good."[157] Insofar as can be understood from Publius' sometimes unclear statements, passion, contrary to private interests based on the ability to acquire property, is the aspiration for power, honor, fame, and influence as goals in themselves, which is not controlled by common sense and judgment. This "private" characteristic of passion is the expression of its tyrannical features: it contradicts the principle of self-government, both in the individual and in society.

Since neither private interests nor passion is neutralized by the equality of citizens as regards virtue and property, and because the causes of faction cannot be eliminated in a free and democratic regime in which the private sphere of all citizens is protected by law, the effects of party formation need to be minimized by means of institutional arrangements. This gives rise to the above-mentioned specific reasoning in favor of the institutional and theoretical modifications of the republican paradigm of order such as the principle of territorial extension, representation, and separation of powers.

The public authority must be organized in such a way that it can guide the passions of society to the benefit of the public good.[158] The point of departure for such a solution can be found in the concepts of passion and interest themselves. According to Reid's modified classical reading of the affects, passion and interest are manifestations of natural desires and emotions, and as such they are animal impulses of action necessary for life, which blindly—that is, as wild desire that is not controlled by reason— lead to the "perturbation" (within the meaning of Cicero) of the human soul, aiming at immediate satisfaction.[159] Under the guidance of a sense of interest and sense of duty, they can cause passionate dedication to achieve the highest of goals.

155. *Federalist No. 63.*
156. *Federalist No. 49.*
157. *Federalist No. 10; Federalist No. 49.*
158. *Federalist No. 13; Federalist No. 16; Federalist No. 48; Federalist No. 72.*
159. Reid, *Works,* II, 551–84.

Naturally, Publius did not formulate such a detailed theory of affects, but it explains the ambivalence of his concept of passion as reflected by the deep respect he had for such emotions as patriotism and love of glory.[160] In addition this allows him to give legitimacy to interest in property within the framework of his anthropology, for example, in the continual praise of the commercial "spirit of enterprise,"[161] which the dogmatic agrarian republicanism could only view with skepticism.

No matter whether a faction has its origins in political or even religious passion, in economic interests, or in a combination of both, its effects can, in any case, be checked. This is first done by having the principle of representation continuously serve the primary goals of all republican politics: "The aim of every political constitution is, or ought to be, first to obtain for rulers men who possess most wisdom to discern, and most virtue to pursue, the common good of society; and in the next place, to take the most effectual precautions for keeping them virtuous whilst they continue to hold their public trust. The elective mode of obtaining rulers is the characteristic policy of republican government."[162] In accordance with Aristotelian tradition, what matters is to filter out a minority of competent and mature citizens from the citizenry to be rulers because "the institution of delegated power implies that there is a portion of virtue and honour among mankind which may be a reasonable foundation of confidence."[163] "There are strong minds in every walk of life that will rise superior to the disadvantages of situation and will command the tribute due to their merit, not only from the classes to which they particularly belong, but from the society in general. The door ought to be equally open to all."[164] In Publius' opinion, the system of representation based on direct and indirect elections provides the public government with the necessary degree of civic virtue and statesmanlike competence. In this respect, Publius believes that such indirectly elected bodies as the senate and such offices as the office of the president, as well as the body of judges, have a higher degree of civic and governing virtues than the directly elected representatives of the people.

The tiered system of representation has a particularly chastening effect on the political life of the citizenry: it makes it possible "to refine and enlarge the public views by passing them through the medium of a chosen body of citizens, whose wisdom may best discern the true interest of their country and whose patriotism and love of justice will be least likely to

160. *Federalist* No. 2; *Federalist* No. 72.
161. *Federalist* No. 7.
162. *Federalist* No. 57.
163. *Federalist* No. 76.
164. *Federalist* No. 36.

sacrifice it to temporary or partial considerations."[165] Thus, contrary to "pure democracy," the principle of representation makes the ruling positions immune to the spirit of faction, letting it find no ways to transform the diverse interests and factions throughout the republic into an "unjust and interested majority." Although the influence of "factious leaders" may give rise to "local fires," such fires will remain restricted to the region—the organization of political passion ("the rage for paper money, for an abolition of debts, for an equal division of property, or for any other improper or wicked projects") by demagogues, political leaders without civic virtue, will be stopped by the national representatives, who stand for the public welfare. Contrary to widespread opinion, Publius did not believe that the pluralism of interest and factions acted as such a stabilizing factor; of decisive importance is the fact that the effectiveness of the "factious leader" remains limited to a certain region or sector, that these leaders are kept within bounds by the ethical qualifications of the national representatives of the people.[166] However, since the holders of public offices are themselves subject to corruptive influences, Publius considers the internal organization of the government institutions, the separation of powers, and the system of checks and balances to be a secondary means of putting an end to the latent temptations, to which even virtuous, wise, and competent citizens may be exposed because of their nature. "This policy of supplying, by opposite and rival interests, the defect of better motives, might be traced through the whole system of human affairs, private as well as public. We see it particularly displayed in all subordinate distributions of powers, where the constant aim is to divide and arrange the several offices in such a manner as that each may be a check on the other—that the private interest of every individual may be a sentinel over the public rights."[167] In fact, "the desire of reward is one of the strongest incentives of human conduct; or that the best security for the fidelity of mankind is to make their interest coincide with their duty."[168] The secondary means of neutralizing political passion appeals to the sense of interest as well as the sense of duty in order to use private impulses for the public good. The mechanism of the Constitution contains numerous devices that can be applied to this end, but they will not be discussed in more detail here. According to Publius, the institutional order of the Constitution as a whole is a unique combination of measures aimed against the fatal illness of the republic, the "spirit of faction." Publius (Hamilton) summarizes this concept at the ratifying convention in

165. *Federalist* No. 10.
166. *Ibid.*
167. *Federalist* No. 51.
168. *Federalist* No. 72.

New York: "We are attempting by this constitution to abolish factions, and to unite all parties for the general welfare."[169]

The constitution as *suprema lex* reflects the logic of the republican principle. Insofar as it is the repository of the primary principles of the moral and political knowledge of the society, the truth of the common sense of man made its historical appearance in it through the genius of the American people. In its consensus on the Constitution, the American nation not only constitutes itself as a body politic but beyond that, the authority of the Constitution is based on an ultimate ground of order common to humanity: the dictates of reason and common sense. The question of whether and to what extent the citizenry is obliged to agree to the Constitution against a minority leads Publius to one of his most profound metaphysical ultimate arguments for the constitutional institutions, inspired by his commonsense philosophy: "to the great principle of self-preservation" and beyond that "to the transcendent law of nature and of nature's God, which declares that the safety and happiness of society are the objects at which all political institutions aim and to which all such institutions must be sacrificed."[170]

Contrary to Jefferson, Publius was convinced of the uniqueness of this collective act of founding a new body politic, and, as discussed above, he never considered the making of the Constitution to be any repeatable event: "The establishment of a Constitution, in time of profound peace, by the voluntary consent of a whole people, is a PRODIGY, to the completion of which I look forward with trembling anxiety."[171] Thus Publius deems it necessary that constitutional amendments refer only to individual passages of the Constitution; by no means does he intend a revision of the entire Constitution. On the contrary, Publius warns of appealing to the people too often with respect to constitutional issues, and he introduces an argument that, over and above the idea of a finite constitutional order, points out their social prerequisite, the sociocultural embodiment in societal self-understanding:

> As every appeal to the people would carry an implication of some defect in the government, frequent appeals would, in great measure, deprive the government of that veneration which time bestows on everything, and without which the wisest and freest government would not possess the requisited stability. If it is true that all governments rest on opinion, it is no less true that the strength of opinion in each individual, and its practical influence on his conduct, depend much on the number which he supposes to have

169. A. Hamilton, *Papers*, V, 85.
170. *Federalist* No. 43.
171. *Federalist* No. 85.

entertained the same opinion. The reason of man, like man himself, is timid and cautious when left alone and acquires firmness and confidence in proportion to the number with which it is associated. When the examples which fortify opinion are ancient as well as numerous, they are known to have a double effect.[172]

These passages from the *Federalist* No. 49 were and still are considered by many interpreters to be an "anti-democratic scandal" because they seem to be a blatant contradiction of the basic republican principle of government by consent. Garry Wills, following in Adairs' footsteps, discovered Hume's influence in these passages.[173] In his essay "Of The First Principles of Government," Hume answers the question as to how government is possible: "It is . . . on opinion only that government is founded." Hume explains that "the opinion of right"—the belief in legitimacy of those governed—is illustrated "by observing the attachment which all nations have to their ancient government, and even to those names which have the sanctions of antiquity. Antiquity always begets the opinion of right."[174] Hume turns against any social-contract theory and interprets government by consent exclusively on the basis of the traditional character of any government. Did Publius really want to move back to Hume's doctrine of the traditional basis of government for the sake of the stability of the political order? If that is so, then Wills would be correct in claiming that "when we see him arguing, from Hume's doctrine of opinion, for reverence to the established order, we begin to wonder if he knew what he was letting himself in for. Did he use Hume with full knowledge of the consequences? If he did we must attribute to him a line of thought at odds with his reputation. But if he did not, then his claim as a serious political thinker is considerably reduced."[175]

I suppose that this contradiction can be solved if one proceeds on the assumption that, as was the case in other passages, Publius combines Hume's opinions with the theoretical position of Reid. In the *Federalist* No. 85, Publius extends Hume's warning that an order established by law needs experience and time to achieve perfection. Within this reasoning, he also accepts Hume's argument that it is only through permanence that a political regime can achieve the aura of venerability required for stability. Publius, however, by no means wants to replace the consensus of the citizens of common understanding as the source of authority with tradition according to Hume. Publius' point is that "reverence for the

172. *Federalist* No. 49.
173. G. Wills, *Explaining America. The Federalists* (Garden City, 1981), 24–33.
174. Hume, *Political Essays*, 24.
175. Wills, *Explaining America*, 32–33.

laws," the indispensable basis for a free and republican order, cannot be ensured by means of the "voice of an enlightened reason" alone because one is not dealing with a nation of philosophers. Wherever the reason of the majority does not reach, the "reverence for the laws" must be secured by opinion.[176] However, opinion is based both on the authority of tradition as well as on the authority of other persons. If opinion is guided by the correct authority, then it will give rise to the "reverence for the laws" in the measure necessary to maintain the stability of the regime. This argument can rely on Reid. Opinion is, as it were, the weaker expression of the power of judgment of the common sense. Contrary to knowledge, opinion is a judgment containing doubts.[177] For this reason, the judgments formulated in an opinion require substantiation through the authority of others: "Society in judgement, of those who are esteemed fair and competent judges, has effects very similar to those of civil society: it gives strength and courage to every individual; it removes that timidity which is as naturally the companion of solitary judgement, as of a solitary man in the state of nature."[178] Insofar as opinion considerably determines the conduct of man, the reasonable shaping of opinion is an indispensable prerequisite for civil government: "Of all instruments of government, opinion is the sweetest and the most agreeable to the nature of man. Obedience that flows from opinion is real freedom, which every man desires." The opinions of the majority of the people are always determined by the teachings of those whom they consider wise and good. Thus, opinions are to a large extent "in the power of those who govern them." Thus, Reid concludes: "I apprehend, therefore, that, if ever civil government shall be brought to perfection, it must be the principal care of the state to make good citizens by proper education, and proper instruction and discipline."[179] Reid also believes that government requires opinion as its basis, insofar as the power of judgment based on common sense does not reach the perfection in all persons that would ensure the complete independence of right judgment. However, right opinions are not the result of tradition; rather, they are brought forth by the educational authority of those who practice "the art of government" in the correct manner. If we interpret Publius' position using Reid's definition of the concept of opinion, we can say that "the reverence for the laws" is based on right opinion. This, however, is borne by the authority of both the tradition-inducing permanence of the constitutional order as well as

176. *Federalist* No. 49.
177. Reid, *Works*, I, 426.
178. *Ibid.*, 440.
179. *Ibid.*, II, 577–78.

the reciprocal confirmation by the citizens. Since, according to Reid, each judgment based on authority, as it is manifested by opinion, is defined also as prejudice, Publius can claim that "the most rational government will not find it a superfluous advantage to have the prejudices of the community on its side." [180] Understood in this way, Publius reveals himself as a veritable political philosopher: He has comprehended that the psychosocial constitution of the political structure of order is based on a common realm of consciousness that creates meaning, from which the legitimacy of the new regime will obtain that historical aura that can no longer be politically doubted.

The founders, who were also instructed in the ancient examples of classical and American history, found a certain truth in Hume's thoughts. They themselves continuously claimed "the sanction of antiquity" for the republican paradigm, at the same time viewing themselves as the founders of a tradition that demanded authority for later generations in accordance with the Roman concept of founding.

The "rituals of acclamation" described by Catherine L. Albanese show how consciously the political leaders wrapped the ratification of the Constitution in a tradition-shaping symbolism of national unity: "Probably the most memorable procession occurred in Philadelphia on the Fourth of July in a spectacle which combined at their height the elaborate stage-managing of the planners and the spontaneous enthusiasm of the people. It was liturgy in its fullest sense. . . . The procession was an elaborate and dramatic sermon on the true source of union among Americans. Representatives of traditional religious bodies had quietly taken their place among the rank and file of the parade, all innocent variations of a unity which had its ultimate ground in the religion of the republic and the Constitution, its most cherished sacrament." [181] No matter how the spiritual communality in the young republic actually stood, in the eyes of its organizers this grand federal procession was the symbolic presentation of a union of souls: "universal love and harmony prevailed, and every countenance appeared to be the index of a heart glowing with urbanity and rational joy." [182] Thus, the act of founding gave rise to the new identity-bearing symbolism of the paradigmatic republic: "In the establishment of a new center of power, the patriots discovered their communality. For those who would follow, the remembrance of the new thing the founders had done would unify and identify the citizen-heirs. This would be evident in the regard for the sacred times and places such as the Fourth of

180. *Federalist* No. 49.
181. C. L. Albanese, *Sons of the Fathers: The Civil Religion of the American Revolution* (Philadelphia, 1976), 212, 214.
182. *Ibid.*, 215.

July and Independence Hall, in the role of the Supreme Court as collective exegete for the Constitution, in the pervading sense in American life of a 'winding-down' of patriotism with accompanying exhortation to draw strength from mythic remembrance."[183]

Americans did in fact accept their founders' experiences of order and developed from them the corresponding behavior patterns, which their institutions expressed. But they also kept the ritual of the spiritual-moral awakening for the purpose of revitalizing their own order. For this they made use of the traditional New England cult of the father and the traditional understanding of history. But their objective now was only indirectly God, for the meaningfulness of the individual and social existence resulted from recurrence to the founding, the words and deeds of the fathers. Only the spiritual communality resulting from participation in the fathers' consciousness produced "reverence for the law" and the "supremacy of the written constitution, built on the balance of diverse interests"; herein lay, as will be shown below, the "cement of a pluralistic society which soon encompassed an enormous area."[184]

Publius, as well as John Adams and the other founders, raised the question that continues to be crucial to this day: "whether the postulate of a free society without the premise of an ethic binding on this society can even have any meaning—and whether a catalog of human rights, which has been resolved into an inflation of entitlements, is sufficient as a societal ethic."[185] The founders answered this question in the negative, theoretically by the truth of their personal existence and practically in its transformation into the truth of American society.

183. *Ibid.*, 9.
184. Stourzh, "Tugendhafte Republic," 261–62.
185. H. Lüthy, "Tugend und Menschenrechte," *Merkur*, CCCIX (1974), 134.

Four

Americanism: The Genesis of a
Civil Theology

I. Monumental History

The process by which the founders' consciousness created itself a social field in the new society and the authority of an ultimate source of order was accrued to them lasted half a century. This process was accelerated because it fit seamlessly into the traditional thought patterns of New England speculation on history and heroes.

New England historiography,[1] formally an Anglo-Saxon variant of reformation historiography, has, since the end of the seventeenth century, dealt with "the wonders of the Christian religion, flying from the deprivations of Europe to the American strand"[2] and thus dealt predominantly with those "godly men" who were at once founders and fathers of

1. Compare Dunn, "Seventeenth Century English Historians of America," in *Seventeenth Century America,* ed. J. M. Smith (Chapel Hill, N.C., 1959), 195–225. On American historiography, see M. Kraus, *The Writing of American History* (Norman, Okla., 1953); E. N. Saveth, ed., *Understanding the American Past* (Boston, 1954); D. D. van Tassel, *Recording America's Past: An Interpretation of the Development of Historical Studies in America, 1607–1884* (Chicago, 1960); H. Wish, *The American Historian* (New York, 1960). For general discussions of the problem of American historical apocalypse, see C. I. Sanford, *The Quest for Paradise* (Urbana, Ill.); M. Eliade, "Paradis et utopie: Géographie mythique et Eschatologie," in *Vom Sinn der Utopie* (Zurich, 1964); H. R. Niebuhr, *The Kingdom of God in America* (New York, 1959); M. Holloway, *Heavens on Earth* (New York, 1966); Tuveson, *Redeemer Nation.*

2. Miller and Johnson, eds., *Puritans,* I, 163.

the New England colonies: "particularly after 1676, a theme receives literary formulation which henceforth was to be a staple of the New England mind: ancestor worship. Virtually every one who migrated as an adult before 1640 was gone; in order to lay the covenant of the golden age upon their descendants . . . , the spokesmen called for such a veneration of progenitors as is hardly to be matched outside China." An impressive document for this attitude was the previously mentioned *Magnalia Christi Americana* of Cotton Mather, who, as the grandson of John Cotton and Richard Mather and the son of Increase Mather, was a legitimate prophet of the Founding Fathers' fame. The *Magnalia* was "under the guise of history, a sustained chant to the glory of might and already misty ancestral heroes."[3] And "it is a monumental piece of ancestor veneration, full to the brim of 'Hero's worthy to have their lives written.'"[4] Perry Miller saw the cause of this phenomenon in that functional nexus of the cult of the founders with the ongoing controversy concerning the right order, which was later to become so important for all modern societies grounded in revolution and which had been anticipated in the New England of the early eighteenth century: "Soon emphasis upon this theme was carried to such length of abjectness . . . , that we marvel how any Protestant culture could so abnegate its Christian liberty, until we remind ourselves that the preachers were fighting tooth and nail for what they considered survival, that these gestures were not so much humble submissions to the past as a discharge of heavy artillery against their antagonists."[5]

The same period saw the beginning of the outward practices of the cult of the hero: in 1729 in Salem for the first time on the American continent a centennial celebration in memory of the Founding Fathers' landing was held, and numerous sermons in Massachusetts recalled the event. Shortly thereafter, Plymouth Rock emerged as a monument to be worshiped and a symbol of the colony's founding. The intensification of outward forms of hero worship does not occur until the prelude to revolution.[6] In any case, at the end of the eighteenth century a "composite ideal called the Pilgrimfathers or the Puritans"[7] emerges; in the years when the republic was being consolidated, this model fused into a unified national symbolism by merging with the more recent small and large, as well as regional and national, heroes, and the symbolism of the Revolu-

3. P. Miller, *New England Mind*, II, 135; compare also Craven, *Legend of the Founding Fathers*, 9–20.
4. P. Miller, *New England Mind*, II, 189.
5. *Ibid.*, 135.
6. Wector, *Hero in America*, 42.
7. *Ibid.*

tion. In this symbolism the heroic fathers of the first founding served as Johannine heralds of the heroes of the Revolution: "The sons of the fathers became fathers themselves in the course of the Revolution." The patriots' "actions possessed warrant and metaphysical validity because they were patterned on the model that had existed from time immemorial: they in the present were secure because they were repeating an exemplary action from out of the past. Yet while still invoking their fathers, the patriots were finding in their actions a creative power without reference to the models from the past. They began to function as self-constituting and self-commanding figures."[8]

The condition for this state was the general acceptance "of propositions identifying the purposes of the original settlers with the cause for which the revolution was fought"[9]—a premise we have already encountered in our examination of Adams' self-understanding. Although this view found its confirmation in the traditions of most colonies, it inevitably led to an overwhelming influence of the New England Puritan tradition on the new republic's understanding of history[10] (which found its analogy in politics and to a lesser extent in the social order, thanks to the Northwest Ordinance of 1777).

In the other colonies there was no cult of the fathers and of heroes that was as lavish, William Penn in Pennsylvania excepted;[11] and the New England historiography, from the chronicles of the first settlers to Thomas Hutchinson's masterwork, *The History of the Colony and Province of Massachusetts Bay* (1764), stood alone at the top. Subsequent historiographic contributions of the Smith clan for the middle colonies, New Jersey, New York, and Pennsylvania descended directly from New England writings. In the South, historical consciousness overstepped the threshold of articulation only in three histories of Virginia, all written between 1705 and 1750.[12]

This supremacy of the New England tradition of history is not accidental; New England historiography was the explication of the City Upon the Hill, its origin and its crisis; it was expressed in an intense intellectualism, which radiated dynamically into the social reality, and this in turn was shaped along the concept of the "New England way of

8. Albanese, *Sons of the Fathers*, 46; compare P. Shaw, *American Patriots and the Rituals of Revolution* (Cambridge, Mass., 1981).

9. Craven, *Legend of the Founding Fathers*, 3.

10. *Ibid.*, 5; see also Colbourn, *Lamp of Experience;* J. T. Berens, *Providence and Patriotism* (Charlottesville, Va., 1978).

11. Craven, *Legend of the Founding Fathers*, 47–48.

12. Dunn, "Seventeenth-Century English Historians of America," in *Seventeenth-Century America*, ed. Smith; Craven, *Legend of the Founding Fathers*, 6–12, 46ff.

life" and established a self-confident political regime. As a jeremiad, created by an awareness of crisis, New England historiography always expressed an interest in the concrete beginnings and in the founders of the New England polities, in order to renew the original substance of society through revivals. Beginnings and founders were, so to speak, on the record and original in the sense of a politically and intellectually autonomously engendered society, which represents itself. Only New England could lay claim to a founding out of a spirit of separatism, outside the British empire, which one had voluntarily joined, and in the realization of an apocalyptically inspired new order (although only Plymouth—but not Massachusetts Bay—had understood itself as a separatist community). Once the self-interpretation of the Revolution had engaged in a speculation on American origins up to illuminating their significance, it necessarily had to cling to the New England tradition.[13]

In spite of Captain John Smith, the beginnings of Virginia were visible only in blurred outline; historiography kept to the reform policy of the Virginia Company (1619–1624), or the transformation of Virginia into a Crown colony (1624); it further saw Virginia closely connected with the political quarrels between Parliament and king and with the opposition to Cromwell—in short, in the imperial context.

Thomas Jefferson and Richard Bland, like Adams, claimed their political and legal privileges as Englishmen in confrontation with Parliament; but they did not invoke any American fathers. They followed the Whig view by transferring the origin of rights, liberties, and self-government to the old Anglo-Saxon order, which was already corrupted by the Norman invasion and was now to be destroyed once and for all in America.[14] This conception was the Whig tradition common to both England and America,[15] but understandably it played a lesser role in New England (Adams thought little of the transfiguration of the old Saxons[16]). Similar difficulties arose concerning the beginnings of the other colonies: the proprietary colonies owed their origins to a feudal institution; Georgia was the failed result of a philanthropic entrepreneurial spirit that

13. The self-consciousness of regional history rejected this tendency well into the nineteenth century.

14. T. Jefferson, "A Summary View," in *Papers*, ed. J. P. Boyd (Princeton, 1950), I, 121–22, especially on the role of the "Saxon ancestors." See also Bland, *Inquiry into the Rights of the British Colonies*, 7.

15. Colbourn, *Lamp of Experience*; B. Bailyn, ed., *Pamphlets of the American Revolution* (Cambridge, Mass., 1965), I, 52ff. For a general discussion of the Saxon origins of the British constitution, see Pocock, *Ancient Constitution*; D. C. Douglas, *English Scholars, 1660–1730* (London, 1951); S. Kliger, *The Goths in England* (Cambridge, Mass., 1952); J. E. C. Hill, "Norman Yoke," in *Puritanism and Revolution* (New York, 1964).

16. J. Adams, *Works*, III, 543.

aimed to empty London's debtors' prisons; and Maryland was a Catholic island in a Protestant sea.

Massachusetts—which offered its sister colonies a self-confident tradition of solid beginnings, solid founders, and an aggregate of motives for self-assertion tested over a long period of time—was both instigator and driving force of the independence movement. Furthermore, the Massachusetts of 1776 was no longer the City Upon the Hill of 1630; and the structure of the cult of the hero and of historiography, formally unchanged, contained a content whose sentiments, doctrines, and attitudes were, not least as a result of the Great Awakening, already shared throughout America to such an extent that they could be accepted by the comrades-in-arms in the other colonies. These concepts included the heroic element of the "errand into the wilderness"; the English elements of traditional rights, freedoms, and self-government; and the Protestant element of the freedom of religion and conscience. Thus the New England tradition of heroes and history substantially encompassed the entire American past: the forefathers came to America as free men paying their own way, took possession of the land by their own blood and sweat, and always proved their original freedom-loving cast of mind by resistance to every imperial encroachment on their privileges and their right to self-government.[17]

The process of becoming a nation is also heralded in the project of an American history. In 1774 Ebenezer Hazard wrote, "When civil States rise into importance, even their earliest history becomes the object of speculation." Since it was therefore important to make available materials "to lay the foundation of a good American history," Hazard proposed a collection of important documents under the title "American State Papers."[18]

But long before Hazard could realize his plans, George Chalmers, a Tory who had returned to England as early as 1775, had composed an American history, *Political Annals of the Present United Colonies* (1780). All the historians of the new Republic learned from this book, and it communicated to them three basic elements of the New England tradition: (1) The beginnings of the colonies, unlike those of the European nations, are known and open to historical examination; (2) Puritan New England, though no bastion of religious freedom, always marched at the head of the colonial civilizational process, and since the transfer of the charter of its Bay Colony to America, it thought of independence within or outside the Empire; (3) The Revolution began and ended as a defense

17. Craven, *Legend of the Founding Fathers*, 57 and *passim*.
18. Ebenezer Hazard to Thomas Jefferson, August 23, 1774, in Jefferson, *Papers*, I, 144.

of existing rights and liberties.[19] It is true that other strata and facets asserted themselves in the historical self-understanding of the Republic; but I am here dealing for the moment merely with the recurrent dominant symbolic pattern in which the New England dovetailing of the cult of the hero and historical thought was effective. In his *History of the United States* (1834–1876), George Bancroft laid down this conception, which was in force well into the twentieth century. Bancroft, a student of Heeren's in Göttingen, follower of Andrew Jackson, and "high priest of American nationality,"[20] located the American mission of a City Upon the Hill in a universal drama written by God and applying to all mankind, whose climax is the realization of freedom in the organization of American society.[21]

The American understanding of heroes and history may be summed up in Friedrich Nietzsche's concept of "monumental history." According to Nietzsche, it is motivated by faith in humanity, with the basic idea that states that "the great moments in the individual battle form a chain, a highroad for humanity through the ages, and the highest points of those vanished moments are yet great and living for men."[22] And Nietzsche further articulates precisely the theme that gave rise to the New England cult of the hero and historiography: "If the man who will produce something great has need of the past, he makes himself its master by means of monumental history."[23]

But Bancroft's monumental history was sufficiently leavened with humanism to keep the national chosenness and apocalyptic structure from overwhelming man entirely, debasing him to the other-determined object of collective-libidinous processes, to which monumental history of the nation-state kind was only too easily inclined at the time. Bancroft's popularity, the product of a style indebted to the romantic aesthetic, corrected the success of such tendencies in America, which appeared in the form of Darwinian historiography of the late nineteenth century. The nexus of hero and history, implied in the concept of monumental history,

19. Craven, *Legend of the Founding Fathers*, 60–65; Boorstin, *The Americans*, II, 368; F. Somkin, *Unquiet Eagle: Memory and Desire in the Idea of American Freedom, 1815 to 1860* (New York, 1967), 184–206.

20. Boorstin, *The Americans*, II, 369–73.

21. G. Bancroft, *History of the United States* (Boston, 1934–74), III, 4–11; G. Bancroft, "The Necessity, the Reality, and the Promise of the Progress of the Human Race," in *Literary and Historical Miscellanies* (New York, 1855). Compare also H. Kohn, *American Nationalism* (New York, 1957), 28–32; Tuveson, *Redeemer Nation*, especially 137 ff.; Somkin, *Unquiet Eagle*, 68–80, 184–206.

22. F. Nietzsche, *Werke*, ed. K. Schlechta (Darmstadt, 1966), I, 220 (English from Nietzsche, *The Use and Abuse of History*, trans. A. Collins [New York, 1949], 13).

23. Nietzsche, *Werke*, 225 (English from Nietzsche, *Use and Abuse of History*, 17).

is expressly turned into the content of history by Emerson: "There is properly no history, only biography."[24] It is also preserved when, as in the democratic cult of the genius celebrated by the Jacksonians, the common man becomes the hero; this variant of hero worship already occurs in the works of Thomas Carlyle. In contrast to Europe, however, America did not furnish any speculative undertaking transcending self-interpretation, such as the work of an American Machiavelli or Carlyle. The few attempts at a theorization of this complex made use of European categories: Emerson reproduced Carlyle; Alexander Everett fell back on Victor Cousin.[25] This did not change until the twentieth century, when American self-understanding became the object of examination; Dixon Wecter, Merrill D. Peterson, Seymour Martin Lipset, Wesley Frank Craven, Daniel Boorstin, all study the figure and role of the hero in America.

I believe that two factors are responsible for this situation. One is the understandable intellectual parochialism of the new nation at the outermost limits of the western inhabited world; the other is the extraordinary functional significance of the cult of the hero.

Beyond this basic difference, Boorstin, though he ignored the New England heroic tradition and the specifically modern European cult of the hero, points out that "in America the compression of time and the extension of space transformed the whole problem." Boorstin compared the rapid exaltation of historical figures through democratic mass literature at the moment of becoming a nation with the long process in which the heroes of the early European period (Achilles, Beowulf, Romulus, King Arthur) gradually changed through oral transmission into figures of a high literature written for a small upper class and eventually became a component in the national cult of the hero. But this is an unacceptable restriction of European phenomena; and correct as the observation of "chronological abridgment" and trivialization through subliterature in a completely literate society may be, it nevertheless seems to me true for all new nation states. A result of American conditions is surely the regional "superman," most often admixed with folkloristic comedy elements, whom Boorstin also differentiates from the consciously constructed national heroes in the manner of George Washington.[26]

John Adams was not alone in harboring a lifelong mistrust of Washington's "apotheosis." For the skeptics Washington was, beyond his real

24. Ralph Waldo Emerson, "History," in *The Complete Works* (Boston, 1903–1904), I, 8.
25. Everett, Origin and Character of the Old Parties. Compare Peterson, *Jefferson Image*, 86.
26. Boorstin, *The Americans*, II, 327–37, 482.

merits as commander in chief and statesman, exclusively the exponent and symbol of the nation; but he was not its creator. Even during the war Adams still vehemently disputed the idea that if outstanding leaders of the revolution were lost by death or corruption, the course of the Revolution could be changed in some way. He included Washington in his judgment, for only the people's "sentiments" were determining.[27]

Washington was merely "the creature of a principle, and that principle was the union of the colonies,"[28] and Washington's character was to be praised only as an "exemplification of the American character."[29] In the same way, when Adams was president his eulogy for Washington in 1799 recalled the greatness of this man from the aspect of an exemplary founder's virtue, an element important to pass on to posterity. "His example is now complete, and it will teach wisdom and virtue to magistrates, citizens, and men, not only in the present age but in future generations as long as our history shall be read."[30] Death freed Washington the hero from an awkward situation. For toward the end of his life he had strayed into the tense field of partisan confrontations and had been seen by many as a tool of the Federalists. In 1798, Adams, a victim of Hamilton's political tactics, had named the old general commander in chief of a de facto Federalist army, with Hamilton as inspector general. This measure had given new nourishment to the widespread fears of a military putsch, with Hamilton as dictator. But Washington's death immediately restored him to his status as *pater patriae,* the Cincinnatus of Mount Vernon, and the Moses of his chosen people in the New World.[31]

II. The Apotheosis of the Founders

In 1800, when the Federalists, after twelve years in power, had lost almost all regional and national offices to the Republicans, the promotion of the cult of Washington was more than a consolation to them; it also gave them an opportunity to use this national symbol to solicit the lost sympathies of the majority of their fellow citizens. Until this time the Federalists, as officeholders, had been able to monopolize the nation's birthday. Now that the Republicans governed the symbols, cult, and rites

27. J. Adams, *Works,* VII, 281–82.
28. John Adams to Lloyd, April 24, 1815, in J. Adams, *Works,* X, 164.
29. John Adams to Webb, September 10, 1885, in J. Adams, *Works,* IX, 541.
30. Quoted in P. Smith, *John Adams,* II, 1022.
31. D. S. Freeman, *George Washington* (New York, 1948–57), VII, 648–53; G. Wills, *Cincinnatus: George Washington and the Enlightenment* (Garden City, N.Y., 1984), 23, 31–35.

of the Fourth of July, they celebrated less the fact of independence (as the Federalists did) than the democratic import of the preamble and its author, Thomas Jefferson, of whom not much had been said until this time.

As a countermove, the Federalists turned to Washington's birthday.[32] Of course, underlying the pragmatic occasion for easy manipulation of the symbols was the general problem of the national cult of the hero. "Is this not a unique practice," asked Benjamin Rush, "in the history of nations thus to perpetuate the memories of their benefactors and deliverers? I exclude from this question the homage that has been paid by all nations to the birthday of the Saviour of the world."[33] Rush believed that the motive was deification of the founders, and that motive surely accounted for the movement's social success. Washington's birthday grew from a Federalists' celebration to a national holiday, and the analogy with Christ, from which Rush recoiled, was finally proclaimed publicly. "From the first ages of the world," Representative Benjamin C. Howard declared in Congress on February 13, 1847, "the records of all times furnished only two instances of birthdays being commemorated after the death of the individual: those two were the 22d of February and 25d of December." The epitaph for Washington's mother consequently also became "To 'Mary the Mother of Washington,'" and alluding to this inscription a clergyman by the name of J. N. Danforth exclaimed on July 4, 1847, "'To Mary the Mother of Washington' . . . we all owe all the mighty debt due from mankind to her immortal son."[34] The parallel between Washington and Christ was reflected very early in *Commemoration of Washington*, a lithograph by J. J. Barralet after the painting of an unknown artist that presented Washington in a typical resurrection scene. He is departing the tomb, which is flanked by the grieving figures of America and Freedom, and he is being guided heavenward by two angels. The ascension itself is shown in a lithograph by H. Weishaupt after a painting by Samuel Moore, *The Apotheosis of Washington* (*ca.* 1800); Washington is borne upward in the arms of Faith and Love, surrounded by the

---

32. A. Mathews, "Celebrations of Washington's Birthday," *Col. Soc. of Mass. Pub.* (1906), 252–58; C. Warren, "How Politics Intruded into the Washington Centenary of 1832," *Proceedings of the Massachusetts Historical Society*, LXIV (1931), 143–64; C. Warren, "Fourth of July Myths," *William and Mary Quarterly*, II (1945), 237–72.

33. Benjamin Rush to John Adams, February 18, 1808, in Rush, *Letters*, II, 960. Even during the American War of Independence, Rush opposed the movement to turn Washington into a hero. In 1777 he was among those critics of the commander in chief who seriously considered replacing him with the victor at Saratoga, Horatio Gates; compare L. H. Butterfield, "Rush and Washington," in Rush, *Letters*, II, 1197–1208.

34. Quoted in Boorstin, *The Americans*, II, 353.

virtues in a wreath of light, while below, Columbia and the orphaned states mourn him.[35]

This transfigured Washington, finally, was granted a certain public status through Constantino Brumidi's fresco, *Apotheosis of Washington* (1865), in the cupola of the Capitol rotunda. With the presence of Washington at the architectural center of the only national temple the American people erected for themselves (Rufus Choate), the elevation of Washington to heroic stature assumed the form of a national cult, the only admissible form for Americans.[36]

The public and the private element, that is, become blurred very specifically in the cult of Washington, as the example of the Washington Monument shows. The 1799 resolution of Congress provided for a tomb in Washington, but regional, political, and family resistance brought this plan to nought. After 1832 private initiative had its turn. In 1848 the Washington National Monument Society laid the cornerstone, but building was stopped in 1856 because of a lack of funds. Only in 1885, after a quite unpleasant confrontation concerning financing, the plans, and the actual construction, was the memorial site finally dedicated.[37]

The nation was more generous with other honors: not only was the capital city named after the hero in his lifetime, but so were a state and countless counties and communities. It is characteristic for the mixing of public and private that the congressional delegates named the new capital in 1791 without having the legal authorization to do so.[38]

But the written and spoken word more than all other cultic acts has anchored the founder in the consciousness of the society. The panegyric to the living, the eulogy to the dead Washington, and the yearly memorial rites, the declamatory liturgy on the birthday of the nation and its founder finally formed a "sacred life" (Boorstin), a binding paradigm of republican existence. The basic pattern was furnished by Mason Locke Weems, an occasional preacher, author, and printer of devotional literature, "an itinerant salesman of salvation and printed matter."[39] His *Life and Memorable Actions of George Washington* (1800) describes the hero of American chosenness as the exemplary reification of virtues (religiosity,

35. Compare illustrations in J. Adams, *Spur of Fame*, between 148 and 150; Wills, *Cincinnatus*, 74–75.

36. Compare illustration and description in *We the People: The Story of the United States Capitol* (Washington, D.C., 1963), 72ff. The quotation from Choate appears in the Foreword.

37. Craven, *Legend of the Founding Fathers*, 105–106; Boorstin, *The Americans*, II, 349–51.

38. Boorstin, *The Americans*, 340.

39. *Ibid.*; Wills, *Cincinnatus*, 39–53.

patriotism, magnanimity, industry, moderation, and fairness), with clearly antimilitary and antiaristocratic tendencies. This paradigm is informed by Fausto Socinus' life of Jesus, humanized and embellished with colonial middle-class morality, such as we find in the syllabus *The Life and Morals of Jesus of Nazareth* by Thomas Jefferson, which is made up primarily of material from Matthew and Luke.[40] This Arian religiosity lightened the parallels between Jesus and Washington and contributed much to the public apotheosis of Washington. Boorstin considers Weems's *Life* to be perhaps the most influential book ever written about American history.[41] It suffices here to refer to Edward V. Everett's *The Character of Washington* (1856), a peroration its author delivered 128 times (from 1856 to 1860) in order to finance the purchase of Washington's home, Mount Vernon, to serve as a public shrine.[42] Today numerous studies deal with Washington's apotheosis in the American consciousness, and it is therefore sufficient to sketch the situation briefly insofar as it is pertinent to our subject.

This political rhetoric even referred back to the ancient sun symbol—the image of a center that moves majestically and throws its light on all that there is—which the preachers of the Great Awakening used constantly with reference to Christ, until, in 1770, it was finally applied to George Whitefield, the Great Awakener, in a eulogy.[43] "Washington is in the clear upper sky. These other stars [Adams and Jefferson!] have now joined the American constellation; they circle around their center, and the Heavens beam with new light,"[44] Daniel Webster exclaimed in 1826. The same metaphor was used by Lincoln: "To add brightness to the sun or glory to the name of Washington is alike impossible. Let none attempt it. In solemn awe pronounce the name, and in its naked deathless splendor leave it shining on." In the invocation of that which is the light and the life ("Washington is the mightiest name on earth") is experienced the

40. Compare H. W. Foote, *The Religion of Thomas Jefferson* (Boston, 1960).

41. W. A. Bryan, "The Genesis of Weems' Life of Washington," *Americana*, XXXVI (1942), 147–65; M. Cunliffe, Introduction to *The Life of Washington*, by M. L. Weems (Cambridge, Mass., 1962); W. A. Bryan, *George Washington in the American Literature* (New York, 1952); Wector, *Hero in America*, 130–36; Boorstin, *The Americans*, II, 340–45. Other important contributions to the "sacred life" were J. Marshall's little-read *The Life of George Washington* (Philadelphia, 1804–1807), J. Sparks's *Life of George Washington* (Boston, 1839), and his edition of the *Writings* (1834–37).

42. E. Everett, *Orations and Speeches on Various Occasions* (Boston, 1868), IV, 3–51.

43. Nathaniel Whitaker, in 1770, commenting on the death of Whitefield: "So bright a sun descending below the horizon, whose benign beams have long enlightened and warmed so great a part of our hemisphere," in Heimert, *Religion and the American Mind*, 147.

44. Quoted in Wector, *Hero in America*, 172.

holy conturbation out of which the way and the goal of right action is found (in this case, freeing man from the slavery of alcohol).[45]

From these testimonials follows the central significance of the apotheosis of Washington for the nexus of founding and order in American self-understanding. This situation is first made clear in all its dimensions on the occasion of an event in consequence of which Webster conjured up the American firmament: On July 4, 1826, Adams and Jefferson both died.[46] The nation was deeply shocked, moved, and gripped by this enormous sign from God. The apotheosis of Washington was followed by the "apotheosis of 1826" (Peterson): "Hitherto, fellow-citizens, the Fourth of July had been celebrated among us, only as the anniversary of our independence, and its votaries had been merely human beings. But at its last recurrence . . . the anniversary, it may well be termed, of the liberty of man—Heaven itself, mingled visibly in the celebration, and hallowed the day anew by a double apotheosis."[47] From the Atlantic to the Pacific, politicians and their electorates, ministers and their congregations, journalists and their readers repeated the single theme: God had given His people a visible sign that He had not abandoned them. "With the simultaneous deaths of Adams and Jefferson, the past seemed ready at last, its contents prepared to be a model."[48] "When Adams and Jefferson died in 1826, their departure separated dramatically the Revolutionary supermen from mortals searching for America's true meaning. Liberty and freedom came to be established national features, not to be criticized. This produced a Trust from the wondrous men of '76."[49]

The "apotheosis of 1826" was prefigured by the "second coming of Washington": Lafayette's journey through the United States from August, 1824, to September, 1825.[50] Lafayette, once a major general in the Continental army, forty years later responded to an invitation tendered by the

---

45. Temperance Address, Springfield, February 22, 1842, in J. Adams, *Works*, I, 279.

46. See M. D. Peterson, *The Jefferson Image in the American Mind* (New York, 1960), 3–14; F. N. Thorpe, "Adams and Jefferson, 1826–1926," *North American Review*, CCXXIII (1926); L. H. Butterfield, "The Jubilee of Independence, July 4, 1826," *Virginia Magazine of History and Biography*, LXI (1953), 119–40.

47. Quoted in Boorstin, *The Americans*, II, 347. See also William Wirt, "A Discourse on the Lives and Characters of Thomas Jefferson and John Adams," in *Eloquence of the United States*, ed. E. P. Willston (Middletown, Conn., 1827), V, 454–503.

48. Nagel, *Sacred Trust*, 56.

49. *Ibid.*, 54. Nagel's study of American self-interpretation in the period 1798–1898 provides a wealth of interesting material and important insights but lacks a clear analytic structure. Nagel interprets the years 1815–1848 as a single epoch, while I agree with Peterson, Somkin, Williams, Anderson, and others in assuming a break to come only during the presidencies of Adams and Jackson.

50. Somkin, *Unquiet Eagle*, 151; compare the detailed account on 131–74.

president and Congress to return to the United States. A guest of state, he traveled through all the states of the Republic, visited the battlefields of the War of Independence, embraced venerable old comrades, and had honors heaped upon him. It was a triumphal procession in the truest sense of the word. Roman rituals were deliberately imitated; but more important was another reference to the classical republics: "A follower of Lafayette's itinerary might well have concluded that Rome was America's principal rival and competitor in a contest of public gratitude."[51] "As men with a classical orientation, the founding generation had been uncomfortably aware of the historic charge that republics were notoriously ungrateful to their benefactors . . . : 'Let it never be said of us as of Rome and of Athens, that ingratitude is the common vice of Republics.' "[52] The people's spontaneous republican gratitude proved, for one, that the American Republic had by no means fallen prey to the errors of the ancient republics, which had doomed them; for another, however, the old European constitutionalist Lafayette was a particularly suitable object to serve as an example of voluntary and free public honor and gratitude, to prove to the aristocratic societies of the Old World, with their pomp-burdened compulsion to venerate princes, the superiority of a republican social order. Fred Somkin described the trip as "something in the nature of a communal pageant, enacted over and over on numerous stages."[53] This "interaction between the American people and the 'Nation's Guest'" was not restricted to paying off a national debt of gratitude; it was given its real social relevance for the American consciousness in the context of the apotheosis of Washington—that is, with the background of the "identification of Lafayette . . . with the most potent father image in American history: George Washington," whose "adopted son" the Marquis de Lafayette liked to call himself.[54] Lafayette's return as the "favorite son" of a "common father"[55] also meant the return of the George Washington of the War of Independence, the hero beyond and outside all subsequent political controversy. Lafayette alone represented the grandeur and virtue of 1776 in all its purity, without the stains inevitably incurred on the harsher side of day-to-day politics. The incarnation of genuine grandeur and virtue in Lafayette was finally confirmed by the historical fact that he fought in the war as a foreigner without personal interest, merely from "love of liberty," inflamed by "an ardent desire for

51. *Ibid.*
52. *Ibid.*, 137.
53. *Ibid.*, 136.
54. *Ibid.*, 149.
55. *Ibid.*, 150.

the general welfare of mankind." He was "publicmindedness" incarnate.[56] "The return of the past in the form of a Washington surrogate was an event all the more thrilling because of Lafayette's long absence from America. He now seemed 'like one arisen from the dead.'"[57]

The American nation experienced a second coming. Somkin shows that the messianic theme was universally present: "Having seemingly come back 'from the tomb,' Lafayette was greeted at Camden, South Carolina, as 'one who redeemed me while yet I was not; and who is the redeemer of posterities which are not.'"[58] Lafayette's self-sacrifice, another passage notes, "came 'nearer the comparison with the saviour, in relation to America, than any other man of whom he had any account.'"[59] This come-again Washington was able to confirm wavering Americans in his own view that the hopes of 1776 had truly come to pass: "No one was so qualified as 'our Father, the good Lafayette' to assimilate the Americans of the 1820's and their material achievements to the value of those who had formulated the original meaning of the republic."[60] "As a triumph over time, and as a symbolic restoration of the era of acknowledged virtue, Lafayette's benison was that of the dead Washington."[61] On one hand the "republican worship" of Lafayette stressed "the transcendent nature of the hero's morality," and on the other it opened "new paths of contact between the heroic model and his republican admirers."[62] This last point indicates Lafayette's role for the psychosocial substantiation of the experience of founding in the post-revolutionary generation. It was this generation, according to the governor of Alabama, that derived the greatest advantage from this "most signal recurrence to first principles, that Lafayette symbolizes."[63] The encounter with Lafayette is an act of return to the original substance of order of the founding principles. By this "patently sacramental function" the American welcome of Lafayette testifies to "a general awareness that the production of the type of virtue upon which 'the purity of . . . republican institutions' depended could no longer be safely left to time alone."[64] Lafayette was thus expected to bridge the abyss between generations, "between the fast-disappearing era of the founders and the al-

56. *Ibid.*, 163.
57. *Ibid.*, 153.
58. *Ibid.*, 164.
59. *Ibid.*, 166.
60. *Ibid.*, 156.
61. *Ibid.*, 157.
62. *Ibid.*, 167.
63. *Ibid.*, 165.
64. *Ibid.*, 169.

ready arrived age of steam."[65] "Only the purity of Lafayette, which had come down stainless from the days of the Fathers, could bring about such a time-defying reunion of the generations."[66] Lafayette's reception made manifest the basic structure of the nexus between founding and order in the American consciousness, but at the same time it becomes evident that the societal legitimation of the content of order of the founding principles in the future will no longer be assured by living persons: "Looking back with a stabbing sense of loss, the nation pressed Lafayette to its heart in a last communion with its youthful self. When he was gone the world of the Founders had vanished forever."[67] This clean break could not be overlooked in the apotheosis of 1826.

Fifty years after the Declaration of Independence, the process of becoming a nation had reached a certain end. The Fourth of July, 1826, "marked the solemn termination of one great epoch of our Republic—it is the sublime commencement of another."[68] The "heroic age" (Jefferson), at the same time a golden age, had found its worth and edifying conclusion. The War of 1812 had intensified the consciousness of shared nationality and had set in motion ample emotional energies to promote national integration, as the failure of the Hartford Convention of 1814 had proved. This consensus tentatively overcame political, regional, and economic tensions and found its expression in a thorough process of democratizing the state constitutions.[69] Property qualifications for white voters were largely eliminated. The Era of Good Feelings had begun around 1815. Such great judges as Lemuel Shaw in Massachusetts modified the common law and adapted it to the social and economic structures already emerging in outline in the society that from then on reached continental dimensions. The population had quadrupled since 1776, roads and canals were opening up the continent, the legendary age of steam began; Eli Whitney had invented the cotton gin and had established the uniform-assembly system, which worked along the lines of modern industrial mass production.

This progress was backed by the political economy of the paradigmatic republic. Henry Clay, John Calhoun, and John Quincy Adams practiced the political economics of the fathers in the "American Sys-

65. *Ibid.*, 170.
66. *Ibid.*, 173.
67. *Ibid.*, 174.
68. Quoted in Peterson, *The Jefferson Image*, 7.
69. Compare M. D. Peterson, ed., *Democracy, Liberty, and Property* (Indianapolis, 1966); C. Williamson, *American Suffrage from Property to Democracy, 1760–1860* (Princeton, 1960).

tem": "In four years the Adams Administration spent almost as much on internal improvements as had been allocated in the previous twenty-four. Indeed, by 1826 the government was the largest single entrepreneur in the country. It handled more funds, employed more people, purchased more goods, and borrowed more operating and investment capital than any other enterprise. For generations that are reputed to have believed in weak and minimal government, the Founding Fathers and their first off-spring created a rather large and active institution."[70] The "American System" had created the psychological and political conditions for development of the productive resources; during the nineteenth century this process was reflected in a dynamic industrial economic society with a capitalist cast. But it was precisely the success of the political economy of the paradigmatic republic that evoked a centripetal reaction: an industrial Northeast, an agrarian West, and a plantation economy in the South increasingly found themselves in political and socioeconomic conflict. Consequently the Era of Good Feelings crumbled in the jubilee year: John Quincy Adams was the president of a minority and had been elected by the House of Representatives; his opponents suspected political logrolling and the dirty work of northern financial and manufacturing interests behind the scenes. With his massive program to modernize the Republic under strict national control ("the American System") Adams stepped before the nation at a moment when the traditional groupings and their complaints were defining the image anew; local rights and states' rights were in greater demand. The followers of the defeated Jackson, especially those in the slave-owning South, were up in arms against Adams' administrative program, which anticipated a centrally controlled expansion of the navy, roads, canals, education, and research with federal funds. Divisiveness was also rife in foreign policy concerning possible support of revolutionary movements abroad in South America and Greece. Not for the last time was the isolationist tradition of Washington's farewell address at loggerheads with the revolutionary tradition of the Declaration of Independence.

In this situation the nation, vacillating between fear and hope, uncertainty and confidence, was fiercely receptive to the good news that God had by no means forgotten it and its benefactors. The providential event of the double apotheosis told Americans that their fathers were philosopher-statesmen, whose divinely inspired words and deeds conveyed the truth of their own existence and made up the spiritual content of the emerging national *corpus mysticum:* "In this most singular coincidence, the finger of Providence is plainly visible! It hallows the Decla-

70. W. A. Williams, *Contours of American History,* 211.

ration of Independence as the Word of God, and is the bow in the Heaven, that promises its principles shall be eternal, and their dissemination universal over the earth."[71]

The simultaneous death of the two fathers blurred those elements that divided Adams and Jefferson. The respectful friendship that had united them was real in this interpretation, but forgotten were the bitter intellectual and political quarrels between Adams the Federalist and Jefferson the Republican. The insults and press feuds between their respective followers, the different casts of mind, all were forgotten and instead were celebrated as variations on the same American spirit. The Era of Good Feelings became spiritually and symbolically fused with the fundamentals of the Republic on which any number—or at least almost any number—of bitter political, intellectual, and socioeconomic conflicts were to be settled.

It was only this foundation that allowed the dynamization of the individualistic self in the movement of the mental, political, and economic laissez-faire, with the result that the failure in the "imperial self" of the present had not robbed the order of the "Common Man" of every substantial reason. "The passing of Jefferson and Adams was a dramatic moment in the growth of American self-consciousness. The imagination working upon the event, made of it a fable of the republic. The fable explained the miraculous, brought man into a community of loyalty and belief, and turned the nation's loss into a triumph. It was the creation of a pervasive national faith reaching for justification and here finding it. Providence, Union, Heritage."[72]

The revitalization and regeneration of the "national faith," however, had to take place through spiritual, ritualistic, and pragmatic recurrence to the Founding Fathers. "The Republic will cease to be, when it ceases to remember, to revere, and to imitate the virtues of its founders."[73] Samuel Knapp recommended to the young men of Boston that they imitate the youth of Rome who were said yearly to have sought inspiration at the tomb of the religious founder Numa: "Go, ye young men of my country, oftener than once a year, to visit the tombs of your fathers. No man was ever great who did not live much among the dead."[74] Here the origin of the American experience and the instrument of its existential liquifaction become palpable; but it also becomes clear why questioning this origin must mean questioning American society itself.

71. Quoted in Peterson, *The Jefferson Image*, 6.
72. *Ibid.*, 5.
73. *Ibid.*, 8.
74. *Ibid.*, 9. Compare also Nagel, *Sacred Trust*, 9, 53, 75–76.

Adams and Jefferson each left behind a kind of Founding Father's last will and testament. Adams did so in his reply to the Boston organizers of the semicentennial celebration, Jefferson in his letter to the mayor of the capital. Let us recall Adams' self-understanding as a Founding Father and his debate with Rush concerning the meaning of such testaments. He was opposed to apotheosis but subscribed to spiritual patriarchy, deeply convinced of the truth that penetrated society through the founders. But there is evidence not only of a common private and individual continuity from the founders to the apotheosis of 1826, but also of a public continuity, which we must briefly document.

On September 15, 1790—representatives and government had just settled in the provisional capital of Philadelphia—the College of Philadelphia issued invitations to a series of lectures "On Law." The lecturer was James Wilson,[75] a prominent leader of the Revolution in Pennsylvania, influential delegate to the Constitutional Convention, a judge of the Supreme Court under the new government, and a tireless land speculator who would come to a bad end in a shabby small-town inn while fleeing from his creditors. This lawyer was one of the most brilliant minds of his generation's political class; his *Lectures on Law* may be considered among the few theoretical achievements in the political literature of his day.

His inaugural lecture was one of the great social events of that December. The president and vice-president, with their ladies, attended, as did the leading figures of the administration and Congress. Before this audience Wilson developed the theme of the founders' self-interpretation, which was to have its national apotheosis in 1826. We are familiar with the argument's elements. The New England understanding of history and heroes, already nationalized in George Chalmers' *Political Annals*—that is, augmented with Penn and Calvert—was brought fully up to date: Wilson designed a "temple of fame" for the American patriots and heroes and furnished the individual niches; one place at the center remained empty: "For the most worthy"—George Washington.[76] The founding of the nation—which, according to its origin in "truth and freedom," goes back to an "original social compact" (the Mayflower Compact)[77]—gave mankind a paradigm surpassing even ancient Greece.[78] The excellence of the nation was expressed in virtue: the foundation of the American char-

---

75. Compare Page Smith, *James Wilson* (Chapel Hill, N.C., 1956), particularly 310–41.

76. J. Wilson, *Lectures on Law* (Philadelphia, 1804), 8, Vol. I of *Works*, ed. B. Wilson.

77. *Ibid.*, 6.

78. *Ibid.*, 4–5. .

acter was "love of liberty" and "love of law"—that is, love for rational principles that are accessible to common sense and are basic to human existence in society purely and simply.[79] Wilson understood the founding of the American nation as the glowing realization of the "just and genuine principles of society."[80] These signified the "foundations of political truth," and in their establishment Wilson saw a "foundation of human happiness" of unknown dimensions.[81] The practice of the basic virtues of the "free and independent man" as the source of sovereignty meant participation in the public affairs of the Commonwealth—that is, acting in "this public character."[82] These intellectual and ethical preconditions of a functioning republic required an enormous education of subsequent generations. According to Wilson, such education is offered by the "science of law": on one hand it is a "historical science," providing access to the ancestors; on the other it is a science of principles—that is, a theoretical science—and communicates the "general principles of law and obligation, law of nature, law of nations, municiple law, man as individual, member of society, of a confoederation and part of the great commonwealth of nations"; finally, it is the "science of government" in the narrower sense, dealing with the law, the constitution, and the government of the United States.[83]

Let us concentrate on the significance of this December 15, 1790: Wilson brought the dead and living founders together with the subsequent generation, the students at the College of Philadelphia. The continuation of virtuousness assembled in the "Hall of Fame," the source of republican order and the excellence of the shining American character in the young people, required the conscious transmission of this virtuousness. Wilson took on this mission as a teacher of the "science of law," which allowed him the understanding of law and liberty from which the basic virtues of love of liberty and love of law grow. This educational process must be gone through by every free citizen of the Republic. "Law education," according to Wilson, is instrumental in preserving the founding's "genuine and just principles of society."

Wilson's inaugural lecture anticipates the crucial passages of Washington's farewell address of 1796, in which Hamilton and Washington, somewhat like a will, expounded in trenchant summary their concept of order:

79. *Ibid.*, 9–10.
80. *Ibid.*, 6.
81. *Ibid.*, 23, 26.
82. *Ibid.*, 11ff.
83. *Ibid.*, 41ff.; compare J. Gebhardt, *Common Sense and Urteilskraft.*

Of all dispositions and habits which lead to political prosperity, religion and morality are indispensable supports. In vain would that man claim the tribute of patriotism who should labor to subvert these great pillars of human happiness—these firmest props of the duties of men and citizens. . . . It is substantially true that virtue or morality is a necessary spring of popular government. . . . Promote, then, as an object of primary importance, institutions for the general diffusion of knowledge. In proportion as the structure of a government gives force to public opinion, it is essential that public opinion should be enlightened.[84]

Our interpretation of Wilson is confirmed by John Adams himself. Influenced by the threat of an American-French passage at arms, young recruits of the city of Philadelphia, the district of South Wark, and the Northern Liberties had directed a declaration of loyalty to President Adams in which, "actuated by the same principles on which our forefathers achieved their independence," they expressed their indignation at French policies.[85] In his reply the president claimed for himself the "privilege of a father" and recommended to the young men constant occupation with science and ethics as the foundation of the nation's well-being. But then he continued: "Without wishing to damp the ardor of curiosity, or influence the freedom of inquiry, I will hazard a prediction that, after the most industrious and impartial researches, the longest liver of you all will find no principles, institutions, or systems of education more fit in general to be transmitted to your posterity than those you have received from your ancestors."[86] This message is not distinguished by any particular originality; of far greater importance is John Adams' commentary in an 1813 letter to Jefferson in which he defended himself against the accusation that he was a bigoted enemy of scientific progress. After expressly stating that John Adams and Thomas Jefferson were to be counted among the cited "ancestors," he elucidated the function, content, and quality of the "general principles." "Who composed that Army of fine young Fellows that was then before my Eyes?" Adams asked himself. "There were among them Roman Catholics, English Episcopalians, Scotch and American Presbyterians, Methodists, Moravians, Anabaptists, German Lutherans, German Calvinists, Universalists, Arians, Priestleyans, Socinians, Independents, Congregationalists, Horse Protestants and House Protestants, Deists and Atheists." The only trait common to

---

84. J. M. Richardson, ed., *A Compilation of the Messages and Papers of the Presidents, 1789–1897* (Washington, D.C., 1896–99), I, 210.

85. Quoted in John Adams to Thomas Jefferson, June 28, 1813, in J. Adams, *Adams-Jefferson Letters,* II, 338.

86. J. Adams, *Works,* IX, 188.

this motley crew, in Adams' view, lay in the fact that all of them were raised "in the general Principles of Christianity: and the general principles of English and American Liberty." From this he concluded, "The general Principles, on which the Fathers achieved Independence, were the only principles in which that beautiful assembly of young gentlemen could unite." For, he noted, there were general principles of Christianity—as mental makeup underlying the respective dogmas—shared by all sects and general principles of American and English liberty, on which all parties in America had agreed by a vast majority in order to claim independence on their basis.

This aggregate of principles, however, is by no means arbitrary in its substance and therefore not dependent on progress in natural science or technology, since it explicates the structures of a reality beyond human grasp. Adams insisted "that those general principles of Christianity, are as eternal and immutable, as the existence and attributes of God; and that those principles of liberty, are as unalterable as human nature and our terrestrial, mundane System." He could not, therefore, imagine any discoveries that would contradict these "general principles."[87]

This commentary already took Adams a considerable step closer to the apotheosis of 1826: the existing mental-political frame of mind of an American citizen is acquired, preserved, and handed down through exegesis of the words, deeds, and writings of the fathers—though Adams would surely have protested energetically against such a formal construction of the tradition. Such a development, after all, debased Wilson's "science of law" and Adams' "science of government" to the handmaiden of monumental history. Its *res gestae* and *personae dramatis* constituted an American cosmos that assured the meaningfulness of the society and allowed broad scope for possible actions, behavior, and decisions within a rapidly changing social and geographic context. From the speculations about founding and fathers—with Washington, the Declaration of Independence, and the Constitution at the core—grew the "social myth" of the nation as a "presentation of the ultimate speculations of metaphysics, including cosmology, in a coherent system of symbols."[88] The concepts "patriotic faith" (Peterson), "social myth" (Elliott), or "civil religion" (Bellah) are here used, pending more detailed analysis.

---

87. John Adams to Thomas Jefferson, June 28, 1813, in J. Adams, *Adams-Jefferson Letters*, II, 339–40. Compare Adams' concept of a "republican religion," in AP, *Diary and Autobiography*, III, 240–41.

88. W. T. Elliot, "The Constitution as the American Social Myth," in *The Constitution Reconsidered*, ed. Conyers Read (New York, 1938), 210. Compare also T. W. Arnold, *The Symbols of Government* (New Haven, Conn., 1935).

III. The Normative Power of the Symbolism
of the Constitution

The aggregate of symbols[89] of self-interpretation was from the beginning extremely flexible, dynamic, fluid, and open to manipulation. For a long time important elements were objects of controversy and were only hesitantly offered up to the *consensus omnium*.

As long as the strong confrontations between the Federalists and Republicans went on, the text of the Declaration of Independence remained controversial; it was only in the Era of Good Feelings and following the democratization of the state constitutions around 1810 that the Declaration of Independence became a noncontroversial component of the national canon as "Charter of the Democracy."[90] The other great normative document of this canon, the Constitution, underwent a similar process. John Adams reflected from the first on the "melancholy lot of humanity," that "any constitution of government within human contrivance" was short of immortality[91]; he, like Hamilton, presumably revered only the English constitution. When, during the 1790s, he was plagued by the fear that the people's moral fiber was weakening and that republican government would drown in bloody anarchy, he entertained the idea of an Anglicization of the Constitution and toyed with the idea of making some offices inheritable. As a result, in his inaugural address (1797) the brand-new president was forced to stress his loyalty to the Constitution.

Jefferson warned of those who "look at constitutions with sanctimonious reverence and deem them like the ark of the covenant, too sacred to be touched."[92] He pleaded for changing the Constitution every twenty years.

From 1787 to 1788, writing under the name of Giles Hickory, Noah Webster spoke out vigorously against a "perpetual constitution on parchment." "Americans' efforts to fix a form of government in 'perpetuity,'" Webster argued, supposed a 'perfect wisdom and probity in the framers;

89. When I make use of the concept of symbol, it refers first of all to Aristotle, *De Interpretatione*, 16a4ff., as language symbols; but it also includes nonverbal symbols insofar as they share with verbal symbols the purpose of interpreting the psychic experience of reality under the irrevocable condition of the intersubjectivity of all human existence in society. I refer here to A. Schütz, *Collected Papers* (The Hague, 1962–66), I, 287–336. For the concept of symbol in general, see K. Jaspers, *Philosophie* (Berlin, 1932), III, 16; E. Cassirer, *An Essay on Man* (New Haven, Conn., 1944), 32ff.; T. J. J. Altizer *et al.*, eds., *Truth, Myth, and Symbol* (Englewood Cliffs, N.J., 1962).

90. P. Detweiler, "The Changing Reputation of the Declaration of Independence: The First Fifty Years," *William and Mary Quarterly*, XIX (1962), 557–74.

91. John Adams to Brand to Hollis, October 18, 1787, in APM.

92. Thomas Jefferson to Kercheval, July 12, 1816, in Jefferson, *Writings*, XV, 35.

which is both arrogant and impudent.' Indeed, 'the very attempt to make perpetual constitutions is the assumption of a right to control the opinions of future generations; and to legislate for those over whom we have as little authority as we have over a nation in Asia.'"[93] Representative George McDuffie uttered similar sentiments in Congress as late as 1824. He spoke against the argument that the constitutional revisions would weaken "the popular veneration for that instrument." "Nothing can be more dangerous than the inculcation of this sort of superstitious idolatry in this country," he elaborated, since such an attitude would obstruct any corrections in a necessarily flawed human institution.[94] It very soon became evident, however, that one need not exclude the other. The alternative, according to Nathaniel Chipman, consisted "'in the idea of incorporating, in the constitution itself, a plan of reformation,' enabling the people periodically and peacefully to return to the first principles, as Machiavelli had urged."[95] The institution of amendments to the Constitution paved the way for the document's dual function. It became both instrument and symbol. "As an instrument it must be viewed hardheadedly and used flexibly to promote the people's welfare in the present and future. As a symbol it is part of the mass mind, capable of arousing intense popular hysteria, loaded with a terrible inertia, its face turned toward the past."[96]

The skill and success of the Federalist leadership of the new government; the powerful propaganda of journalists, ministers, teachers, and politicians; and a certain economic prosperity—all allowed, after the anti-Federalists had been mollified by the formulation of a Bill of Rights, the Constitution to disappear as the object of controversy concerning the basic order of the nation. In answer to the Alien and Sedition Acts of 1798, Madison and Jefferson had formulated the Virginia and Kentucky Resolutions, furnishing the opposition with their own interpretation of the Constitution; this step had major consequences. It was based on recognizing the sovereignty of the individual states and their right to nullify unconstitutional laws.

93. G. S. Wood, *Creation of the American Republic,* 377, 379.
94. C. S. Hyneman and G. W. Carey, eds., *A Second Federalist* (New York, 1967), 51.
95. G. S. Wood, *Creation of the American Republic,* 613. For the genesis of the amendment clause in the state constitution, see Adams, "Republikanismus," 541–45.
96. M. Lerner, "Constitution and Court as Symbols," *Yale Law Journal,* XLVI (1937), 1224. Also E. S. Corwin, "The Constitution as Instrument and Symbol," *American Political Science Review,* XXX (1936), 1071–75; Elliot, "Constitution as the American Social Myth"; Schechter, "The Early History of the Tradition of the Constitution," *American Political Science Review,* XXIX (1915), 707 ff. It is worth noting that H. E. Holst, in *Verfassung und Demokratie der Vereinigten Staaten von Amerika* (Berlin, 1884), I, 56–69, already gave a detailed account of the "canonization of the Constitution."

The decision by Jefferson and his Republicans, after assuming power, to accept the frame established by the Constitution put an end to controversy on principles concerning the Constitution. "A leaning toward constitutional literalism, a tendency engendered by some of the strongest currents in Anglo-American thought and powerfully reinforced by Antifederalist prophecies of constitutional decay, prepared the way for constitutional apotheosis. It also does much to explain the appearance of an opposition party which would quickly elevate the constitution as the palladium of American liberty."[97] When, in 1854, the abolitionist William L. Garrison burned copies of the Constitution, this deed alone placed him outside the national consensus. His action, like Seth Luther's "Address to the Working Men of New England" (1833) and Frederick Douglass' "The Meaning of July Fourth for the Negro" (1852), was in the tradition of the "Fourth of July heresies" that emerged in the 1830s; these protested against the national ritual in antipatriotic speeches and reminded their listeners on the Fourth of July of the unfulfilled promises in the Declaration of Independence and the Constitution.[98]

By such behavior, however, even protest confirmed the canonical nature of the documents. Heresy presupposes national consensus. As a rule all political and social conflicts were now waged within the terms of the Constitution. From this time on, in its battles with the administration the opposition accused those in power of betraying the Constitution and of passing unconstitutional laws. The written Constitution became the outward and visible symbol of all society's aspirations, its unity and continuity. The Constitution was the link connecting the revolutionary ferment of 1776, the institutional arrangement of the political class of 1787, and the "revolution" of 1800. It concretized the ordering power accumulated by the fathers: "Here was the document into which the Founding Fathers had poured their wisdom as into a vessel."[99] Constitution and Declaration of Independence, together with other sacred documents, are exhibited in the entrance hall to the National Archives, for public worship. "Around the turn of the century . . . the Constitution actually became, quite literally, the people's political Bible. Children learn at their mother's knee the belief that they are to consider it as such. The paternal *sic credo, stat fides mea pro ratione* guaranteed the correctness of the belief. What was later read into the Constitution was another matter. The more wildly the battle of the tongues raged, the more loudly was heard

---

97. Banning, "Republican Ideology and the Triumph of the Constitution," 179.
98. Compare Lynd, *Intellectual Origins,* 140–41.
99. Lerner, "Constitution and Court as Symbols," 1299.

the call for a Constitution, the more fervently each voice swore not to deviate from it by so much as a hair." [100] North and South waged the Civil War in the name of the Constitution, but this event nevertheless taught Americans that there were limits to what the symbolism of the Constitution could encompass, and since that time they have more cautiously distinguished between the instrumental and the symbolic nature of the Constitution. But in spite of the Civil War and other violent internal confrontations, the Constitution as symbol of the nation's consciousness has penetrated so far as to create a series of habitual reactions in specific social and political situations. This "cultural constitutionalism" (Kammen) is reflected in democratic practices, most particularly those relating to cooperation and the solution of conflicts in private and public affairs.

A further product of the specific American experience, the "divine right of judges" (of the Supreme Court) moved only slowly toward the noncontroversial sector. In spite of *Marbury* v. *Madison,* the Court had not become a noncontroversial element in the political process. Jefferson was a bitter opponent of judicial review. [101] Lincoln was willing to grant it only in specific cases, while he rejected the constitutional implications of judicial review. [102] Max Lerner regarded the divine right of judges as the result of a pattern that consists of the "fetishism of the Constitution," the claim by the Supreme Court to exercise the office of guardian of the Constitution, and the Anglo-Saxon cult of the independent and infallible judge.

In 1861, when the insufficient capacity of the constitutional symbolism to solve conflicts became evident, the question concerning a better instrument became urgent. "The fetishism of the Constitution, as a flexible instrument open to various constructions, was in itself inadequate. In short, a faith was not enough. It had to be a faith deposited in a power. That power was the judicial power. The function of interpreting the con-

---

100. Holst, *Verfassung und Demokratie,* I, 58. The belief in the integrating power of the constitutional symbolism found its classical expression in Daniel Webster's "Second Speech on Foot's Resolution" of January 26, 1830, in *Writings and Speeches* (Boston, 1903), VI, 3–75. To the present, the Constitution as an instrument has been far from adequate to the American reality in its pragmatic compromise between nation and confederation.

101. Thomas Jefferson to Torrance, June 11, 1815, in Jefferson, *Writings,* XI, 471–75. Compare C. G. Haines, *The American Doctrine of Judicial Supremacy* (Berkeley, Calif., 1932).

102. Abraham Lincoln, "First Inaugural Address, March 4, 1861," in *Collected Works,* IV, 269.

stitution had to be specialized in a single tribunal."[103] But the precondition was that the intellectual order objectified in the normative document as the expression of a "higher law" accessible to the justices in their judicial decisions was not only bound by but also recognized as mandatory in the society. "We transfer our sense of the definite and timeless character of the constitution to the judges who expound it"; if the Constitution incorporates the "ultimate wisdom of government," it follows "that men versed in its lore must reach their conclusions, not by the paths of ordinary men, but by some mysterious and inspired processes." They are the discoverers of an ultimate truth, "priests in the service of a godhead."[104] Only with this condition can the normative oracle of the Supreme Court justices be released from the sphere of controversy. Wilson's description of the Supreme Court as a permanent constitutional convention again leads to a direct reference to the apotheosis of 1826: at "the moment of Truth" of the Supreme Court decision, the justices, representing the nation, vitalize the original substance of the founding, repeat the work of the fathers in the political and social context of their own time, and thus authenticate the meaning and security of the society—elements that always remain questionable on the pragmatic level of power and social existence.

With the exception of Washington, all the Founding Fathers had, of course, to travel the road from the controversial to the noncontroversial sphere. Franklin, Jefferson, and Lincoln accomplished the journey more rapidly than did Madison and Marshall.[105] Hamilton and Adams had to wait until the middle of the twentieth century to become noncontroversial. A congressional resolution for July 4, 1926, commemorated the centennial of Jefferson's death and the sesquicentennial of Independence Day, but John Adams was not mentioned.[106]

However, as soon as the controversial and noncontroversial symbols had sufficiently penetrated the consciousness of the members of society, they also became a manipulatable medium on every level of the political and social process. The venerable principles, norms, and traditions were from the beginning weapons in the war for power, the names of the Founding Fathers symbols for parties and movements and their "cause"; all the combatants on the extended field of privately motivated interest battles, the fabric of everyday politics, made use of the language of the

103. Lerner, "Constitution and Court as Symbol," 1308; J. Gebhardt, "The Federalist," in *Klassiker des politischen Denkens*, ed. H. Maier *et al.* (Munich, 1968), 101–102.

104. Lerner, "Constitution and Court as Symbol," 1312.

105. Wector, *Hero in America*; Peterson, *The Jefferson Image*.

106. Thorpe, "Adams and Jefferson," 234.

socially dominant interpretation of order. In its name the old settlers, the Know-Nothings, defended their social and political attitudes against immigrants. By basing themselves on the "sacred right of property" (Adams), company lawyers attempted, for the most part successfully, to block government intervention in industry by means of laws and regulations, in particular the issuing of antitrust laws. They did so by extending the "person" of the fifth and fourteenth amendments to the legal person of the corporation.[107] Each symbol or aggregate of symbols was at one time or another used to legitimate material interests. Henry S. Randall, author of a "Democratic" biography of Jefferson (1859), defended himself against the accusation of party bias: "What American biography is not partisan, i.e. what biography of our political great men."[108]

Thus, around 1840 there existed a fourfold Jefferson: the upright Democrat of the Jacksonians, the wicked demagogue and anti-Christ of the conservative Old Federalists, the liberal and pragmatic statesman of the Whigs, and finally, the defender of states' rights of the Old Republicans. The modern liberal may refer to Jefferson for democracy and to Hamilton for the security of acquired rights and a limited democracy.

But even this use of the symbols reveals their role as communicators of the rightness and truth of existence, which must ever and anew assert itself against the fears nourished by the doubt about one's own origin and end. But since the dominant symbols of the American interpretation of order are irrevocably tied to the *res gestae* and *personae dramatis* of the founding, it is understandable that it became necessary to reassure oneself of their truth in both the spiritual and the historical sense. This explains the constant protestations concerning the historicity of one's own beginning, which contrasted so favorably with the "mythic" origins of the nations of the Old World. This claim is found in George Chalmers, James Kent,[109] James Wilson,[110] and even as late as Francis Parkman[111]; in short, it goes hand in hand with the genesis of the basic pattern of the traditional American monumental history. It is not here exclusively a matter of a judgment by the historian about his materials. For the linking of self-understanding to founding suggests a dependence of existential truth on historical truth. This is a specific outgrowth of the Protestant heritage in which the written word of God, which anyone can read and interpret, is the source of the Christian life. The documentation of

---

107. P. A. Freund *et al.*, eds. *Constitutional Law* (Boston, 1942), II, 1282ff.
108. Quoted in Peterson, *The Jefferson Image*, 113.
109. Craven, *Legend of the Founding Fathers*, 63–64.
110. J. Wilson, *Works*, ed. R. G. McGloskey (Cambridge, Mass., 1967), I, 6.
111. Boorstin, *The Americans*, II, 377.

the beginnings, universally accessible, corresponds to the fixed self-documentation of God in Holy Scripture.

The nexus is seriously endangered when the interpretation of social existence assumes the form of "monumental history." For it is precisely this, according to Nietzsche, that leads to the circumstance that there are times when "there is no possible distinction between a 'monumental' past and a mythical romance, as the same motives for action can be gathered from the one world as the other." [112] In other words, the conception of order that regards itself as the construction of the unfolding of the founding experience and is construed as monumental history inevitably contains a permanent element of unrest, crisis, and fear, since the tendency of monumental history to historical fiction must of necessity be understood by Americans as existential fiction—that is, the untruthfulness of their conception of order. Proof that such fictions exist—as such, a continuous phenomenon of human history—is amply at hand, but more important than the concrete occasion for such fictitious creations is the fact that the fictions took their place in the national symbolism, and thus in the consciousness of society, with extreme rapidity, as several examples will show.

The most famous exclamation of the Revolution, Patrick Henry's "Give me liberty, or give me death," supposedly the climax of a speech delivered on March 23, 1775, in the Virginia House of Burgesses, was the invention of a biographer, William Wirt, who was intent on turning his subject into a hero and consciously constructed the *paradigma* of a life of a Founding Father.[113] The silversmith and courier of the Continental army, Paul Revere, owes his fame as patriotic hero to the fact that in 1860 Henry Wadsworth Longfellow climbed the tower of the Old North Church. The result of this adventure was the poem "Paul Revere's Ride." [114] Although independence was declared on July 2, 1776, the occasion is celebrated on July 4, the day on which nothing happened except that Jefferson's phrasing of the declaration was ratified. When Davy Crockett—intermittently *the* national hero of frontier culture, whose variety he exemplified as a hunter, soldier, politician, and poet—was a congressman, he broke with Jackson over the latter's support of land speculation. The Whigs tried to exploit the situation to gain western votes; in

---

112. Nietzsche, *Werke,* I, 223 (English from Nietzsche, *The Use and Abuse of History,* 15).

113. Boorstin, *The Americans,* II, 309. In general, see S. G. Fisher, "The Legendary and Myth-Making Process in Histories of the American Revolution," *Proceedings of the American Philosophical Society,* XL (1912).

114. Wector, *Hero in America,* 87.

a well-organized campaign they created a legend for the elections. Nevertheless, Crockett was not reelected in Kentucky and moved to Texas; his martyr's death at the Alamo posthumously lent the semblance of veracity to the fiction invented for the campaign.[115]

The assumption that present existence is merely the development and interpretation of the founders' lives naturally assigns a special role in America to the institutions of national history—the regional and local historical societies with antiquarian interests, the genealogical societies, and so forth, which we find in one or another form in all modern nations. They secure for the collective (state, community) and the individual a manifest, immediate participation in the founding that goes far beyond external sharing in the ritual and an inner frame of mind. As it did elsewhere, genealogy in America served to elevate the individual's humdrum life by focusing on eminent ancestors. These ancestors need not have performed great deeds, for the dogma that anyone who had come to these shores before 1776 had helped to found the nation provided everyone with a *bona fide*—a Founding Father on the family tree. But beyond this, a bloodline extending back to the founding promised a truer, more substantial, more American existence in the present. Conversely, this criterion in effect excluded all groups whose genealogy forbade presumed participation in the creation because they were slaves of African origin, original Indian inhabitants, or immigrants from Europe who had come only after the event. Until the great national crisis in the second half of the nineteenth century, the tradition was cultivated and interpreted by a Protestant intelligentsia of Anglo-Saxon descent. Most controversies centered on the share and precedence of various groups from this milieu in the founding. Thus, the South attacked the predominance of the New England tradition. Presbyterians and Quakers claimed to rank above the Puritans as the standard-bearers of religious tolerance. But the colossal shock of the Civil War, industrialization, corporate capitalism, and the rising self-confidence of the newcomers changed the picture in various aspects.

The relevance of the traumatic experience of the Civil War for American self-understanding is difficult to overestimate, since even the historical interpretation of the *res gestae* of the Civil War, its causes and consequences, is in turn an integral element of the process of the self-understanding of American society.[116]

---

115. Boorstin, *The Americans*, II, 327–33.

116. Compare K. M. Stampp, ed., *Causes of the Civil War* (Englewood Cliffs, N.J., 1959).

IV. The Symbolic Renewal of the Paradigmatic Republic: Abraham Lincoln

Within the context of the present inquiry, the analysis of Abraham Lincoln and the Civil War is to be limited to a few crucial points. First, the Civil War clearly signaled the collapse of the common national world of symbols. As long as the national symbolism retained its functional efficacy, conflicts could be solved on a political level or held in abeyance by the application of different mechanisms of interpretation. In the context of the successful establishment of the republic as a power unit capable of political, diplomatic, and economic action, however, the dynamics of the social process simultaneously dissociated contradictory components of political reality to the point at which two social orders confronted each other. To that extent we can agree with Barrington Moore when he speaks of the "irreconcilability of two different forms of civilization."[117] If originally the balance of power had allowed the Union to exist—indispensable premise for the realization of the "paradigmatic republic"—only at the price of accepting possibly temporary socioeconomic, political, and psychological structures of dubious "republican" character, the preservation of the Union now enforced a military conflict on the level of power. Moore's overall analysis is correct in stating that neither superficial socioeconomic nor political or even simple moral questions caused the Civil War. But Moore's pointing to "fundamental causes . . . of an economic nature"—that is, the existence of two different economic systems, giving rise to two different capitalist civilizations—touches on only part of the reality. Moore clearly sees that the question of slavery was in fact a matter of the political realization of divergent interpretations of man's entire existence in society: "Slavery was a threat and an obstacle to a society which in fact was heir to the Puritanical, the American, and the French Revolutions. Southern society was founded firmly on inherited rank as the basis for judging a man." Moore correctly sees the victory of the North as the revolutionary justification for a firmly rooted democracy of an industrial-capitalist nature. But it must be pointed out that he inadmissibly simplifies and thus suppresses a crucial dimension of reality. For as Louis Hartz has brilliantly shown, the alternative interpretation of the national symbolism was tied to the overall American self-understanding to such an extent that the corporative-conservative language of the South time and again reflected the doctrine of republicanism. In the South the criterion of inherited rank was applied only to the African, whether slave or free; for the rest, espe-

117. B. Moore, *Social Origins of Dictatorship and Democracy* (New York, 1963).

cially in the South, the republican "ideal of equal opportunity" (to acquire a slave) was of great significance for social mobility and social self-understanding of whites on all social levels. In this sense, outlined by Moore, the emphasis on the contradictory forms of civilization within a nation is vague insofar as the respective "ideal" was not simply reflected in a particular economic collective condition; the economic makeup of the South or the North and West in the early 1860s had, in turn, resulted from a complex process of consciousness and social history. Moore indicated as much when he raised the question of "what would have happened if the South's plantation system had found a foothold in the West in the middle of the nineteenth century and had encircled the North."[118] One should, more correctly, ask what would have happened if slavery as a national institution (which it was before 1776) had remained an integral element of the whole nation's economic conditions. Paradoxically, the collapse of the consensus resulted from the psychosocial establishment of the "paradigmatic republic" in the North and West as far as the so-called border states, that followed from the founders' politics. To this extent the Civil War was certainly the "second revolution," forced into being by the logic of the "paradigmatic republic," in that its laissez-faire individualistic component brought about the mobilization of the common man (which we shall examine more closely below), the sociopolitical conditions for the supremacy of the farmers of the West and the industrial North, and the interpretation of order that they advocated. This interpretation was irreconcilable with the institution of slavery as a national institution, such as existed in the colonies before 1776. As already noted, the founders eliminated slavery as a national institution from the American cosmos, reducing it to the "peculiar institution" of one region. As such it was legitimized in the Constitution of the United States in the categories available to the founders' set of symbols. As a man, the slave was a person; but in his social existence, he was property. This regulation was enshrined in the Constitution (Article I, Section 2 and Section 9; Article IV, Section 2) without explicit mention of the institution of slavery: "Its anomalous existence was forced to depend on elaborate circumlocutions and tacit understanding." "The evidence there permits the conclusion that the future, with respect to possible public action against slavery, was left open on purpose, at the insistence of such delegates as James Madison, Governeur Morris, and James Wilson."[119] Madison explicitly stated that the conception of the "paradigmatic republic" was

118. *Ibid.*, 187–88.

119. D. L. Robinson, *Slavery in the Structure of American Politics, 1765–1820* (New York, 1971), 246, 424.

irreconcilable with slavery: "Mr. Madison thought it wrong to admit in the Constitution the idea that there could be property in men."[120] Tolerated by the Constitution though continually repressed into the social unconscious, where it had a traumatic effect, slavery was preserved de facto in the southern states, thanks to their political and economic power within the federation.

But the congressional debates on the Missouri Compromise had raised the question in principle as early as 1819.

> Underlying this debate was a conflict over the meaning of the fundamental principles of the regime, and it was no coincidence that it produced the first extended consideration by Congress of the meaning of the Declaration of Independence and the Constitution. The Northern Position was straightforward: the doctrines of the Declaration were basic commitments, providing substance for the "republican form" of government guaranteed to every state by Article VI, Section 4 of the Constitution. In framing the constitution, the equalitarian thrust of republicanism against slavery had been set aside in deference to the predicament of the Southern states, where slavery was already entrenched beyond uprooting. But in legislating for the territories, where social patterns were not yet set, Congress should consider itself bound by the standards of republicanism, by which slavery could not be justified.[121]

Jefferson, an old man by now, persuaded of the necessity of a tacit arrangement between North and South for the sake of preserving the Union until slavery could be eliminated gradually, was horrified to glimpse a novel sort of constellation: "A geographical line, coinciding with a marked principle, moral and political, once conceived and held up to the angry passions of men, will never be obliterated."[122] Nevertheless, until the 1830s, with Jeffersonianism the South remained aware of the irreconcilability of this institution with the symbolism of national self-interpretation. Only the threat to the South's power from the long-range political and economic developmental trends in the nation, combined with the consolidation within the society of the plantation states, promoted a variant of the American symbolic form. This variant interpreted the independent political and socioeconomic structure in such a way as to give the South a social identity without entirely forfeiting the authoritative truth of the founders' order. A "heresy bound by geography"[123] was cre-

120. Farrand, ed., *Records of the Federal Convention*, II, 417.

121. D. L. Robinson, *Slavery in the Structure of American Politics*, 409.

122. Thomas Jefferson to John Holmes, March 22, 1820, in Jefferson, *Writings*, XII, 158–59.

123. Bratford, *A Rhetoric for Continuing Revolution*, 2.

ated; that is, a completely heterogeneous sectional group of political units turned into a closed society, "the South." [124] This new entity was by no means the same as the geographic region of the southern United States; on one hand it was only conditionally possible to include the states of the "upper South," whereas on the other hand the Southwest, most especially Texas, felt itself to be part of the South. The common element in such a symbolization of the South's psychosocial field was the traditional interpretation of the Constitution, stressing states' rights and limited federal power, the agrarian republicanism of the Jeffersonians with the recognition of slavery as a political and economic institution, justified by the inferiority of the omnipresent Afro-Americans and by the civilizing superiority of white culture. The Old South's Virginia-dominated gentry society, with its country republicanism, was becoming transformed into a large-scale, dynamically capitalistically diversified, agrarian society; commercially run plantations, which powered the economy, existed at the center of the mass of white yeomanry living on family farms without significant urban centers, but most especially without the basic structure of the town constitution peculiar to New England; here and there the white population was even sparser. The pressure of this transformation distorted the consciousness and symbolic structure of the general American tradition in various ways. The white minority within a black majority, whose political and social control alone promised to overcome the deep-seated anxiety of a mass rising on the model of Haiti, took seriously the biological version of the chain of being, as they did the ethnic attribution to the American apocalypse to turn it into a historical-speculative progressivism of the white race, which received the blessing of a fundamentalist belief in the Bible. In the minds of the slaveholders and those who wanted to own slaves, the property-individualistic component became separated into a laissez-faire individualism *sui generis;* eventually this attitude openly reduced the society's *sensus communis* to the civilizing ethos of white Americanism. The synthesis of these elements in the symbolism of "romantic nationalism" (Hartz) as a coherent interpretation of order came too late for the white masses. George Fitzhugh's "Sociology of the South" remained merely an isolated episode, in spite of the beginning of speculative exegesis of the southern experience by John C. Calhoun, Hughes, Theodore R. Dew, and J. D. B. De Bow, as well as in the romantic literature. The "sociology of the South," as a paradigmatic counterpart to the "political economy of the North," attempted to mobilize in equal measure the tradition of Western civilization and the new social science of positivism to enhance the dignity of the southern ethos.

---

124. W. McWilliams, *The Idea of Fraternity in America* (Berkeley, Calif., 1973), 267.

Fitzhugh and his fellows reconstructed a historical depth dimension of civilizing greatness for the South; its referents included ancient Egypt, Israel, Greece, Rome, and feudal Europe, as well as counterrevolutionary conservatism and antiliberal socialism. Slavery was shown to be the ethically, politically, and economically appropriate social way of organizing work to establish the "good society," since it does not leave unprotected men exposed to the anarchic forces of laissez-faire, the conflict between capital and labor. Historically, the so-called free society of the modern world was seen as a decline from a healthy, beautiful, and natural order; this decline would inevitably drive a free society to its own defeat in the socialism of a Saint Simon, a Fourier, or a Blanc; however, this is no more than an attempt to restore the old order of the slave society. "All concur that free society is a failure. We slaveholders say you must return to domestic slavery, the oldest, the best and most common form of socialism. The new schools of Socialism promise something better, but admit, to obtain that something better, they must first destroy and eradicate man's human nature." [125] But here human nature is no longer experienced in a philosophical or Christian way; it is defined "scientifically." It is the new certainty of Comtian sociology and of biologistic anthropology, which describes man as a datum—that is, reifies him. It is this which "first allows" us to recognize the "great truth which lies at the foundation of all society—that every man has property in his fellow man." [126]

The South's self-understanding—which dealt with the tiny minority of the large planters (about 2 percent of the slaveholding families) and the group of those who owned from ten to twenty slaves (about 24 percent of the slaveholding families), along with the mass of those who owned fewer slaves, as well as the 75 percent of the white population that owned no slaves at all—could, on the basis of economic reality, nevertheless refer to a certain rationality in the system. The southern economy was thoroughly profitable in the capitalist sense; agriculture in particular was considerably more efficient than the system of western family farms. A similar situation prevailed in reference to the use of slaves in urban industry. As Moore had already unequivocally noted, slavery was by no means

---

125. George Fitzhugh, "Sociology of the South," in *Antebellum*, ed. H. Wish (New York, 1960), 85.

126. *Ibid.*, 83. Compare the anthology edited by McKitrick, ed., *Slavery Defended* (Englewood Cliffs, N.J., 1963); J. Calhoun, *Works* (New York, 1851–56). See also R. Hofstadter, "Calhoun," in *The American Political Tradition and the Men Who Made It* (New York, 1961), 68–92; L. Hartz, *The Liberal Tradition in America* (New York, 1955), 145–200; W. J. Cash, *The Mind of the South* (New York, 1969), especially 91–100; McWilliams, *Idea of Fraternity*, 258–70. On the anthropological discussion in the United States, see W. D. Jordan, *White Over Black* (Chapel Hill, N.C., 1968), 482–538.

irreconcilable with industrial capitalism. Just the opposite was true; the cotton of the South was the principal impetus to industrialization in the North and played an important role in the industrial revolution in England.[127]

The economic rationality of the southern variant of the economic system also worked in other regions in principle, to the extent that throughout the United States the situation was one of a national economic system with a considerable rate of growth.[128] Economic contradictions by no means need have evoked armed conflict before the backdrop of the economic rationality embracing the whole of society.[129] But the economic rationality operating in society is not its constitutive basis, no matter how important a factor the economic structure might be. It was precisely the Civil War that showed how forcefully the South, in spite of its economic inferiority, could hold its own against the North and West.[130] What was crucial on the level of power politics was the confrontation over control of the constitutional power center, the federal government—that is, the future direction of national policy.

Here too the question of power was instrumental, for it arose only when the principal order of the United States as a continental empire was questioned. But in this way the truth and authority of the founders were at stake. A logical reaction to the question with Fitzhugh's attempt to create for the South its own interpretation of order, reasoning that the work of the fathers had failed and that the ancient order of things would have to be reestablished. The social order of the South had the truth and authority of history on its side; the factuality of the South's history and "sociology"—to this extent Fitzhugh's recourse to European experiences was thoroughly "modern"—replaced the fathers' consciousness as the center of order. It followed therefore for those few southern thinkers who cared about a radical justification of their social existence that the Constitution of the United States must be revised to reflect the southern principles of order. "Social forms so widely differing as those of domestic

---

127. D. C. North, *The Economic Growth of the United States* (Englewood Cliffs, N.J., 1961), 67 ff.; Moore, *Social Origins of Dictatorship and Democracy;* D. L. Robinson, *Slavery in the Structure of American Politics,* 432–33; A. H. Conrad and J. R. Meyer, "The Economics of Slavery in the Ante-Bellum South," *Journal of Political Economy,* LXVI (1958), 95–130; R. W. Fogel and S. L. Engerman, *Time on the Cross: The Economics of American Negro Slavery* (Boston, 1974).

128. I use the term *economic society* here with the meaning given it by E. Heimann, *Soziale Theorie der Wirtschaftssysteme* (Tübingen, 1963).

129. Compare especially Moore, *Social Origins of Dictatorship and Democracy.*

130. This fact continued to perplex Friedrich Engels, among others, and occasionally made him doubt whether the North would win. Compare K. Marx and F. Engels, *The Civil War in the United States* (New York, 1961), 239–52.

slavery and (attempted) universal liberty cannot long co-exist in the Great Republic of Christendom. They cannot be equally adapted to the wants and interests of society."[131]

"The sociology of the South" states logically that "slavery will everywhere be abolished, or everywhere reinstituted."[132] The secession of the South was only a minor program in the worldwide dispute concerning the future order of society; the long-range debate was over the replacement of the "free Society." In principle the debate also involved slavery as a principle of social organization, independent of the American case involving slaves of African descent. This implication, which Lincoln immediately understood and exploited for his own ends, also underlies, as we will show, the crucial challenge to the fathers' concept of order. But Fitzhugh and his allies never understood the consciousness-shaping form of the "paradigmatic republic." Louis Hartz has described at length how the southerners were unable to free themselves of the ordering impact of the fathers' consciousness and concomitant symbolization they sought to destroy. "Long before, in the seventeenth century, America had laid this trap for the Southern thinkers. By being 'born equal,' by establishing liberalism without destroying feudalism, it had transformed the rationalist doctrine of Locke into the traditionalist reality of Burke so that anyone who dared to use conservativism in order to refute liberalism would discover instead that he had merely refuted himself."[133] There is no solution to the dilemma: "the more consistently a man advanced the antiliberal arguments of Burke, the farther away he got from the traditionalist substance they were designed to protect. The more he cherished the traditionalist substance, the farther away he got from the antiliberal arguments. The only question was on which horn of the dilemma he wanted to impale himself. Most southerners, unlike Fitzhugh . . . actually embraced both."[134] In the consciousness of the South, the old Jeffersonianism was to be resurrected in a New Burkean traditionalism. "Calhoun exemplifies it perfectly, a man whose thought it cut into two by the tug of the liberal past and the pull of the reactionary present. He slays Jefferson only to embrace him with a passion on the end, he destroys the Founding Fathers only to carry their work forward."[135]

The logic of this contradiction required a revision of the work of the founders under the horizon of the *status quo ante*. Calhoun fell back on

131. Quoted in Wish, ed., *Antebellum*, 8.
132. Fitzhugh, "Sociology of the South," in *Antebellum*, ed. Wish, 95.
133. Hartz, *Liberal Tradition*, 151.
134. *Ibid.*, 153–54.
135. *Ibid.*, 166.

institutionalism as the instrument of order. The southern interpretation of the Constitution, with the explicit recognition of slavery as a political and social institution, had to become the basis on which the Union was reorganized. The principle of a "concurrent majority" and a dual executive was to defuse the sectional conflict by means of "political equilibrium" (William H. Seward). In this way Calhoun hoped in at least one section to protect slavery as the social organization of Afro-Americans and at the same time to preserve the republican principle of order for the whites. Such was the South's actual intention around the middle of the century. In my view, Calhoun best formulated the South's position: the distortion of the "paradigmatic republic," which the founders accepted for the sake of pragmatic power, was to be raised to the principle of the empire. Unlike Fitzhugh's sociology, however, this position could be justified only by accepting a speculation on race that identified African-Americans scientifically, that is, authoritatively, as inferior. But this solution merely led back to the historical and depth-psychological dimension of the common American consciousness: the contradiction between the philosophical and Christian experience of the potential equality of all men and the actual and historical experience of the coexistence of ethnically and racially different forms of humanity in a society in which the African minority was de facto and de jure robbed of the spiritual-political dimension in its social existence. Inevitably the southerners had to fail in solving this common American dilemma.

> Thus if the racial theory tried to save the whites from the attack on Locke, an inescapable reality kept pulling them into its orbit, since their common humanity with the Negroe could not easily be denied. Indeed the very compulsion they felt to attack Locke betrayed them on this score, since Locke had been concerned with men in general, not with Negroes in particular. Or the negroe was not a Lockian "man," why bother to attack Locke? If the Negroe was a parcel of property rather than a human being, why bother to attack Jefferson? Certainly Jefferson had believed in property rights. The Southerners could not remove from the human category, and, not being able to do so, their logic of inequality was bound to backfire on themselves. [136]

But the pressure of social reality allowed only a few, such as Moncure Conway, to arrive at a theoretical decision: "the Negroe must either be an 'inferior animal' or a 'man and a brother.' Eventually coming to accept the truth of the latter alternative, Conway felt a deep sense of his

136. *Ibid.*, 170.

own inferiority and lack of humanity in ever having doubted, and spent much of his life trying to make up for it." [137] Understandably most of the southerners were so frightened at losing the foundation on which their social world was constructed that, in spite of all the inconsistencies of their position, they could not abandon the truth and authority of the fathers and thus carried the illogicality of their revisionism to the point where even after secession the constitutional order of the fathers was taken over in toto in establishing the Confederate States of America. Before that time Calhoun's position still seemed to promise a constitutional solution on the level of power—an illusion with the paradoxical outcome that each step in a successful assertion of southern interests in national politics inevitably brought the South closer to defeat, to the point where Southern republicanism was excluded from the dominant frame of consciousness and symbolism, driving them to the underground of tolerated illegal social practice. In this area, however, North and South had little cause to accuse each other after Reconstruction.

In the years after 1820 it became increasingly clear that the quarrel over the basic principles of American order—that is, the question about the realization of the founders' "paradigmatic republic" through the social expansion of New England culture and its spiritual-political dynamic, not least raised by the engagement of the sons of the federalist founders who were driven out of the political process by the rise of Jackson—disturbed arrangements made on the basis of elitist interests. But the threshold for mass mobilization on questions of principle could be passed only under specific socioeconomic conditions: population growth through immigration into the Midwest and North, redirection of midwestern agriculture to the North, growing independence of the North's industrial interests in contrast to the traditional southern-oriented finance and trade interests, expansion and internal consolidation of the South, and so forth. The call for regeneration of the truth of the fathers in a spiritual-political movement of awakening and reformation could meet with a response only after the southern strategy of challenging the prevailing interpretation of man and society became obvious to a majority of the white workers and farmers in the West and North that felt threatened by southern attacks on the free-soil and free-labor policies in the West.

We should point out that in terms of policy the experience of the search for lost justice in the republican experiment motivated only isolated groups. The majority of the northern population did not share the

137. McWilliams, *Idea of Fraternity*, 266–67.

abolitionists' bursts of moral outrage; their fundamentalist dogmatism often repressed the more complex social problems.

But the spirituality of New England culture, embodying the truth and authority of the fathers, preserved its political expression not only in the organizational form of the civil association, but also in the medium of public order, as is shown by countless ordinances issued in the congresses of both the various New England states and the new states in their social hemisphere. For the New Englanders, slavery and slave labor were the permanent degradation of humanity and justice; they represented a violation of the "dictates of Christian religion" and the "higher law of God," as well as the "supreme law of the Land," along with the national Constitution and the Union.[138]

What is decisive in this regard is not that the scale of judgment was naturally taken from the traditional, symbolic cosmos of the founders, but that an intellectual minority focused on those symbols which express immediate person-centered existential virtue and that the constitutional order was placed in the context of an overarching experience of order. By recurring to the fundamental experience of order, sensitive minds became so much aware of the principled untruth of the status quo that the link between the psychic order and the societal order once more came within the view of political action and practice. Inevitably, morally motivated political practice gained influence over the majority through the shared symbolism of republicanism only after this majority felt the threat of impediment to its laissez-faire individualistic understanding of the republic as the place for free personal development. This understanding was described by the key symbols free soil, free men, and free labor. But in my view William Appleton Williams is mistaken in seeing the social materialization of the laissez-faire morality of total individualized freedom in religion, politics, and economics through revision of the Constitution as the decisive cause for the mobilization of the North and West in the Civil War.[139] Of course there is no gainsaying that in the symbolization of the Republican party the laissez-faire concept of the common man asserted itself at the same time that it expressed the position of interests of different social and regional groupings in the respective realization of the promise of this concept. Nevertheless, it required a conscious or unconscious recourse to the psychological depth dimension of the dominant form of consciousness, in which the prevalent reality image of the society

138. For example, see *Acts and Resolves of Massachusetts, 1846–1848*, 541–42; *Acts and Resolves of Massachusetts, 1854–1855*, 946–47 and *passim*.

139. W. A. Williams, *Contours of American History*, 252 ff., 285–86.

as a community of free and equal men had its empirical origin and ground. Only this psychosocial condition explains why the prospect of danger to the whole order of society from slavery could become socially relevant to such a degree that a great number of individuals suddenly saw their immediate social existence threatened, though such a thing was out of the question, especially as the interests of the majority of the political and economic elites pointed in the direction of compromise. The indistinct reactivation of a trapped experience of order in the concrete consciousness of many people led the Republican party to find in Lincoln a representative figure. In the course of his political life, he was able to rediscover the meditative depth dimension of the "paradigmatic republic" beyond its laissez-faire curtailment.

Before that time, however, an impersonally materialized dogmatism of national consensus still covered up the conflict, as proved by the success of the Clay-Webster Compromise of 1850, with its confirmation of the Fugitive Slave Acts, as well as the balanced admission of slave and free states into the Union and the election of Franklin Pierce to the presidency in 1852.[140] In Clay's and Webster's self-understanding the nexus of order and founding was still present through biography. Their tormenting fear of decline was, first of all, fear that the new nation would break apart. Increasingly they took the continental empire of the American Republic as an end in itself. Its meaning in history resulted from the successful historic mission of the national collectivity, predestined by God, and less from the quality of the good life in society. Webster and Clay gave absolute precedence to the perpetuation of the social organization of the founders. This twist made it biographically understandable as well as characteristic for the process of dogmatizing the symbolic self-interpretation of the founders in a complex of doctrines that stabilized the social consensus. The content of "nationality" was not the reconstruction of the experiences of order, but the duty of preserving and increasing the national polity by applying the precepts of the founders. This was the key symbol for "harmony," "peace," and "security" as the criteria of social order. The secondary virtue of "duty" became the carrying theme of a political ethic whose content was determined by a preserving constitutionalism and nationalism and whose form was the practice of mutual compromise. In their defense of the Compromise of 1850, Webster and Clay logically interpreted the existential virtues as peripheral to the person. The American Republic, they noted, was substantially identical

---

140. Compare A. Nevins, *Ordeal of the Union* (New York, 1947–71), I; W. E. Binkley, *American Political Parties* (New York, 1963), 179–80; Moore, *Social Origins of Dictatorship and Democracy.*

with the continental empire; freedom, equality, justice, and morality were inevitably subordinated to imperial existence. But unwittingly Webster and Clay thus turned the person-centered existential virtues, the precondition for the goodness of society, into the constitutional way to regulate conflicts among the members of society. This is equally true for the conflict concerning the question of the content of humanity and its order. Webster and Clay were forced by the logic of the power process to absolutize the institutionalism and power-political pragmatism of the Founding Fathers at the cost of relinquishing those motivating experiences of order that alone serve to legitimate the experiment in power politics carried out by the republican Union. The Union's existence, in turn, was now meant to sanction *any* constitutional pragmatism.[141]

Finally, this change in the traditional symbolism of order positively defines a dynamic sociopolitical power complex as the anonymous center of historical order. An orthodox power-pragmatic nationalism arose at the center between the romantic nationalism of the South and the spiritual-political nationalism of New England culture. Rufus Choate, one of Webster's New England followers, in a speech delivered on July 4, 1858, offered a good example of such reification of a social artifact to the center of order.

> Think of [nationality] as a state of consciousness, as a spring of feeling, as a motive of exertion, as blessing your country, and as reacting on you. Think of it as it fills your mind and quickens the heart of millions around you. Instantly, under such an influence, you ascend above the smoke and stir of this small local strife; you tread upon the high places of the earth and of history; you think and feel as an American for America; her power, her eminence, her consideration, her honour are yours; your competitors, like hers, are kings; your home, like hers, is the world; your path like hers, is on the highway of empires; our charge, her charge, is of generations and ages. . . . Think of it [nationality] as an active virtue. Is not all history a recital of the achievement of nationality, and an exponent of its historical and imperial nature? Even under systems far less perfect than ours, and influences far less auspicious than ours, has it not lifted itself up for a time above all things meaner, vindicating itself by action, by the sublimit of working hope.[142]

In his obituary for Webster, Choate logically stressed that the preservation of the Union was to be preferred to any discussion of slavery for the

---

141. Compare Nagel, *Sacred Trust*, 160ff.
142. Quoted in Kohn, *American Nationalism*, 109.

sake of America's progress.[143] This concentration of self-understanding on organized society itself as the ground and source of all that gives meaning to the life of the members of society made quite an impact on the political consciousness of Americans.

The social relevance of this reduction of the dominant symbolic form to national patriotism unquestionably lies in the fact that structures of social organization can be taken for the quality of society itself, and the unquestioning loyalty to the whole of society relieves the citizen of the question of his own quality without any loss in the terms of meaning for his existence. The language of this early form of patriotic orthodoxy transfers the spiritual and symbolic consensus to the social unconscious; for that very reason it was so important to the survival of American society well into the twentieth century. Even more characteristic of this aspect than Clay and Webster are the messages and addresses of President Pierce. Here the fathers appear as efficient and practical patriots who wasted no energy "upon idle and delusive speculations." The belief in the national institutions and the preservation of the grand constitutional doctrine, along with renunciation of all wild and chimerical plans for change brought forth by the unstable minds of visionary sophists and self-seeking demagogues, the "restless spirit," now elevates a mature nation in the fulfillment of its purpose to the "Great Republic of the World."[144] Although power-pragmatic nationalism broke down in the crisis of divergent interpretations of reality, at the same time it established the indissolubility of the continental empire on the psychosocial level to such an extent that the idea of secession, which had until this time been symbolically legitimated, was rejected with horror by both New England abolitionists and southern romantics as rebellion against what seemed the truth and authority of the order of the paradigmatic republic. Only the background of this crucial success of the power-pragmatic idea of unity can explain the circumstance that, in the discussions on principle concerning the order of man and society in the Republic, Lincoln was able to firmly link the program of spiritual-political awakening with the preservation of the Union. "The Union must be preserved in the purity of its principles as well as in the integrity of its territorial parts."[145] For Lincoln, the Union was the *conditio sine qua non* to preserve that "form and

143. Compare Nagel, *Sacred Trust*, 160.

144. Quoted in Nagel, *Sacred Trust*, 154–55.

145. Lincoln, *Collected Works*, II, 341. Lincoln always understood himself as the executor of Clay's policies, and he always interpreted Clay, though sometimes it took an effort, as the purest representative of the Founding Fathers' tradition; see his obituary for Clay of June 6, 1852, in *Collected Works*, II, 121–32.

substance of government whose leading object is to elevate the conditions of man" in the world.[146] The plausibility of this argument of the majority of those involved presumed the consciousness-shaping power of the power-pragmatic doctrine of the Union of Lincoln's opponent Stephen Douglas.

On his way to the White House, Lincoln, from the beginning the common man as *zoon politikon* par excellence, apparently came to understand increasingly the meditative origins of the forms given to consciousness and symbolism by the Founding Fathers, without losing his own ability to engage in pragmatic politics. It was surely this skill that allowed him to understand that Douglas' revision of the Missouri Compromise of 1820 in the Kansas-Nebraska Bill of 1854 and the Supreme Court's 1857 Dred Scott decision opened the door to a thorough revision of political power relations in the Union. The alliance of the New England spiritual-political awakening with a broad spectrum of sociopolitical and regional interests of workers, farmers, some industrialists, new immigrants and nativists, old Whigs and anti-Dixie Democrats, abolitionists, Negrophobes, and temperance advocates into a new party furnished the social basis for a regeneration of republicanism on the model of the Founding Fathers. The laissez-faire concept of the common man, wrapped in the tradition of the "American System," promised an industrial economic society of autarkic producers (in agriculture, trade, and industry) beyond the conflict of capital and labor, in which the virtuous republic achieves full maturity to the extent that everyone is granted unlimited access to the realm of public happiness according to his abilities. "Free Soil, Free Labor, Free Speech, Free Men" meant, according to Lincoln, "that education—cultivated thought—can best be combined with . . . any labor, on the principle of thorough work. . . . Let us hope, that by the best cultivation of the physical world, beneath and around us; and the intellectual and moral world within us, we shall secure an individual, social, and political prosperity and happiness, whose course shall be onward and upward, and which, while the earth endures, shall not pass away."[147] According to Eric Foner, the fundamental achievement of the Republican party before the Civil War consisted in the formulation of an interpretation of order "which blended personal and sectional interest with morality so perfectly that it became the most potent political force

146. *Ibid.*, IV, 438.

147. *Ibid.*, III, 481–82. Compare the detailed account of the sociopolitical and programmatic genesis of the Republican party in E. Foner, *Free Soil, Free Labor, Free Men: The Ideology of the Republican Party Before the Civil War* (New York, 1970), and Binkley, *American Political Parties*, 206–37.

in the nation." [148] This Republican interpretation of order contained the implication "that North and South represented two social systems whose values, interests, and future prospects were in sharp, perhaps mortal, conflict with one another." [149]

Lincoln perceived the conflict of two types of transcendental truths in American society, though they could represent only one truth—that is, the truth of the fathers. Lincoln consciously and emphatically accepted the claim to truth of Fitzhugh's "Sociology of the South": American society can be based on but *one* principle.

> A house divided against itself cannot stand. I believe this government cannot endure, permanently half slave and half free. I do not expect the Union to be dissolved—I do not expect the house to fall—but I do expect it will cease to be divided. It will become all one thing, or all the other. Either the opponents of slavery will arrest the further spread of it, and place it where the public mind shall rest in the belief that it is in course of ultimate extinction; or its advocates will push it forward, till it shall become alike lawful in all states, old and new—North as well as South. Have we no tendency to the latter condition? [150]

Lincoln transformed a theoretical insight into a plausible symbolic formulation by taking Fitzhugh's argument seriously and turning it against him. It is a matter of slavery as a principle of social order, not of the particular institution in the South. The politics of the South in the Union signaled the "nationalization of slavery"—that is, the alteration of the dominant pattern of institution and behavior—as well as the order of consciousness encompassing the former in the Union in the sense of "the sociology of the South." "Our government rests in public opinion. Whoever can change public opinion, can change the government, practically just so much. Public opinion, on any subject, always has a 'central idea,' from which all its minor thoughts radiate. That 'central idea' in our political public opinion, at the beginning was, and until recently has continued to be 'the equality of men.' And although it was always submitted patiently to whatever of inequality there seemed to be as a matter of actual necessity, its constant working has been a steady progress towards the practical equality of all men." But the election of James Buchanan in 1856 was "a struggle, by one party, to discard that central idea, and to substitute for it the opposite idea that slavery is right, in the abstract, the

148. Foner, *Free Soil, Free Labor, Free Men*, 309.
149. *Ibid.*, 310.
150. Lincoln, *Collected Works*, II, 461–62.

workings of which, as a central idea, may be the perpetuity of human slavery, and its extension to all countries and colors."[151]

Lincoln's interpretations of events during the 1850s take up the theme of the jeremiad with new urgency: the "central idea" of the Republic is not only put in question, it is already well on the way to becoming lost. The new Republicans of 1854 organized a political mass movement, not because Lincoln demanded the immediate elimination of the "peculiar institution" of the South, but because he made people understand the immediate danger "that slavery would become a nation-wide American institution if its geographical spread were not severely restricted at once."[152] Regardless of whether Lincoln's opinion regarding long-range trends in the United States was justified, however, the fear of the "nationalization of slavery" took its vitality from the meaningful connection of founding and order. The new "central idea" of slavery stood for all the social developments that ate away at the order of the fathers. That was why Lincoln's response to the crisis had to be: "with steady eye on the real issue, let us reinaugurate the good old 'central idea' of the Republic. We can do it. The human heart is with us—God is with us."[153]

In word and deed Abraham Lincoln was a unique exponent of the "political faith" of his fathers. In Lincoln the form the fathers gave to consciousness and symbol became present under the horizon of nineteenth-century experience to such a degree that Lincoln's self-understanding became identical with his symbolic function in the consciousness of society. But at the same time the structure of American consciousness gained a new kind of authenticity in Lincoln's psyche, for the peculiarly Western spiritual-political background of experience of an Adams or a Jefferson was lacking. The nexus of founding and order was, for Lincoln, the self-evident principle of American existence. All Americans, the descendants of the founders as well as all later immigrants, form a *corpus mysticum* with the fathers, in which the presence of God through the symbolic mediating role of the fathers in the Declaration of Independence is guaranteed for all past, present, and future generations. "We find a race of men living in that day whom we claim as our fathers and grandfathers; they were iron men, they fought for the principle that they were contending for; and we understood that by what they then did it has followed that

151. *Ibid.*, II, 385.
152. Hofstadter, *American Political Tradition*. Later, Marx was to adopt this belief of Lincoln's: "The war of the Southern Confederacy is, therefore, not a war of defense, but a war of conquest, a war of conquest for the extension and perpetuation of slavery" (Marx and Engels, *The Civil War in the United States*, 73).
153. Lincoln, *Collected Works*, II, 385.

the degree of prosperity that we now enjoy has come to us." The anniversary celebration of independence ties the grandfathers to the fathers at the same time that it brings the individual into harmony with himself, his fellowmen, and his country. But alongside those citizens who are immediately descended from the blood of the fathers, there is still that half of the American people

> who are not descendants at all of these men, they are men who have come from Europe . . . and settled here, finding themselves our equals in all things. If they look back through this history to trace their connections with those days by blood, they find they have none, they cannot carry themselves back into that glorious epoch and make themselves feel that they are part of us, but when they look through that old Declaration of Independence they find that those old men say that 'We hold these truths to be self-evident, that all men are created equal,' and then they feel that the moral sentiment taught in that day evidences their relation to those men, that it is the father of all moral principle in them, and they have a right to claim it as though they were blood of the blood and flesh of the flesh of the men who wrote that Declaration . . . and so they are. That is the electric cord in that Declaration that links the hearts of patriotic and liberty-loving men together, that will link those patriotic hearts as long as the love of freedom exists in the minds of men throughout the world.[154]

This theology of the national *corpus mysticum* stands at the center of the Lincolnian reform movement: "The mystic chords of memory, stretching from every battlefield, and patriotic grave, to every living heart and hearthstone, all over this broad land, will yet swell the chorus of the Union, when again touched, as surely they will be, by the better angels of our nature," Lincoln's first inaugural address noted in the year of crisis, 1861.[155] The fathers as mediators to God and guarantors of the mystical community find their collective reincarnation precisely in this: "this nation, under God, shall have a new birth of freedom—and that government of the people, by the people, for the people, shall not perish from the earth."[156] The "new birth of freedom" is the collective work of reconstructing the founding in order to restore it in all its truth and purity: "Our republican robe is soiled, and trailed in the dust. Let us repurify it. Let us turn and wash it white, in the spirit, if not the blood, of the Revolution."[157]

---

154. *Ibid.*, 499–500. For here and for what follows, compare W. J. Wolf, *Lincoln's Religion* (Boston, 1970).

155. Lincoln, *Collected Works*, IV, 271.

156. *Ibid.*, VII, 23.

157. *Ibid.*, II, 276.

Lincoln's logical recurrence to the substance of the symbolism of American self-understanding, that is, the nexus of founding and order, was persuasive because of the spiritual authenticity of this recourse in the person of Lincoln; in him the form of consciousness and its critical symbolic form once again became genuinely united. This circumstance, finally, explains Lincoln's ability to mobilize large sections of the nation and unite them in a political movement overreaching separate socioeconomic interests and his elevation to their charismatic leader; it also accounts for the disintegration of the movement into its original elements after his victory and death.

Lincoln's "republicanism" was the permanent interpretation of the words of the fathers and always circled around the symbols of order of the Declaration of Independence. Lincoln perceived that the sacredness of the document is no longer a given; its words were mangled; its meaning distorted, even despised and denied.[158] With the denial of the Declaration of Independence, America, however, also denied the order of the founding: the Founding Fathers "meant to set up a standard maxim for free society, which could be familiar to all, and revered by all; constantly looked to, constantly labored for, and even though never perfectly attained, constantly approximated, and thereby constantly spreading and deepening its influence, and augmenting the happiness and value of life to all people of all colors everywhere. . . . Its authors meant it to be, thank God, it is now proving itself a stumbling block to those who in after times might seek to turn a free people back into the hateful paths of despotism."[159]

Lincoln drew on the language of the fathers for the power of persuasion with which he made it absolutely plain to his fellow citizens that "nationalization of slavery" meant the recantation of the Declaration of Independence: "if free negroes should be made things, how long think you, before they will begin to make things out of poor white men."[160] And he graphically listed the possibilities of such a process of turning men into objects:

> You say A. is white, and B. is black. It is color, then; the lighter, having the right to enslave the darker? Take care. By this rule, you are to be slave to the first man you meet, with a fairer skin than your own. You do not mean color exactly?—You mean the whites are intellectually the superiors of the blacks, and, therefore have the right to enslave them? Take care again. By this rule, you are to be slave to the first man you meet, with an intellect

158. *Ibid.*, 404.
159. *Ibid.*, 406.
160. Quoted in Hofstadter, *American Political Tradition*, 113.

superior to your own. But, say you, it is a question of interest; and if you can make it our interest, you have the right to enslave another. Very well. And if he can make it his interest, he has a right to enslave you.[161]

By this reflection Lincoln demonstrated his sensitivity to the implicit theoretical problems: the reduction of man to an object contradicts the premise laid down in the Declaration of Independence of the essential equality of all human beings as such, which alone justifies the *corpus mysticum* of American society, beyond all differences in the actualization of this essential humanity. Lincoln also logically understood that the motive for the objectification is to be found in the disorder of the psyche by which the relationship between reason and emotion is reversed. Disavowal of the Declaration of Independence in this spirit was a recantation of human nature, for to the extent that it clearly robs men of their humanity and turns them, like household pets, into objects, the principle of slavery is grounded in the "selfishness of man's nature" and declares "self-interest" to be the sole proper principle of action. The principle of order of the Declaration of Independence, on the other hand, is realized in the "love of justice,"[162] forbidding any denial of the Negroes' humanity. But Lincoln also lived so exclusively in the authoritative symbolic world of the fathers that he and the whole Republican movement had to run aground on its sociopolitical and theoretical limitations as soon as it became a question of a possible integration of the Afro-American as a *zoon politikon* in the nation's *corpus mysticum*—though "slavery" as a principle of social organization contradicted the substantial order of the fathers, "the Republican desire to place this great question of slavery on the very basis on which our fathers placed it, and no other."[163] But what can it mean that "our Fathers did not make this nation half slave and half free. . . . I insist that they found the institution of slavery existing here. They did not make it so, but they left it so because they knew of no way to get rid of it at that time"? By prohibiting slave trading and slavery in the new territories, where these had not been practices, "they placed it where they understood, and all sensible men understood, it was in the course of ultimate extinction."[164] Accordingly, Lincoln continued, the Constitution recognized no right of property in human beings, avoiding the words *slave* and *negro race* and speaking only of *persons*.[165] But how were the fathers to be interpreted if slavery was to be abolished? Lincoln's

161. Lincoln, *Collected Works*, II, 222–23.
162. *Ibid.*, 255, 271.
163. *Ibid.*, IV, 21–22.
164. *Ibid.*, III, 276.
165. *Ibid.*, 307ff., 522–45.

exegesis of the tradition resulted in an attempt to differentiate between the actualizations of humanity in society. As a first step, the Declaration of Independence included the potential equality of all human beings: the Negro was "entitled to all natural rights enumerated in the Declaration of Independence, the right to life, liberty, and the pursuit of happiness."[166] Accordingly, the Negro was entitled to all civil rights which virtually circumscribe the private realm of social existence: the individual right to life, liberty, and property imply the status of a legal subject, insofar as the protection of individual rights must be guaranteed by the legal order of society. Lincoln proclaimed the natural and legal equality of the Afro-Americans—"he asserts for them a perfect equality of civil and personal rights under the constitution," explained the New York *Times* after his election[167]—but with the majority of Republicans, he believed that neither the Declaration nor the Constitution inevitably required that "social and political equality between whites and blacks" be realized in the political order.[168] Since the authority of the fathers did not demand "political friendship" between black and white, did not compel the admission of the Afro-American to the "public happiness" of political life, as the radical Republicans derived from the New England ethos, Lincoln could justify the politics of suppression: "Free them, and make politically and socially, our equals?" he asked himself as early as 1854. "My own feelings will not admit this; and if mine would, we well know that that of the great mass of white people will not. Whether this feeling accords with justice and sound judgement, is not the sole question, if indeed it is any part of it. A universal feeling, whether well or ill-founded, can not be safely disregarded. We can not, then, make them equals."[169]

Although Lincoln believed that the granting of citizenship was constitutional, he was influenced by the basic psychological makeup of the white majority and was persuaded of its very real import on any political decision—probably correctly. The insurmountable obstacle in the conscious and unconscious mind of Lincoln and his fellow citizens consisted of the consequence of the realization of the "republic of virtue" for the Afro-American as *zoon politikon*, for which an exegesis of the fathers' symbols of order was hardly suitable: racial integration. The pressure of the historical and psychic depth dimension in American society proved from the beginning to be stronger than the existential truth of the experience of order. The European interpretation of the experience of the Af-

---

166. *Ibid.*, 222.
167. Quoted in Foner, *Free Soil, Free Labor, Free Men*, 294.
168. Lincoln, *Collected Works*, III, 328. Compare also III, 16, 146; II, 520 and *passim*.
169. *Ibid.*, II, 256.

rican as the other and stranger in a counterpart of human deficiency, in which one's own emotional nature was projected, was in some form or other part of every image of reality. Winthrop D. Jordan has shown that it was only the presupposition of this reverse image that allowed slavery to arise in the colonies, and that consequently racial integration to the point of miscegenation seemed a psychological and social danger to personal human essence.[170] For Lincoln the alternative of racial integration was out of the question.[171] He opted for separation of the races through colonization. When this alternative failed, what remained, in spite of the formal extension of political rights to Afro-Americans, was social separation through segregation. "All I ask for the negro is that if you do not like him, let him alone. If God gave him but little, that little let him enjoy."[172]

Lincoln's spiritual-political reform remained focused on slavery as the expression of all the evils of the world, bemoaned in the jeremiad. It addressed the purification of the individual psyche of those who shared in the national *corpus mysticum,* that is, the return to the purity of the fathers' origins. The republicanism of 1860 mobilized for its second revolution, the Civil War, the established symbolic pattern of the first Revolution, complete with the underlying structure of revolutionary consciousness; it included apocalyptic undertones as well, as proved by "The Battle Hymn of the Republic" (1862).[173] At the center of this revolutionary con-

170. Jordan, *White Over Black,* xff. Compare also D. L. Robinson, *Slavery in the Structure of American Politics,* 430; Foner, *Free Soil, Free Labor, Free Men,* 261–300.

171. Lincoln, *Collected Works,* V, 370ff.

172. *Ibid.,* II, 520.

173. First stanza:

> Mine eyes have seen the glory of the coming of the Lord:
> He is trampling out the vintage where the grapes of wrath are stored;
> He hath loosed the fateful lightning of his terrible swift sword;
> His truth is marching on.

Chorus:

> Glory! Glory! Hallelujah . . . .

Fifth stanza:

> In the beauty of the lilies Christ was born across the sea;
> With a glory in his bosom that transfigured you and me;
> As he died to make men holy, let us die to make men free,
> While God is marching on.

The author, Julia Ward Howe, was far from being a dogmatic Christian; rather, she belonged to the "enlightened" Boston reformers surrounding Theodore Parker, closely connected with radical Republicans. "Thus the fact that she was the poet of the American apocalyptic faith is significant, it shows how deeply such ideas must have penetrated the

sciousness of the radical Republicans we find once more the acute experience of an existential tension between want and plenty, disorder and order, time and eternity, which causes a collective process of "conversion" in the spiritual-political revival: "the radicals . . . rejected a cardinal principle of American politics, that of compromise. They were as much moralists as politicians, using political means to eradicate a sin from American society." [174]

The politics of the Republicans once more raised the patterns of consciousness and symbolism of revivalism and millenarianism from the underground of the social subculture of churches and sects to the national level in a design for existence socially dominant for the North. Its interpretation of the Civil War, with the victory of the truth of spiritual-political reform over the untruth of the South, became once and for all the definitive integral element of the national symbolic universe. The Civil War achieved the public status of a spiritual-political reformation—of course, first of all, in the life and death of Lincoln as the Redeemer. In his beginnings, of course, Lincoln, a local politician, was no political-ethical revivalist, as were his later allies Charles Sumner, Thaddeus Stephens, Joshua Giddings, William Seward, and others from the New England belt, who called themselves "political abolitionists." But his regional revivalist background, together with his nonsectarian, national-American, biblical-Unitarian religiosity marked by "faith in the Fathers," allowed Lincoln to discover a persuasive interpretation of his political actions in the symbolism of spiritual-political awakening and restoration.[175] "A redeeming nation, a Redeemer-President: the combination is appropriate. The fact that, in the crucial hour, there was elected a President who did

---

national mind" (Tuveson, *Redeemer Nation*, 198). Tuveson's brilliant interpretation of the song shows it to be an "Americanized" paraphrase of the apocalypse of Saint John; see 199–202. Compare also E. Wilson, *Patriotic Gore: Studies in the Literature of the American Civil War* (New York, 1962), 91–96, and W.-A. Clebsh, "Christian Interpretations of the Civil War," *Church History*, XXX (June, 1961), 212–22.

174. Foner, *Free Soil, Free Labor, Free Men*, 114. Characteristically, Moore, *Social Origins of Dictatorship and Democracy*, simply bypasses this motivational center in his account of the radical Republicans.

175. Compare Lincoln's "Address Before the Young Men's Lyceum of Springfield, Illinois, January 27, 1838," in *Collected Works*, I, 108–15; "Temperance Address, February 24, 1842," *ibid.*, 279: "And what a nobel ally is this, to the cause of political freedom. With such an aid, its march cannot fail to be on and on, till every son on earth shall drink in rich fruition the sorrow quenching draughts of perfect liberty. Happy day, when all appetites controlled, all passions subdued, all matters subjected to mind, all conquering mind, shall live and move the monarch of the world. Glorious consummation! Hail fall of Fury! Reign of Reason, all hail." See also C. Sandburg, *Abraham Lincoln: The Prairie Years and the War Years* (New York, 1954), 14, 575, 641; McWilliams, *Idea of Fraternity*, 276–78; Wolf, *Lincoln's Religion*.

indeed have the qualities of such a figure was further proof that the millennial mission was no dream."[176] The repolitization of the awakening of the national *corpus mysticum* proceeded in the reinstitutionalization of the fathers' traditional rituals; during the crisis, the representative of the "people under God" called for public meditation, for penance and thanksgiving. The proclamation of fast days on August 12, 1861, and March 30, 1863, and of thanksgiving on July 15, 1863, and the president's second inaugural address, of March 4, 1865, all furnish the authoritative symbolic interpretation of the *res gestae* of the Civil War under the horizon of the collective experience of spiritual regeneration of God's people in America. Public mortification, public prayer, and fasting meditatively disclose the ground of all being, God, who not only permitted the affliction of the Civil War but actually sent it as punishment for individual and collective sinfulness. The decline from the original excellence of the fathers' order, the fall of the nation, was essentially manifested in the evil of slavery; but slavery stood, in a way, for all other forms of corruption: the ever-present greed for power and possession, sexual dissipation, and the abuse of alcohol—that is, the overall complex of private and public viciousness—become the occasion for public confession of sin and guilt and for the prayer for forgiveness and mercy as well as for the grace to allow conversion. This conversion is also understood as national reformation, for the Civil War is not only God's punishing affliction but also a wondrous proof of God's grace. The war represented the public act of collective, active remorse and purification of the sinners; the war was the process by which submission to divine Providence took place. The return to God in a well-ordered spiritual-political existence was identical with the return to the "truth" and order of the fathers. In 1863 Lincoln gave exemplary expression to the principle of the political revival:

> And insomuch as we know that, by His divine Law, nations like individuals are subjected to punishments and chastisements in this world, may we not justly fear that the awful calamity of civil war, which now desolates the land, may be but punishment, inflicted upon us, for our presumptuous sins, to the needful end of our national reformation as a whole people? We have been the recipients of the choicest bounties of Heaven. We have been preserved, these many years, in peace and prosperity. We have grown in numbers, wealth and power, as no other nation has ever grown. But we have forgotten God. We have forgotten the gracious hand which preserved us in peace, and multiplied and enriched and strengthened us; and we have

176. Tuveson, *Redeemer Nation,* 206. Compare Nagel, *Sacred Trust,* 156–57, 191ff.

vainly imagined, in the deceitfulness of our hearts, that all these blessings were produced by some superior wisdom and virtue of our own. Intoxicated with unbroken success, we have become too self-sufficient to feel the necessity of redeeming and preserving grace, too proud to pray to the God that made us!—It behooves us then, to humble ourselves before the offended Power, to confess our national sins, and to pray for clemency and forgiveness.[177]

.   .   .   .

I invite the People of the United States to . . . render homage due to the Divine Majesty, for the wonderful things he has done in the Nations behalf, and invoke the influence of His Holy Spirit . . . to lead the whole nation, through the paths of repentance and submission to the Divine Will back to the perfect enjoyment of Union and fraternal peace.[178]

In the inaugural address of 1865 he described the catharsis of the Civil War in an apocalyptically tuned theodicy.

The Almighty has its own purposes, "Woe unto the world because of offences! For it must needs be that offences come; but woe to that man by whom the offence cometh!" If we shall suppose that American slavery is one of those offences which, in the Providence of God, must needs come, but which, having continued through his appointed time, He now wills to remove, and that he giveth to both North and South, this terrible war, as the woe due to those by whom the offence came, shall we discern therein any departure from those divine attributes which the believers in a Living God always ascribe to him? Fondly do we hope—fervently do we pray— that the mighty scourge of war may speedily pass away. Yet, if God wills that it should continue, until all the wealth piled by the bond-man's two hundred and fifty years of unrequited toil shall be sunk, and until every drop of blood drawn with the lash, shall be paid by an other drawn with the sword, as was said three thousand years ago, so still it must be said "the judgements of the Lord, are true and righteous altogether."

Lincoln' version of Matthew 18:7 is placed right beside the Revelation of Saint John in order to incorporate the affliction of the war in a divine plan of salvation, which removes the "scandal" of slavery from the world and allows the victory of the North to be understood as the Lord's righteous punishment of the sinners in the South. Lincoln's concluding words present the ethic of the purged psyche: "With malice toward none; with charity for all; with firmness in the right, as God gives us to see the right,

177. Lincoln, *Collected Works,* VI, 156,
178. *Ibid.,* 332.

let us strive on to finish the work we are in . . . to do all which may achieve and cherish a just and a lasting peace, among ourselves, and with all nations." [179]

Lincoln does not, however, mistake the purification of the national psyche with the salvation of man in the world; he warned against any apocalyptic exaltation that prophesied the realization of the kingdom of God in the here and now of the United States: "Human nature will not change. In any future great national trial, compared with the men of this, we shall have as weak, and as strong; as silly, and as wise; as bad and good. Let us, therefore, study the incidents of this, as philosophy to learn wisdom from, and none of them as wrongs to be revenged." [180] Lincoln's symbolism blended seamlessly with the other components of societal self-interpretation. In the "Founder and Restorator," the national revival had once more brought the nation symbolically into harmony with the fathers, with God, and with the cosmos. The work of reconciliation seemed completed by Lincoln's sacrificial death. [181]

The apotheosis of Lincoln as father and restorer gave to society a new source of order, a new standard for the interpretation of the existential truth of the order of the fathers. But Lincoln's spiritual strength was not communicated to enough members of society to allow the spiritual-political reformation of the depth dimension of the psyche to be touched to this extent and to allow the authentic experiences of order to evoke socially relevant changes in the socially dominant mental pattern. Reconstruction was important within the prevailing symbolic form, since in the long term it implicated the inclusion of all the people on the continent in the paradigmatic republic. Because of its advanced concretization, however, the prevailing symbolic form largely swallowed all attempts at intellectual breakthroughs beyond the established image of reality. Only briefly did recurrence to the fathers in the crisis seem to restore the nexus between order and founding in the real experience of the national *corpus mysticum*. But the consciousness of society, without foundation in pre-dogmatic reality of knowledge, clung to the handed-down symbolic form to obviate the permanent danger of the loss of substantial solidarity. The impetus of the spiritual-political awakening failed after 1865 as it ran increasingly into those socioeconomic processes that evoked the socio-political implications of spiritual-political revivals in society. As early as 1876 the centennial was once again marked by the sign of the jeremiad

179. *Ibid.*, VIII, 333. Compare the precise interpretation of the text in Tuveson, *Redeemer Nation*, 206–207, as well as Nagel, *Sacred Trust*, 130, 134, 145ff., 156–57, 165ff.

180. Lincoln, *Collected Works*, VIII, 101.

181. Nagel, *Sacred Trust*, 191ff., 195, 198ff.

concerning universal corruption. The latent search for the order of man in the Republic was shaped by the medium of the meditative visualization of the founding and the associated methodologies of the social communication of the symbolic forms under changed social conditions.[182]

V. The Social Function of the World of National Symbols

Even before 1860, the infinite variety of civic associations of every sort and with different public and private goals included veterans' societies from the wars of 1776, 1812, and 1846, as well as such patriotic groups as the New England societies of transplanted New Englanders, the xenophobic organizations of the Know-Nothing movement, and the Mount Vernon Ladies Association, which had for its purpose the care and preservation of Mount Vernon.[183] But it was not until after the Civil War that the fear of danger to social order became so widespread that it led to socially relevant defensive measures. Paul C. Nagel has described the "psychic crisis" of 1876 to 1898 in detail.[184] Once again, however, Americans could describe the experience of disorder only in the jeremiad; they chose to oppose it by insisting on the beginnings. "Americans began incessant calls for 'a revival of patriotism.'"[185] The language is revealing: the revival, the "restoration" of the authentic self through the existential act of turning to the order of the founders became the demand for restoration of symbolic order and behavior. Although it was of necessity verbally linked to the ethos of the virtuous citizen's fathers, the person-centered core of this design for living was no longer understood. The supplicating patriotism of a Woodrow Wilson or Carl Schurz,[186] in that it expressed hope for a renewal of the political wisdom and morality of the fathers, was traditional by comparison with the "noble vision of race patriotism" that reinterpreted the past more or less openly in terms of instinct psychology. The existential truth of the founders was reduced to the successful actualization of a specifically Anglo-Saxon instinct in history. Logically, then, in this case monumental history presented itself as a natural process of man's evolutionary ascent to the Anglo-Saxon race. The meaning of the American order could be scientifically assured. The expansive dynamic of American society implies the unfolding of the truth of its

182. *Ibid.*, 207–23, 242–46.
183. Here and the following, see Craven, *Legend of the Founding Fathers;* W. E. Davies, *Patriotism on Parade* (Cambridge, Mass., 1955).
184. Nagel, *Sacred Trust,* 247–324.
185. *Ibid.*, 247.
186. *Ibid.*, 281–85.

order in history; fear, doubt, and unrest are resolved in the apocalyptic process. "It is God's great purpose made manifest in the instincts of our race, whose present phase is our personal profit, but whose far-off end is the redemption of the world and the christianization of mankind." For Albert J. Beveridge, the nucleus of the "imperial policy" was thus delineated. "His acceptance of Saxon instinct as fundamental to an inevitable national development made other spokesmen cautious by comparison. Greed and demagoguery would be dangerous, according to Beveridge, only until America's character emerged. This was a biological event, for 'we must obey our blood.' "[187] The "revival of patriotism" that was called for inevitably had to limit itself to organization and indoctrination in order to be effectively socially relevant. The kind of patriotism that emerged was dogmatically rigid, institutionalized, socially isolated. It carried considerable political weight as an answer to the modern age's challenge to the viability and spiritual quality of the American design for existence.

It makes sense that this fear tormented the New Englanders most especially. James Phinney Baxter, president of the New England Historical-Genealogical Society, traditionally identified the "New England Idea" with the "American Idea" and complained that "the New England type of civilisation give way here in Massachusetts to that of the Old World races who have been reared in subjection, ignorance and poverty." But Baxter could counter only with the methods of the cult of the hero: he left $50,000 to the city of Boston with the charge of erecting a "New England Pantheon or Temple of Honour" to celebrate those men "who laid in New England the foundation of popular government."[188] But Boston, in 1921 already strongly under the influence of the Irish Catholics, refused the gift. Millions of immigrants, without a knowledge of the English language, from different cultural milieus, unfamiliar with the rules and possibilities of American politics, vegetated in the slums of the large American cities. Let us recall James Wilson: the free citizen, existentially shaped from the knowledge of justice and freedom, is the precondition of a functioning republican government. These qualities, established society feared, were increasingly lacking in the Republic's new citizens, and the original fear that the American experiment might fail was given new nourishment. Only if these huddled masses could be brought successfully in contact with the founding substance could the experiment be saved.

But first the knowledge of the founding itself had to be salvaged. For this purpose a highly unusual type of civic association was created: the

187. *Ibid.*, 294–95.
188. Quoted in Craven, *Legend of the Founding Fathers*, 166.

patriotic society with hereditary membership on the basis of genealogy. Its objective was "to associate men of a similar ancestry, to teach revered regard for the founders and the patriots, to preserve historical records and monuments, to commemorate appropriate historic events, and to serve other historical and patriotic purposes."[189] Briefly, the most important of these "hereditary societies" are: Sons of the Revolution (1876), Sons of the American Revolution (1889), Daughters of the American Revolution (1890), Colonial Dames of America (1890), Daughters of the Revolution (1891), Daughters of the Cincinnati (1894), Colonial Order of the Acorn (1894), Children of the Revolution (1895), Colonial Daughters of the XVIIth Century (1896), Order of the Descendants of Colonial Governors Prior to 1750 (1896), Order of the Founders and Patriots of America (1896), Society of the American Wars of the United States (1897), Society of Mayflower Descendants (1897), Daughters of the Founders and Patriots of America (1898). The flood tide of these new organizations ended in 1933 with the Descendants of the Colonial Clergy.[190] Sociologically, these groups are the nub of a ruling minority; significantly, they establish American women as a social and political force exclusively on the criterion of sharing in the founding substance.

"Unless there is an eternal readiness to respond with the same faith, the same courage, and the same devotion in the defense of our institutions which where exhibited in their establishment we shall be dispossessed, and others of sterner fiber will seize on our inheritance," declared Calvin Coolidge as honorary president of the United States Flag Association, which, after the First World War, attempted to coordinate all patriotic societies and to mitigate the impact of the Continental European revolution on America.[191]

To the extent that the new immigrants differed from the ruling white Protestant leadership of Anglo-Saxon origins on religious, ethnic, and cultural levels, as well as from the African-American minority and the Indians, who in fact had not been assigned a place in the American universe, they could be integrated into it only by absorbing the American experience through the medium of the founding symbolism. Only this process of a mental Americanization made possible the social and political integration that is tantamount to the end of collective proletarian

---

189. Quoted *ibid.,* 161.

190. *Ibid.,* 158 and *passim;* W. E. Davies, *Patriotism on Parade,* 44–73. This phenomenon began with veterans' associations that provided for inherited membership. But most of the veterans' organizations were in first-line interest groups; the cult of patriotism became their principal purpose only later. We should also remember that the 1880s through 1890s was a time when all sorts of societies sprang into being.

191. Quoted in Craven, *Legend of the Founding Fathers,* 183.

existence in the urban or rural slum. The immigrant accepted this criterion and tried to meet it. He felt deeply injured by the claim "that he had no part in the founding of the country." He suspected that this claim compromised his very dignity as a citizen, implying a lack of respect for his humanity.

"He has accepted the tradition in all its essentials, and he has accepted it by making it his own. In so doing, he has not quarreled with the rules of the game as established by those who played it before him. He agrees that this country owes its greatness to the ideals of those who first established it, and he agrees that it was established some time before 1789." He chose the alternative designated for him by the intellectual structure: "He argues only that his own people were here before that date and that they played the part they should have played."[192] The expansion of the monumental history is carried out in two steps: in the sequence of their emancipation, Irish, Germans, French (Huguenots), Italians, Poles, Asian-Americans, and African-Americans organized themselves into historio-patriotic societies to affirm and document their presence at the beginnings (not without frequently floundering in the maelstrom of mythic romance). Once a sufficient historiographic corpus had come about to legitimate Irishmen, Germans, or blacks as participants—though at times quite marginal ones—in the historic moments of the nation, then society would accept them, albeit grudgingly, and assign them niches in the national pantheon, that is, in the schoolbooks and devotional literature, in the patriotic cults, and in ritual.

Our analysis of the emergence and function of the symbolic apparatus of the self-interpretation of American society from the nexus of founding and order will, in conclusion, be supplemented and, especially as concerns the function on all levels of social life, be confirmed by the results of empirical social research in the first half of the twentieth century. In his work *The Living and the Dead: A Study of the Symbolic Life of Americans* (1959), Lloyd Warner studied the meanings and social functions of the political and historical symbolic system of contemporary America, including in his research all social classes. The focus of Warner's study rests on a community he called Yankee City. It is easy to recognize that this is Newburyport, Massachusetts. To that extent the result has only a limited indicative value, but significantly Warner explains, "The nature of symbolic life in this country is such that, despite of important variations, the basic meanings of our secular and religious symbols are much the same in all regions . . . much of what is learned holds for the

192. *Ibid.,* 167.

rest of the nation."[193] The inventory of the whole apparatus of symbols in connection with its ritual submergence in social processes and complex behavior patterns resulted, according to Warner, in two types of symbolic systems. "Segmentary systems provide the symbolic means to express the sentiments of members within the limited solidarity of autonomous structures" (that is, churches, societies, ethnic groups—also called subcultures). "Integrative systems allow common sentiments present in every one to be expressed, giving participants the necessary symbols to express the unity felt by all members of the community."[194] Warner also called them "private symbols" and "public symbols." "Complex societies must have a common core of basic understanding and used by every one or their complex and diverse symbolic superstructures will not stand. They need general symbol systems that everyone not only knows but feels."[195] What is important for our line of argument is that form, content, and function of the public symbols are perceived exclusively in the shape of the ritual incorporation of the past—in the event of the tricentennial celebration of the city, and especially in the parade organized on this occasion, and in the yearly celebration of Memorial Day, as well as in "the heroic Myths . . . of Lincoln and Washington."[196] The public symbols of the tricentennial "contribute to the integration of all the citizenry for enterprises common and important to the total community."[197] The parade was the symbolic presentation of the *res gestae* and *personae dramatis* of American history under the horizon of Newburyport local history. But it is almost entirely the history of the founding that was presented; the hundred years since 1830 seemed merely a kind of epilogue. It must, of course, be borne in mind that by then the town had lost its former political and economic stature. It remains to be noted that in the social reality of the twentieth century the public symbols must materially and structurally be assigned to monumental history. But their actual effectiveness in the form of specific processes of consciousness also confirms our presentation to this point, as Warner's description of the participants' mental states shows.

> For that moment [of marching past] the lives of those who viewed the spectacle were suspended and timeless. In them the meanings of the Eternal

193. W. L. Warner, *The Living and the Dead: A Study of the Symbolic Life of Americans* (New Haven, Conn., 1959), 4.
194. *Ibid.*, 231.
195. *Ibid.*, 233.
196. *Ibid.*, 234.
197. *Ibid.*, 331.

City of St. Augustine were present. Coming from the past, time moved by them. . . . The meanings of objective time were non-rationally contradicted . . . to those in the stationary reviewing stand their own time stood still. All the scenes were part of one timeless thing. In this symbolic unity the simultaneity of 1630 and 1930 was non-rationally stressed. The great past of the ancestors was evoked and symbolically lived in the present . . . In their diversity [of the images presented] there was logical empirical time; within the non-rational meanings of their unity was the static, fixed quality of being. The timeless sense of species existence, felt as eternity, was present.[198]

Warner exposed the experiential basis to which the symbols owe their existential social function. He described a religious experience—the encounter of man with his ground—by way of a mystic union with the beginnings. The integrating effect of the aggregates of symbols, it seems to me, results from the collectively experienced tension with the shared origins. The ceremonies of Memorial Day are, according to Warner, "rituals comprising a sacred symbol system which functions periodically to integrate the whole community with its conflicting symbols and its opposing, autonomous churches and associations." The cult of the dead allows a "sacred unity" to be experienced. Its "principal themes are those of the sacrifice of the soldier dead for the living and the obligation of the living to sacrifice their individual purposes for the good of the group so that they, too, can perform their spiritual obligations."[199] The *bonum*, however, is the realization of the "Fathers' heritage," Washington and Lincoln's; from it stems the obligation. Warner's concluding description shows once again that the ritual practice of Memorial Day in turn represents a collective meditation toward the ground of being *sub specie mortis* in the medium of the symbolism of society's self-interpretation: "The Memorial Day rite . . . dramatically expresses the sentiments of unity of all the living among themselves, of all the living with all the dead, and of all the living and dead as a group with God. God, as worshiped by Catholic, Protestant, and Jew, loses sectarian definition, limitations, and foreignness as between different customs and becomes the common object of worship for the whole group and the protector of everyone"[200]—for, as a highly judicial formula words it, "we are a religious people whose institutions presuppose a Supreme Being."[201]

This state of affairs was also worked out by Supreme Court Justice

198. *Ibid.*, 223.
199. *Ibid.*, 248–49.
200. *Ibid.*, 279.
201. E. S. Corwin, *The Constitution and What It Means Today* (Princeton, 1948), 193.

Felix Frankfurter in his opinion in *Minersville* v. *Gobitis,* in which symbols of theory coincide with those of the American self-interpretation. The decision empowers state legislatures to force schoolchildren by law to participate in the ritual of saluting the flag. "National unity is the basis of national security."[202] But what is decisive is not the unity of public order, of the state and social apparatus; rather, "the ultimate foundation of a free society is the binding tie of cohesive sentiment. Such sentiment is fostered by all those agencies of the mind and spirit which may serve to gather up the traditions of a people, transmit them from generation to generation of a people, and thereby create that continuity of a treasured common life which constitutes a civilisation."[203] The "national cohesion" flows from the "common life," the *xynon.* From this premise it follows, just as the necessity of measures followed in James Wilson's 1790 argument, "to evoke that unifying sentiment without which there can ultimately be no liberties, civil or religious."[204] For "only a persistent translation of the faith of a free society into the convictions and habits and actions of a community is the ultimate reliance against unabated temptations to fetter the human spirit."[205]

But after this precise definition of the problem of translating the intellectual substance of order into behavior, Frankfurter once again referred to the only method America knew to accomplish this end—the experience underlying the American design for existence can be revitalized only through national symbolism: "We live by symbols." The medium in which the experience of order becomes visible is considered its source. Thus Frankfurter granted the local authorities the right to use the salute to the flag in order to establish compulsory "training of children in patriotic impulses" and a "subtle process of securing effective loyalty to the traditional ideals of democracy."[206] "The flag is the symbol of our national unity, transcending all internal differences . . . it signifies government resting on consent of the governed; liberty regulated by law; the protection of the weak against the strong; security against the exercise of arbitrary power; and absolute safety for free institutions against foreign aggression"[207]—in other words, the sum of the doctrines, institutions, and behaviors that were given in the origins and that found their realiza-

---

202. *Minersville School District* v. *Gobitis* (1939), 310 *U.S. Supreme Court Reports,* 595.
203. *Ibid.,* 596.
204. *Ibid.,* 597.
205. Frankfurter, Dissenting Opinion, *West Virginia State Board of Education* v. *Barnette* (1943), 319 *U.S. Supreme Court Reports,* 671.
206. *Minersville School District* v. *Gobitis* (1939), 310 *U.S. Supreme Court Reports,* 598.
207. *Ibid.,* 596.

tion in the specific American context. But neither Frankfurter nor those who dissented from his opinion reflected on whether a "universal gesture of respect for the symbol of our national life" alone could in the long run guarantee education for the "common life." There is no indication of an alternative, or at least supplementary, method of meditation to reactivate the symbols of motivating experience. The horizon of experience is limited to the traditional meanings and contexts. Both Justice Harlan Stone's dissenting opinion in the Minersville case and the majority decision in *West Virginia State Board of Education* v. *Barnette,* which overturned Frankfurter's ruling, subscribe to Frankfurter's theoretical premise, objecting merely to the compulsory performance of a patriotic rite in a public school: first, on constitutional grounds, since it goes counter to the First Amendment and Section 2 of the Fourteenth Amendment, which guaranteed the religious freedom of the plaintiffs (who were Jehovah's Witnesses); and second, from common-sense considerations: patriotism as a binding routine, an encroachment on intellectual freedom, presents a danger to national unity and cohesion.[208]

VI. On the Concept of Civil Theology

The American self-interpretation fused the cult of the hero and monumental history, Christian spirituality, philosophical and political doctrines of the Enlightenment with very concrete behavior patterns, institutional arrangements and social practices into a whole encompassing all of man's existence in society and history. In spite of all its vagueness, blurredness, and amorphousness, it always appeared with the claim of truth. The symbolism of this "patriotic faith" or "social myth" encompasses the dominant field of consciousness of organized society.

Tocqueville treated this situation at length. No society, he noted, exists "without such common belief . . . for without ideas held in common there is no common action, and, without common action there may still be men, but there is no social body. In order that society should exist and, *a fortiori,* that a society should prosper, it is necessary that the minds of all the citizens should be rallied and held together by certain predominant ideas."[209] For, he went on, there is hardly any human activity "that does not originate in some very general idea men have conceived of the Deity, of his relation to mankind, of the nature of their own souls, and of their duties to their fellow creatures."[210] In the American case this meant that

208. Majority Opinion of the Court, *West Virginia State Board of Education* v. *Barnette* (1943), 319 *U.S. Supreme Court Reports,* 625–42.
209. A. de Tocqueville, *Democracy in America,* ed. P. Bradley (New York, 1945), II, 9.
210. *Ibid.,* 21.

"almost all the inhabitants of the United States use their minds in the same manner, and direct them according to the same rules; that is to say, without ever having taken the trouble to define the rules, they have a philosophical method common to the whole people."[211] But this eighteenth-century philosophical method rests on a strong basis. One must not forget, Toqueville pointed out, "that religion gave birth to Anglo-American society. In the United States, religion is therefore mingled with all the habits of the nation and all the feelings of patriotism, whence it derives a peculiar force."[212] The twentieth-century observer is presented with a picture that has not changed: "America . . . has the most explicitly expressed system of general ideals in reference to human inter-relationships. . . . The American Creed is not merely—as in some other countries—the implicit background of the nation's political and judicial order as it functions. . . . It is the cement in the structure of this great and disparate nation."[213] Sidney E. Mead takes the title of his essay on American self-interpretation from Chesterton's characterization of the United States as "a nation with the soul of a church." By analogy, it is a spiritual core, without which the American nation cannot understand itself as such. A definitive element of this spiritual core "is the conception of a universal principle which is thought to transcend and include all the national and religious particularities brought to it [the nation] by the people who come from all the world to be 'Americanized.'"[214]

But Mead ignores the question of spiritual experience by considering the spiritual core synonymous with the "religion of the republic," which confines him to the level of symbolism. To determine the nature of this "American religion," he has recourse to a "cosmopolitan, inclusive, universal theology" of the founders. Their "theology of the synergistic and theonomous religion" beyond the specific Christian denominations constitutes for him almost the "invisible church" of the national *corpus mysticum,* incarnate in a "cosmopolitan commonwealth."[215] But the analysis of central components of self-understanding made these absolute in the concept of the "theonomous cosmopolitism" and led to the one-sided assertion that "the religion of the Republic is essentially prophetic, which is to say that its ideals and aspirations stand in constant judgment over the passing shenanigans of the people, reminding them of the standards

211. *Ibid.,* 3.
212. *Ibid.,* 6.
213. G. Myrdal, *An American Dilemma* (New York, 1944), 3. Characteristically, Myrdal begins his study with a detailed account of the "American creed," pp. 3–25.
214. S. E. Mead, "The Nation with the Soul of a Church," *Church History,* XXXVI (1967), 273.
215. *Ibid.,* 270, 282.

by which their current practices and those of their nation are ever being judged and found wanting."[216] The genuine public-political dimension of any paradigm of social order has vanished under Mead's hand. For this reason it is tempting to describe the American self-understanding by using Robert Bellah's borrowing from Rousseau: "civil religion." Bellah describes the situation as we have already come to recognize it: "What we have, then, from the earliest years of the republic is a collection of beliefs, symbols, and rituals with respect to sacred things, and institutionalized in a collectivity."[217] This writer, too, noted that the civil religion is neither synonymous with Christianity in its various guises nor a replacement for Christianity. His examination of proclamations and public messages from George Washington to John F. Kennedy lists the decisive elements of the order of symbols: "The God of the civil religion is not only rather 'unitarian,' he is also on the austere side, much more related to order, law, and right than to salvation and love."[218] This civil religion is marked by "biblical archetypes": "Exodus, Chosen People, Promised Land, New Jerusalem, Sacrificial Death and Rebirth. But it is also genuinely American and genuinely new. . . . It is concerned that America be a society as perfectly in accord with the will of God as men can make it, and a light to all the nations."[219] But Bellah raised the crucial point that the separation of church and state "has not denied the political realm a religious dimension." "Certain common elements of religious orientation . . . still provide a religious dimension for the whole fabric of American life, including the political sphere."[220] Bellah also understood completely that a social self-interpretation owes its social function to the underlying experiences: "civil religion at its best is a genuine apprehension of universal and transcendent religious reality as seen in, or, one could almost say, as revealed through the experience of the American people."[221]

But it remains questionable whether the term *religion* is not burdened by a multiplicity of connotations; furthermore, it does not seem to express sufficiently the specific nature of the social field of consciousness of an organized society, as the term *civil* is meant to express. Similar problems arise with the use of the concept of the "public philosophy," which Walter Lippman and John C. Murray proposed. Murray listed a triple function for the "ensemble of truths that makes up the public consensus

216. *Ibid.*, 275.
217. R. N. Bellah, "Civil Religion in America," *Daedalus*, XCVI (1967), 8.
218. *Ibid.*, 7.
219. *Ibid.*, 18.
220. *Ibid.*, 3–4.
221. *Ibid.*, 12.

or philosophy." First, it determines "the broad purposes of our nation as a political unity organized for action in history." This purpose is a moral act. Second, it sets "the standards to which judgement is to be passed on the means that the nation adopts to further its purposes." These measures determine the area of the "policy." Third, the public philosophy creates "the basis of communication between government and the people and among the people themselves." "It furnishes a common universe of discourse in which public issues can be intelligibly stated and intelligently argued."[222] But in its origin, content, and function, public philosophy is not identical with philosophy as the source of order for concrete consciousness, in which the *realissimum* is meditatively disclosed. Rather, the secondary phenomenon of communicating concepts of order, designs for existence, and the like, is addressed to an organized society as its carrying self-interpretation. I therefore consider the concept of civil theology, a phrase coined in antiquity for this phenomenon, more appropriate.[223]

Before we continue to explore the concept, we must point out the insufficiency of some current social-science ideas. This is especially true for the concept of ideology. Insofar as it is understood as an "untrue" mode of consciousness and symbolism, with the assigned function of occasional or permanent legitimation of power, social self-understanding with critical intention may, in principle, correctly or incorrectly come under "suspicion of ideology" or even lose any element of truth, like any other symbolism and its attendant forms of consciousness.[224] In any case, the term does not adequately describe the social field of consciousness predominant in any society when it deals with its symbolic explication. The structural-functional generalization of the concept, therefore, remains merely a "general system of beliefs held in common by the members of a collectivity."[225] A similar objection applies to Philip Converse's substitution of "belief system": "We define belief systems as a configuration of ideas and attitudes in which the elements are bound together by some form of constraint or functional interdependence."[226] C. J. Fried-

222. J. C. Murray, *We Hold These Truths* (New York, 1960), 80–81. Compare also W. Lippmann, *The Public Philosophy* (London, 1955), 97 ff.

223. Compare W. W. Jaeger, *Theologie der frühen griechischen Denker* (Darmstadt, 1964), 9–17; E. Voegelin, *Die Neue Wissenschaft der Politik* (Munich, 1959), 125ff., and E. Voegelin, *Anamnesis* (Munich, 1966), 342; E. Sandoz, "The Civil Theology of Liberal Democracy: Locke and His Predecessors," *Journal of Politics*, XXXIV (1972), 2–36.

224. Compare K. Lenk, ed., *Ideologie* (2nd ed.; Neuweid, 1964), 17–59; J. R. Plamenatz, *Ideology* (London, 1970).

225. T. Parsons, *The Social System* (Glencoe, Ill., 1951), 349; C. Geertz, "Ideology as a Cultural System," in *Ideology and Discontent*, ed. D. E. Apter (London, 1964).

226. P. E. Converse, "The Nature of Belief Systems in Mass Publics," in *Ideology and Discontent*, 207.

rich attempts to recapture the dimension of organized society by establishing a limitation: "Ideologies are sets of ideas related to the existing
political and social and intended either to change it or to defend it."[227]
But "action-related systems of ideas" are symbol aggregates inherent to
the respective symbolic order, insofar as all social existence is permanently in flux. This attempt, however, reifies sets of symbols into objects
and reduces them more or less at will to functional aggregates whose
meaning must be determined arbitrarily by the observer, since the symbols lose transparency for their own structural meaning to the degree that
they are divested of their character as medium of the interpretation of
human existence in society and history in experienced participation in an
overarching reality. Only this substratum of motivating experience reveals the structure of symbolisms and permits an evaluation of their loss
of meaning by the erosion of the psychosocial foundation. The elimination of consciousness as the center of order, from which symbol forms
become understandable, compels us to assign an external order to symbol
constructs as "systems." This is most especially true for the interpretations of order and self that imbue an organized society; such interpretations always appear empirically as interpretations of the total existence
of the members of the society, including the organizational structures for
safeguarding physical existence—that is, of production and regeneration.

Before resuming our reflections, the "political culture approach"
needs to be touched on briefly. For on the basis of its claim, this conception seems to take into account the objections raised here. After all, it is
defined as the "psychological dimension of the political system" and its
content determined by "attitudes, beliefs, values, and skills which are
current in an entire population."[228] Lucian W. Pye—along with Gabriel
Almond, Sumner C. Powell, and Sidney Verba one of the protagonists of
this attempt—makes an argument that seems plausible at first glance in
view of the findings at hand: "in any operating political system there is
an ordered subjective realm of politics which gives meaning to the polity,
discipline to institutions, and social relevance to individual acts. The concept of political culture thus suggests that the traditions of a society, the
spirit of its public institutions, the passions and the collective reasoning
of its citizenry, and the style and operating codes of its leaders are not
just random products of historical experience but fit together as a part of
a meaningful whole and constitute an intelligible web of relations." "In
essence, thus, political culture, as Verba indicates . . . , consists of the
system of empirical beliefs, expressive symbols, and values which define

227. C. J. Friedrich, *Man and His Government* (New York, 1963), 89.
228. G. A. Almond *et al.*, *Comparative Politics* (Boston, 1966), 23.

the situation in which political action takes place. It encompasses both the political ideals and the operating norms of a polity."[229] "A political culture . . . has deep emotional dimensions involving the passions of loyalty and community identity, the sentiments of human and geographical attachment."[230]

In these statements the political culture seems unequivocally bound up with the self-understanding of society to the extent that this is essential for its organization and, as the dominant interpretation of the whole existence of man in society, communicates meaningful order explicated in the language and actions of concrete individuals. But the impression is deceptive, for Pye explains: "In sum, political culture provides structure and meaning to the political sphere in the same manner as culture in general gives coherence and integration to social life."[231] Political culture is reduced to the political dimension of social existence: "The concept makes it easier for us to separate the cultural aspect of politics from other aspects (as well as the political culture from other forms of culture) and to subject it to more detailed and systematic analysis."[232] Our analysis of the American self-understanding thus far clearly shows that such a separation is empirically impossible and methodologically absurd.

> The distinction between political culture and the more general cultural system of a society is an analytical one. Political culture is an integral aspect of more general culture, the set of political beliefs an individual holds, being of course part of the totality of the beliefs he holds. Furthermore the basic belief and value patterns of a culture—those values that have no reference to specific political objects—usually play a major role in the structuring of political culture. Such basic belief dimensions as the view of man's relation to nature, time perspective, as the view of human nature and of the proper way to orient toward one's fellow man, as well as orientation toward activity and activism in general would clearly interdepend with specifically political attitudes. . . . The focus on the relationship between basic belief structure and political beliefs is of great use in determining what political attitudes are important to consider in describing a political culture.

Without considering this positivistic linguistic rubble more closely, we may note that all those forms of consciousness and symbolism that are empirically essential to social self-understanding do *not* fall under this

229. L. W. Pye and S. Verba, eds., *Political Culture and Political Development* (Princeton, 1965), 7–8.
230. *Ibid.*, 9.
231. *Ibid.*, 8.
232. *Ibid.*, 515.

original conceptualization of political culture. "Though political culture is closely connected with other aspects of the cultural system the analytical separation from general culture of those values, cognitions, and expressive states with political objects is useful." [233] The question is merely: for whom?

The attempt by Almond, Verba, Powell, and others to make the concept operational reveals the implications of this dissociation of political culture from culture in general. "We can speak of a political culture just as we can speak of an economic culture or a religious culture. It is a set of orientations toward a special set of social objects and processes." [234] The existential realm of man (in society and history) is reduced to the Hobbesian relationship structure of things to each other. "The political culture of a nation is the particular distribution of patterns of orientation toward political objects among the members of the nation." [235]

Elsewhere mention is made of a "pattern of individual attitudes and orientations toward politics among the members of a political system." [236] The discussion deals with a subject-object relation between the individual in his cognitive, affective, and evaluative subjectivity on one hand and in his orientation to an object projected as "political sphere," "political system," "political objects," "entire scope of political activities" on the other. This realm of the political is concretized in the institutions of public domination, separate structures, and roles of public authority, as well as the "self" of the individual as political actor. In this last example the quantifiable subject-object relation of the knowing, feeling, and judging individual to himself, now presented as political activity, becomes a case of split personality. This construction is meaningful, of course, only with the assumption that reality is system-forming and that the structure of relations has the nature of a system and through this in turn receives the appearance of order, that is, the order qua system. The premise of system formality, however, is by no means sufficient to answer the question about calling a system area "politics." The declaration of system units as political is achieved not system-immanently but decisionally. Dirk Berg-Schlosser summed up the system-analytical, structure-functional concept of politics: "The basic unity of a political system is political action, whereby all those actions of a society are seen as political that concern the legitimate, authoritative decisions that affect at least potentially all members of a society. The application of this decision through public

233. *Ibid.*, 521–23.
234. G. A. Almond and S. Verba, *The Civic Culture* (Boston, 1965), 12.
235. *Ibid.*, 14.
236. Almond *et al.*, *Comparative Politics*, 50.

organs is marked by the monopoly of legitimate physical force."[237] Berg-Schlosser, however, does not demonstrate with sufficient clarity that this concept of politics, wherever and however it is formulated by the adherents of the various structure-functional and system-analytic schools, always represents no more than a paraphrase of Max Weber. Any attempt at an analysis of "the political" ends with a reformulation of Weber's concept of politics in the guise of power, domination, and state as essential forms.[238]

I am concerned here not merely with the paradoxical situation governing the theoretical definition of political reality, but also with the fact that a system-analytical or structure-functional paradigm of political science was never capable of attempting such a theoretical definition. The same is true for Berg-Schlosser's expansion of the "purely system-related concept of the 'political,'" which he considered too narrow. "All those attitudes and values found in a society are . . . therefore to be understood as political which, directly or indirectly, play a part in the process of authoritative, public decisions."[239]

To comprehend the heuristic value of political culture, we must examine the concept in the context of Weber's definition of "politics." What is meant is the measurable pattern of "political orientations" (also, by the

---

237. D. Berg-Schlosser, "Die Erforschung 'politischen Kultur'" (Ph.D. dissertation, Munich, 1971), 42. This study provides an extensive and critical introduction to the problems of "political culture."

238. For example, Almond *et al.* claim that the special identity of a political system consists in the fact "that its relation to coercion is its distinctive quality" (*Comparative Politics*, 18). This is a paraphrase of M. Weber's "state" or "political association." D. Easton, *The Political System* (New York, 1939), 134, 146, states: "My point is . . . that the property of a social act that informs it with a political aspect is the act's relation to the authoritative allocation of values for a society." And, "Political Science is the study of the authoritative allocation of values as it is influenced by the distribution and use of power." Here the emphasis has shifted away from Weber's concept of domination. K. W. Deutsch, *The Nerves of Government* (Glencoe, Ill., 1966), 254, writes: "we define the core area of politics as the area of enforceable decisions, or more accurately of all decisions backed by some combination of a significant probability of enforcement." R. Dahl, *Modern Political Analysis* (Englewood Cliffs, N.J., 1963), 6, claims: "A political system is any persistent pattern of human relationships that involves, to a significant extent, power, rule, or authority." And R. C. Macridis and B. B. Brown, *Comparative Politics* (3rd ed.; Homewood, Ill., 1968), 1, contend that "a political system is, above all, a mechanism for the making of decisions. It is endowed with legitimacy, that is, decisions made by the various organs of Government are expected to be widely obeyed." Deutsch, Dahl, and Macridis and Brown stick closely to Weber's phenomenology of power, state, and domination. Compare the relevant passages in M. Weber, *Wirtschaft und Gesellschaft* (Cologne, 1964), I, 38–39; II, 695–96, 1042–43.

239. Berg-Schlosser, "Erforschung 'politischen Kultur,'" 95.

way, a term in Weber's concept of social action)—that is, "attitudes" and "values" held by individual members of society insofar as they relate to the area of government (to use Weber's phrasing) altogether and its organizational subsections (institutions, persons, and decisions) as well as to the perception of the role of the individual as active and passive participant in political life, in Weber's words, or, to use Almond's terminology, "the self as political actor."[240] The distinction, taken over by Edward Shils and Talcott Parsons, of an intellectual, emotional, and judgmental component of such orientations takes its beginnings from the model of a reductionist psychology without personal center and proves useless in the empirical experience of the actual case. "In his actual typology Almond drops this differentiation silently."[241] Finally, the concept of political culture includes that sector of the dominant plausibility structures that is limited by the institutional sphere of public order both representatively and explicitly as regards the tools and methods of empirical social science. In this framework the study of political culture furnishes valuable material for the analysis of social self-understanding. Besides this obvious methodological limitation of an empirically existent social self-understanding, its main component—that is, the interpretation of man's whole existence, which is explicitly assigned the nature of a basic condition—remains outside the grasp of studies in political culture. Furthermore, the concept suffers under the positivistic syndrome of the reification of psyche, consciousness, and symbol. The psychic dimension of "consciousness" is refused its essential function as the center of order, and the total sphere of the motivating experiences, especially those of nonobjective reality, must by definition be omitted from the analysis. With reference to new nationhood and the question of national identity, Berg-Schlosser also noted, "In the last resort it is only a certain 'intellectual' unity which concerns the solidarity of certain intellectual, emotional, and judgmental attitudes toward a shared object, the nation, which can be taken as the ultimate criterion for the definition of being a nation."[242] But correct as this insight is, no theoretical conclusions are developed from it; the discussion is limited to measuring the variables of "feeling of belonging together"; the essential connection of substantial solidarity through essential experiences of order is not examined.

A similar problem arises in a subsequent contribution by Pye:

240. Weber, *Wirtschaft und Gesellschaft*, II, 1100; Almond and Verba, *Civic Culture*, 16.
241. Berg-Schlosser, "Erforschung 'politischen Kultur,'" 54.
242. *Ibid.*, 104.

The concept of political culture does imply that there is an underlying and latent coherence in political life. Among political scientists there has been a long-standing acceptance of the idea of such a basic and implicit force in human societies. . . . At the same time political scientists tend to treat such underlying forces as being somewhat vague and only a determining factor at the extremes of behavior—it is accepted that within the limits of the constitutional consensus, that is of the political culture, there can be a fair variety of behavior that is still "consistent," and hence culturally acceptable.

These sentences, Pye's contribution to the unsolved problems of the concept of political culture, confirm the paradoxical nature of the attempt, for the "underlying forces" of intellectual solidarity would have to be the onset of a revised and broadened concept of political culture if this is to encompass all the dimensions of societal self-understanding and not merely the "constitutional consensus," that is, explicit opinions on "politics" in Weber's spirit.[243] This argument suggests that the analysis penetrates to the civil-religious or civil-theological core of any political culture.

My presentation of the material so far should have made it clear that from the first I placed the weight of the study on presenting the constituents of the "underlying and latent coherence in political life" of American society. An explication of the theoretical background of the foregoing inquiry is necessary only to the extent that the choice of the term "civil theology" needs further justification and that the theoretical implications of the concept must be briefly developed. The attempt at such an elaboration takes its bearings from the analyses of the social world carried out by Alfred Schütz and his students as well as the works of Eric Voegelin, who undertook the integration of these analyses into a theory of political reality under the contemporary horizon of the scientific experience of man and beyond dogmatic reifications.

In continuing the work of Max Weber, Edmund Husserl, and Max Scheler, Schütz showed that before there is any social science, the social world has a meaningful structure for those who live in it. "Now this same social world which we immediately experience as meaningful is also meaningful from the standpoint of the social scientist."[244] The methodical study of the "meaningful structures within the social world," the discovery of its basic elements, as well as the boundaries of the individ-

243. L. W. Pye, "Culture and Political Science," *Social Science Quarterly,* LII (1972), 296.

244. A. Schütz, *Der Sinnhafte Aufbau der sozialen Welt* (2nd ed.; Vienna, 1960), 7 (English from A. Schütz, *Phenomenology of the Social World,* trans. G. Walsh and F. Lehnert [Evanston, Ill., 1967], 10).

ual and separate layers subsequently engaged Schütz and his followers and resulted in important contributions to the analysis of social self-understanding. The volume *The Problem of Social Reality* in Schütz's *Collected Papers,* as well as the works by Thomas Luckmann and Peter Berger, furnishes a number of insights germane to our purpose precisely because the perplexities that emerge compel further theoretical penetration of the problem. If the research on "political culture" leaves the constituent elements of a significant construction of the social sphere methodologically uninferable and therefore mere speculation along social-science common-sense lines, for Schütz and his followers the phenomenon of meaningful construction forms the beginning of their analysis of social order as well as of its underlying pattern of consciousness and symbolism. The phenomenology of social reality, following Husserl, starts from the social reality par excellence, the reality of everyday life: "Everyday life presents itself as reality interpreted by men and subjectively meaningful to them as a coherent world. . . . I apprehend the reality of everyday life as an ordered reality. Its phenomena are prearranged in patterns that be independent of my apprehension of them upon the latter. . . . The reality of everyday life is organized around the 'here' of my body and the 'now' of my present. This 'here' and 'now' is the focus of my attention to the reality of everyday life. What is the 'here' and 'now' presented to me in everyday life is the realissimum of my consciousness." The everyday world I share with others is a commonsense world; its "fabrics of meaning," without which society cannot exist, are commonsense knowledge that structures the social reality of everyday life according to self-evident criteria of the relevance of social action for the individual members of society. Individual participation in the commonsense world of everyday life is shaped according to the shared participation in the available social stock of knowledge, which may assume quite different forms for the individual members of society, from marginal participation to extensive power of disposing over the pool. Commonsense knowledge is largely pragmatic knowledge of order.[245] In this knowledge, past experiences are deposited like sediments, furnishing patterns of interpretation for individual experience, primarily those of the everyday world. This always occurs in the medium of language; through it they become my biographical experiences "ongoing subsumed under general orders of meaning, that are both objectively and subjectively real."[246]

245. P. L. Berger and T. Luckmann, *The Social Construction of Reality* (New York, 1966), 19, 21, 22, 42–45. Compare also Schütz, *Collected Papers,* I, 7–26, 207–28, 341–42, and *passim.*
246. Berger and Luckmann, *Social Construction,* 39.

Occasionally Schütz applies Scheler's term *relative natural weltan-schauung* to this knowledge; the "natural attitude" of commonsense practices underlies this term. It implies symbolization, of necessity—that is, because it is a subjectively meaningful interpretation of a shared social world that transcends the immediate experience of a concrete person here and now (in his fellow men, for example). For Schütz, symbolization constitutes among other things the complex of organized society [247] insofar as its members experience the commonsense world as specific transcendence, that is, as society. This symbolic form is a construct of common sense, and at the same time it explains a reality beyond the commonsense world, though the symbols in turn refer to it in that they motivate our actions in it.[248] Schütz calls this the "symbolic appresentation of society." This analysis exhibits a certain contradictoriness, which is probably grounded in its phenomenological roots and which will be briefly explicated in what follows. The commonsense world of everyday life is a finite province of meaning (in James's sense) in which is inherent an "immanent transcendence" (fellow man); this does not require symbolization but can make do with appresentation of a lesser order (marks, indications, signs). The meaningfulness of this world, the thing that constitutes its reality, is grounded in the highest possible level of conscious life, the "wide awakeness" of the "working self." It is fully turned toward life: "It lives within its acts and its attention is of the working self traces out that the segment of the world which is pragmatically relevant, and these relevances determine the form and content of our stream and thought." "Working acts" of the *ego agens* constitute a meaningful context of communication, that is, the commonsense practice of everyday life.[249]

Berger and Luckmann interpret the privileged position of the everyday world: "The tension of consciousness is highest in everyday life, that is, the latter imposes itself in the most massive, urgent and intensive matter . . . it forces me to be attentive to it the fullest way. I experience everyday life in the state of being wideawake. This wideawake state of existing in and apprehending the reality of everyday life is taken by me to be normal and selfevident, that is, it constitutes my natural attitude."[250] Schütz now saw only too clearly that though empirically commonsense practice as a shared reality of the "working selves" actually is "paramount reality" in the immediate "face-to-face" experience, it

247. Schütz, *Collected Papers*, I, 353.
248. Schütz, *ibid.*, 331 and 343, defines "symbolization" as an interpretive reflection on the contents of experience of transcendence of the "here" and "now" of the everyday world.
249. *Ibid.*, 212–13.
250. Berger and Luckmann, *Social Construction*, 21.

merely describes a plurality of biographically determined social situations, the sum of which by no means makes up the social world: "the We-relation, although originating in the mutual biographical involvement, transcends the existence of either of the consociates in the realm of everyday life. It belongs to a finite province of meaning other than that of the reality of everyday life and can be grasped only by symbolization."[251] "Society," that is, a shared social world overarching the everyday worlds, is a permanent experience of transcendence of a specific kind, a province of meaning whose characteristic symbol forms are needed to confer reality on the order of organized society. As noted above, Schütz named this situation "symbolic appresentation of society" and described it as a special case of the constitution of such provinces of meaning, which take their meaning from experiences of transcendence, that is, from beyond the everyday world. This remains as the archetype of experience of reality, since Schütz is unwilling to grant all other provinces of meaning ("dream," "religion," "science," "politics") anything more than modifications.[252] Such provinces of meaning come into being through an experience shock that compels us to break through the boundaries of the provinces of meaning of the everyday world to constitute a province of meaning of transcendence experience, whose realities are explicated through symbolization in the commonsense world. Schütz describes this process as a "leap" in consciousness, modifying the *attention à la vie* and in its content suspending in whole or in part belief in the evidence of the reality of the everyday world.[253] This construction presupposes a phenomenological concept of reality that grants to all concrete experience of transcendence only the nature of subjective meaning and is willing to acknowledge a *realissimum* only in the "here" and "now" of the immediate experience of social action. The reality content of the transcendence experience laid out meaningfully in symbols is disputed (it is a "quasi-reality"), though the analysis itself by no means justifies such a decision. This holds true in particular for the symbolic appresentation of society, since the "symbolic universe" society, even according to Schütz, is an integral and essential element of that social world. If Schütz's analysis were strictly followed, consciousness would constantly be found in the leap within the province of meaning called politics, so that society would be beyond the "paramount reality" of the everyday world. From this it would follow that in principle the "wideawakeness" of the "working self" cannot be the paradigm of a form of consciousness that confers

251. Schütz, *Collected Papers*, I, 218.
252. *Ibid.*, 232.
253. *Ibid.*, 233.

community and meaning; on the contrary, a "wideawake self" is articulated only in the symbolic explication of transcendence experience, at least in that of society.

The assumption becomes compelling that the "working self" need not absolutely be that form of conscious life that constitutes the significance of the commonsense world. This idea leads to the thought that everyday life can be described phenomenologically as the "paramount reality" simply because it is so in a psychosocial sense for the members of society, but that they find the meaning of their social existence as well in the everyday world in the transcending experiences of reality, and that it is only this circumstance that allows men to consciously order the various spheres of their social existence. The everyday world of common sense would thus become a dimension of social existence whose respective sense and relevance structures are determined by overarching interpretations of reality. Schütz tacitly acknowledges the aporias concerning the symbolic appresentation of society only to the extent that he took over for this realm Voegelin's analysis of specific appresentation of social and political organizations.[254] The consequence, the concept of the self-interpretation of political society, will engage our attention below.

On several crucial points Berger and Luckmann also appear able to resolve the aporia in the concept of the symbolic appresentation of society by reconstructing a process they call "social construction of reality." Here, then, the paramount reality of the world of daily life is seen from the aspect of total society from the first. Schütz's distinction between the everyday world and society no longer consists of membership in different provinces of meaning. Although symbolization continues to be a reflection of transcendence on the experience of the everyday world, symbolism has become an integral structural element of this dimension: "Language is capable not only of constructing symbols that are highly abstracted from everyday experience, but also of 'bringing back' these symbols and appresenting them as objectively real elements in everyday life. In this manner, symbolism and symbolic language become essential constituents of the reality of everyday life and of the commonsense apprehension of this reality. I live in a world of signs and symbols every day."[255] Symbolization coordinates the experience of a world of multiple realities. Consciousness continues to move by shifting its attention—the shock or leap—in the provinces of meaning beyond the everyday world, but here these are described more precisely as enclaves within the paramount reality of everyday life: "Enclaves . . . marked by circumscribed

254. *Ibid.*, 336, 355.
255. Berger and Luckmann, *Social Construction*, 40–41.

meanings and mode of experience. The paramount reality envelops them on all sides, as it were, and consciousness always returns to the paramount reality as from an excursion."[256] The phenomenon of multiple realities within and beyond the everyday world leads secondarily to a strictly societal definition of reality: "a stable symbolic canopy for the entire society."[257] "Symbolic universes . . . integrate different provinces of meaning and encompass the institutional order in a symbolic totality."[258] The symbolic universe is comprehended as "the matrix of all socially objectivated and subjectively real meanings."[259] "Experiences belonging to different spheres of reality are integrated by incorporation in the same, overarching universe of meaning."[260] The problem of the provinces of meaning is solved for the purpose by noting that a symbolic universe guarantees for society a common structure of plausibility, though it is assumed that its reality is constructed exclusively on the social level, that is, that the symbolic explication of experiences does not make any statement about its content as such. The symbolic structure has merely a functionally ordering character, not a substantial one; it is secondary in that concrete consciousness and its experience of order do not stand at its point of origin but rather a new version of the "working self." The symbolic universe is a subsequent interpretation of institutional complexes, but according to Berger and Luckmann, it is not related to the process of institutionalization, of "founding," in its inception; it is not present *ab initio*.[261]

Since symbolization can arise, not from an authentic experience of reality, but only as the final step in the legitimation process of institutional order, and since, conversely, Berger and Luckmann must assume meaningfulness inherent in the founding of institutional order, the cause of the meaning of any social beginning by the *ego agens* must be sought elsewhere. Berger and Luckmann find it in a conception of institutionalization that is a variation of Schütz's formulation of the *ego agens*. Both unconditionally claim the meaningful nature of individual social action. But Berger and Luckmann see it as constituting not only the everyday world but also institutional order, that is, the social world of society.

The habituation of individual social action, according to Berger and Luckmann, automatically produces something like shared meaning, which furnishes the basis for institutionalization processes. But such in-

256. *Ibid.*, 25.
257. *Ibid.*, 86.
258. *Ibid.*, 95.
259. *Ibid.*, 96.
260. *Ibid.*, 97.
261. *Ibid.*, 99.

stitutionalization of social interaction presumes a common pattern of consciousness and symbolism. Empirically, the meaning of action is the self-interpretation of the actor, and institutionalization requires collectivity in self-interpretation, including the motivating experiences, so that action in the sense described can be institutionalized. The symbol ordering of a society, then, is also necessary from the outset as consciousness, and the founder as symbolic for present rather than secondary legitimation of institutional order against the onslaught of the chaos of multiple realities.

This critique returns us to the theory of the founding in which the aporia of a phenomenological theory of institutionalization is proved. This is also evident as regards the discussion of overlapping designs for existence within a symbolic universe, with the extreme case being a conflict in which divergent interpretations take the field in the battle for social representation. Although Berger and Luckmann limit their inquiry to the modern case of a revolutionary ideologue who forces his deviant conception—his symbolic subuniverse—on society as a symbolic universe,[262] and though in analyzing historical transformation of symbolic universes they fall back on a vague historical-speculative sequence of phases of consciousness,[263] their analysis of the social construction of reality is headed toward the question of the motivating experiences required to constitute social reality as meaningful order qua symbolic universe.

The phenomenology of social reality decodes the structure relations of the meaningful composition of the social world as a psychosocial symbolic universe grounded in consciousness, which unites the physical existence of concrete individuals in a shared objective reality experienced as ordered and meaningful beyond the realm of immediate provision (the realm of necessity) to such an extent that the form of order of political society acquires historical existence. To put it in Schütz's terms, the pattern of the transcendence experience, which is essential to the province of meaning or world of politics, is synonymous with the symbolic appresentation of society.

The analysis leaves open the content and structure of the motivating experiences, since reality is defined only by meaningful experience but is not described as structured as far as its content is concerned. Since the problem cannot be ignored, Schütz immediately introduces the basic ex-

262. *Ibid.*, 127–28.
263. *Ibid.*, 110, 203. This is also opposed to J. Habermas, who assumes that the "steering imperatives of highly complex societies" might in themselves drop problems of legitimation. This thesis can be shown to be wrong at any time: a society without self-interpretation sooner or later empirically loses its status as an organized society. Compare J. Habermas, *Legitimationsprobleme im Spätkapitalismus* (Frankfurt, 1973), 62–68.

perience of death—he calls it the "fundamental anxiety." From it grow "the many interrelated systems of hopes and fears, of wants and satisfactions, of chances and risks which incite man within the natural attitude to attempt the mastery of the world, to overcome obstacles, to draft projects, and to realize them."[264] The concentration on the everyday world gains its meaning not last from the suspension of doubt in its reality, that is, the fundamental fear of death. Berger and Luckmann also see death as the individual's "marginal situation par excellence," the most serious threat to the self-evident reality of the everyday world; but they extend Schütz's analysis by viewing the central nomic function of death to be its integration within an overarching symbolic universe. In the context of death, they identify fear as the motivating experience of the social ordering of symbols. "The symbolic universe shelters the individual from ultimate terror by bestowing ultimate legitimation upon the protective structures of institutional order."[265] Berger generalizes this thesis: "The socially established nomos may thus be understood, perhaps in its most important aspect, as a shield against terror. Put differently, the most important function of society is nomization. The anthropological presupposition for this is a human craving for meaning that appears to have the force of instinct."[266] Even phenomenological analysis cannot evade the question of the content of the motivating experiences of symbolic forms of order, but it does not analyze experiential processes that bring forth symbols of order; rather, it selects the experience of the fear of death as the *summum malum*. In this attempt, however, the correct observation that the majority suppresses the fear of death by absorbing it in the immanent ordering of symbols is confused with the paradigmatic experiences that interpret reality beyond the spatial-temporal constellation of life and death in the dimension of mortality and immortality. It seems to me correct, however, even on this plane of phenomenological analysis, to observe that for the symbolic universe, in which society interprets itself, a basic structure is given by the question of man's origins and ends, for which equivalents of content and function exist in all societies.

Even the more advanced phenomenological analysis of "symbolic appresentation of society" given by Berger and Luckmann does not yet permit adequate theorization of the previously analyzed modes of American self-understanding to the extent that all the empirically available lines, patterns, and structures of meaning, as well as their interrelations, could be represented in such a way that the proposed theoretical concept of

264. Schütz, *Collected Papers*, I, 228.
265. Berger and Luckmann, *Social Construction*, 102.
266. P. L. Berger, *The Sacred Canopy* (Garden City, N.Y., 1969), 22.

civil theology can be used with sufficient justification. Schütz combined his phenomenological investigation of the symbolic appresentation of society with Voegelin's analysis of societal self-interpretation—though he did not adopt Voegelin's principle of theorization (as is also true for Berger and Luckmann) from which Voegelin developed a structural model for the interpretation of order in human affairs.[267]

What follows is intended to show his heuristic relevance to further theoretical clarification of the phenomenon of "self-understanding," with a result that is intended to supplement the outcome of our theorizing about the problems of founding. The experience of the specific symbolic appresentation of social and political organization (Schütz)—that is, the establishment of a "stable symbolic canopy for the entire society" (Berger and Luckmann)—is analyzed by Voegelin in a first step as self-interpretation of a society:

> Human society is not merely a fact, or an event, in the external world to be studied by an observer like a natural phenomenon. Though it has externality as one of its important components, it is on the whole a little world, a cosmion illuminated from within by the human beings who continuously create and bear it as the mode and condition of their self-realization. It is illuminated through an elaborate symbolism, in various degrees of compactness and differentiation . . . and this symbolism illuminates it with meaning insofar as the symbols make the internal structure of such a cosmion, the relations between its members and groups of members, as well as its existence as a whole, transparent for the mystery of human existence. The self-illumination of society through symbols is an integral part of social reality, and one may even say its essential part, for through such symbolization the members of a society experience it as more than an accident or a convenience; they experience it as of their human essence. And, inversely, the symbols express the experience that man is fully man by virtue of his participation in a whole which transcends his particular existence.[268]

Voegelin proceeds from the results of phenomenological analysis but eschews the questionable privileging of the everyday world. It is surely understood more adequately as a dimension of overall social structures of meaning, which are required to constitute collectivity. Those symbols by which a society interprets the meaning of its existence claim to be true. In the medium of its symbolism each society claims to be the representative of a truth. From this circumstance Voegelin concluded that, empirically, the existential representation of a society in history, its articulation

267. Compare Voegelin, *Anamnesis*, 348ff.
268. Voegelin, *Neue Wissenschaft der Politik*, 49–50.

as a discernible authority capable of acting, always has a context by which "society itself represents something that goes beyond itself, a transcendent reality."

The American case is absolutely typical for this constellation. Only the dimension of the representation of truth confers on the actions of the existential representatives of a society a legitimating meaning and integrates the individual members in the plausibility structure of the society in such a way that domination in the sense of Weber's definition becomes possible.[269] Thus "for every society . . . the self-understanding of its order [is] constitutive; and therefore every known society in history brings forth to us symbols . . . , through which it expresses its experience of order."[270] Methodologically, it follows that "every study of order must concentrate on the acts of self-understanding and then pursue from this center the ramifications into the order of the collective existence."[271] For this purpose Voegelin uses the concept of the social field to describe adequately, that is, as distinct subjects, the individual levels and structures of social reality. Voegelin speaks of social fields, whose dimension and relative stability in time allow them to be identified as discernible power units capable of acting in history, as organized, that is, political, society. It is dominated by the respective interpretation of order, the symbolic universe in the language of phenomenology. The basic prerequisite is the physical dimension of human existence: the basic pragmatic structure of power and economic conditions of existence in the form of organized rulership; that is, the experience of order always includes the experience of the concrete and material foundation of human existence as partially constitutive in that this is where the multifunctional steering system is rooted that directs the elementary life process. Power relations and economic structures manifest man as conditioned materially and concretely, but the structures are ordered from consciousness, for power relations and economic structures are shaped by the order of consciousness, exhibited in the order or symbols. In the medium of symbolization every organized society is supported by a dominant social field of consciousness

---

269. *Ibid.*, 82–83, 110–11, and others. Schütz refers specifically to this analysis; it is this same state of affairs that provides Marx with the authority for his statement "The individuals composing the ruling class possess . . . consciousness . . . thus their ideas are the ruling ideas of the epoch" (K. Marx, *Die deutsche Ideologie* [Berlin, 1953], 44 [English from R. C. Tucker, ed., *The Marx-Engels Reader* (2nd ed.; New York, 1978), 173]). Nevertheless, the context of the argument, to the extent that it is defined at all, is aporetic.

270. Voegelin, *Anamnesis*, 284.

271. *Ibid.*, 345 (English from *Anamnesis*, trans. G. Niemeyer [Notre Dame, Ind., 1978], 205).

insofar as it constitutes the pattern of habitual action, the ethos of the members of the society, down to the institutional ramification of social order.

The compactly experienced life ambience of each organized society as a rule represents itself as *the* reality of society and obfuscates other experiential inventories of man and society.

Of course the evidence of the structural and relational conditions of a social order is analytic, since empirically it is experienced only under the horizon of participation in a multidimensional overarching reality. Analytically, we are dealing with a configuration in which psychic structure, symbolic structure, and behavioral and institutional structure can all be identified. This structural pattern gains process reality in the various dimensions of social existence: in spiritual processes, power and domination processes, and economic and generative processes. Two points are important for relational conditions. The first is primarily the area of the psyche, with the illumination dimension of consciousness as the center of order, from which the described structural constellations are determined and the respective dimensions of the social processes are shaped. Second, the establishment of a social field of consciousness qua organized society necessarily sets up a determination of the particular consciousness of the majority of the members of society through the shaping solidarity in psyche, symbol, behavior, and institution. Marx linked this insight to the determination of individual existence through dominant psychosocial fields with the fact of the material foundation of existence and the consequent dependence of all social order on an economic structure and turned it into a causal relationship. By changing words—*conditioning* becomes *determining*—consciousness loses its status as the primary center of order to a "social being." The statement "the mode of production of material life conditions the social, political and intellectual life process in general" cannot lead to the conclusion that "it is not the consciousness of men that determines their being, but, on the contrary, their social being that determines their consciousness."[272] No matter how carefully the terms of the economic structure (relations of production, material forces of production, social production of life) were explained in detailed analyses, the reciprocal relations of the structural conditions remain unclear. The general concepts of "being," "social being," and "consciousness" continue to lack specific meaning; they are placed in a causal relation that is nowhere elaborated but feeds on the theoretical intention that all structures of order are to be interpreted in the human realm of being from

272. Marx, *Werke*, VI, 839; Tucker, ed., *Marx-Engels Reader*, 4.

the bottommost level—that is, the "material basis of every specific social organization."[273]

But it must be emphasized that the analysis of social self-understanding deals only with a specific type of social field of consciousness—organized society, whose basis in the material existence of concrete persons marks it as a power unit identifiable in space and time. The term *civilis* in the concept of civil theology expresses this state of affairs. Such other over-arching or particular social fields of consciousness or frames for the power process as civilization and global economy are not here further illuminated.

The determination of organized society as a social field of consciousness has its empirical justification in the assessment of consciousness as the *sensorium* of those experiences of order in which society expresses its truth symbolically. Of course the word *society* is a code here, for—and with this we return to our reflections on the theory of founding—we are dealing with "the process by which concrete persons create a social field, i.e., a field in which their experiences of order are understood by other concrete men who accept them as their own and make them into the motive of their habitual action."[274] The essential factor of a social field of consciousness therefore lies within the dimension of experience—not qua experience, as Schütz would have us believe, but in the interpretation of an experience of reality that by its content confers collectivity. We are dealing with primary knowledge of the logos as the shared quality (Heraclitus was the first to call it *xynon*), in which all human beings as human beings participate, regardless of their actual differences. This primary experience, undifferentiated and reduced as it may be, must in some form be present at least within the framework of a social field in order to allow the particular experience of order of concrete persons and the corresponding interpretations in the meaning described to be socially relevant and socially dominant. For the content of experiences of order proves to be a justified depth dimension of the reality of knowledge of the *xynon* in that it interprets order on its basis. "The various modes of the experience, with their corresponding multiplicity of symbolic expressions, all

273. *Ibid.*, 425. Compare U. Sonnemann, *Negative Anthropologie* (Hamburg, 1969), 43. Marx thought a "critical history of technology" to be desirable. "Technology reveals man's active relation to nature, the immediate production process of his life, and therefore also his social living conditions and the mental expectations arising from them." It is only the execution of such a "developmental history of the productive organs of social man" that justifies Marx's statement concerning the causal relations of "infrastructure" and "superstructures" in the structural relations of social formations. All existent research, however, points in a direction opposite to Marx's.

274. Voegelin, *Anamnesis*, 342 (English from *Anamnesis*, trans. Niemeyer, 202).

revolve around the founding of right order through insight into the ground of order. The multiplicity of interpretations, even when known, can never be understood as referring to a multitude of grounds, but the interpretation is always joined to the consciousness that it expresses the experience of the *one* ground. . . . Behind the historical variety of interpretations, then, we find the unity of the question about the ground." [275] From the quest for the ground there emerges the experiences on which the images of reality are erected. These experiences, however, are of a nonobjective nature, "the intangibility of the reality, which is no ineffability, allows room for a variety of experiences that motivate a corresponding number of symbolic expressions of the experience. In the dynamism of the effort to find the right expression of order we find the origin of the tensions in political reality." [276] From this standpoint it also becomes clear why the order of symbols that interprets a social field of consciousness in organized society is called by Voegelin *civil theology*.

The term, taken by Saint Augustine from Varro's *Antiquitates*,[277] referred with apologetic intention to the archaic-compact self-interpretation of ancient Rome which, already with an analytic purpose, was distinguished from other types of the interpretation of order. The implications of this concept must be briefly explained with a view to its application to the sphere of social self-understanding. A part of it is, for one, the realization that the Romans were referring to a term that, unlike modern concepts, belonged from the beginning to the area of politics. Plato introduced the word *theology* in the *Republic* to apply to a specific circumstance. The subject is types of theology. But in which connection are these discussed? The context is unmistakably political. It is a matter of educating youth in politics in general and the politics of the rulers in particular. From this point of view Plato and his students, acting as *oikistes poleos*, founders of a polis, discuss the question of primary socialization, which they believe to be crucial to any social order. Because, as Plato argues, it brings about the crucial personality structures, it is therefore of extreme importance for the development of the virtues of communal life as citizens. The formation of the psyche in the primary phase of socialization is identical with the structure of reality images in the verbal communications of teachers. This comes about through "speeches," "stories"—that is, simple symbolizations that reveal to the children the sources of the primary experience of order and develop the psyche as the site of such

275. *Ibid.,* 288 (English, *ibid.,* 148).
276. *Ibid.,* 287–88 (English, *ibid.,* 147).
277. Compare R. Agahd, *Der Varronis rerum divinarum* (Leipzig, 1896) and Aurelius Augustinus, *De Civitate Dei*. See also Jaeger, *Theologie der frühen griechischen Denker*, 10ff.

experience. The "speaking of gods" means nothing other than a symbolic form that, correctly or falsely, informs the psyche about "what is" (*peri ta onta*). A false picture of reality evokes existential ignorance in the souls of those who have been duped, which can be overcome only with difficulty.[278] That is why Plato developed criteria for true theology—that is, the correct explication of the "divine" as the origin of the good and the "daimonion" as the center of order in the psyche. It is against this background that the subsequent use of the concept in the Roman context must be understood: the Varronian classification of the *genera theologiae* is concerned with differentiating among various symbolic forms, in which consciousness interprets the experience of the ground of order. Unlike the theology of the mythic tradition of the "poets" and the theology of the Greek philosophers, *theologia civilis* is the theology of citizens of political societies—in this context, the symbolic explication of the sacred authority of the Roman founding, the order of its profane and sacred affairs, with which the citizen's private and public existences are linked. According to Varro, the specific aspect of a civil theology was logically that it grew from the founding of political society; that is, the *res divinae*, the statements concerning spiritual order, result from the *res humanae*, the political order of the *civitas*.[279] "The notion of a spiritual tradition and of authority in matters of thought and ideas is here derived from the political realm and therefore essentially derivative."[280] Civil theology, "as secondary dogmatization and systematization of realizations of the speculative exegesis of primary experiences of order," is "therefore the stabilizing element through which the cultic and mental coherence of a political society is assured and in which at the same time the organizational form of society itself experiences its apologetics."[281]

Varro's *theologia civilis*—developed in the crisis of ancient Roman self-understanding—has its functional equivalent in the symbolic universes of political societies, whenever the social field of consciousness as self-interpretation of society, sustaining organized society, can be distinguished from other social fields of consciousness and their respective symbolisms in the social reality. Inevitably this also includes the case of the plurality of political societies with divergent self-interpretations, that is, competing claims to representing transcendent truth. Beyond this

---

278. Plato, *The Republic* (London, 1969–70), 337a–382a; E. Voegelin, *Order and History* (Baton Rouge, 1956–74), II, 173–74.

279. Voegelin, *Neue Wissenschaft der Politik*, 126–27.

280. H. Arendt, *Between Past and Future* (Cleveland, 1963), 124. Compare Cicero, *De Natura Deorum*.

281. P. Weber-Schäfer, *Oikumene und Imperium* (Munich, 1968), 19.

point, equivalences in the medium of symbolization itself can be sufficiently recorded to show that the inevitable images of reality in the interpretation of social order as concerns their ground are reality-formed to the extent that the empirical share in the various dimensions of reality is reflected in some manner in the postulate of an interpretation of man's entire existence. Much as this may vary as far as reality content is concerned, the various structure spheres nevertheless always recur in some form in the symbolization. Finally, civil theology, like other symbolic forms, always expresses a social field of concrete consciousness and—this must be especially stressed here—of the concrete unconscious[282] in which experiential fields become manifest. The equivalence of the experiences justifies the equivalence of symbolizations.

The constant that underlies the equivalent patterns in the experiential field is man himself in search of his humanity and its order. This constant, however, is the process of experience of the structure of existence as it is arranged in the tension that exists between eternity and time, immortality and mortality, completion and incompleteness, order and disorder, abundance and want, truth and untruth, meaningfulness and meaninglessness.[283] When existence becomes transparent as an "intermediate sphere," the underlying process of "reality" is itself experienced equivalently as a shared depth dimension of men that primarily makes them partners in their own affairs, that is, turns them into *zoon politikon*, which in a civil theology creates the symbolic universe of their existence in a respective society, a cosmos they imbue with meaning, as the American self-understanding claims.

The self-interpretation of American society was correctly covered by the expression *Americanism*. It functions as the instrument of the self-understanding of a national universe; it also, however, takes the stage with a universal claim and constructs a cosmos that encompasses God, the world, man, society, and history in the American grain. The word *Americanism* originally referred to transatlantic neologisms but was used

282. This dimension of the psychosocial field seems to me of not inconsiderable significance, though this can be determined here only tentatively. Voegelin touches on only the edges of this problem. Jung's archetypes hypostatize this dimension as a quasi-natural structure of a primal substance in an inherited apriority, thus destroying the concrete psyche as the center of order and cutting both dimensions off from the motivating experiences; see H. Herwig, *Therapie der Menschheit* (Munich, 1969), 80–81, 83–84. Kilian's attempt at an analysis of the collective historical and social unconscious fails because of the elimination of concrete consciousness in favor of an eschatologically pure consciousness in *statu nascendi;* this elimination is motivated by historical speculation; see H. Kilian, *Das enteignete Bewußtsein* (Neuweid, 1971), 7–11 and *passim.*

283. See. E. Voegelin, "Equivalences of Experience and Symbolization in History," in *Eternita e Storia* (Florence, 1970), 215–34.

as early as the era of the Founding Fathers as a symbol for an American interpretation of order. In the domestic and international conflict situation of 1797, with the increasing hardening of partisan fronts, Jefferson demanded "the dictates of reason and pure Americanism" for the basis by which to arrive at political decisions.[284] Similarly, John Adams spoke of Americanism: "Patriotism in this country must be tinctured with English and French devotion or be without support and almost without friends. Independent, unadulterated, impartial Americanism is like Hayley's old maid, a decayed tree in a vast desert plain of sand."[285] In using the term, Jefferson and Adams expressed their critical view of dangerous entanglements in domestic and foreign policy. In this context Americanism means no alliance with France or England and no forming of parties on the basis of this worldwide political conflict but rather awareness of a specific American mode of existence.

Even the early concept of Americanism hints at its fragmentary nature and its universalist claim. The political and mental process of fragmentation that grew out of the disintegration of medieval Europe created isms: beginning with anarchism in the seventeenth century, it became established in the eighteenth as a description of concepts of order that absolutized fragments of experience from concrete experiential occasions and in their totality allowed the emergence and persistence until well into the twentieth century of a pluralistic universe of two mutually antagonistic isms, each of which laid claim to the truth. In this way Americanism is also to be understood as a general Western phenomenon.[286] However, a peculiarity appears insofar as it actually does have a substratum of a sociocultural fragment. According to Hartz, Americanism is the "result of the extrication of a bourgeois fragment from the turmoil of seventeenth century Europe."[287] Unrestricted by the pressure of the social structures of the Old World and in an infinite continent with unsuspected material resources, the fragment became transformed into the totality of a nation, and bourgeois Whiggism turned from the intellectual segment of European origin into "Liberalism as the American way of life" and into the universalist interpretation of all reality.

284. Thomas Jefferson to John Rutledge, June 24, 1797, in Jefferson, *Writings*, IX, 409. Compare G. Chinard, *Thomas Jefferson: The Apostle of Americanism* (Boston, 1929); Chinard used the life of his protagonist to construct a finite conception of American order.

285. John Adams to Benjamin Rush, July 7, 1805, in Adams, *Old Family Letters*, 70.

286. Compare the study by R. Michels, *Der Patriotismus* (Munich, 1929), Chap. 1, "Der Mythus des Vaterlandes."

287. L. Hartz *et al.*, *The Founding of New Societies* (New York, 1964), 4.

Five

The Crisis of Americanism

I. The Destructive Tradition of Spiritual-Political Individualism

"The decade of the nineties is the watershed of American history. As with all watersheds the topography is blurred, but in the perspective of half a century the grand outlines emerge clearly." [1] On the level of pragmatic existence, the watershed results from the civilizing process. Self-contained, autonomous, independent agrarian America is transformed into urbanized, industrialized America, and this new entity was, by force of its stage of development, inevitably drawn into the tension field of world economics and world politics. The apocalyptically motivated idea of the nation of 1776 had, by the time of the Civil War, been realized in the continental American empire that not only had freed itself from the threat posed by the competing imperial enterprises of the European powers, but had also risen to be the hegemonic power in the Western hemisphere.

The internal consolidation of this empire had progressed to the point at which the mechanism, inherent in American society, of solving conflicts through avoidance, the principle of separatism or secession, had become ineffective. The Civil War proved that any antagonism taken to the extreme between two types of social organizations could no longer be solved in this empire through the collective secession of one, so that

---

1. H. S. Commager, *The American Mind* (New Haven, Conn., 1959), 41.

one had to fall back on the instrument for solving conflicts employed in such cases in the Old World—armed confrontation. In 1890 the "frontier of settlement" first disappeared from the federal census. It was with this consideration in mind that Frederick Jackson Turner published his famous essay, "The Significance of the Frontier in American History" (1893), in which he announced the end of the frontier. The westward movement had come to a standstill; an American civilized world now existed from which no one could any longer separate himself. After the collective secession, therefore, individual secession from society as an alternative had also ceased to exist. We see secession as a viable substitute for revolution and intensive social conflicts in the first founding of the seventeenth century, which was an exodus from seventeenth-century English society; in the second founding of 1776, the separation from the English empire; and in the mass emigrations from nineteenth-century Europe. Under the geographic conditions of the vast and seemingly inexhaustible continent, separatism became the fundamental social experience. From Thomas Hooker and Roger Williams to the mass migration of the southern African-Americans into the slums of the North, it marked social behavior in cases of conflict.[2]

The epochal understanding of the events of 1826 finds its correspondence in the interpretation of the break of the 1890s: "The frontier has gone, and with its going has closed the first period of American History."[3] Even if in no case the symbols of self-interpretation furnish an adequate medium for dividing the structure of the historical process into periods, epochal consciousness and the fact of such division in themselves point to the shape of American history: the period between 1830 and 1890 emerges as a specifically structured phenomenal unit.[4] The governmental machinery established by the founders for the federation and the states, an adequate local administration, and safe borders, together with Americanism, served as the main field of consciousness of society, under the presupposition of the social mechanism of separatism sufficiently integrative to be able to keep the divergent social forces in balance; further, they created a frame for an explosive development of the nation's physical, material, and spiritual potential. Only the evolutionary achievements of the American system[5] furnished the conditions for the repudiation of

2. Compare Hartz, *Liberal Tradition*, 64–65.

3. F. J. Turner, *The Significance of the Frontier in American History* (Madison, Wis., 1894), 62.

4. William A. Williams has brilliantly developed the unity of this period in *Contours of American History*, 225–338.

5. For a summary, see S. M. Lipset, *The First New Nation* (New York, 1963), 35–60; W. A. Williams, *Contours of American History*, 149–200.

its representatives Adams and Clay in 1828. This event strengthened the position of liberalism that fed on the traditions of the classical agrarian republicanism of the founding period and which now, in view of the domestic and international stabilization and the enormous material resources, eclipsed the public sphere of society in favor of a prevailing notion of human individuality. Our recapitulation of these events at this point in our investigation is not focused on the structural changes in the American civil theology in which the spiritual, political, and economic mobilization of the libidinous ego is reflected. Rather, here a brief overview of this phenomenon will explore its long-range destructive consequences for the psychic order of society.

With the sociopolitical realization of the paradigms of the *zoon politikon* in the republic of the founders, the membership of society down to the last individual had articulated itself politically (with the obvious exceptions!), and society had become its own representative. To that extent the rise of the Common Man under Jackson was the historically necessary sociopolitical substratum of Americanism. But this movement already made manifest those elements of a deformation of consciousness implied by the destruction of the form given to consciousness and symbolism by the founders; that is, it could not help but dissolve the content of the nexus of founding and order. The collectivity of "public happiness" is based on a balance of the psychological forces in consciousness that is maintained by the ordering function of the authentically reasoning self of the citizen. The crisis of a civil theology is announced in the explicit and implicit erosion of the ordering force of reason and the advancement of the libidinous ego as the guiding principle of political existence.

As early as the first half of the nineteenth century we find exemplary evidence of elements of the libidinous ego in reductionist designs for existence. De Tocqueville analyzed their destructive consequences, subsuming these designs for existence under the concept of individualism. Unlike *egoism*, selfishness, a vice shared by all forms of society in equal measure, individualism grows out of man's isolation under the social conditions of democratic society. Individualism is the specific form of *amour-propre*, self-love, in such a society. It even expresses the negative phenomenon of a domination of the "private world" of man's emotional nature in a democratic society that the fathers—even de Tocqueville is still firmly convinced of this—successfully fought against by establishing the "public happiness" of shared action in political life. For de Tocqueville, the effective remedy for the evils of individualism consisted of political liberty.[6]

6. Tocqueville, *Democracy in America*, II, 109ff.

De Tocqueville's picture of the "Age of the Common Man" in the United States appeared so plausible to American self-understanding to the present day—regardless of the fact that it was not, of course, possible to consider socioeconomic equality throughout the Republic—that, like him, Americans did not recognize that the psychosocial syndrome of individualism might have a greater significance for America; in the Anglo-Saxon world, the relevance of de Tocqueville's generalization was not understood at all. Americanism continued to discuss *amour-propre* in the language of John Adams, that is, of the anglicized ethos of philosophical-Christian provenance.[7]

De Tocqueville diagnosed the manifestation of the privatist existence of individualism under the conditions of democratic civilization in its basic structure with extraordinary caution:

> Individualism is a mature and calm feeling, which disposes each member of the community to sever himself from the mass of his fellows and to draw apart with his family and his friends, so that after he has thus formed a little circle of his own, he willingly leaves society at large to itself. . . . As social conditions become more equal, the number of persons increases who, although they are neither rich nor powerful enough to exercise any great influence over their fellows, have nevertheless acquired or retained sufficient education and fortune to satisfy their own wants. They owe nothing to any man, they expect nothing from any man; they acquire the habit of always considering themselves as standing alone, and they are apt to imagine that their whole destiny is in their own hands.

This acute social-psychological description of the common man led him to the crucial existential-analytic conclusion: thus democracy affects every man and "throws him back forever upon himself alone and threatens in the end to confine him entirely within the solitude of his own heart." But this means nothing other than the destructive reduction of man to his libidinous self, which, as it were, endangers the order of the individual psyche as well as the order of republican society: "Selfishness blights the germ of all virtue; individualism, at first, only saps the virtues of public life; but in the long run it attacks and destroys all others and is

7. Compare the commentary of Henry Reeve, an Englishman, whose translation (1835) first brought de Tocqueville to the attention of an English-speaking public: "I adopt the expression of the original [individualism], however strange it may seem to an English ear, partly because it illustrates the remark on the introduction of general terms into democratic language which was made in a preceding chapter, and partly because I know of no English word exactly equivalent to the expression." Quoted in Tocqueville, *Democracy in America*, I, vi.

at length absorbed in downright selfishness."[8] This turn of the paradigm from the common man to absolutizing the American bourgeois is already marked at an early stage. James Fenimore Cooper spoke for many when he wrote in 1828: "The secret of all enterprise and energy exists in the principle of individuality. Wealth does not more infallibly beget wealth, than the right to the exercise of our faculties begets the desire to use them. The slave is everywhere indolent, vicious and abject; the freeman active, moral and bold. It would seem that is the best and safest, and, consequently, the wisest government, which is content rather to protect than direct the national prosperity, since the latter system never fails to impede the efforts of that individuality which makes men industrious and enterprising."[9] Thomas Skidmore, a spokesman for the New Yorker Workingmen's Party at the same time, radicalized this property-individual position: "Title to property exists for all; . . . BECAUSE THEY ARE: BECAUSE THEY EXIST! I AM; THEREFORE IS PROPERTY MINE."[10]

Once again it speaks for the intellectual power of New England that it ranked among the transcendentalists those thinkers who speculatively articulated the intellectual core of this eruption of man from society. Emerson determined it as the deification of the self in mystic union with the universe.[11] He gave to the American apocalypse the form of a vision of the collective existence of the individual who has been rendered divine, freed from the problems of social existence. Of course this in turn is backed by the principle of separatism, as was proven by the exodus from society practiced by the transcendentalist Henry David Thoreau.

Quentin Anderson calls this phenomenon "imaginative desocialization."[12] He analyzes the deification of the self as a "secular incarnation," "the act not of identifying oneself with the fathers, but of catching up all their powers into the self, asserting that there need be no more generations, no more history, but simply the swelling diapason of the expanding self."[13] This emergence of the "imperial self" was the answer to the latent identity crisis suffered by sensitive psyches in response to the uncertainty of an order without its original guarantors, the fathers. "If on the wider

8. Tocqueville, *Democracy in America*, II, 104–105.
9. Quoted in R. B. Perry, *Puritanism and Democracy* (New York, 1964), 535.
10. Quoted in Somkin, *Unquiet Eagle*, 81.
11. Compare especially Emerson's "Divinity School Address, July 15, 1838," in Emerson, *Works*, II, 111–43, and "Politics, 1841," *ibid.*, 399–416. See C. J. Friedrich, *The New Belief in the Common Man* (Boston, 1942), 15–20; L. Baritz, *City on a Hill* (New York, 1964), 205–69.
12. Q. Anderson, *The Imperial Self* (New York, 1971), 4.
13. *Ibid.*, 58.

public scene it was an age of political parties, of revivalism, of utopianism, and the growth of associations for benevolent purposes, it was likewise on every man's inner stage an age of revolt against earlier certainties." The younger generation of the 1820s still grew up with the immediate accessibility of the nexus of founding and order in the form of living fathers; this same generation was of necessity thrown into an identity crisis by experiencing the death of the fathers. The crisis was to be overcome in the imperial self as the origin of all order: "I am saying no more than that we have not taken quite literally and naïvely enough the crucial fact that the generations of the founding fathers was gone or going."[14] "Americans appear to have suffered a punishing psychic blow in the generation of Emerson's youth, to have lost the assurance provided by their sense of the presence of leaders and an instituted order." The imperial self reconstructed order from within itself: it is "a self which assumed psychic burdens because outer supportive structures of custom and institutions had disappeared or lost imaginative authority."[15] The shock of fatherlessness is resolved in the libidinous ego's claim to command reality:

> Many Americans were more or less attempting the emotional task Emerson had undertaken: that of incorporating the powers of the fathers who no longer seemed to be present, qua father, or minister, or state. There came a moment when the loose texture of developing American life made it impossible to credit the authority of those filling these roles. At the outset this drift in the direction of an imperial separateness made itself felt only as a symptom, not a central fact about the life of the masses of Americans. . . . We must be clear about the kind of effect we attribute to Emerson and Emersonianism before 1850; it was a highly important symptom, and what it portended was centrally exhibited later, in industrial America following the Civil War.[16]

The continuity of the imperial self became evident only retrospectively, after the social breakthrough of this dynamic-expansive ego to the dominant type that attempted to reconstruct the lost reality in its own image.[17] But even during the incubation phase of the spiritual, political, and economic dynamization of the person, this concentration on the individ-

14. *Ibid.*, 40.
15. *Ibid.*, 234–35.
16. *Ibid.*, 56.
17. Compare also E. Voegelin, "The Eclipse of Reality," in *Phenomenology and Social Reality*, ed. M. Natanson (The Hague, 1970), 185–95.

ual under American conditions unleashed powerful energies: Jackson's so-called revolution perfected political democracy.[18] Taney's decision in *Charles River Bridge* v. *Warren Bridge* (1837)[19] ceded the order of the conditions of production to the liberal politics of laissez-faire. This statement, however, should not be misunderstood in the sense of the doctrine of the "free enterprise" of a liberal "competitive capitalism" that hovers over the textbooks of liberal political economics (and its critics). It means, rather, that the psychosocial structural patterns of industrial economic society were accorded *public* status—that is, the original conception of the political solution of economic problems was replaced by a laissez-faire attitude. Although the circumstance that economic decisions remained in the medium of public government was unchanged, this transformation implied a shift of the level of decision making from the federal government to the political institutions under the immediate control of the common man in the community and the state, though traditionally, under the American system of the fathers, these had already been the centers of public economic policy. The decentralized politics of laissez-faire meant aligning the patterns of decisions of all the representatives of society in the federation, the state, and the community according to that dynamic psychosocial structure of individualism whose plausibility must be seen in the clear victory of an expanding industrial economic society over hunger and disease.[20] The politics of laissez-faire, then, is determined less by the elimination of economic decisions from the public sphere—they were omnipresent there—than by its increased domination

18. In the Introduction to his *United States Magazine and Democratic Review,* I (October, 1837), 1–15, John L. Sullivan formulated the policies of the Jacksonians better than Jackson ever could. Sullivan's Introduction was reprinted in J. Blau, ed., *Social Theories of Jacksonian Democracy* (New York, 1954), 21–38, where there is also further material on the Jacksonians' self-interpretation. Compare also A. M. Schlesinger, Jr., *The Age of Jackson* (Boston, 1945); Hofstadter, *American Political Tradition,* 45–67; Hartz, *Liberal Tradition,* 89–142; E. Pessen, *Jacksonian America* (Homewood, Ill., 1969); M. Meyers, *The Jacksonian Persuasion: Politics and Belief* (Stanford, Calif., 1957); Dorfman, *Economic Mind,* II, 601–37.

19. 11 Peters, 420 (1837).

20. For the role of the public hand in the nation and individual states in the nineteenth century, see A. Shonfield, *Geplanter Kapitalismus* (Cologne, 1969), 356–66. For the mercantilist tradition of public intervention in the economy of the individual states, see L. Hartz, *Economic Policy and Democratic Thought: Pennsylvania, 1776–1860* (Cambridge, Mass., 1948); O. Handlin and M. Handlin, *Commonwealth: A Study of the Role of Government in the American Economy, Massachusetts, 1774–1861* (New York, 1947); J. N. Primm, *Economic Policy in the Development of a Western State: Missouri 1820 to 1860* (Cambridge, Mass., 1954); M. S. Heath, *Constructive Liberalism* (Cambridge, Mass., 1954).

through the reality picture of the libidinous ego. "Usually thought of as a philosophy of individualism, by which is meant the single human being, the competition and conflict of laissez faire actually occurred at many different levels. In addition to the individual, there were organized groups such as corporations, labour unions, and reformers; political subdivisions such as parties and the states; social and economic units which became self-conscious sections or regions; and, in the broadest sense, nations themselves in the world arena."[21]

William Appleton Williams described critically the intellectual, political, and socioeconomic atomization of the "paradigmatic republic," which, granted, need not immediately attack its substance. But what was more serious was that this phenomenon concealed a decision that in the long run sanctioned the transformation of the socially dominant hierarchy of goods in the public sector. *Charles River Bridge* v. *Warren Bridge* would once again elucidate this argument: Taney took his point of departure from the fathers' principles of order in arriving at his decision: "the object and end of all government is to promote the happiness and prosperity of the community by which it is established; and it can never be assumed that the government intended to diminish its power of accomplishing the end for which it was intended. . . . While the rights of private property are sacredly guarded, we must not forget that the community also have rights, and that the happiness and well-being of every citizen depends on their faithful preservation." Laissez-faire, therefore, means not that economic affairs are no longer subject to the public sector and its order, but that the public regulation of production relations is to occur according to new standpoints, for Taney declared the mercantilist institution of the privileged company to be unconstitutional because it hindered the government in its pursuit of the public interest. In republicanism, the "incorporated economic enterprise" was the expression of the public nature of private property, the instrument for increasing the national wealth through the promotion of private interests in agriculture, trade, and industry, including science, as well as the dominant form of public control of social relations insofar as these were not regulated by direct ordinances of the executive and legislative branches. Consequently the Founding Fathers viewed the economy—of whose pervasiveness of the social reality they needed to convince no one—in terms of the human condition. Thus, they strove to place material prosperity in the service of the overarching purpose of public justice and to prevent its potentially destructive effects on society through political order: "the ideal of secular corporate justice . . . was . . . the kind of an internalized restraint that

21. W. A. Williams, *Contours of American History*, 247.

had to be developed if self-interest and private property were to function satisfactorily as means to the general welfare. Along with Adams, Jay, Jefferson, Monroe, and other mercantilists, Madison persistently emphasized the vital role of a strong sense of justice: the ideal had to be pursued with vigor if the constitution were to produce the good society—'the national welfare'—that he sought."[22] Taney correctly concluded that "incorporated property" with a claim to monopoly must lead to an inadmissible restriction of the aims of public rule if the property guarantees of the Constitution were claimed for the monopoly. In *Charles River Bridge* v. *Warren Bridge,* however, Taney gave an entirely new interpretation to the "public benefit"[23] implied in incorporation. He understood it as the best possible use to be made of modern science, and of progress in general, to increase wealth and prosperity, the comfort and ease of life. The monopoly claim of the owners of the Charles River Bridge is a misuse of property and a restriction of public purposes, since property can be of use to the public goal of improvement only in competition; in this case progress lies in the establishment of technically advanced means of transportation and communication. Taney's decision not only allowed the mercantilist institution of incorporated enterprise to disappear but also determined the imperative of technical-economic progress as the goal of political order in regard to economic decisions. Taney's interpretation of the constitutional order obligates public action, at least in this case, to submit to the organizational principles of industrial economic society. But in my view this was the substance of the liberal politics of laissez-faire. The indisputable success of the publicly legitimated competition of owners, with the goal of continuous production and productivity increases, more and more rooted the coordination of Americanism in the growth of economic production of goods in the dominant consciousness, symbolism, and behavior patterns of American society. John Kenneth Galbraith properly described this development:

> The industrial system identifies itself with the goals of society, and it adapts these to its needs. . . . It is the genius of the industrial system that it makes the goals that reflects its needs—efficient production of goods, a steady expansion in their output, a steady expansion in their consumption, a powerful preference for goods and leisure, an unqualified commitment to technological change, autonomy of the technistructure, an adequate surplus of trained and educated manpower—coordinate with social virtue and hu-

---

22. *Ibid.,* 158–59. Compare also J. J. Spengler, "Political Economy of Jefferson, Madison, and Adams," in *American Studies in Honor of William K. Boyd* (Durham, N.C., 1940), 3–59; Dorfman, *Economic Mind;* Dauer, "Political Economy of John Adams."

23. See particularly *Dartmouth College* v. *Woodward,* 1818.

man enlightenment. These goals are not thought to be derived from our environment. They are assumed to be original with human personality. To believe this is to hold a sensibly material view of mankind.[24]

This form of Americanism as economism created for itself a field of consciousness in the corporation, and in the twentieth century this social field finally spread beyond the borders of organized American society, though not without legitimating itself within society through recourse to civil theology. Galbraith, himself a victim of his concretized language, forgets that the transformation of Americanism originated with the growing impact of pragmatic-functional rationality of the industrial system on the doctrine of the common man, insofar as this doctrine involved the idea of the "imperial self." But as early as the mid-nineteenth century, Emerson proved that turning the common man into a hero would turn back on him until he would have no choice but to call on society for protection against the dynamics of the expanding self. For in social practice the liberated self only too quickly yielded to the pleonexia of the driving force of his behavior. The idea that "in a free and just commonwealth, property rushes from the idle and imbecile to the industrious, brave and preserving" was the final conclusion even of transcendentalist wisdom.[25] No rational model of human existence could be developed from the autonomy of the deified self; the dynamic of individualism transformed the paradigm of the common man into a Horatio Alger and produced the entrepreneur as the ideal type and a Rockefeller and Carnegie in the social sphere in which pleonexia was given its socially most powerful form.

At the end of the century the expectations of the common man had not been fulfilled. Instead of holding unrestricted sway over society's means of power, he saw himself exposed to bosses, political machines, and the spoils system. Instead of being a member of a democratic economic society of private capitalist entrepreneurs, he was confronted by an unavoidable process of economic concentration. From this situation corporate capitalism emerged as the prevailing organizational form of the means of production. Instead of an agrarian-republican idyll of free farmers—beneficiaries of a liberal distribution of land by the public hand—the "embattled farmer" experienced nothing but want; the number of the dispossessed and of dependent tenant farmers rose. "The end of the frontier" meant, finally, only territorial satiation of the "paradig-

24. J. K. Galbraith, *The New Industrial State* (New York, 1967), 350–51. Compare also Heimann, *Soziale Theorie der Wirtschaftssysteme;* M. Hereth, *Freiheit, Politik und Ökonomie* (Munich, 1974).

25. R. W. Emerson, "The Conduct of Life," in Emerson, *Works,* VI, 106.

matic republic"; but the dynamic of the spiritually, politically, and economically expanding self had found a power base in this continental empire. This empire promised that the obvious insufficiency of one's own social existence could be overcome in the fulfillment of apocalyptic yearnings. Economic-social Darwinism and idealist power-political symbolism in American self-understanding made the episode of direct imperialism of 1898 and the long-range policy of indirect imperialism seem plausible, though even this plausibility threatened repeatedly to obstruct an evaluation of the power structure of the global civilized world corresponding to the Americans' situation.

In terms of world history, the imperial republic understood itself primarily as the new Rome, destined to spread throughout the world the *novus ordo seclorum,* that is, the republican order. The expansion not of imperial power but of republican order, whether in the form of a republic encompassing the entire continent or in the form of a republican federation of states, was the primary objective of the founders, and in this they cleverly combined the power-political continental claim with clear economic-political interests.[26] But the Roman model and the fathers' own theoretical insight similarly planted the seeds for justified doubts about the possibility of combining imperial politics and republican order. This contradiction intensified in the latent psychic crisis at the end of the nineteenth century, when increasingly libidinously motivated apocalypses were substituted for the original consciousness-shaping spiritual-political experiences of order, and when Manifest Destiny treated other people and nations as objects of one's own *libido dominandi.* So, on one hand, imperial foreign policy was always tied to the mental, political, and economic crisis within the country, thus also the crisis of Americanism. On the other hand, time and again, foreign-affairs dealings by the political leadership and the majority that supported it showed that the various strands of motivation were intertwined: republican pathos, the modes of imperial apocalyptics, and the power-political and economic-political pragmatism of dominant social interests.

But what is crucial is the fact that all the actors moved in the continuity of the symbolic cosmos of Americanism and perceived the structures of the global civilized world only in the context of their own symbolic universe, where even the individual American always derives his point of view within his world. On this point the latent contradiction between imperial politics and republican order deepens into the contradiction between the American world and the competing symbolic worlds

26. Compare R. W. Van Alstyne, *The Rising American Empire* (New York, 1960), 78–79.

of contemporary humanity to the point at which regularly, to the present day, the search for a finite world order in the sense of the perfection of the founding in the world proves useless. The thoroughly reasonable insight into the vanity of imperial efforts, however, turns just as often into an attempt to retreat from the inevitable international entanglements into its own closed universe.[27]

Objectifying national expansionism into an imperial operation merely served to make very clear to sensitive Americans the progressive loss of republican humanity by which their own existence was measured. Before long this experience of frustration was critically captured only in American literature—given its social standing, a marginal product to this day. Washington Irving, Johnson J. Hooper, Edgar Allan Poe, Joseph G. Baldwin, George W. Harris, Nathaniel Hawthorne, Herman Melville, and Mark Twain alone were sensitive enough to measure the pathos of civil theology against the American reality. They somehow subjected the cities of the East, the plantations of the South, and the camps of the West to harsh criticism and, as Miller noted in speaking of Melville, offered "a long farewell to national greatness."[28] Not until the 1890s did the awareness of crisis spread until it produced an extensive literature of American self-criticism that reached its apex in the middle of the twentieth century.

Our observations so far make it seem understandable that the literature of crisis is invariably linked to the symbolism of Americanism, so that it operates in the medium of the dominant social field of organized society's consciousness. Underlying its premises there is, thanks to the transparency of social and political processes in American democracy, highly developed pragmatic criticism, by which I mean the detailed analysis of specific social phenomena and the investigation of singular circumstances, followed by proposals for reform. A splendid example of such pragmatic criticism grew out of the collaboration of the progressive politician Robert La Follette with the University of Wisconsin, where social analysis was converted into reform politics. But behind the pragmatic criticism—which, as will be shown, transformed American society from

27. For this complex in general, compare besides Van Alstyne, *Rising American Empire*, and W. A. Williams, *Contours of American History*, in particular W. A. Williams, *The Roots of the Modern American Empire* (New York, 1969); W. La Feber, *The New Empire: An Interpretation of American Expansion, 1860–1898* (Ithaca, N.Y., 1963); F. Merk, *Manifest Destiny and Mission in American History* (New York, 1963); E. R. May, *American Imperialism* (New York, 1968); Nagel, *Sacred Trust*, 247–324; H.-U. Wehler, "Der amerikanische Imperialismus vor 1914," in *Der moderne Imperialismus*, ed. W. J. Mommsen (Stuttgart, 1971), 172–92; H.-U. Wehler, *Aufstieg des amerikanischen Imperialismus* (Göttingen, 1974).

28. Quoted in K. S. Lynn, *The Comic Tradition in America* (Garden City, N.Y., 1958), 109.

Wilson's New Freedom through Roosevelt's New Deal to Kennedy's New Frontier under the horizon of Americanism—there gradually arose doubt in its substance. The doubts were expressed both in a stiffened patriotism and in criticism of the established understanding of history. But criticism could not achieve any genuine theoretical dimension, remaining linked to the American beginnings and mired in historical reinterpretation.

Turner claimed that the American spirit, character, and politics are the result of a pioneer culture unique in history. Having proclaimed the end of the frontier, he insisted staunchly on the unbroken shaping force of the "American spirit" and the "American ideals"; "However profound the economic changes, we shall not give up our American ideals and our hopes for man, which had their origin in our own pioneering experience. . . . We shall continue to present to our sister continent of Europe the underlying ideas of America as a better way of solving difficulties. We shall point to the Pax Americana, and seek the path of peace on earth to men of good will." [29]

Turner's thesis of the frontier merely gives new form to monumental history; he and his time did not yet doubt its substance; only its material substratum strays into the zone of doubt. Consequently criticism, in a Protestant manner, addresses itself to the fictional elements in the cult of the hero and monumental history. The reception of the critical methods of Continental European historians between 1890 and 1925 led to a demythologizing of American salvational history.

Sydney G. Fisher examined the *Legendary and Myth-Making Process in Histories of the American Revolution* and learned that the apotheosis of the Revolution and its heroes hardly presented a picture of historical reality. He suggested that what was needed was "to substitute truth and actuality for the mawkish sentimentality and nonsense with which we have been so long nauseated." [30] Searching for the truth, he composed a *True History of the American Revolution* (1902), a *True Benjamin Franklin* (1900), and a *True William Penn* (1900). As early as 1897, Paul L. Ford had written *The True George Washington;* in the book the apotheosis was recanted, and Washington was humanized so as to turn a historical figure into a man.[31] Turner, Fisher, Ford, and their fellow writers were interested not merely in historical accuracy; along with such figures as Henry Adams, Thorstein Veblen, Woodrow Wilson, John Dewey, William James, H. L. Mencken, Brooks Adams, and Charles Beard, they were part of a broad intellectual movement that articulated a

29. F. J. Turner, *The United States, 1830–1850: The Nation and Its Sections*, 152f.
30. Fisher, "Legendary and Myth-Making Process," 54.
31. P. L. Ford, *The True George Washington* (Philadelphia, 1897), 6.

crisis of American society in order to find a new connection with reality on the far side of the symbolism apparatus of orthodox Americanism.

The problem of the search for reality becomes clear in the concept of *debunking,* a term coined by the writer William E. Woodward in 1923 to designate the critical abolition of the cult of the hero: "Why, debunking means simply taking the bunk out of things. . . . You've heard of deflation—of prices, wages, and so on—taking the fictitious values out of merchandise. Well, debunking is an intellectual deflation. It's the science of reality."[32] Debunking alone, however, was no substitute for the critical history that, according to Nietzsche, corrects and destroys the past.[33] Woodward himself proved, in his *George Washington* (1926), that debunking leads not to reality but, at best, to banality.[34]

II. Republicanism and Industrialism: The Progressive Attempt at Renewal

The example of Charles Beard shows how little the intellectual revolt before the First World War was able to free itself from the ties to its own beginnings. He developed his progressivist attack on the "American Way of Life," led by covetousness, greed, and acquisitiveness, in his *Economic Interpretation of the Constitution* (1913), which revealed that among the members of the Constitutional Convention special interests were tied to decision making. Similarly, Louis Boudin published his radical attack on judicial review as a device to block all social progress in a historical tract, *Government by Judiciary* (1911).

What is true for the critical literature of Progressivism applies even more to the Progressive political and social protest movement as well as to the earlier mass movement of Populism. Progressivism and Populism articulated the psychological makeup of the Republic in the late form of civil theology of the waning nineteenth century.[35] Both have a place in the continuum of the spiritual-political movement of awakening. They are, with characteristic differences, the specifically American answer of those social groups that were most violently deprived of the realization of the world of the common man by the real consequences of Jacksonism, the organized oligarchy of bosses and corporations. Their basic structure contains all the elements of traditional political revivalism. The social-critical jeremiad takes the separate analysis of economic crisis, social con-

32. Quoted in Craven, *Legend of the Founding Fathers,* 188.
33. Nietzsche, *Werke,* I, 229.
34. Craven, *Legend of the Founding Fathers,* 196.
35. Hartz, *Liberal Tradition,* 228–55.

flicts, misuse of power, and concentration of power in economics and politics in particular, and a chaotic urbanism and industrialism in general, and shapes it into an apocalyptic pattern of corruption and vice. The looming punishment of a dissolution of the American order had to be countered with a national purification and reformational awakening of the citizens in order to restore the order of man and society. This political revivalism extended from the vulgar evangelism of a William Jennings Bryan through the militant moralistic national-republicanism of a Theodore Roosevelt to the ethical-political spiritualism of a Woodrow Wilson.[36] "All of the society was felt to be threatened—not by economic breakdown but by moral and social degradation and the eclipse of democratic institutions. This is not to say, however, that the men of the age gave way to despair; for they believed that, just as the sinner can be cleansed and saved, so the nation could be redeemed if the citizen awoke to their responsibilities."[37] Populism and Progressivism, social movements that, as such, had encompassed broad sections of society beyond their respective party organizations, were, according to Richard Hofstadter, reforming attempts "to hold on to some of the values of agrarian life, to save personal entrepreneurship and individual opportunity and the character type they engendered, and to maintain a homogeneous Yankee civilization."[38]

But the spiritual impetus of this movement no longer touched the deeply rooted pattern of consciousness in the majority of Americans; rather, it worked itself out primarily in the effort to imagine the established symbolic world in pragmatic-organizational terms. In this sense it was a matter of claiming the spiritual, political, and economic autarky of the common man against the superior power of the political and economic big businesses as the new unit of the national power game. The encompassing reformation programs of the era before the First World War were, accordingly, a recourse to the institutionalism of the fathers with the objective of restoring the citizen to his place as the ultimate political unit in the society of big business. But the organized interests' competition for optimal economic growth had entered Americanism through laissez-faire politics and had become indispensable as an integral premise of thriving industrialism; the dogmatic-individualistic patriotism of this movement therefore remained ineffectual as far as the specific new structures of American society were concerned. Populism organized the

36. Compare Hofstadter's biographical essays in *American Political Tradition*, 186–282.
37. R. Hofstadter, *The Age of Reform* (New York, 1955), 11; J. D. Hicks, *Populist Revolt* (Lincoln, Nebr., 1967).
38. Hofstadter, *Age of Reform*, 12.

social protest of the provincial yeomen, the agrarian-republican frontier culture, which was increasingly losing its social basis, though it continues to exist to the present day as a social fragment, like a social facet of agrarian-provincial America, along with the Populist tradition. The Populism of the free farmer was wrecked on the structural change of agriculture. But the successful commercial and industrial agriculture of a few producers who had taken the place of the farming majority of yeomen realized the Populist forms of political self-organization and the claim to sweeping public protection and subvention by the federal government to such a successful extent that in the twentieth century agriculture as a powerfully organized and special interest could become an important factor in the new political equilibrium of group interests to which William Appleton Williams gave the name of American syndicalism.[39]

The contradictoriness of restoration and reform becomes even more evident in Progressivism. Unlike agrarian-provincial Populism, Progressivism, which included important Populist elements, was a national movement of the new urban middle class, which for its part was already a product of the social-structural change brought about by industrialism. Progressive social criticism still judged the conditions of American society mainly according to the standards of the Jacksonian variant of Americanism, the republicanism of the individual entrepreneur and virtuous citizen. The "trust" and the "machine" were the root of all evil, of "mammonism," which was suddenly undermining the republican substance. The Progressivist psyche also gave a prominent place to pragmatic reform in the context of the revivalist recourse to traditional doctrine: "the trust in America was a significant part in intellectual technique for defining economic problems in terms of a Locke no one dared to transcend. If the trust was the heart of all evil, then Locke could be kept intact simply by smashing it, it was a technique by which a compulsive 'Americanism' was projected upon the real economic world."[40] For L. Hartz, the whole complex of the antitrust laws is the expression of a Progressive variation of Americanism; the same is even more true for all initiatives to democratize the political process:

> It does not take a deep analyst to see that the whole issue of "direct government," that passionate symbol of the progressive days, was involved root and branch in this problem. Why smash bosses and elect senators directly? . . . The answer was: to give every last individual an equal chance to govern. . . . Here was the equity of the Alger world flowering into

39. W. A. Williams, *Contours of American History*, 384.
40. Hartz, *Liberal Tradition*, 232.

politics. . . . Indeed the political energies premised by Progressivism were no less astounding than the economic energies it premised, so that the good American was not only a frantic economic dynamo rising to the top after trusts were shattered but a frantic political dynamo voting by referendum and recall after bosses were shattered.[41]

Trusts and machines were the targets of the Progressive revival, and the cathartic impetus of the movement was proved by their being shattered: the world was cleansed of all corruption. Here was found the specific connection of economic power and political corruption "which made the abolition of both simultaneous questions. . . . The point of connection, of course, was the charge that trusts and monopolies extracted special benefits from the state . . . , so that a restoration of the true 'American' world automatically called for elimination of the political corruption which its economic corruption inspired."[42] But Hartz ignores what is peculiarly paradoxical in the Progressive contribution to Americanism. He insists on including in the symbolic universe of society the organizational structure of industrial society as well as the principles of efficiency and functionalism that embody it and that were allegedly being attacked. Unlike those of Populism, the spokesmen of Progressivism were in a position to understand the irreversible nature of the historical process of the evolution of modern science, technology, industry, and bureaucracy, not least on the basis of their strong following among the new middle class. The Progressive movement began as a protest of the "unorganized public" against the new large organizations of capital and labor, as well as, implicitly, against the imperative of functional rationality inherent in industrialism. Under the pragmatic pressure of the reciprocal dependence of material prosperity and rational efficient organization, the restitution of the "paradigmatic republic" on the basis of the organizational principles of industrial society increasingly became the focus of the Progressive reformers' attention. Roosevelt and Wilson thought Taney through to his logical conclusion when they ultimately made efficiency the criterion for the political evaluation of big business: "That is the difference between a big business and a trust: A trust is an arrangement to get rid of competition, and a big business is a business that has survived competition by conquering in the field of intelligence and economy. A trust does not

41. *Ibid.*, 240.

42. *Ibid.*, 241. Compare also R. H. Wiebe, *The Search for Order* (New York, 1967); J. Weinstein, *The Corporate Ideal in the Liberal State, 1900–1918* (Boston, 1968); D. M. Kennedy, ed., *Progressivism* (Boston, 1971); D. S. Kirschner, "The Ambiguous Legacy: Social Justice and Social Control in the Progressive Era," *Historical Reflections*, II (1975), 69–88.

bring efficiency to the aid of business; it buys efficiency out of business."[43] A trust is artificially created by powerful men; it is a product of "greed," and therefore an expression of social corruption. Big business, on the other hand, grows naturally. "I admit that any large corporation built up by the legitimate processes of business, by economy, by efficiency, is natural; and I am not afraid of it, no matter how big it grows." "Big business is no doubt to a large extent necessary and natural. The development of business upon a great scale of cooperation, is inevitable, and . . . is probably desirable."[44] Like Marx, Wilson is convinced that "major industry" is essential to modern production: "I am not jealous of any process of growth, no matter how huge the result, provided the result was indeed obtained by the processes of wholesome development, which are the processes of efficiency, of economy, of intelligence, and of invention."[45] Consequently this insight into the organizational structure of industrial society had to alter the direction of political reform:

> A simple and poor society can exist as a democracy on a basis of sheer individualism. But a rich and complex industrial society cannot so exist; for some individuals, and especially those artificial individuals called corporations, become so very big that the ordinary individual . . . cannot deal with them in terms of equality. It therefore becomes necessary for these ordinary individuals to combine in their turn, first in order to act in their collective capacity through that biggest of all combinations called the government, and second, to act also to their own self-defence, through private combinations, such as farmers' associations and trade unions.[46]

In Herbert Croly, the author of *The Promise of American Life* (1909), this change from urban-industrial Progressivism to recognition of the organizational principles of the industrial economic society, which the agrarian-republican Populist Jeffersonians in the West and the South could not easily espouse, found its civil-theological interpreter. Croly— the son of devout Comtians, a student of Santayana, Royce, and James— wrote under the influence of the politics of Roosevelt, whose implications and underlying intentions he not only understood better than the president himself but also knew how to turn into theory. His book became the bible of the intelligentsia with a revivalist bent, who expressed themselves after 1914 in the *New Republic:* John Dewey, Walter Lippman,

43. W. Wilson, *The New Freedom* (Englewood Cliffs, N.J., 1961), 109.
44. *Ibid.*, 102–103.
45. *Ibid.*, 115.
46. J. M. Blum, *The Republican Roosevelt* (Cambridge, Mass., 1954), 110; also quoted in Hofstadter, *Age of Reform*, 247.

Walter Weyl, George Soule, and Bruce Bliven. "While many of Croly's ideas were later substantially modified and expanded, they served as the point of departure for an entire generation of writers who believed that America could be fundamentally transformed without having to endure a violent revolution."[47] Croly remained strictly within the context of founding and order when he described the conditions that would allow sociopolitical reformation in the United States, which at heart is an ethical-spiritual revival of the nation. In order to remain true to the traditional vision of the promise, the American must sacrifice the traditional means of fulfillment; otherwise American life will gradually lose all specific promise. For Croly, American history after Jefferson and Hamilton is a sequence of abortive attempts at realization, thanks not least to the reduction of political faith of the Americans to a national optimistic fatalism: "The substance of our national Promise has consisted . . . of an improving popular economic condition, guaranteed by democratic political institutions, and resulting in moral and social amelioration. These manifold benefits were to be obtained merely by liberating the enlightened self-interest of the American people. . . . The fulfillment of the American Promise was considered inevitable because it was based upon a combination of self-interest and the natural goodness of human nature."[48] The optimistic fatalism of an automatic fulfillment of the American promise and the social-Darwinist economic form of American civil theology I have described above were the core of Croly's critique. Reform of the political institutions in the state and federal governments, with the inclusion of organized labor and organized capital in a constructive regulation of industrial corporations, were to be the principles of big business, placed in the service of an ethical-spiritual renewal of the nation. This he described as "constructive individualism," the contents of which were based on the representative humanity of Abraham Lincoln:[49] "these very qualities of high intelligence, humanity, magnanimity and humility are precisely the qualities which Americans, in order to become better democrats, should add to their strength, their homogeneity, and their innocence; while at the same time they are just the qualities which Americans are prevented by their individualistic practice and tradition from attaining or properly valuing."[50] Although the apotheosis of Lincoln furnished the paradigm for the Progressive revival, the prevailing individualism prevented a return to Lincoln. Croly called for such a return as a collective

47. R. H. Pells, *Radical Visions and American Dreams* (New York, 1973), 4–5.
48. H. Croly, *The Promise of American Life* (Cambridge, Mass., 1965), 22.
49. *Ibid.*, 89–99.
50. *Ibid.*, 99.

act, that is, a national education. It involved the moral and intellectual emancipation of the individual, which was to occur in a system of collective responsibility that allowed the process of social reform to become altogether identical with that of individual reform.[51] Croly was aiming at the restoration of the truth of individual existence, but he determined it from the excellence of those activities whose ethical and intellectual meaning consisted in the material disinterest of the actors. The citizen's organized material autarky was the precondition for the "declaration of intellectual independence," the "emancipation of the individual"; that is, political and economic Americanism would henceforth have to be followed by the "intellectual basis of Americanism," in which the standards of technical excellence (in the sense of *techne*) are tied into the standards of moral and intellectual excellence. The training of some individuals who are competent in the sense of Croly's ethics is the first condition of national reconstruction, for it is only such persons whom the people will ultimately prefer as reformers over the traditional political leaders. To Croly reform meant regeneration of the national *corpus mysticum* in the form of a "religion of human brotherhood," in which "a democratic scheme of moral values" achieves its perfect expression. The ordering force of "loving-kindness" toward one's fellow citizens would meaningfully unite the different technical excellence of competent individuals in the work of social reorganization and individual emancipation. The end of this work, according to Croly, may consist in an "outburst of enthusiasm," inspired in part by a democratic evangelist: "some imitator of Jesus who will reveal to men the path whereby they may enter in to spiritual possession of their individual and social achievements, and immeasurably increase them by virtue of personal regeneration." Croly's Progressive revival combines Comtian symbolism with the tradition of Americanism. Democracy—and with this Croly takes up the leitmotif of the fathers—*is* virtue. "The common citizen can become something of a saint and something of a hero, not by growing to heroic proportions in his own person, but by the sincere and enthusiastic imitation of heroes and saints, and whether or not he will ever come to such imitation will depend upon the ability of his exceptional fellow-countrymen to offer him acceptable examples of heroism and saintliness."[52] Croly's Americanism saves him from the Comtian implication of ascension to the superman: the restitution of virtue under the conditions of the organizational principles of industrial society is placed in the continuity of the revivalist reconstruction of the paradigmatic humanity of a national hero: Abraham Lincoln.

51. *Ibid.*, 409.
52. *Ibid.*, 453–54.

Progressivism was successful, not as an organized political awakening movement, but in its dominance as the vehicle of a form of consciousness and symbol in whose medium the structures of the industrial-technical organization in society could first develop without breaking apart its collectivity. This Americanism of the Progressive movement was also shared by the socialist variants of the waning nineteenth century, especially the Socialist party, insofar as they did not, like the Marxists, persist in their "Europeanism," thus giving up their effectiveness in the American world. The socialist alternative proposed by the American radicals, as W. A. Williams never ceases to insist, was rooted in the old tradition of a Christian-cooperative commonwealth grounded in the great debates of Cromwell's forces in the English revolution.[53]

Heedless of the decay of the "movement" with the end of World War I, Progressivism left behind an all-American consensus concerning the dominant sociostructural components of the industrial society of the United States. This genuine product of progressivist politics was, for one thing, a saturation of politics with the principles of industrial organization. The organization of social groups along the lines of function and efficiency gave to the political process a new structure; agriculture, labor, and capital became the constitutive units of American politics. But what was decisive was the social breakthrough of a specific Progressive component: the bureaucracy as the vehicle for public reform. The community, the state, and especially the nation were subjected to bureaucratization in an effort to coordinate the organized special interests cooperatively through a powerful central organization of the public interest. To these sociostructural components was added the elements of the functional leadership elite in the form of the professional politician. Its highest objective was the political and bureaucratic power center of this new structure of society: the office of the president. Complementing the social group of professional politicians is the shifting and fluid group of reforming and consulting intellectuals. Together they form the functional leadership elite—what Williams calls American syndicalism. Theodore J. Lowi uses the term *interest-group liberalism* for the current manifestation of this phenomenon.[54] It is the organizational form of industrial

53. W. A. Williams, *Contours of American History*, 386–89, 486ff. However, Williams turns Marx into a secularized leveler. Compare also A. Fried, ed., *Socialism in America* (New York, 1970), 1–15; Hartz, *Liberal Tradition*, 233–36.

54. W. A. Williams, *Contours of American History*, 384ff., 470–73; T. J. Lowi, *The End of Liberalism* (New York, 1969), 55–97. Compare also H.-J. Puhle, "Der Übergang zum organisierten Kapitalismus in den USA," in *Organisierter Kapitalismus*, ed. H. A. Winkler (Göttingen, 1974), 172–94, and E. W. Hawley, "New Deal und 'organisierter Kapitalismus' in internationaler Sicht," in *Die große Krise in Amerika*, ed. H. A. Winkler

America, whose stability is based on including the new structural elements into the social plausibility structure of Americanism. The symbolic universe mediated among the sociostructural outcomes of private-libidinous segments with the public-rational claim to order of the socially dominant form of consciousness in such a way that the crucial contradictions could be successfully suppressed. The deformation of consciousness and of symbol forms in the waning nineteenth century was the common denominator for such mediation.

In any case, the symbolism proved its worth once more in the serious crisis of the sociopolitical order in 1929, and at the same time it allowed the pragmatic reorganization of the New Deal. "If the great Depression of the 'thirties' suggested anything, it was that the failure of socialism in America stemmed from the ideologic power of the national irrational liberalism rather than from economic circumstance."[55] This is how Hartz described the decisive function of the American civil theology at the time when the organizational structures of the early form of the syndicalist system collapsed. It was crucial to preserve the public sphere, the politics, as the locus of the social totality in the symbolic universe; that is, the constitutional order and its institutions remained untouched, and therefore the crisis could be surmounted through collective political action of the crucial segments of the syndicalist system under the leadership of a determined executive. J. C. Davies speaks of a revolution that did not happen, though the socioeconomic preconditions for it were at hand. But the apathy and despair of the affected masses continued to be on principle embedded in the plausibility structure of Americanism. "The great majority of the public was committed to the virtues that represented public dogma since 1776, and not the oppositional program of an alienated intelligence. . . . Those who were least affected by the crisis—businessmen from the upper middle class, the clergy, lawyers, and intellectuals, remained committed not only to the egalitarian values and the established economic system, but also to the constitution."[56] The minimal effectiveness of alternative interpretations of order is, of course, also connected to the fact that the ethos of the ruling symbolism of order of the spiritual-moral authority was more easily assumed to reside in "public persons" than in the words and books of the intelligentsia. The literary man as the

---

(Göttingen, 1973). The term *organized capitalism* as applied generally to a number of *essential* aspects of the social reality of completely different political societies does not seem to me very instructive for theory, since it arbitrarily reduces a common component of the socioeconomic structure that can be found in different forms to an absolute.

55. Hartz, *Liberal Tradition*, 259.

56. J. C. Davies, "Theorie der Revolution," in *Theorien des sozialen Wandels*, ed. W. Zapf (Cologne, 1968), 411–12.

"conscience of the nation" did not exist in this American universe, except possibly as a columnist for a powerful newspaper. Richard H. Pells, who has traced the struggle of American intellectuals in pursuit of a radical alternative during the 1930s, has shown the social irrelevance of any attempts to reconcile Marx and Locke in an "American-style socialism." The deep contradictoriness of all alternative symbolisms proposed by the radical intelligentsia consisted not only of the insistence by organizationally splintered Marxism on its Europeanism and the ambivalence of the Soviet Union's communist model, but most especially the underlying existential stamp by the Americanist symbolism of the Progressive orientation. In Pell's view, Lewis Mumford, John Dewey, Helen and Robert Lynd, Sidney Hook, and Reinhold Niebuhr carried Croly's Progressive revivalism almost to the point of no return, to the essential nexus of founding and order. In the long run, however, the representatives of American radicalism were neither willing nor able to bring the sacrifice of self-destruction in favor of a rebirth under the sign of European ideology. The quenching of the American self for the sake of entry into the "second reality" of European ideology was, in the 1930s, the radical alternative from which, understandably, the radicals' common sense shrank back. In representative cases a symbolic "half-way covenant" was all it came to this:

> By combining traditional liberal values, new socialist insights, and a profound moral passion, they hoped to give their fellow citizens a means of understanding and solving the crisis in which everyone found himself. . . . In sum, Mumford, Dewey, Lynd, Hook, and Neibuhr had managed momentarily to join ideas that seemed otherwise contradictory. They succeeded in preserving a tenuous balance between liberalism and Marxism, morality and politics, private thought and collective action, individual freedom and the search of community, a cultural critique of industrialism and an ideological analysis of capitalism, the desire for psychologically satisfying myths and the need of coherent social theory. But it would prove increasingly difficult to sustain this equilibrium in the later years of the decade. What they were asking Americans to do was hold two opposing ideals in their minds at the same time.[57]

While in 1932 the radical intelligentsia was still discussing the relative merits and drawbacks of William Z. Foster, the Communist candidate, and Norman Thomas, the Socialist one, the overwhelming majority of Americans had already made up its mind in favor of the "Christian" and "Democratic" Franklin Delano Roosevelt. In the beginning the reform

57. Pells, *Radical Visions*, 148 ff.

program of the "'sublimated' Americanism" (Hartz) of the New Deal alienated the radical intelligentsia to the same degree that it fulfilled the voters' expectations. The commonly perceived American reality was the psychic effort to overcome the Depression; this loss of material sustenance had turned latent existential anxiety into palpable experience. For the radical break with the self-evidence of infinite progress in material prosperity affected the faith in the American experiment, whose substance it had become. The restitution of the promise of American life must be proved in the vigorous reorganization of material living conditions, thus preserving the majority's trust in the ordering power of *politics* in the paradigmatic republic. The New Deal was certainly not an extrapolation of the Progressive movement. Nor was it "different from anything that had yet happened in the United States,"[58] even less an "abrupt break with the continuity of the past."[59] From the point of view of the history of society and consciousness, the New Deal is preformed to such a degree that the traits of pragmatic-political reform affecting all of society such as had not before been recognized in the United States became all the more apparent. In other words, the New Deal was not a movement of political awakening like Progressivism, though many revivalists participated in it, and the thrust of pragmatic reform took a different direction, responsive to the conditions of the Depression. But pragmatism was possible only in the medium of an unchallenged civil theology, where the Progressives had placed industrial society in the continuity of founding and order. Furthermore, the institutional and structural reforms rested on the organizational form of American syndicalism, which in its basic structure was already fully developed and—not least, in turn, through the politics of Progressivism—had symbolically become part of the civil theology:

> The leading models of the new order grew for the most part out of the ideas of the innovators of the past reform period. They grew out of the experiences of these people from the planned economy of the wartime period and from the "teachings" and "logical conclusions" that one apparently felt it necessary to draw from Hoover's experiences and from his methods. The United States now no longer adhered to the problem solving of the 1920s, and Americans professed their loyalty to the encompassing movement toward socioeconomic integration. But in this they continued . . . in the past, and their behavior can be understood only in the context of the total national history.[60]

58. Hofstadter, *Age of Reform*, 303.
59. S. Lubell, *The Future of American Politics* (New York, 1955), 3.
60. Hawley, "New Deal und 'organisierter Kapitalismus,'" 17.

Williams' analysis very precisely depicted the connection and trenchantly concluded: "the New Deal is often viewed as a major turning point in American history. A bit more perspective suggests that it represented a reaction to a severe crisis in which most of the elements, attitudes, and policies of the Progressive Movement were finally consolidated in one short period under the leadership of a particularly dramatic politician."[61] The experimental practices of Roosevelt's pragmatism and of his heterogeneous following based its implicit theory on the common sense of the Americanisms of the preceding spiritual-political awakening movements, though without signs either of their spiritual impetus or their underlying experiences.

Certainly Williams was not incorrect when he described Roosevelt as a representative of the "American feudal gentry" and pointed to its traditional "spirit of noblesse oblige," "disinterested humanitarianism," and "buoyant confidence." This ethos of the old leadership elites of the United States is the tradition of the political class since Washington. Nevertheless, the European analogy to the terms *feudal* and *gentry* conceals the fact that we are dealing with a leadership ethos *sui generis:* the mentality of the existential-political republicans is psychosocially rooted in the form of consciousness of common sense. True, in the case of Roosevelt it takes its vitality less from authentic spirituality than from the certainty of a self-evident symbolic order as the source of order. Its primal thrust in the symbolic world of the republic enables it to exercise the bold *eupraxia* of the true dilettante, though its borders lie precisely in this world of Americanism. Roosevelt's naïveté toward a world in whose structures the symbolic universe of his civil theology does not appear reveals the limits of this particular universe.[62] Roosevelt came to power neither as a pragmatic reform technocrat with a closed mind about ways to overcome the Depression nor as the clever "virtuoso of opportunism" (Hofstadter), who allowed himself to be guided by the "attitude" of practical performance in the permanent experiment of crisis resolution—though both the technocratic and the opportunistic element were present.

---

61. W. A. Williams, *Contours of American History,* 439.

62. For Roosevelt, compare Hofstadter, *American Political Tradition,* 315–52; A. M. Schlesinger, Jr., *The Age of Roosevelt* (Boston, 1957–60); J. M. Burns, *Roosevelt: The Lion and the Fox* (New York, 1956). The account of the New Deal in American historiography, of course, depends in turn on the particular position within social self-understanding. Besides the noted contributions by Hartz, Hofstadter, Hawley, Schlesinger, Burns, and Williams, compare also the anthology by E. C. Rozwenc, ed., *The New Deal* (Boston, 1968). See also W. E. Leuchtenburg, *Franklin D. Roosevelt and the New Deal, 1932–1940* (New York, 1963); P. K. Conkin, *The New Deal* (New York, 1967); Shonfield, *Geplanter Kapitalismus;* A. A. Berle, *The Twentieth Century Capitalist Revolution* (New York, 1954); J. K. Galbraith, *American Capitalism* (Boston, 1952).

Rather, he rose to be the political leader of a new majority of the impoverished masses of the "forgotten man" by his promise to actively restore social justice in the paradigmatic republic under the new conditions of industrial society. "Social justice" called first of all for the effective establishment of all possible measures to abolish material want in its various guises. The civil-theological content of this program of social justice was illustrated in Roosevelt' famous Commonwealth Club address, which the early New Dealers helped to write. "Faith in America, faith in our tradition of personal responsibility, faith in our institutions, faith in ourselves demand that we recognize the new terms of the social contract. We shall fulfill them, as we fulfilled the obligation of the apparent Utopia which Jefferson imagined for us in 1776, and which Jefferson, Roosevelt and Wilson thought to bring to realization." The end of the frontier, the speech noted, meant the end of freedom for farmers, and the highly organized financial-industrial corporate complex meant the end of the free-enterprise system. The socioeconomic premise—the right to property and independence through property—of the political order of the founders was thus turned into its opposite: the economic power of an oligarchy not only threatened the individual's material existence but also affected the public welfare, the purpose of government. But just as formerly uncontrolled political power in a social contract was subjugated to the public interest through constitutional democratic government, today, he said, it was a matter of modifying and controlling economic power in an "economic constitutional order." Roosevelt's declaration of economic rights follows Jefferson's declaration of political rights. In the crisis of 1932 the social contract of the Declaration of Independence needed to be newly defined. An "economic constitutional order" is what the "new terms of the old social contract" meant.[63] Because Roosevelt saw himself as the Jefferson of the twentieth century, he follows the tradition of republicanism in viewing the current economic crisis not in economic terms, as a structural defect of the economic system, but in political terms, as a structural defect of the constitutional order.

Roosevelt's principled political understanding of order resulted in the New Deal's confusing multiplicity of conceptual initiatives, ideas, and programs for institutional reform and the contradictory complexity of experiments and techniques for problem solving. In the social context of the basic syndicalist structure, it was essential that the federal authorities proceed democratically in solving the power problems of industrial society in an "economic republic"; this method would supposedly guarantee that both social welfare and economic growth be preserved. The eco-

63. F. D. Roosevelt, *Public Papers and Addresses* (New York, 1953), I, 742–56.

nomic republic had, in the words of the New Dealer A. A. Berle, "integrated the democratic process by which we operate our politics with visible or indirect controls of the private decisions by which we work our economics."[64] In his attempt to describe the results of the New Deal, Berle certainly defined the intention of Roosevelt, whose close adviser he was.

This is not the place to discuss the six hectic years from 1933 to 1938 but only to note that the New Deal, despite considerable failures, was successful on at least one point: it salvaged for organized society the social field of consciousness that exemplified it. From this time on, organized society would on the whole arrange itself according to the syndicalist principles of the large organizing units. The restoration of constitutional civil government in all the areas of the syndicalist structure institutionalized a tentative equilibrium among the various components for the time being. The institutional center of order was the office of the president, around which were grouped a variety of bureaucracies in a singular "fragmentation of governing power" (Shonfield) in which the public power of the nation exercised its constitutional government syndicalistically. This complex federal reform bureaucracy was linked with the municipal and state bureaucracies in exercising its tasks, and, tied to the political process, it recognized the organized interests as concerted participants in power; its rise marked the specific republicanism of the New Deal. At the same time it established for the duration the reform intelligentsia in the various ranks of the welfare-state bureaucracy in such a way that the social relevance of an alienated intelligentsia was blunted. Not only the professional politicians as the de facto trustees of the public sphere but also the leadership elite of big labor and big business decided the power questions in organized society, at least until the time when the socioeconomic unit of the corporation began to go beyond the social field of organized society in the context of a global economic community. As long, however, as this state of affairs ran parallel to the international policies of the American empire, Americanism covered over a potential contradiction between imperial policy and global economy.

In the practices of the New Deal, pragmatic rationality with a bureaucratic-economic orientation inevitably attained the status of a social principle of order: "At the core of the New Deal, then, was not a philosophy . . . but an attitude, suitable for practical politicians, administrators and technicians."[65] To put it in negative terms: "The personal condescension of the New Deal, allied with the doctrine of the liberal

64. A. A. Berle, *The American Economic Republic* (New York, 1963), vii.
65. Hofstadter, *Age of Reform*, 325.

tradition, encouraged it to be satisfied with giving Americans a greater share in material goods—and even within this standard, to measure success by quantitative 'indices' of well-being that masked the unevenness of the economy's performance."[66] This functional-rational part of the New Deal is revealed especially clearly in the relationship of the New Dealers to the symbolic dimension of American existence. The social success prevailing over other symbolic worlds lay not least, as already shown, in recourse to the traditional symbolism; Pells correctly points to Roosevelt's attraction for American intellectuals: "many writers in the late 1930s were attracted to the New Deal precisely because it seemed to utilize the traditional rhetoric, images, and slogans of American culture far more effectively than any of the parties farther to the left, thereby uniting people around the lowest common denominator of belief and action."[67] Roosevelt's minimizing of the national crisis in a symbolic popular consensus, which took political shape in the election of 1936, as well as the looming international crisis, compelled a departure from the European ideologies; consequently the American radical intelligentsia, including the Communists, renewed their efforts to join with the masses in the shared symbolic world of Americanism: "the search for an alternative social philosophy gave way in the late 1930s to a renewed appreciation for the habits and precedents that had sustained the country through previous crises."[68] "Now, as the Left discovered the value of patriotism and as intellectuals displayed a new found respect for the underlying vigor of the national character, the past was being transformed into precisely the sort of compelling 'political myth' that could comfort the populace in an age of chaos and uncertainty."[69] This turn toward Americanism arose less from the search for the sources of order of the republic in traditional symbolism than from the insight into the functional achievement of civil theology, preserving the patterns of social behavior; this phenomenon was noted by such prominent figures of the left as Helen and Robert Lynd in their study *Middletown in Transition* (1937), in which they used the methods of empirical social research.

The attitude coincided on one point with the functional rationalism of the New Deal elite: social self-understanding having already largely lost its motivating experiences, doubt now also arose whether implicit rational knowledge of order could be involved. Here lies the break with the tradition of spiritual-political revivalism: the truth of the existence of

66. McWilliams, *Idea of Fraternity*, 547.
67. Pells, *Radical Visions*, 326.
68. *Ibid.*, 314.
69. *Ibid.*, 315.

homo Americanus was disputed. The liberal Frederick Schumann, in 1932 a cosigner of an appeal to the Communists, persuaded of the synthesis of pragmatism and Marxism, began from then on to deny that the masses employed reason; they were, he claimed, moved "by emotions, mysticism, and mythology." Not last, in connection with the new forms of mass communication, public recourse to the symbols of self-interpretation was understood as functionally steering the citizens to their best interests in the sense of behaviorist psychology. Harold Laswell and most especially Thurman Arnold absolutized symbol functionalism, which they considered to be the theory of the New Deal. "We find a sharp and sustained attack upon ideologies, rational principles, and moralism in politics."[70]

Arnold's *The Symbols of Government* (1935) and *The Folklore of Capitalism* (1937) seek to demonstrate that all social organization is based on the symbols of self-understanding. But "social and political beliefs had 'no meaning whatever' apart from the organization and movements to which they were 'attached.'" Arnold "interpreted every doctrine as a semantic instrument for the regulation of human activity."[71] Symbolism, here called folklore, was no longer granted any wisdom; the motivating order of consciousness was replaced by the structure of drives: patterns of behavior and organization expressed the satisfaction of needs identified by utilitarian determinants—that is, guarantees of optimal production and distribution of material goods. Although Arnold understood the instrumental character of civil-theological symbolism, he disputed its order content; he therefore transferred the authoritative justification of reform within a social order—in the sense of that very order content—to the depths of unconscious instinct. Arnold's "fundamental axiom that man works only for his fellowman"[72] was the final conclusion of pragmatic wisdom. "What Thurman Arnold failed to see was that the technical pragmatism he wanted was nourished by the very 'folklore' he blasted. An irreversible ethics made all problems technical."[73] Arnold as well as Laswell documented the functional connection of founding and order, at the same time making clear the social consequences of the reification of the symbolic order in its instrumentalization of all symbols; all "national mythology" was a means to further steering of other-directed man by the standards of the calculating self-interest of organized groups. The institutions of the republic were redefined in the spirit of the func-

---

70. Hofstadter, *Age of Reform*, 319.
71. Pells, *Radical Visions*, 324.
72. T. W. Arnold, *The Folklore of Capitalism* (London, 1937).
73. Hartz, *Liberal Tradition*, 271.

tional rationality of organized industrial society. Certainly Arnold represented not even the majority consciousness of the New Dealers, Roosevelt included, and as Hartz correctly stressed, the social reforms of the New Deal could be effected successfully only in the symbolic medium of the dominant social field of consciousness of American society. But he signaled the erosion of the psychic substratum of Americanism, an erosion that intensified with the manifest crisis of the sociopolitical arrangement of the New Deal in the second half of the twentieth century. Until this time the United States could still absolutely interpret itself on a continuum of tradition: "America, so it was argued, had succeeded in breaking through to a magnificent fusing of two worlds into a system that combined technocratic rationality, social security, and stable growth with a large arena for democratic decision processes and decentralized initiative. And this breakthrough . . . was said to have made the 'American way' into the embodiment of economic and social progress. America's way was the way that a large part of the rest of the world would eventually take."[74] Using the terms of civil theology, Arthur Schlesinger, Jr., noted: "The New Deal took a broken and despairing land and gave it new confidence in itself. Not perhaps new confidence; but rather a revival of the ancient faith in the free people which, speaking through Jefferson and Jackson and Lincoln, had been our great source of national strength. Roosevelt had the vision of democratic America and the strength to realize a good part of that vision."[75] Schlesinger remained caught in the spell of a monumental history whose consciousness-shaping power would no longer be able to withstand the pressure of pragmatic reality. On the other hand, since all problems of order were raised in the language of this monumental history, including even Arnold's symbol of nihilism, the American self-critique and self-analysis of the present in its search for the lost order center on the quest for the theoretical dignity of Americanism.

III. Self-Criticism Between Affirmation of the Status Quo and Revival of the Tradition

Only after the convulsions of World War II did American self-criticism very reluctantly abandon the influence of monumental history. The search of representative minds in the humanities, the churches, and the media for a nondogmatic interpretation of Americanism in postwar

74. Hawley, "New Deal und 'organisierter Kapitalismus,'" 32.
75. A. M. Schlesinger, Jr., "The Broad Accomplishments of the New Deal," in Rozwenc, ed., *The New Deal,* 28.

America will be demonstrated by an analysis of the works of Ralph Barton Perry, Daniel J. Boorstin, Seymour Martin Lipset, Reinhold Niebuhr, John Courtney Murray, Walter Lippmann, and Louis Hartz.

This literature of self-criticism and self-analysis is given its coherence by the articulation, or at least the discussion, of an American awareness of consciousness of crisis as well as a constant effort to confer meaning on the power complex that the North American empire has become in the twentieth century. A certain lack of coherence resulted from the fact that the actual impulses, the special intentions, the material examined, and the symbol constructs, as well as the horizons and intellectual states of mind of the authors differ (the social attitudes are remarkably uniform). The writers were variously affected by such general Western crisis elements and factors as the Western civilizations' merging into one global community, the pragmatic pressure, the emergence of the modern political mass movements, or the industrial organization of production relations. These mingled with such experiences of crisis of a specifically American nature as the end of isolationism or the role of America as an interventionist world power from World War I to the Vietnam War, which finally defined the limits of America's power potential, and the internal antagonisms of "society in excess"—for example, the economic crisis or the insufficient social integration of the African-American minority. All these factors solidified into the suspicion that Americanism was proving to be an unsuitable instrument for understanding the domestic and international situations; and in the background loomed a questioning of the society's sense of order, as Perry expressed it in 1944: "There is no cardinal principle of American life, no article of our central faith, that had not during the early decades of the present century been challenged and, by some critic or dissenting group rejected. . . . In 1914 there was only one question: Shall America, or shall America not resort to arms in defense of Americanism? Twenty-five years later, in 1939, there were two questions: First shall America intervene, and if so, in what way and in what time? Where does its frontier lie?" The questions lost none of their weight and urgency under the conditions of the 1960s. "But to these questions of defensive strategy . . . there was now added a second question: For what should America intervene? What was that Americanism, other than bodily lives and possessions, which was worth defending? Even if America was to withdraw within its narrowest territorial frontiers, to what end should it devote itself in its own house?"[76] The existing answers to the questions give essentially three alternatives: the affirmation of the status quo, the postulate of recourse to tradition, and finally,

---

76. Perry, *Puritanism and Democracy*, 17.

the proclamation of a breakthrough to a reality beyond status quo and tradition. These categories are of a formal nature to begin with; their content determination will emerge only from the material.

All the writers carry out their exploration of the American consciousness in the form of an interpretation of history that is informed by a central thesis, which differs from author to author. Daniel J. Boorstin speaks of the "declining sense of American uniqueness" as the "great trauma of the American mind in the last half century,"[77] and he expresses the experience of crisis in the form of a biblical metaphor: it is the fall of the "American Adam." "The American gradually discovered that he was no longer living in the Garden of Eden. How had it all happened? What was he to do about it? Should he try to recapture his innocence, or should he try to atone for his Fall? These are the deep questions which have come to disturb the American mind and conscience." The American discovered that he was "doctrinally naked" and sought desperately to cover his nakedness. "It was thus loss of our feeling of the 'givenness' of our values that led us to a serious and general search for an 'American Philosophy.'"[78] Each national crisis of the twentieth century, Boorstin notes, had intensified the call for an explicit "democratic faith" or a "philosophy for democracy." But, according to this thinker, Americans are not in a position to undertake such a theoretical venture, since every abstract formulation of the principles of political life, especially in the form of a "blueprint for society" in the manner of the ideologues of the eighteenth and nineteenth centuries, would destroy the tacit solidarity of the actual political life of American society. Boorstin clearly supports the Burkean misunderstanding of political theory and describes American democracy and its institutions as the result of the "unprecedented opportunities of this continent" and as an "unrepeatable combination of historical circumstances." He foregoes a thorough study of the problems of the American order, assigns to democracy a genius in the sense of ancient Rome, and understands it to be a characteristic disposition of American culture.[79] The American ethos excluded the "theoretical crotchets" of the European type, since from the beginning it took its vitality from a "mystical faith in a preformed national theory." "Our American past and the theories of politics which it is thought to imply, have become the yardstick against which the national life is measured. This is the deeper meaning of the criterion of 'Americanism.'"[80] In the "unity of American life" the boundaries between "community values" and "personal belief,"

---

77. D. J. Boorstin, *America and the Image of Europe* (New York, 1960), 121.
78. *Ibid.*, 123.
79. D. J. Boorstin, *The Genius of American Politics* (Chicago, 1953), 1.
80. *Ibid.*, 22.

between "political philosophy" and "religious faith" become blurred. The "givenness of community values" also orders individual existence:[81] "Givenness is the belief that values in America are in some way or other automatically defined: given by certain facts of geography or history peculiar to us."

Boorstin distinguishes three levels of this "givenness": (a) "Values" as a gift from the past: "the earliest settlers or Founding Fathers equipped our nation at its birth with a perfect and complete political theory, adequate to all our future needs." (b) "Values" as a gift of the present: "our theory is always implicit in our institutions. This is the idea that the 'American way of life' harbors an 'American way of thought,'" as well as the idea that American political theory always appears in the guise of a specific American experience, which is in first line the experience of the American landscape. (c) Past and present, history and geography are axiomatically linked by belief in the continuity and homogeneity of American history: "It is the quality of our experience which makes us see our national past as an uninterrupted continuum of similar events, so that our past merges indistinguishably into our present. . . . Our feelings of continuity in our history makes it easy for us to see the Founding Fathers as our contemporaries." In the feeling for continuity were fused the belief in the preformed, original theory of the fathers and the idea of a theory underlying all current experience into "givenness."[82] Boorstin uses three major crises of American history—Puritanism, the War of Independence, and the Civil War—to illustrate the essential role of the "sense of 'givenness'" for American history.

Boorstin traces this sense of givenness back to the American historical apocalypse, to the belief "that God himself drew the plans for our career and marked its outlines in our history and our very ground."[83] The fall of the American Adam thus consists of the realization that it was not providential predetermination that determined the American role in the drama of world history but that world history must stage its own production.[84]

Thus Americans face the truly confusing situation that their economic and military preeminence in the world might enable them to realize the concept of "manifest destiny" from the power-political aspect under the horizon of a global community, while at the same time this very "destiny" threatens to be deprived of its "manifestness."

81. *Ibid.*, 157–58.
82. *Ibid.*, 9–10.
83. *Ibid.*, 161.
84. *Ibid.*, 163.

Boorstin's reply to the "declining sense of 'givenness'" is influenced by Edmund Burke's prohibition against theory. He draws a false conclusion from the correct insight that the crisis cannot be overcome through still another variation of eighteenth- and nineteenth-century speculations on systems. Therefore he does not see the phenomenon of Americanism as requiring any continuing theoretical analysis but continues to regard it as natural that the symbols and behaviors cannot be investigated for their reasoning content. Once again Boorstin looks to Burke for a way out of the crisis: he proposes "to try to bring to the surface those attitudes which have been latent in the notion of 'givenness' itself, to discover the general truths about institutions by which we have actually lived."[85]

But since precisely these institutions are nothing other than meaningful behavior patterns that remain constant over long periods of time and are conveyed by social fields of consciousness, the impetus from Burke merely throws Boorstin back on a phenomenological description of Americanism. He refuses to set philosophy in the place of history: "we will be humble before our past and the past of other nations; for we will seek the wisdom in institutions."[86] But the lover of wisdom simply does not find it in any institutions but only in the philosophical reflection upon human existence in society and history. Boorstin distinguishes between singularists and pluralists. The former take literally the American theme of people of God, and in the spirit of patriotic orthodoxy, preach a literal return to the beginnings, insisting on the uniqueness of the "American way of life." Singularists have their counterpart in universalists, who are driven by the millennial motive in Americanism to play an exemplary role in world history in one form or another. To these Boorstin opposes the pluralists:

> They are aware that we are and have always been only one among many nations; and they respect differences. They see history as a continuum. They do not expect that men or nations are ever likely to change much. . . . They are not alarmed by recent history, for they are not obsessed by the uniqueness of the American past, and they remind us that we have never been quite as unique as we have supposed. . . . These Pluralists see our hopes, not in denying the past nor in affirming the future, but in understanding ourselves, accepting both the unique and the universal in our character. . . . Satisfied by moderate objectives, they unashamedly plead for defense of the national interest.[87]

85. *Ibid.*, 169.
86. *Ibid.*, 170.
87. Boorstin, *America and the Image of Europe*, 134–37.

Pluralists draw the inference from the critique of monumental history, eliminating the apocalyptic elements from Americanism, and for the rest, they trust in its genius. Boorstin's reply to the crisis of American consciousness is an affirmative historicism. But this affirmative historicism simply dresses the premises of American self-understanding in new garments, for "it is not surprising . . . that much of our self-criticism has taken the form of historical reinterpretation. In periods of disillusionment we have expressed ourselves not so much in new philosophies, in dogmas or dictatorship or existentialism, as in earnest . . . reinterpretation of the American past."[88]

This thesis testifies that the enterprise of self-analysis can best be accomplished in the guise of an interpretation of one's own history. The work of Seymour Martin Lipset, a sociologist, also prefers this solution. The German sociologist Ralf Dahrendorf has made some interesting observations concerning the role of sociology in the context of the development of the American self-understanding; they form a valuable introduction to our examination of Lipset's *The First New Nation*. To this day, according to Dahrendorf, American sociology "is fed primarily by the problem of the recognition of their own society in its principle and its elements."[89] It is a vehicle of social self-interpretation, grown out of the "unrest of the New World in modern times" during the final decades of the nineteenth century. This theme of unrest is revealed negatively in the sociologists' fear of anomie: "The apparent dissolution of all ties and certainties became an occasion for worry." Positively, it is expressed in the "search for community . . . for certainty and ties."[90]

Since that time, Dahrendorf feels, two tendencies can be distinguished in American sociology. There is a conservative mainstream that "unmistakably" supports "the sign of the justification of social conditions"; the other is "the very much narrower stream of self-criticism," from Thorstein Veblen to C. Wright Mills.[91] But how to explain the fact that in America, unlike other industrial nations, sociology was so extraordinarily successful as an "attempt at self-understanding of a society in change"?[92]

In explanation Dahrendorf offers a Hegelian variation of the monumental-historical factor in Americanism, which also illuminates the specific character of the American crisis. "American history might be

88. Boorstin, *Genius of American Politics*, 19–20.
89. R. Dahrendorf, *Die angewandte Aufklärung* (Frankfurt, 1968), 14.
90. *Ibid.*, 116.
91. *Ibid.*, 19.
92. *Ibid.*, 110.

understood as the evolution of a single principle, a process of rationalization, democratization, mobilization, and collectivism—that is, as the realization of impulses already established in the beginnings of this society." "The dynamic of the process of evolution of the American idea is exhausted, America has lost its goals,"[93] "the old structures of America [have] completed their evolution . . . ; the question therefore is: what now?"[94] Dahrendorf sees the motivating center of this process in the principle of applied enlightenment. In this instance enlightenment justifies man's enfranchisement, since reason is the instrument for shaping his world in the experimental process of "trial and error." This stance of applied enlightenment and its embodiment in fluid social structures surely furnish an essential reason for the increasing significance of sociology as an element of American self-interpretation, even though it must be remarked in qualification that the concept of applied enlightenment by no means represents the exclusive theme in Americanism and that American history cannot be grasped unconditionally as the evolution of the "idea of democracy."

But it seems to me that there is one thing Dahrendorf and the materials he analyzed have proved anew: American civil theology was still so lively even in the nation's crisis that it was able both to communicate its premises to the social sciences and to attempt to stop the decline of truth by the authority of a "scientific" truth. This explains why sociology offered interpretations of American society from its own findings and why the speculative assumptions of Comte and Marx failed to gain a foothold.

Lipset attempted to restore Americanism with the methods of sociology. He disputed that a fundamental change was occurring in American society, such as the critics claimed. He claimed "that it is the basic value-system, as solidified in the early days of the new nation, which can account for the kinds of changes that have taken place in the American character and in American institutions as these faced the need to adjust to the requirements of an urban, industrial and bureaucratic society."[95] For, he declared, "the same basic values which arose in the American Revolution have shaped the society under changing geographical and economic conditions"; he referred to American historiography.[96] Like Boorstin, Lipset stressed the "effective continuity of the fundamental ideals of the society."[97] With regard to content, he spoke of "equality and achievement" as "America's key values," arising "from our revolutionary

93. *Ibid.*, 100–101.
94. *Ibid.*, 106; compare also 196.
95. Lipset, *First New Nation*, 104.
96. *Ibid.*, 105.
97. *Ibid.*, 106.

origins." In his study of specific traits of American social behavior, of American religiosity, and of the American trade-union movement, Lipset demonstrates that this basic value system had not lost its power to shape attitudes. A considerable amount of monumental history, however, has mingled with the historical analysis: "The United States may properly claim the title of the first new nation. It was the first major colony successfully to break away from colonial rule through revolution. . . . For this reason, to see how, in the course of American history, its values took shape in institutions may help us to understand some of the problems faced by the new nations emerging today on the world scene."[98] And from this Lipset concludes: "So perhaps the first new nation can contribute more than money to the latter-day ones; perhaps its development can give us some clue as to how revolutionary egalitarian and populist values may become incorporated into a stable nonauthoritarian polity."[99] These sentences call for interpretive comment.

Lipset does point out that his comparative theory of how a nation comes into being had to take the "uniqueness" of the American situation into account; he also shows that in fact certain structural problems of the emerging nation state are accessible to comparative analysis. But the expectation of determining paradigmatically, as it were, the conditions for establishing a stable democratic polity should dampen the empirical findings slightly. For the proper insight into the constitutive function of the value system calls for a more extensive study of the *differentia specificae* in content of the value systems that respectively became part of the nations founded on revolution. For even Lipset's material urges the realization that success and failure of the Western model of democracy can be explained in part by the nature of the value systems incorporated in the founding.[100]

And this brings me to a further crucial point: although during revolutionary wars colonies have risen against their masters, it was the immigrated colonists who fought their mother countries, rather than autochthonous populations revolting against foreign rule. From this point of view the American Revolution is no doubt closer to the independence movements of the Central and South American Creoles, as well as those of the colonists in South Africa, Algeria, and Rhodesia, than to the anticolonial revolutions of the native populations in Africa and Asia, whose activities correspond more closely to the Mexican Revolution staged by the Indian population. Lipset and many other American scholars forget

98. *Ibid.*, 2–3.
99. *Ibid.*, 16.
100. Compare the detailed treatment of this problem in P. Weber-Schäfer, "'Sozial' und 'Rational,'" *Staat*, VII (1968), 17–40.

this state of affairs, since in the course of Anglo-Saxon colonization the original Indian population was decimated and ceased being a social factor and was displaced from the American consciousness until well into the twentieth century.

This is not to say that the model of Western democracy, taking into regard the rational assumptions, could not be a paradigm for the new nations of the twentieth century; nevertheless it is not enough to claim that the United States is the "first new nation." Further, this criticism does not imply that the anticolonial process of nation building in Africa and Asia is identical with the "metaphysical revolution" of the Marxist-Leninist-Maoist sort. Such an argument would, in turn, simply be accepting the dogma of the "bulwark of progress," but this time as the dogma of the Communist revolution as a competing apocalypse to the American apocalypse.

The materials Lipset examines show that traditional behavioral patterns are still largely intact. But that is no proof against the crisis of those concepts of order in Americanism that have to date sustained those behavioral and institutional structures. For it takes several generations from the disintegration of the mental order to the dissolution of behavior patterns, most especially their stabilizing core, the institutions. This set of problems remains inaccessible to Lipset, since he works uncritically with the complex symbols of value and value systems; they prevent him from distinguishing between the experiential substratum of consciousness, the interpretation of experience in conceptions of order, and their formation into patterns of behavior. From the standpoint of our formulation of the problem, the concept of the first new nation and the evidence "that the American Creed . . . is still a dynamic part of our culture"[101] identify Lipset as representative of affirmative sociology.

If American sociology is deeply embedded in American self-understanding, this is all the more true for political science. In the contemporary context of crisis literature, we can touch briefly on some results of our earlier reflections. For "in America, political science was felt to exist already in the conduct of her own statesmen."[102] John Adams had understood the founding as an act within the nomothetic science of politics. This identification was common to all the Founding Fathers. James Wilson's example showed us that the preservation of the founding was to occur through a process of education, which constantly concretized the principles of the nomothetic science of politics in the citizen's

---

101. Lipset, *First New Nation*, 318.

102. B. Crick, *The American Science of Politics* (Berkeley, Calif., 1959), 5. The opening chapters of every textbook on American government provide evidence for this claim.

existential virtue. This link among the traditional symbol aggregate of the founders, social self-interpretation, and civic education mark American political science to the present day. It is an element of Americanism, even while its history is the history of Americanism: "the science of politics assumes a peculiar fourfold relationship between a common notion of science as it is found in ordinary American social thought; the idea of a common citizenship training; the generalization of the habits of American democracy, and, tending to embrace all these, the common belief in an inevitable progress of a manifest destiny for American society." [103]

It is therefore understandable that political science up to the time of the Civil War was merely a didacticism of Americanism: "It was conceived as a mere method—a technique for sustaining a preexistent American liberalism, not as a critical or speculative method." [104] With the social change at the end of the nineteenth century, political science, now saddled with self-consciousness through the assumption of the European scientific ethos, becomes organized into college departments and, like sociology, begins to be effective by systematically stabilizing. It served the precise experience of the social process and of national self-understanding under the altered conditions without reflecting the premises of Americanism: "this political science did not take the form of political theory or philosophy." It developed as a "technological science." [105] In this role American political science to this day has contributed substantially to the preparation and execution of the pragmatic reform of society and thus, unconsciously, furnished significant proof for the quality of the Americanism implicit in it. As long as reason was alive in Americanism, the pragmatic rationality of a "problem-solving" political science was enough. But the evaporation of the rational substance from the traditional pattern of thinking and behaving, which continued to be socially dominant, caused American political science, like sociology, to seek a basis for the truth of Americanism in the speculative postulates of European scientism from positivism to Freudianism: "A science of Politics would give a total explanation that would restore the sense of shattered 'givenness,' a movement in the plane of abstract thought parallel to the totalitarian movements of European politics in the plane of action. . . . They thought to transcend politics, not in a philosophic sense, by seeking to understand the limits of politics that follow from a belief in the moral structure of human reality, but in a scientific sense, although, palpably and happily, they remained as liberal at heart as before." [106]

103. *Ibid.*, xv.
104. *Ibid.*, 8.
105. *Ibid.*, 36.
106. *Ibid.*, 140.

Bernard Crick correctly saw as a symptom of the erosion of "American Liberalism" the civil theology of society, whose habituating force had until then removed the totalitarian implications of such a scientism and at the same time utilized its technology to shape social reality and make it transparent. But this placed political science in an unavoidable dilemma: "For while it throve upon a belief in a natural unity and unanimity in American thought, yet it has cut itself away from the actual reasonings and experience that underlay the great political literature of the early Republic." [107] The givenness of American life is no longer a matter of course, and, Crick concludes, "neither can it be rescued by an intellectually empty citizenship training, nor by the attempted reduction of liberalism to scientism." [108] The liberation of American political thought from the narrowness and sterility of the "idea of a science of politics" requires, not a direct change of the political and social structures, but merely an indirect change in the understanding of these structures. Crick is an acute critic of the American political scientists, but he is linked to them in the overall Anglo-Saxon self-understanding and therefore sees the renewal of the civil theology of constitutional democracy as the first task and, *cum grano salis,* as the subject of a political theory pure and simple: "A restoration of political thought is more likely to come through what is needed to tackle the problem and subject matter of a clearer national self-understanding." [109] Modern political theory then becomes "in its highest form . . . concerned with the historical grounding and the internal logic of what is most clearly called 'Constitutional Democracy.'" Crick sees the alternative to scientistic political science as recurrence to the core of "constitutional politics," which he makes coincident with Aristotelian politics. Politics in this sense—for Crick the only possible concept of politics—does not make man good because only good men can guarantee a secure and worthy politics. But "when a habit of disinterested moral speculation is no longer of a piece with an understanding of a national history, a political culture loses any ability both to be itself and to be a wider example." [110]

From his understanding of the rational premise of Anglo-Saxon democracy, Crick is eager to revive its commonsense Aristotelianism, which, however, presupposes the presence of a sizable measure of this very common sense; this is a hope the reader cannot share with Crick without further reservations.

107. *Ibid.,* 234.
108. *Ibid.,* 247.
109. *Ibid.,* 233.
110. *Ibid.,* 245–46.

American political science is of necessity overwhelmingly an instrument to affirm the social status quo; therefore, it also reflects its crisis symptoms. To the extent that impulses for a renewal of American self-understanding are expected, this desire is directed to a revival of the rational substance inherent in the beginning by recourse to the traditions of the founding. This is the direction chosen by most of our writers as a way out of the current crisis.

Very early on, Ralph B. Perry expressed his great distress at the crisis that had been advancing since 1900; furthermore, as a clear oppositional stance to the totalitarian regimes, he attempted to furnish a rejuvenated theory of the "good life" on the basis of "Christianity" and "democracy," the two idea systems that respectively marked an epoch of American history and together make up the substance of order: "it is proposed that we, as Americans, take Puritanism and Democracy as symbols of piety, reaffirming that which we find true; looking for their constituents of truth in order that we may affirm them; reaffirming them in order thereby to maintain our moral identity and the stream of the national life." [111] Puritan Christianity and democracy "have been particularly pervasive, reaching not only through the whole length of American history, but breadthwise from center to extremities, touching American experience and behavior at every point; religious, moral, social, cultural, and political. Puritan ideals were acquired before and during the revolutionary period, so that both may be said to have moulded the American mind from the beginning. They originated in the prenatal phase of American life and have predetermined the whole of its later development." [112] According to Perry, the crisis of Americanism calls for a conscious response: "Many Americans have become doubtful of the traditional creed which is the basis of their culture, the presupposition of their institutions and the essence of their nationalism." [113]

Once this national credo has strayed into the shadow realm of doubt, its content cannot be revived in the form of monumental history; [114] it can be assured only through conscious decision. But what can save Americanism is not conquering doubt through the abolition of reason and dogmatic insistence on "irrational beliefs"; rather, "the critical faculties themselves should appraise a creed, or reappraise an old creed, by seeing the reason for its adoption. This alternative implies that there are reasons or grounds for the preference of one creed to another, and that when a

---

111. Perry, *Puritanism and Democracy*, 631.
112. *Ibid.*, 34–35.
113. *Ibid.*, 36.
114. *Ibid.*, 50–55.

creed is defined by these reasons, it possesses a claim upon the acceptance of all rational men." What is called for is not the renaissance of dogmas but the rational rebirth of the original reasonableness: "The past is viewed from the present, and judged in terms of the present."[115] Perry's study, therefore, attempts "to *determine* how far the ideals of puritanism and democracy are acceptable. To this end it will be necessary that these ideals should be so conceived as to mean something now, mean something definite, refer directly or indirectly to the present field of experience, and satisfy present logical standards."[116] Perry is not satisfied with Boorstin's institutionalist effort or Lipset's behaviorist approach. He is guided by the interaction between ideas and institutions. For Perry, ideas are intellectual sketches that produce a "community of emotion and will" in the form of ideals among individuals. This in turn gives rise to behavior patterns encompassing and dominating all areas of human existence in society. "When thus socialized and charged with emotion durable ideas constitute the essence of culture and civilization."[117]

Materially, the study consists of a representation of the ideas of the Puritan fathers and founders of the Republic and the origins of Americanism. But this is not done by understanding intellectual history, but under the horizon of the truth of human existence. The measure "which may appropriately be called the 'moral standard,' the standard of standards, the standard by which all others shall be judged"[118] originates in a vague "European tradition from Plato to Kant"; Perry, echoing William James, calls it the "'philosophical' standard." "It follows that the philosopher, pledged to take the rounded and detached view of life, must take as his 'guiding principle' the satisfaction of as many demands as possible."[119] Even when we know that Perry takes his standard from man's nature, his theoretical foundation remains mired in the surface; it lacks the force of meditative effort. For only the experience of truth in the fathers' concrete thought and action, communicated to Perry by the study of the materials, charges the American order existentially and confers to the pale formal standard existential binding character so much that the complexes of order under examination will be seen according to the criterion of their reality content: "There must be a congruence between Christian-Puritan democracy and the condition of existence." "The true ground of hope for Christian democracy lies, then, in its correspondence with the nature of things through enlightenment, and in its correspon-

---

115. *Ibid.,* 36–37.
116. *Ibid.,* 43.
117. *Ibid.,* 27.
118. *Ibid.,* 48.
119. *Ibid.,* 50.

dence with human nature through its provision for human faculties and human solidarity." The truth of human existence here means, not a piece of reified dogma in behavior and institutions, but truth in concrete action, which correctly orders individual existence and society under present-day conditions. But Perry remains tied to the premises of Americanism: he can imagine the meditative reenactment and renewal of the truth of the fathers: "But by imputing essential truths to our fathers we can acknowledge them with filial piety, nourish ourselves upon them, and at the same time resolve to transmit to our children a wider and fuller inheritance." [120] Consequently, he also proclaims recurrence to the founding: "the chief source of spiritual nourishment for any nation must be its own past, perpetually rediscovered and renewed. A nation which negates its tradition loses its historic identity and want only destroys its chief source of spiritual vitality; a nation which merely reaffirms its tradition grows stagnant and corrupt. But it is not necessary to choose between revolution and reaction. There is a third way—the way, namely, of discriminating and forward-looking fidelity." [121] Finally, tradition overwhelmed even Perry; it caused him to run aground in his search for the "chief source of spiritual vitality" beyond society and history, with which any healing of the crisis would have to begin.

But this problem should be dealt with most effectively by a theologian. Reinhold Niebuhr treats the American crisis in the context of the crisis of Western "bourgeois civilization"; but he, too, cannot change his American spots. His analyses of bourgeois and Communist cultures, the two predominant forces of modern civilization, as aberrations of Western Christianity are superficial and colorless and do justice to the complexity of the historical process only with qualifications: "Modern man's confidence in his virtue caused an equally unequivocal rejection of the Christian idea of the ambiguity of human virtue. In the liberal world the evils in human nature and history were ascribed to social institutions or to ignorance or to some other manageable defect in human nature or environment. Again the communist doctrine is more explicit and therefore more dangerous. It ascribes the origins of evil to the institution of property." [122] Bourgeois culture transforms "everything in the Christian faith which points to ultimate and transcendent possibilities" into simple historical achievements—though only in confrontation with feudalism and without allowing the masses to participate in its success. Communism protests against the illusion and sentimentalities of the bourgeois world

---

120. *Ibid.*, 59.

121. *Ibid.*, 627.

122. R. Niebuhr, *The Irony of American History* (New York, 1952), 4. See also R. Niebuhr, *The Children of the Light and the Children of the Darkness* (New York, 1960), 5.

view and tries in desperation to take these seriously and either carry them out or oppose them with similarly absurd and contradictory concepts.[123] "In every instance communism changes only partly dangerous sentimentalities and inconsistencies in the bourgeois ethos into consistent and totally harmful ones."[124] Niebuhr attempts to summarize the consequences of the modern distortion of the structure of reality of man and history under the concept of irony. "If virtue becomes vice through some hidden defect in the virtue; if strength becomes weakness because of the vanity to which strength may prompt the mighty man or nation; if security is transmuted into insecurity because too much reliance is placed upon it; if wisdom becomes folly because it does not know its limits—in all such cases the situation is ironic." It is ironic because the situation is abolished "if men or nations are made aware of their complicity in it." This rise to consciousness means the discovery of a hidden vanity or arrogance by which a comedy is transformed into irony. These realizations lead either to abandoning the arrogance, that is, remorse, or to a despairing emphasis on the vanities to the point, at which irony turns to pure rottenness. Modern liberal culture "is involved in many ironic refutations of its original pretensions of virtue, wisdom, and power," which have attained their full development only in Communism, and the efforts to remove the ironic contrast between the original dreams of virtue and justice and reality have dissolved irony into pure evil.[125] To Niebuhr, America is "a vivid symbol of the most characteristic attitudes of a bourgeois culture" and therefore the actual object of his observations.[126]

It is therefore a matter of overcoming the "irony of American history" by reflection and returning to a genuine knowledge of order, which for Niebuhr means a "Christian realism." "The ironic elements in American History can be overcome . . . only if American Idealism comes to terms with the limits of all human striving, the fragmentariness of all human wisdom, the precariousness of all historic configurations of power and the mixture of good and evil in all human virtue."[127]

The *modus procedendi* is already familiar to us. A critique of the monumental history of the "American Israel" lays bare the illusions of a "new beginning," which Puritan Calvinism and Jeffersonian deism built into the founding, as the cause of an aberration resulting in the current frustration.[128] This political theory of America suppresses Christian real-

---

123. R. Niebuhr, *Irony of American History*, 12.
124. *Ibid.*, 15.
125. *Ibid.*, viii.
126. *Ibid.*, 3.
127. *Ibid.*, 133; see also R. Niebuhr, *Children of the Light*, 17.
128. R. Niebuhr, *Irony of American History*, 24ff.

ism in early American culture represented by Madison, Adams, and the American Constitution.[129] This Christian realism was derailed into the political practice of institutions: "We may claim that the unarticulated wisdom embodied in the actual experience of American life has created forms of justice considerably higher than our more articulate unwisdom suggests."[130] Niebuhr calls this the "triumph of the wisdom of common sense" over the bourgeois and Marxist types of wisdom, and he identifies the "wisdom of common sense" with the "wisdom of democracy."[131] "The national consciousness must have been informed by some hidden resources of common sense which have been withheld from both the wise and the simple."[132] The irony of American history, therefore, is carried out in the recurrence to a Christian realism inherent in the social practices—the concretized common sense of the nation. This rise to consciousness of the ironic situation is inspired by the Christian belief "that life has a center and source of meaning beyond the rational and social sequences which may be rationally discerned." Because the divine origin and center of this given meaning is experienced in faith, the basis of all meaning remains a mystery. "So discerned, it yields a frame of meaning in which human freedom is real and valid";[133] "the spirit of humanity is . . . preserved . . . by an existential awareness of the limits, as well as the possibilities of human power and goodness."[134]

But beyond recourse to the intellectual and linguistic tradition of America, Niebuhr does not proceed to a theory of politics that might be able to promote the existential renewal of society through the Christian spirit. Rather, he contents himself with an imitation of Abraham Lincoln: "This combination of moral resoluteness about the immediate issues with a religious awareness of another dimension of meaning and judgment must be regarded as almost a perfect model of the difficult but not impossible task of remaining loyal and responsible toward the moral treasures of a free civilization on the one hand while yet having some religious vantage point over the struggle."[135]

The Protestant theologian refers to biblical-Christian *fides* as the source of order.[136] The Catholic theologian John Courtney Murray attempted to reconstruct Americanism from the *ratio* of Christian philoso-

129. *Ibid.*, 96–97.
130. *Ibid.*, 106.
131. *Ibid.*, 107.
132. R. Niebuhr, *The Godly and the Ungodly* (London, 1958), 22.
133. R. Niebuhr, *Irony of American History*, 167–68.
134. *Ibid.*, 170.
135. *Ibid.*, 172.
136. *Ibid.*, 158.

phy. Murray's definition of Americanism—he called it "the American Proposition"—as the "public philosophy" or the "public consensus" is already familiar to us. Murray exemplifies the complete Americanization, social integration, and increasing self-confidence of American Catholics—an evolution that in 1960 placed a Catholic in the White House for the first time. It is "classical American doctrine," Murray declares, that the new nation the fathers founded was dedicated to a "proposition." "The American Proposition . . . presents itself as a coherent structure of thought that lays claim to intellectual assent; it also presents itself as an organized political project that aims at historical success. Our fathers asserted it and most ably argued it; they also undertook to 'work it out,' and they signally succeeded." But their historical success cannot be accepted as a matter of course and is not absolute. The American proposition must be constantly newly acquired as doctrine and practice.[137]

Such a moment is the current crisis in which, for many reasons, the public philosophy is in a state of total disintegration, in which consensus extends only to the formal democratic procedures, and in which a moral vacuum has arisen that increasingly makes impossible a rational pursuance of public affairs in domestic and international politics.[138] A not inconsiderable segment of the American population, however, keeps the "original American consensus" alive—in the "Catholic community." The cause is "the evident coincidence of the principles which inspired the American Republic with the principles that are structural to the Western Christian political tradition." The Catholic community speaks in the political and ethical idiom of its fathers—"both the Fathers of the Church and the Fathers of the American Republic."[139] The American proposition, therefore, is supported by the twofold authority of the Church Fathers and the Founding Fathers. This claim allows Murray to turn the absolute beginning into a relative event, for in the American founding what he sees as being developed is merely the principles of the Western political tradition; Murray subsumes this under the concept of natural law: "only the theory of law is able to give an account of the public moral experience that is the public consensus. The consensus itself is simply the tradition of reason as emergent in developing form in the special circumstances of American political-economic life."[140]

The public philosophy thus derives its claim to truth from the knowledge of order given by philosophy: "Like the whole of the *philosophia*

137. Murray, *We Hold These Truths*, vii–viii.
138. *Ibid.*, 24, 40–41, 16 ff., 95, 275–94.
139. *Ibid.*, 43.
140. *Ibid.*, 109.

perennis, the doctrine of natural law is oriented, toward constant contact with reality and the data of experience." [141] The "public philosophy" incorporates "the dictates of God, who is Eternal Reason, the Logos." From this fact results its binding character: "Their ultimate origin is divine though the mode of their knowing is human and rational." [142] Murray correctly sees that Americanism has absorbed essential elements of Christian-philosophic tradition, but his identification of Americanism with the scholastic natural law is surely not admissible without reservations. Murray understands the "natural consensus," which takes its bearings from the Thomistic model, as other than "static quantity." "It is indeed a legacy from the past, but not in the form of a deposit that is closed to all change and addition . . . it is an open-ended action." [143] But surmounting the crisis nevertheless requires a renaissance of some sort of the scholastic natural law, a recourse to the modes of traditional philosophizing, which might not be so natural to the non-Catholic American. Murray discovered in the natural law those resources "that would make it the dynamic of a new 'age of order.' . . . It can claim to be only a 'skeleton law,' to which flesh and blood must be added by that heart of the political process, the rational activity of man, aided by experience and by high professional competence." But since it was precisely the fundamental structures of the political, social, and economic order that today are most vigorously questioned, it is "the skeleton that we mostly need." "In a word, the doctrine of natural law offers a more profound metaphysic, a more integral humanism, a fuller rationality, a more complete philosophy in his nature and history." [144] But Murray leaves Americans alone with the doubt whether resort to philosophical dogma would be able to restore the rationality of philosophizing, especially since he believes that it is possible to foist Thomistic dogmatics on Americanism without much difficulty.

The other theoretician of "public philosophy," Walter Lippman, also seeks refuge in natural-law dogmatics, even without religious auspices, from the disorder of the times. Like Niebuhr, he sees these as merely a part of the precipitous and calamitous decline of Western society after 1917. [145] The victims of this crisis are the first-line liberal democracies of the Atlantic community: "They have suffered great disasters in this century and the consequences of these disasters are compounding them-

141. *Ibid.,* 331.
142. *Ibid.,* 116.
143. *Ibid.,* 99.
144. *Ibid.,* 335.
145. Lippmann, *The Public Philosophy,* 15.

selves."[146] "They were sick with some kind of incapacity to cope with reality, to govern their affairs, to defend their vital interests and, it might be, to insure their survival as free and democratic states."[147] The diagnosis takes its point of departure from the central function of order of the public philosophy of an organized society: "the democracies are ceasing to receive the traditions of civility in which the good society, the liberal democratic way of life at its best, originated and developed. They are cut off from the public philosophy and the political arts which are needed to govern the liberal democratic society."[148] And he comes to a conclusion: "with the disappearance of the public philosophy—and of a consensus on the first and last things—there was opened up a great vacuum in the public mind, yawning to be filled."[149] The "western traditions of civility" are the content of the public philosophy and prerequisites of the institutions of Western society, such as popular elections, majority rule, representative bodies, freedom of speech, loyalty, property, and voluntary associations.[150]

Lippman, too, sees the basic elements of the "traditions of civility" in natural law: "For over two thousand years," he quotes Ernest Berker, "European thought has been acted upon by the idea that the rational faculties of men can produce a common conception of law and order which possesses a universal validity." The concept of classical natural law was shared by the Stoics, the Roman jurists, the Fathers of the Church, Thomas Aquinas, the Renaissance and the Reformation, the English Revolution of 1688, and the American Revolution of 1776, and it provided the Western political societies with a foundation in the mind.[151] The American form of public philosophy derives from the founding, but like Murray, Lippman goes beyond the American fathers in that he sees them as men who legitimately continue and revive a two-thousand-year-old tradition that starts from the premise that "man's second and more rational nature must master his first and more elemental." The traditions of civility thus also imply the sovereignty of *ratio* in the private and public sector; its decay means the emergence of the instinctive impulse in man and society. This counterrevolution of the passions became historic, according to Lippman, in the movement from Rousseau through the Jacobins and Marx to the totalitarian movements of the twentieth century: "The Jacobins and their successors made a political religion founded

146. *Ibid.*, 61.
147. *Ibid.*, 6.
148. *Ibid.*, 96.
149. *Ibid.*, 100.
150. *Ibid.*, 101.
151. *Ibid.*, 104.

upon the reversal of civility. Instead of ruling the elemental impulses, they stimulated and armed them. Instead of treating the pretensions to being a god as the mortal sin original, they proclaimed it to be the glory and destiny of man." This state of affairs gave rise to the permanent war, with that *conditio humana* explicated in the traditions of civility and articulated in the public philosophy.[152] Neither this libidinously motivated counterreformation nor "public agnosticism" controls the "rational order of human society," whose conditions must be fulfilled if man's aptitude for the good life in this world is to be reflected.[153] The dysfunction of the democratic institutions and the disintegration of society in the private worlds of antagonistic groups can be prevented only by the "renewal of the public philosophy."

But the solution is not neoclassical or neomedieval restoration: "The revival of the public philosophy depends on whether its principles and precepts—which were articulated before the industrial revolution, before the era of rapid technological change, and before the rise of the mass democracy—depends on whether this old philosophy can be reworked for the modern age." [154] In model analyses of such central concepts as the sovereignty of the people, property, freedom of speech, and education, Lippman demonstrates impressively the mind of a *homo politicus* shaped by the *ratio*. But only in relation to communicating the insights of the public philosophy and accommodating the heterogeneous designs for existence in society to the truth of the public philosophy does Lippman touch on the basic problem of all acquisition of the knowledge of order by recurrence to the traditions. For "the principles of the good society call for a concern with an order of being—which cannot be proved existentially to the sense organs—where it matters supremely that the human person is inviolable, that reason shall regulate the will, that truth shall prevail over error." [155] Until recently this tension could be resolved by the interpretation of reality in verbal and nonverbal symbols; but today the critical question is not "whether men do or do not believe in an imagery. It turns on whether they believe that a man is able 'to experience a reality absolutely independent of himself.'" Nietzsche's proclamation that God is dead is not, that is, directed to a symbol, a concrete image of God; rather, it eliminates "the recognition that beyond our private worlds there is a public world to which we belong." Lippman takes his stand at the point at which he realizes that appeals can be meaningful only as meditative processes to regain reality. But the analysis breaks off with an ap-

152. *Ibid.*, 86–87.
153. *Ibid.*, 123.
154. *Ibid.*, 161.
155. *Ibid.*, 165.

peal to the philosophers "to alter the terms of discourse."[156] For "if the philosophers teach that religious experience is a purely psychological phenomenon, related to nothing, then they will give educated men a bad intellectual conscience if they have religious experiences. The philosophers cannot give them religion. But they can keep them away from it"[157]—although, one is tempted to add, they could also help them to a correct order of their existence through philosophizing.

There also remain, therefore, the various recourses to the spiritual traditions of the West that are meant to undergird the tradition of the American founding by means of "secondary ideologies." According to Eric Voegelin: "There have been attempts of return, motivated by the totalitarian climax of the rebellion, but these attempts could not go beyond the older dogmatism, to the reality of knowledge itself. They therefore have produced a curious gray zone of thought about order that is as characteristic a phenomenon of the time as the ideologies themselves, to which it is opposed. One might speak of an area of secondary ideologies."[158]

An inherent logic drives the crisis of American consciousness to the point at which the resistance to a rigid Americanism must shift to a demand for critically reflecting on the nexus between founding and order. But this development occurred almost below the threshold of consciousness of those in the universities, churches, and mass media, in administrations and parliaments, who were celebrating "the death of the earlier metaphysical impulse"[159] as a "de-ideologization";[160] it transformed pragmatism, now deprived of its mentality, into a political doctrine of corporation economics subjugated to social-technological rationality. Theoretically this means no more than that Saint Simon was elected to be the *spiritus rector* of American history. This step, however, only intensified the movement to deprive the political and social institutions, and the patterns of thought and behavior that express them, of meaning. Yearning for a rational attitude of man in relation to God and the world, society and history were no longer satisfied with affirmation or recurrence on the level of intellectual discourse but produced a massive resistance to Americanism.

156. *Ibid.,* 180.

157. *Ibid.,* 178–79.

158. Voegelin, *Anamnesis,* 329 (English from *Anamnesis,* trans. Niemeyer, 188–89).

159. H. von Borch, *Amerika—Die unfertige Gesellschaft* (Munich, 1964), 18–19.

160. Compare E. Shils, "The End of Ideology?," *Encounter,* V (1955), 52–58; D. Bell, *The End of Ideology* (New York, 1960); S. M. Lipset, *Political Man* (Garden City, N.Y., 1959); J. La Palombara, "Decline of Ideology: A Dissent and an Interpretation," *American Political Science Review,* LX (1966), 5–16.

C. Wright Mills, spokesman for "radical" sociology, clearly outlined the situation. "It is not only the skills of reason that they [men] need—although their struggles to acquire these often exhaust their limited moral energy. What they need, and what they feel they need, is a quality of mind that will help them to use information and to develop reason in order to achieve lucid summations of what is going on in the world and of what may be happening within themselves." [161] Unfortunately his moral impetus and deficient theoretical discipline did not allow him to go beyond diagnosis to make his admirable sensitivity to the malaise of American society useful for remedial action.

Two entirely different attempts to eradicate Americanism will now be briefly introduced: Roland van Zandt's *The Metaphysical Foundations of American History* and Louis Hartz's *The Liberal Tradition in America* and *The Founding of New Societies*.

"The historic vision of the American people is in deep trouble today," van Zandt noted.[162] "American history as it has been known is finished." [163] "We now know that the apparatus of ideas with which the American founders started, however deftly used, cannot be made to perform the task for which it was invented." But in what does van Zandt see the purpose of the symbol apparatus?

> If in science this task was first, to understand the world of nature, and second, to understand it so that it could be controlled and organized for the welfare of human society, in history the task was to understand and establish the world of human society so that mankind would have a "new chance" to redeem one of its most ardent dreams, the establishment on this earth, here and now, of a "heavenly city" of man's own deliberate invention. Such was the intent of the American founders when they spoke in the name of the "New World." But in the fifth decade of this century so systematic is this failure that there is hardly a detail of the original American "dream" or "metaphysic" that is not directly contradicted by the "facts." [164]

The nexus of founding and order is equally obvious to van Zandt: "Whatever American History is, it is only that which is defined by the theories, principles, and ideas of those who first established and identified it." [165] The American founders undertook a "great experiment," and this experiment failed. Our knowledge, according to van Zandt, is for the

161. C. W. Mills, *The Sociological Imagination* (New York, 1959), 5.
162. R. Van Zandt, *The Metaphysical Foundations of American History* (The Hague, 1959), 12.
163. *Ibid.*, 78.
164. *Ibid.*, 84.
165. *Ibid.*, 36.

most part negative: "It knows that the intellectual inheritance of the seventeenth and eighteenth century must go; but it has not been able to establish either for itself or society as a whole any system of ideas that can replace that inheritance."[166]

For van Zandt, the American crisis is part of the twentieth-century revolt in the field of the natural sciences against the seventeenth century and its "basic concepts" and "generative ideas."[167] Van Zandt forces the epistemology of Whitehead, Northrop, Cohen, and Mead into an illegitimate bond with Comte's speculation on history. Inside man's head, impelled by an immanent logic, a process of conceptualization of physical reality occurs, and this process is concretized in the expanding control of man over the conceptualized structures of the universe. "History" and "society" are exclusively epiphenomena of this process—that is, the institutionalization of formalized "laws and relations within the world of nature" in the form of a "closed system of ideas," which van Zandt calls "metaphysic." With every "step forward in organized control," the terms of an "enveloping conceptual world of man's own creation" prove to be not false but limited, and they cause frustration, inhibition, and confusion; this unease can be relieved only through new modes of institutionalization, through a more adequate and encompassing "conceptual symbolism."

> Man in this manner finds himself at the helm of a process which, so long as he understands it and obeys it, contains its own innate principle of self-perpetuation and proceeds on the basis of constant change and increased power. This process is self-evidently irreversible: so long as man willfully maintains it, it can only go forward in time without permitting man to revert to a previous and more primitive mode of existence, a previous stage of history. Hence man knows what he calls "progress," a goal that can only be limited by the unspecifiable limits of nature itself, and a goal that is constantly known in its own achievements as the perpetual fulfillment, in a richer and more bountiful form of life, of the very limitations that had been imposed by a previous achievement.[168]

The speculative premise that the interpretation of experience of physical reality alone can bring into being the order of man in society and history makes every theory of man's realm of being into an appendix of theoretical physics. "The social sciences, and especially the field of political

166. *Ibid.*, 60.
167. *Ibid.*, 10, 81.
168. *Ibid.*, 67–68.

theory, have not kept pace with the striking innovations that have occurred in the natural sciences in the present century," van Zandt com-
plains, adding that it was in this circumstance that "the notorious scandal
of contemporary thought throughout the world" consisted. With this he
also revealed the cause for such a construction: "While man has unprecedented power over the world of nature, he has an unprecedented lack of
power over his own world of history and society." [169] The prevailing social and historical ideas still adhere to the principles of a "former scientific conception that have been repudiated in their own original field of
application," that is, in the classical physics of Newton. Van Zandt sees
these principles as the chief obstacle "to the rational control of that
[modern] civilization. Thus while science and man's control of nature
continues to advance, human society, or the end of which this advance
exists, reverts to barbarisms that can bring both itself and that scientific
achievement to an end." [170]

Thus, American history has the same basis as Newtonian science; it is
nothing more than the application of the methods of the natural sciences.
Van Zandt attempts to prove this thesis by identifying American society
in history with its historic self-understanding in Americanism, and the
latter with Jeffersonian thought. "The present study which deals with the
metaphysical foundations of American history, does so almost entirely
through the thought of Jefferson. Just as Burtt assumes that science is . . .
synonymous with Newtonianism, so this study assumes that the subject
of American history is synonymous with Jeffersonianism." [171]

We are not concerned here with discussing the inadequacy of extending the banal insight that Jefferson's cosmology derives from Newton to
all the symbolic material and political actions of the Founding Fathers. I
limit my remarks to van Zandt's argument. The decline of Americanism
forces van Zandt to a transformation of *homo Americanus*. In the place
of the antinomies of individual versus society and the one versus the
many he sets the "unity of process." This category, institutionalized in
social reality, abolishes the myth "that the individual is . . . ruled by laws
that are outside him in nature, that are transcendental to his life." This
dogma is "the greatest single obstacle . . . to the rational control of man's
own life." For "order is the unity of process as organized by man in terms
of definite rules of procedure." [172] Van Zandt's approach makes it clear
that he is intent not only on abolishing Americanism as the dominant

169. *Ibid.*, 79.
170. *Ibid.*, 80.
171. *Ibid.*, 104.
172. *Ibid.*, 264.

conception of order, but also on promoting the intellectual revolution of natural science to the "reformation of political and historical man." [173]

In van Zandt, Newton's Fifth-Monarchy Man has, as it were, been resurrected. Van Zandt accuses classical physics of the sin of the "fallacy of misplaced concreteness," [174] only to commit the same sin himself with the greatest zest under the assumptions of modern physics. Finally, however, the effort at an apocalypse of "groundless" autonomous pragmatic reason remains groundless because the "conceptual world" of modern physics results from the experience of an intelligible whole beyond physical reality.

In the search for "rationality with reason" (Mills), Americans must of necessity one day encounter the limitations of their very national existence. Louis Hartz has taken a decisive step in this direction. We owe to him one of the most persuasive reinterpretations of American history, with the claim of introducing a resolution of Americanism. He reminds us of the significant fact "that instead of recapturing our past, we have got to transcend it. As for a child who is leaving adolescence, there is no going home for America." [175] Hartz—we are already familiar with some of his arguments—used his analyses, based on a wealth of material, to show America as a fragment of Europe that grew into the whole of a nation. For Hartz, Americanism is the total mentality of the "liberal substance," the dominant interpretation of order of "Lockeanism," and the established behavior patterns of the "American way of life"—in short, the American's total existence in history and society. This Americanism as an explication of an autarkic political society isolated within world politics is, according to Hartz, "at once heightened and shattered by the crashing impact of the rest of the world upon it." [176] This double effect is seen both as "national blindness"—that is, as isolationism or Messianism—and as "national enlightenment," through which the fragmentary nature of national existence becomes conscious and releases that "spark of philosophy," "that grain of relative insight that its own history has denied it." But the result of this process can no longer be furnished by an analysis of American history. "What is at stake is nothing less than a new level of consciousness, a transcending of irrational Lockeanism, in which an understanding of self and an understanding of other go hand in

173. *Ibid.*, 237.
174. A. N. Whitehead, *Science and the Modern World* (New York, 1967), 52. In my opinion, this work, as well as Whitehead's *Adventures of Ideas*, refutes van Zandt's speculative program under the horizon of modern science alone.
175. Hartz, *Liberal Tradition*, 32.
176. *Ibid.*, 287.

hand." [177] Inevitably the return of the fragment into the world from which it had been separated would lead to a traumatic experience. But this effects a "moral liberation" and a "broadening of consciousness" that are entirely worth the struggle. "It brings, for the first time in the fragment settings, the hope of philosophy." [178]

This statement by Hartz may serve as the springboard for a concluding reflection on the rise and fall of American civil theology.

IV. The Political Culture of Americanism and the New Political Revivalism

The implicit Americanism of the consciousness and behavior patterns of the majority of the population continues well into the 1960s to substantiate that multiplicity of heterogeneous investigations mostly of a quantitative sort which, produced in connection with the study of voting behavior, analyzed the data to document Americans' statistical-representative "beliefs," "values," "opinions," "attitudes," and "behavior." [179]

No matter whether the empirical structural analyses of "political life," including the in-depth studies of individuals and groups, are intended to supplement, deepen, or confirm an understanding of the manifold manifestations of the American *zoon politikon* in a quantitative-empirical dimension, all—regardless of the differing conclusions drawn from the far-reaching sociopolitical changes in formal and informal government—are in agreement that the continuity of the political process, in the absence of intense polarization of society, allows the conclusion that a "basic consensus" exists. This cautious formulation results from a methodological

177. *Ibid.*, 308.

178. Hartz *et al., Founding of New Societies*, 23, 122.

179. The theoretical problems of such attempts were discussed earlier, and this is not the place to examine the inherent methodological questions of statistical measurements, any more than the subliminal predetermination of results through unreflective research paradigms, such as "democratic personality" and "liberal-conservative continuum," which in themselves could only come into being in the context of Americanism. Besides the major voting studies of P. F. Lazarsfeld *et al., The People's Choice* (New York, 1968); Bernard Berelson, P. F. Lazarsfeld, and W. N. McPhee, *Voting: A Study of Opinion Formation in a Presidential Campaign* (Chicago, 1954); A. Campbell *et al., The American Voter* (New York, 1960); and A. Campbell *et al., The Voter Decides* (Evanston, Ill., 1954), we should here take into account as well attempts at more encompassing empirical evidence of United States political life: R. E. Lane, *Political Life* (Gelncoe, Ill., 1959); R. E. Lane, *Political Ideology* (New York, 1962); V. O. Key, Jr., *Public Opinion and American Democracy* (New York, 1961); V. O. Key, Jr., *The Responsible Electorate* (Cambridge, Mass., 1966); R. S. Erikson and N. R. Luttbeg, *American Public Opinion: Its Origins, Content, and Impact* (New York, 1973).

premise that, though it can state a specific consensus of opinion, can reveal the consensus only in the guise of a quantifiable, that is, statistically significant, formulation of explicit political principles in society.[180] Beyond the methodological concretization of a symbol consensus, the behaviorist majority opinion also confirmed the indicators for its existence into the 1960s. "As we have already seen," Robert Dahl stated his position, "perhaps more than any other people in the world, Americans have been united in expressing faith in a democratic ideology, even if they often have not acted on what they claimed to believe. Since their ideology is a source of unity rather than cleavage, the moment in which to observe the American as an ideologist is not when he talks about domestic politics, but when he talks about international politics, and especially when he talks about America in relation to the rest of the world." Lloyd A. Free and Hadley Cantril conclude their presentation of the "political beliefs of Americans" with a sense of satisfaction:

> Our study has shown that the underlying personal political credos of the majority of Americans have remained substantially intact at the ideological level. But the objective environment in which people live has obviously changed immeasurably. . . . Our study has revealed the amazing elasticity of the American experiment and the rather rapid devising and acceptance of practical programs of action to accommodate both the continuing and the emerging needs and aspirations of the nation's citizens. Because of these, practical adaptations to emerging situations, the majority of the American people have never become so dissatisfied with their political ideology as to feel intensely and continuously frustrated.[181]

180. See Key, *Public Opinion*, 27–50. Erikson and Luttbeg, *American Public Opinion*, draw conclusions from the fact that a range of "terminal values" raised in a sample of adults in Florida in 1969 provides no evidence of agreement but rather hints at wide differences in American "values." "Thus a value consensus is clearly absent" (113). The mischief, of course, lies in the authors' honest belief that a series of eighteen so-called values (from world peace to fun) allows statements about consensus in society. Key's thinking on this point is more cautious: "Whatever the characteristics of popular attitude that permit governments to operate as if a basic consensus existed, they do not seem to consist of ideas that amount to a consensus on political fundamentals unless we mean by that phrase nothing more than a popular recognition of the legitimacy of the regime" (50). For more recent methodological discussion, see A. R. Wilcox, ed., *Public Opinion and Political Attitudes* (New York, 1974), and S. Welch and J. Comer, eds., *Public Opinion: Its Formation, Measurement, and Impact* (Palo Alto, Calif., 1975).

181. R. Dahl, *Democracy in the United States* (Chicago, 1972), 333. Compare also R. Dahl, *A Preface to Democratic Theory* (Chicago, 1956); L. A. Free and H. Cantril, *The Political Beliefs of Americans: A Study of Public Opinion* (New York, 1968), 176, 178.

In *The Political Culture of the United States,* Donald J. Devine made a secondary analysis of the opinion polls of the last thirty-five years (1935–1970) in an attempt to provide empirical-quantitative documentation for Hartz's thesis of the continuity of the liberal tradition, which Devine equates with the political culture of the United States. Devine takes his point of departure from the assumption of "consensual political culture" that has existed essentially unchanged throughout American history. "In summary, the American political culture can be referred to as the liberal tradition. It is maintained that the values of Locke, Madison, and the other liberals of the seventeenth and eighteenth century represent essentially the same values which comprise the American political culture at the present." [182] Hartz's thesis serves as a working hypothesis and is made operational with the help of the structural-functionalist concept of the political culture. "Each element of the system model will be investigated to test the extent to which the United States fulfills adherence to the liberal tradition. The data to be investigated will, hopefully, reveal the degree to which the tradition is shared as the American political culture." [183] In the course of making the thesis operational, of course, Hartz's liberal tradition is considerably simplified, though not necessarily falsified; the same is inevitably even more true for the heterogeneous material of the secondary analysis, which also forces the scholar to pose very simple questions. Even considering such basic methodological objections, Devine's results remain remarkable. "At the mass level, for both the masses and their major social groupings, the liberal tradition is supported as a consensual political culture. Although one could never, in some absolute sense, demonstrate the existence of the liberal tradition as the political culture of the United States, I will argue that the widespread agreement on political values reported above and the depth of support shown here represent a reasonable empirical demonstration of the descriptive hypothesis. Lockean liberalism may be used as an empirical description of the core of the member political culture of the United States." [184]

At present the disorders of the 1970s probably present us merely with something like a blurred snapshot of unspecified processes of change; nevertheless, with all due caution we may look at the results and conclude that the fields of consciousness, symbolism, and behavior of Americanism is being restructured, though a secondary analysis of the data

182. D. J. Devine, *The Political Culture of the United States* (Boston, 1972), 65.
183. *Ibid.,* 65.
184. *Ibid.,* 286.

does not justify more than tentative statements about the content of the changes. As early as 1970 Philip Slater boldly diagnosed two separate cultures in the United States: "the opposition between the old scarcity-oriented technological culture that still predominates and the somewhat amorphous counterculture that is growing up to challenge it." "So long as our society had a common point of moral references there was a tendency for conflicts to be resolved by compromise, and this compromise had a moral as well as a practical basis. Today this moral unity is gone, and the only basis for compromise is a practical one. Whenever moral sentiments are aroused, the opposing groups are pulled in opposite directions, and mere experience is usually too weak a consideration to counteract this divergence."[185] But like other thinkers of the counterculture of the sixties and seventies, such as Theodore Roszak and Charles Reich, Slater saw himself as part of the changing America; this function weakens his analysis. On the other hand, the protracted process of self-doubt in the minds of sensitive observers during the 1960s actually grew into the phenomenon of a mass rebellion against the dominant symbols of society that, unlike similar movements of the 1930s, seriously aimed at escape from the context of founding and order: the psychedelic sects, the God-is-dead movement, ecumenical underground churches, the women's liberation movement, the black-power ideologies, the "lust of Apocalypse" (Mailer), the New Left—all these are factors in a far-reaching process of restructuring American consciousness; this attempt at renovation shuttled between recourse to Continental European ideological traditions and tentative mystical attempts at breaking out.[186] The first tendency applies to the Marxist-revolutionary components of American radicalism in the sixties. A stringent application of the Marxist categories of the critique of political economics revealed American society to be an all-encompassing and self-destructive arena of irrationality, which will of historical necessity perish in the contemporary process of world revolution.[187] But when it becomes a matter of fixing the position of American society as a whole

185. Slater, *The Pursuit of Loneliness* (Boston, 1970), 97–98.

186. See H. von Borch, "Leiden am Imperium," *Süddeutsche Zeitung*, no. 126 (May 18–19, 1968); D. Salomon, ed., *LSD* (New York, 1966); T. J. J. Altizer, ed., *Toward a New Christianity* (New York, 1967); W. A. Beardslee, ed., *America and the Future of Theology* (Philadelphia, 1967); S. Carmichael and C. V. Hamilton, *Black Power* (New York, 1967); P. Jacobs and S. Landau, eds., *The New Radicals* (New York, 1967); J. A. Newfield, *Prophetic Minority* (New York, 1967); N. Mailer, *The Armies of the Night* (New York, 1968); P. Baran and P. M. Sweezy, *Monopoly Capitalism* (New York, 1966).

187. This form of classical Marxism is best expressed in Baran and Sweezy, *Monopoly Capitalism*, and in P. Baran, *The Political Economy of Growth* (New York, 1951). The position is polemically presented in the anthology edited by T. Christoffel *et al.*, *Up Against the American Myth* (New York, 1970).

in the world-historical process and of determining unmistakably the social substratum of a revolutionary movement within this society, recurrence to classical Marxism invariably replicates the complex pattern of past heretical revisionism.

Herbert Marcuse's search for the revolutionary subject is only one famous example of such revisionist attempts. In this effort the United States, as the most advanced capitalist society, immediately regains the status of world-revolutionary avant-garde: "It is precisely the unprecedented capacity of twentieth century capitalism which will generate the revolution of the twentieth century—a revolution, however, which will have a base, strategy, and direction quite different from its predecessors, especially the Russian Revolution." This form of capitalism would bring about "the first truly world-historical revolution." "The historical site of the revolution would be that stage of development on which the satisfaction of the basic needs creates needs that transcend the state-capitalist and state-socialist society."[188] Marcuse once more links Marx's Europe-centered apocalypse to capitalism to such an extent that it becomes easily reconcilable with the Americanism-conditioned apocalypse of domestic capitalism. This explains Marcuse's popularity with the New Left. In its beginnings the common denominator of this revolutionary movement, regardless of its different social and organizational components, was shot through with a common critical sentiment of starting out and breaking out, which made eclectic use of all radical symbolisms, including the Marxist ones. Until the movement splintered into a multiplicity of movements, each with its own reality image, it exhibited the typical traits of any political-spiritual revival. The Port Huron Statement of Students for a Democratic Society of 1962 gave evidence of the spiritual-political impetus that, committed to the traditional form of consciousness, was intent on making it once again the principle of social order in a radical transformation of the structures of the existing social world. It begins with a logical critique of the concretization of all social order through the principle of metrical reality and the functional reality assigned to it: "Human brotherhood must be willed . . . as the most appropriate form of social relation." A truly humane society will come into being only "when a love of man overcomes the idolatrous worship of things." "Politics has the function of bringing people out of isolation and into community, this being a necessary though not sufficient means of finding meaning in personal life." From this follows the objective of restoring the paradigmatic republic: "We seek the establishment of a democracy of individual participation, governed by two central aims: that the individual share in

188. H. Marcuse, *Counterrevolution and Revolt* (Boston, 1972), 8, 16, 26.

those social decisions determining the quality and direction of his life; that society be organized to encourage independence in men and provide the media for their common participation." [189] This original attempt at a radical reordering of society from an altered consciousness was reflected in the plurality of efforts at a spiritual-political revivalism that Roszak first described in detail in his *The Making of the Counter Culture* (1969). Using the concept of "counter culture," he described the social substratum of resistance to the ultimate consolidation of a dictatorship of the technocratic principles of ordering (including the economism of the various Marxisms) as well as the environment in which tentative experimentation with indefinite alternatives exist.

As Slater did before him, Charles Reich also dogmatizes this social environment and, with apocalyptic undertones, announces a unique revolution, the "greening of America." Reich sees the heterogeneous components of the counterculture as the social genesis of a new consciousness—consciousness here representing the ideal type of a picture of reality encompassing the total existence of man. Reich's "Consciousness III" successfully shakes the premises of the two socially prevalent types of consciousness of American society. Consciousness I probably arose with the principle of nineteenth-century property individualism; Consciousness II is expressed in the principle of functional rationality. The "new consciousness is based on the present state of technology, and could not have arisen without it. And it represents a higher transcendent form of reason; no lesser form of consciousness could permit us to exist, given the present state of technology." [190]

> This transcendent reason has made its first appearance among the youth of America. It is the product of the contradictions, failures, and exigencies of the Corporate State itself. . . . It is now in the process of rapidly spreading to wider and wider segments of youth, and by degrees to older people, as they experience the recovery of the self that marks conversion to a different consciousness. The new consciousness is also in the process of revolutionizing the structure of our society. It does not accomplish this by direct political means, but by changing culture and the quality of individual lives, which in turn change politics and ultimately structure. [191]

Reich proclaims: "There is a revolution coming. It will not be like the revolutions of the past. . . . It promises a higher reason, a more human

---

189. Students for a Democratic Society, "The Port Huron Statement," in Jacobs and Landau, eds., *The New Radicals*, 153.
190. C. Reich, *The Greening of America* (New York, 1970), 13.
191. *Ibid.*

community, and a new liberated individual. Its ultimate creation will be a new and enduring wholeness and beauty—a renewed relationship of man to himself, to other men, to society, to nature and to the land." [192]

The abolition of the corporate state—the embodiment of all experience of deficiency in the contemporary American crisis—through a "revolution by consciousness" à la Reich was the main theme of the new political revivalism. Reich's impressionistic phenomenology of the social field of Consciousness III fed on the countercultural life-styles, including music, fashion, and the like. Manfred Henningsen quite properly objected that these countercultural movements all too frequently and all too quickly deviated into the apolitical-privatistic area of existential *divertissements*.[193] Reich by no means proves that the factors of the counterculture do indeed signify a socially relevant reversal in the spirit of Consciousness III—that is, restoration of the person-centered experience of order. Regardless of the question whether the described social phenomena actually are in the nature of such a revolution of consciousness, however, it should be noted that Reich's concept of the "Greening of America" expresses the specific American understanding of revolution: Reich develops the program of a spiritual-political reformation movement in the tradition of revolutionary revivalism: "this new age is not a repudiation of, but fulfillment of, the American dream." [194]

> The new age of man can take the best from the ages which preceded it. From the pre-industrial age it can take the integration and balance of life, the sense of God in everything. From the industrial era it can take technology and the steady rise to a higher level of life. From its own age it can take the control and use of technology, and the way of life of satisfaction, community and love, a way of life that aspires higher and higher, without forgetting its human source . . . it will not only release but augment and inspire, and make that the chief end of society. And it will do so within a society that makes the Judeo-Christian ethic not merely an ignored command, but a realistic way of life.[195]

This theme of a spiritual-political awakening may correctly be understood as part of the tradition of American self-consciousness. "The new consciousness . . . seeks restoration of the non-material elements of man's existence, the elements like the natural environment and the spiritual that were passed by in the rush of material development. It seeks to transcend

---

192. *Ibid.*, 1.
193. M. Henningsen, *Der Fall Amerika* (Munich, 1974), 253.
194. Reich, *The Greening of America*, 261.
195. *Ibid.*, 287.

science and technology, to restore them to their proper place as tools of man rather than as the determinants of man's existence. It is by no means anti-technological. . . . It makes the wholly rational assertion that machines should not do the bidding of man, of man who knows and respects his own nature and the natural order of which he is a part."[196]

In the European view of Jean-François Revel, a Frenchman, this moment of revivalist "hope of philosophy" vanishes, though like Reich, he is convinced of an American revolution *sui generis*. "The revolution of the twentieth century will take place in the United States. It is only there that it can happen. And it has already begun. Whether or not that revolution spreads to the rest of the world depends on whether it succeeds first in America." This American revolution is of quite a different sort than the "museumlike reconstruction of the revolutions of the nineteenth century."[197] Like Reich, Revel sees in the countersociety of the counterculture, "which has nothing marginal about it," a "revolutionary galaxy, marked by a configuration of appearances which all point to the breakthrough of a homo novus."[198] A new man such as the counterculture anticipates, however, can of necessity be realized only in the context of the pragmatic reality of an industrialized civilization. Economic prosperity and constant growth, technological expertise and a high level of basic research are among the premises of this revolution, as are the countercultural aspects of cultural futurism, affirmation of personal freedom and equality, rejection of authoritarian controls, and an increase in creative initiatives in every field, especially in the "'value free' areas: art, life-style, forms of sensibility, diversity in the coexistence of numerous supplementary and alternative subcultures."[199]

It seems questionable, however, whether the basic premise of these suggestions—a newly achieved balance of material and functional reality—shaped the countercultural attitude to the extent assumed by these writers. Otherwise Peter Berger would be correct when, analyzing the youth culture and the counterculture as expressions of demodernizing consciousness, he sees them only as a rejection of the functional rationality of technology and bureaucracy. Berger correctly demonstrates that the radical elimination of the mental and symbolic structures that are inherent in bureaucratic and technological processes destroys the pragmatic basis of modern social existence itself: "our analysis suggests that the demodernization, at least in its more radical manifestations, is faced

196. *Ibid.*, 259.
197. J.-F. Revel, *Without Marx and Jesus* (Garden City, N.Y., 1970), 11.
198. *Ibid.*, 112.
199. *Ibid.*, 139.

with the very definite limits in any such projects. These limits are imposed institutionally by the simple fact that short of unspeakable catastrophe, contemporary society cannot divest itself of its technological or bureaucratic structures in toto."[200] These limits "may be shifting but are nonetheless quite firm . . . grounded in the necessity of maintaining the fundamental technological and bureaucratic machineries of the society."[201] For this reason Berger foresees the creation merely of socioeconomically dependent—parasitical—countercultural enclaves that, given continuing economic growth, may in the future be able to institutionalize symbolic counterworlds within specific social spheres, such as the educational system. Such enclaves would serve, not as alternatives to the dominant social field of consciousness, but as a coexisting social field, one unable to support organized society.

Berger's objection correctly touches on the real problems of countercultural behavior patterns, though even in these "a rumor of angels" can be heard: "some have entertained angels unawares," Berger elsewhere quotes Hebrews 13:2. Finally, "openness to the signs of transcendence, the new vision in appropriate situations"[202] also characterizes the beginnings of a spiritual-political revival, at least in the analytic understanding of Reich and Roszak. Beyond this, in my opinion, Berger overlooks the crucial point: Although the pragmatic reason of the ends-means rationality of technology and bureaucracy determines modern industrial society to such an extent that in fact its destruction through the demodernizing consciousness would endanger social existence on the pragmatic level, it is nevertheless no substitute for noetic-substantial reason in the person-centered sense and the rational action associated with it in the area of material psychic and social order. Roszak's "true post-industrialism" attempts to open itself to this dimension:

> Politics of our time must reopen the metaphysical issues which science and sound logic have for the last two centuries been pleased to regard as closed. For to expound upon social priorities of the quality of life without confronting those issues is the very folly of alienation. It is . . . the half person prescribing the whole person's needs. But it is *experience* that must reopen those issues, not academic discourse. We must learn once more to discriminate experimentally between realities, telling the greater from the lesser. If there is to be a next politics, it will be a religious politics . . .

200. P. L. Berger *et al.*, *The Homeless Mind* (Harmondsworth, Eng.), 192–93.
201. *Ibid.*, 198.
202. *Ibid.*, 134.

religion in the oldest, most universal sense: which is vision born of transcendent knowledge.[203]

Although Roszak's revivalist enthusiasm is not without its gnostic-eschatological traces, it nevertheless exhibits a theoretical striving for extradogmatic and predogmatic reality that, having sought in vain for Hartz's "hope of philosophy" in the sterility of university departments of philosophy and the social sciences, has shifted to the divisions of religion, literature, and history.

In the search for a postindustrial paradigm of social order, the "hope of philosophy" often overlaps with the broad stream of reforming criticism of the institutional ramifications of society: the power apparatus of the nation, states, and localities; federalism; the educational establishment; the mass communication media; and the conditions of production. Scholars in every field, politicians, foundations, and the like, following the pragmatic reform movement, have insisted on resolving the crisis through an institutional arrangement.[204] This effort is very clearly based on that belief in institutions we have examined in the self-understanding of John Adams, the Founding Father. This is as true for the "new politics" of Schlesinger, who wishes to restore the intentions of the fathers in a "constitutional presidency cleansed of Watergate," as it is for James McGregor Burns, who wants to cure the current crisis with the medicines of 1776 or 1789: "to rediscover our overarching values, to recommit ourselves to them, to restructure our institutions to fulfill them, and to support and sustain leaders who will serve them. Who will emerge as the Franklin, Washington, Jefferson, Adams, or Madison of our time?"[205] Theodore Lowi's response is equally antifederalist-republican in that for him, this cult of the leader is merely the expression of contemporary institutional atrophy; his antidote is the restoration of the "rule of law" in a reform program of "juridical democracy."

In their most significant moments, the outlined changes in America's self-understanding during the 1960s and 1970s are indebted to spiritual-political revivalism. Although this revivalism left unmistakable traces on

203. T. Roszak, *Where the Wasteland Ends* (New York, 1973), 420–21.

204. Among the wealth of the relevant literature, exemplary contributions are the report of the Committee on Political Parties of the American Political Science Association, *Toward a More Responsible Two-Party System* (N.p., 1950); J. M. Burns, *The Deadlock of Democracy* (Englewood Cliffs, N.J., 1963); J. M. Burns, *Uncommon Sense* (New York, 1972); A. M. Schlesinger, Jr., *The Crisis of Confidence* (Boston, 1969); A. M. Schlesinger, Jr., *The Imperial Presidency* (Boston, 1973); Lowi, *The End of Liberalism;* T. J. Lowi, *The Politics of Disorder* (New York, 1971).

205. Burns, *Uncommon Sense,* 181.

the outward appearance of society, it was not able to break-up the continuity of the *sensus communis,* as the successful countermovement of the other tradition of spiritual-political individualism in the 1980s once again proved.

As ever, the American political process finds its intellectual and cultural frame of reference in the civil theology of Americanism, whose symbolic modes present historical structural change with its own peculiar sociocultural form in that they prescribe their political agenda according to the respective changes. Looking back upon the past decades, these circumstances, though they already had been noted previously, were picked up again by several authors: Schlesinger speaks about "the cycles of American politics: Let us define the cycle as a continuing shift in national evolvement, between public purpose and private interest."[206] The civil-theological origins of these swings of the pendulum in American politics become apparent in Schlesinger's description of these "cyclical alternation of public purpose and private interest: . . . in the American republic conservativism and reform, capitalism and democracy, private interest and public purpose, join to define the political tradition. The two jostling strains in American thought agree more than they disagree. Both are committed to individual liberty, the constitutional state and the rule of law. Both have their reciprocal functions in preserving the body politic. Both have their roles in the dialectic of public policy."[207] Whereas Schlesinger postulates a thirty-year cycle—that is, not differentiating between large or small swings—S. P. Huntington works out those civil-theological turning points that are the object of our study: "American society seems to evolve through periods of creedal passion and creedal passivity." This process articulates the tension between the aspirations of the identity-giving American creed and societal reality; in each case, it expresses the crisis in which Americanism finds itself.

> The 1960s thus had much in common with other periods of creedal passion, when the values of the American Creed had been invoked to challenge established institutions and existing practices—periods such as the Revolutionary era of the 1770s and 1780s, the Jacksonian Age of the 1820s and 1830s, and the Populist Progressive years of the 1890s and 1900s. In a sense, the gap between ideal and institution condemn Americans to coexist with a peculiar form of cognitive dissonance. At times, the dissonance is latent; at other times, when creedal passion runs high, it is brutally mani-

206. A. M. Schlesinger, Jr., *The Cycles of American History* (Boston, 1986), 27.
207. *Ibid.,* 7.

fest, and at such times, the promise of American politics becomes its central agony.[208]

Creedal passion is a civil-theological way of recourse to the original source of ordering at the founding; it is the response to politics inspired by cynicism, self-satisfaction, and hypocrisy, whose objective it is to try to restore the "paradigmatic republic." "Creedal passion periods," Huntington summarizes his findings, "involve intense efforts by large numbers of Americans to return to first principles. They are characterized by a distinctive type of political cleavage, major efforts at reform, and significant shifts in alignments between political institutions and social forces."[209] W. G. McLoughlin goes one step further, defining the periods of creedal passion as phases of the "Great Awakening and revivals," which form the basis for the historical development of American self-understanding. "Great Awakenings (and the revivals are part of them) are the results . . . of critical disjunctions in our self-understanding. They are not brief outbursts of mass emotionalism by one group or another but profound cultural transformations affecting all Americans and extending over a generation or more. Awakenings begin in periods of cultural distortion and grave personal stress, when we lose faith in the legitimacy of our norms, the viability of our institutions, and the authority of our leaders in church and state."[210] The great awakenings are movements of revitalizing American self-understanding, recovering the sense of American existence, redefining political and social goals, and reconstructing the institutions. According to McLoughlin, the five great awakenings in America—from the Puritan awakening in the seventeenth century, whose City Upon the Hill gave America's self-interpretation its "cultural core," through the first Great Awakening from 1730 to 1760, from which the Republic was born, through the Great Awakenings of 1800 to 1830 as well as 1890 to 1920, to the fourth Great Awakening of the 1960s and 1970s—warded off the recurring ideological and social crises in a "process of reorientation and redefinition of the core of beliefs and values that has enabled us to emerge from each crisis with renewed self-confidence as a people."[211] Thus, McLoughlin, as a radical Protestant civil theologist, ascribes contemporary spiritual-political revivalism to its Puritan origins: "Americans, in their cultural mythology, are God's

208. S. P. Huntington, *American Politics: The Promise of Disharmony* (Cambridge, Mass., 1981), 4.

209. *Ibid.*, 129.

210. W. G. McLoughlin, *Revivals, Awakening and Reform: An Essay on Religious and Social Change in America, 1607–1977* (Chicago, 1980), 2.

211. *Ibid.*, xv.

chosen, leading the world to perfection. Every awakening has revived, revitalized, and redefined that cultural core."[212]

Despite all differences in analytic details, the historian, the political scientist, and the historian of religion agree that the American process of civilization must be viewed on the basis of the self-understanding prevalent in American society, that is, Americanism. However, each in his own way sees that the diversity of forms prevalent in American symbolism developed historically from the civil-theological tradition. This tradition is the frame of reference for the value-giving ordering experience, which, altogether, forms the basis of the common substance of American politics. It is in this context that these interpreters once again discover "American exceptionalism." In Schlesinger's opinion, "one signal advantage over most nations" is the valid standards of the Founding Fathers, incorporated in the American creed, "by which to set our course and judge our performance," so that the "American experiment" may reach its destiny beyond the flux of events.[213]

Huntington puts it more precisely: The problems of the twentieth century affect only the incidental elements of American exceptionalism—those of power, wealth, and security; they do not touch upon "the historically most exceptional aspect of the United States: The United States has no meaning, no identity, no political culture or even history apart from its ideals of liberty and democracy and the continuing efforts of Americans to realize those ideals. Every society has its own distinctive form of tension that characterizes its existence as a society. The tension between liberal ideal and institutional reality is America's distinguishing cleavage. . . . If that tension disappears, the United States, as we have known it, will no longer exist."[214] The crisis of Americanism in the twentieth century is supposed to be mastered through a historical retrospective by pointing out the historical ordering function of civil theology, without, however, going beyond the semantic influence of the civil-theological discourse. Yet this confirms the view that, throughout their history, Americans have not identified with the American nation on the level of power and dominion, economics and society; rather, such identification attained plausibility through their consciousness and symbols: "the changes in the regime could hardly have been greater if we had a violent revolution," Elmer Eric Schattschneider correctly observes.[215]

A radically phenomenological description by fixing each piece of so-

212. *Ibid.,* 19.
213. *Ibid.,* A. M. Schlesinger, Jr., *The Cycles of American History,* 21.
214. Huntington, *American Politics,* 260–61.
215. E. E. Schattschneider, *The Semisovereign People* (New York, 1960), viii.

cial reality in time would demonstrate an enormous discrepancy between the America of Jackson and that of Nixon. The Constitution of 1789 is valid today, not because the constitutional reality has not altered in the past hundred years or because the document can still meet all the needs of the adequate organization of government—it probably never could— but because it maintained the stability of the social field of consciousness, nourished since the founding and expressed in Americanism, and because it allowed the individual American to experience in his consciousness the radical changes in the government and its underlying socioeconomic structures on a person-peripheral level—that is, not as a substantial change in his status of *homo Americanus*. The social and political change initiated by the mental resources of Americanism is experienced as a continuum that threatens to rupture only when the order of consciousness itself disintegrates. But this would mean quite simply the dissolution of the common sense of American society.[216]

V. Epilogue

We have already encountered common sense as the symbol of American self-understanding. This historic state of affairs, given a theoretical turn, brings us closer to the problem, repeatedly referred to above, of the reality content or rationality of Americanism.

The *Oxford English Dictionary* defines common sense as "an internal sense which was regarded as the common bond or centre of the five senses"; as "the general sense of mankind, or of a community"; and as "ordinary, normal, or average understanding (without this a man is foolish or insane)."[217] But common sense as "the logic of inquiry which is derived altogether from experience and from reflection upon it"[218]—that is, the judgmental and behavioral attitude of a man formed by reason—has first and foremost become an element of Anglo-Saxon self-interpretation. To acquire this, the American has traded a self-evidence that cut him off from his spiritual roots in philosophic meditation. Common sense here is no more than a code for the complex process by which a specific form of classical politics was established in the Anglo-Saxon culture area from the commonwealth's-men of the seventeenth century to the Scottish school of philosophy of the eighteenth century.[219] It is there-

---

216. This retreat of common sense, which now allows only a pluralism of private worlds, is a characteristic of modernity, according to Arendt, *The Human Condition*, 272 ff.

217. *Shorter Oxford Dictionary*, 351.

218. S. Hook, *Common Sense and the Fifth Amendment* (Chicago, 1957), 15.

219. See Robbins, *Eighteenth-Century Commonwealth Man;* Bailyn, *Ideological Origins of the American Revolution.*

fore not surprising that the lexical definition of common sense is synonymous with Thomas Reid's "philosophy of common sense."

Beginning in the middle of the eighteenth century, this philosophy of common sense rebelled in the name of humanity against a dominant "philosophy" that it identified as Humean skepticism, against the denaturing of reason and its deflection into the reflex of emotional life or the structural principle of logic, against the destruction of the general world of commonsense experience necessary to allow the meaningfulness of existence. Against this philosophy Reid declared, "I despise philosophy and renounce its guidance; let my soul dwell with common sense."[220]

First of all, common sense explicates our primary experience of the intersubjective everyday world by grasping its reality in structures of type, in "principles . . . which we are under a necessity to take for granted in the common concerns of life, without being able to give a reason for them."[221] Common sense "knows" what it is that is to be taken as original, both in action and in thought.[222] But it is absurd to speak of an antinomy between common sense and *ratio,* for it is only the intersubjectivity of the everyday world that establishes common sense as that "degree of reason" found "in the greater part of mankind": "It is this degree that entitles them to the denomination of reasonable creatures."[223] Such a degree of reason is necessary "to our being subjects of law and government, capable of managing our own affairs, and answerable for our conduct to others; this is called common sense, because it is common sense to all men with whom we can transact business or call to account for their conduct."[224] This function or this branch of reason can be acquired and become habitual, allowing us "to draw conclusions that are not self-evident from those that are."[225] "This is reasoning or dianoia"—that is, the dianoetic or discursive function of the *ratio*—commented William Hamilton, the editor of Reid's works.[226] But what is crucial is that self-evidence does not hang in the air but is disclosed by that function or that degree of the *ratio* that allows man to share in the divine; this function is

220. Reid, *Works,* I, 147. Compare L. Stephen, *History of English Thought in the Eighteenth Century* (New York, 1962), 49ff.

221. Reid, *Works,* I, 108.

222. Funke, *Gewohnheit* (Bonn, 1961), 387. The author concentrates almost entirely on the epistemological aspect of common sense. A substantial contribution is made by Henningsen, "Wirklichkeit des Common Sense." Further important insights into the problem of common sense are contained in B. J. Lonergan, *Insight* (London, 1963), 173–242, 289–99, and others.

223. Reid, *Works,* I, 425.

224. *Ibid.,* 422.

225. *Ibid.,* 425.

226. *Ibid.,* II, 791.

"to judge of things self-evident." It is "the province, and the sole province, of common sense, it coincides with reason in its whole extent,"[227] and is "purely the gift of Heaven. And where Heaven has not given it, no education can supply the want." The "noetic function"[228] of common sense is here explicitly identified with the *nous*.[229] This reformulation of the Aristotelian paradigm of man's rational nature justifies in some sense Hamilton's claim "that the doctrine of Common Sense . . . is the one catholic and perennial philosophy" and "that this is too the name under which that doctrine has for two thousand years been most familiarly known, at least, in the western world."[230] It seems to me admissible to say that in self-evident common sense of Anglo-Saxon self-consciousness, including its special form of Americanism, Aristotelian rationality was sufficiently creative to prevail in the modern conflict "of ideology against the Mediterranean mind"[231] expressed in that rebellion which, according to Camus, is the action of educated man aware of his own rights.[232]

Along with the discovery of a nature common to mankind, Aristotelian rationality also conferred on self-evident common sense the "measure and the limit which are the very principles of this nature."[233] According to Camus, "The rebel is a man who is on the point of accepting or rejecting the sacred and determined on laying claim to a human situation in which all the answers are human—in other words, formulated in reasonable terms."[234] Reason then feeds on understanding or *nous,* so that the rebellion "aspires to the relative and . . . promises an assured dignity coupled with relative justice,"[235] creating a solidarity of humanity. Aristotle's *philia politike,* freed of all socially conditioned limitations, establishes within this solidarity a society of the free and equal that alone has the power to confer on modern times the legitimacy they demand. George Bancroft, for his part, explicitly reclaimed this substantial commonsense reason for the experiment of the American polity: "Reason exists within every breast. I mean not that faculty which deduces inferences from the experiences of the senses, but that higher fac-

227. *Ibid.,* I, 425.
228. *Ibid.,* II, 791.
229. *Ibid.,* I, 550.
230. *Ibid.,* II, 757. The essay by Reid's editor, William Hamilton, "On the Philosophy of Common Sense," in Reid, *Works,* II, 742–803. Voegelin, *Anamnesis,* 352, should be amended to note that at least Reid and Hamilton were aware of noetic experience as a precondition for common sense.
231. A. Camus, *The Rebel,* trans. A. Bower (New York, 1956), 299.
232. *Ibid.,* 20.
233. *Ibid.,* 294.
234. *Ibid.,* 21.
235. *Ibid.,* 290.

ulty, which from the infinite treasures of its own consciousness, originates truth, and assents to it by the force of intuitive evidence; that faculty which raises us beyond the control of time and space, and gives us faith in things eternal and invisible."[236]

This common sense, which in its concrete American manifestation absorbed diverse Christian-Protestant and Puritanical-apocalyptic elements and was inevitably marked by the specific social experience of colonial existence, was the state of mind of the *homines politici* of the founding, creating for it a social field in the civil theology of the new nation.

But since even the Founding Fathers already understood that the "original truths and first principles" of ethics and politics were the "natural and unsophisticated dictates of the common sense"[237]—that is, they allowed its theoretical preconditions in the effort of noesis to fall below the threshold of consciousness—recurrence itself is in danger of being wrecked on the attitude of common sense if the behavior and decision-making pattern ingrained in this attitude is no longer a match for the challenge of an altered historical situation because this requires a new typology of social action. This demand is radical because it compels meditation to go back beyond the principle of self-evidence to the noetic origin of the order of consciousness.

236. Bancroft, "The Office of the People in Art, Government, and Religion, 1835," in *Literary and Historical Miscellanies,* 409.
237. *Federalist* No. 31.

Bibliography

Unpublished Sources

Boston Public Library, Rare Book Collection
    Library of John Adams.
Chicago Historical Society
    Adams Manuscripts.
Henry E. Huntington Library, San Marino, Calif.
    Cooper, Sam. Papers.
Historical Society of Pennsylvania, Philadelphia
    Adams, John. Manuscripts.
Library of Congress, Manuscript Division, Washington, D.C.
    Adams Papers.
Massachusetts Historical Society, Boston
    Adams, John. Papers, in Adams Family Microfilm.
    Cushing Papers.
    Dana Papers.
    Davies Papers.
    Follen Papers.
    John Quincy Papers.
    Pickering Papers.
    Putnam Papers.
    Smith-Carter Papers.
    Tudor Papers.

Warren Papers.
Waterston Autographs.

Printed Sources and Secondary Literature

Aaron, D., ed. *America in Crisis,* New York, 1952.
The Acts and Resolves, Public and Private, of the Province of Massachusetts Bay. Boston, 1869–1922.
Adair, D. "The Authorship of the Disputed Federalist Papers." *William and Mary Quarterly,* I (1944), 97–122, 235–64.
———. "That Politics May Be Reduced to a Science: David Hume, James Madison and the Tenth Federalist." *Huntington Library Quarterly,* xxix (1957), 343–60.
———. "Fame and the Founding Fathers." In *Fame and the Founding Fathers: Essays,* edited by Trevor Colbourn. New York, 1974.
Adams, A. *Letters.* Edited by C. F. Adams. 2 vols. Boston, 1841.
———. *New Letters.* Edited by S. Mitchell. Boston, 1947.
Adams, H. *History of the United States of America During the Administration of Thomas Jefferson.* 2 vols. New York, 1930.
———. *History of the United States of America During the Administration of James Madison.* 2 vols. New York, 1930.
———, ed. *Documents Relating to New England Federalism,* 1800–1815. Boston, 1877.
Adams, J. *The Adams Papers.*
  Series I:
  The Earliest Diary. Edited by L. H. Butterfield. Cambridge, Mass., 1966.
  Diary and Autobiography. Edited by L. H. Butterfield. 4 vols. Cambridge, Mass., 1961.
  Series II:
  Adams Family Correspondence. Edited by L. H. Butterfield. 2 vols. Cambridge, Mass., 1963.
  Series III:
  Legal Papers. Edited by L. K. Wroth and H. B. Zobel. 3 vols. Cambridge, Mass., 1965.
———. *Papers.* Edited by R. J. Taylor. Vols. I, II. Cambridge, Mass., 1978.
———. *Works.* Edited by C. F. Adams. 10 vols. Boston, 1850–56.
———. *The Political Writings.* Edited by G. A. Peek. New York, 1954.
———. *The Selected Writings.* Edited by A. Koch and W. Peden. New York, 1946.
———. "Letters from a Distinguished American." *General Advertizer and Morning Intelligencer,* August 23–December 26, 1782.

———. "Correspondence of the Late President Adams." Boston *Patriot,* April 10, 1809–May 16, 1812. Excerpts in *Correspondence of the Late President Originally Published in the Boston Patriot.* Boston, 1809.

———. *Catalogue of the John Adams Library in the Public Library of the City of Boston.* Edited by L. Swift. Boston, 1917.

———. *Familiar Letters.* Edited by C. F. Adams. Boston, 1876.

———. *Letters.* Edited by C. F. Adams. Boston, 1841.

———. *The Adams-Jefferson Letters.* Edited by L. J. Cappon. 2 vols. Chapel Hill, N.C., 1959.

———. *Old Family Letters: Copied from the Originals for Alexander Biddle.* Philadelphia, 1892.

———. *The Spur of Fame: Dialogues of John Adams and Benjamin Rush.* Edited by J. A. Schutz and Douglas Adair. San Marino, Calif., 1966.

———. *Warren-Adams Letters: Being Chiefly the Correspondence Among John Adams, Samuel Adams, and James Warren.* 2 vols. Boston, 1917–1925.

———. *Correspondence Between the Hon. John Adams and the Late William Cunningham.* Boston, 1823.

———. *Statesman and Friend: Correspondence of John Adams with Benjamin Waterhouse.* Edited by W. C. Ford. Boston, 1927.

———. "Correspondence Between John Adams and Professor John Winthrop." *Collections of the Massachusetts Historical Society,* IV (1878), 287–313.

———. "Correspondence Between John Adams and Mercy Warren." *Collections of the Massachusetts Historical Society,* IV (1878), 315–511.

———. "Some Unpublished Correspondence Between John Adams and Richard Rush." *Pennsylvania Magazine of History and Biography,* LX (1936), 419–54; LXI (1937), 26–53.

———. "John Adams, Knox and Washington." Edited by B. Knollenberg. *Proceedings of the American Antiquarian Society,* LVI (1947), 207–38.

———. "The Correspondence of John Adams and Horatio Gates." Edited by B. Knollenberg. *Proceedings of the Massachusetts Historical Society,* LXVII (1945), 135–51.

———. "The Papers of the Adams Family: Some Account to Their History." *Proceedings of Massachusetts Historical Society,* LXXI (1959), 328–56.

———. "The Revolutionary Correspondence of Nathanael Green and John Adams." Edited by B. Knollenberg. *Rhode Island History,* I (1942), 45–55, 73–83.

———. "John Adams Speaks His Mind." Edited by B. J. Hedges. *American Historical Review,* XLVII (1942), 806–809.

———. "Letters of John Adams." *Bulletin of the New York Public Library,* X (1906), 227–54.

———. "Queries Relating Slavery in Massachusetts." *Collections of the Massachusetts Historical Society,* III (1877), 401–16.

————. "Correspondence of John Adams." *Quarterly Review,* LXIX (1842), 245–79.

————. Letters of John Adams, addressed to his wife. In John Adams, *Letters,* edited by C. F. Adams. Boston, 1841.

————. "John Adams as He Lived: Unpublished Letters." *Atlantic Monthly,* MCMXXXIX (1927), 610–19, 774–83.

————. Individual letters in, among others, *New England Historical and Genealogical Register,* V (1851), 414–16; W. S. Bartlet, *The Frontier Missionary* (Boston, 1853), 34–35; *Historical Magazine,* IV (1868), 218–19; *Magazine of American History,* XX (1888), 304–308; *Bulletin of the Boston Public Library,* VI (1901), 342–44; *Proceedings of the Massachusetts Historical Society,* XLIV (1911), 422–28; XLV (1912), 24–25; XLVI (1913), 410–12; XLVII (1914), 466; XLVIII (1915), 507–508.

Adams, J. T. *New England in the Republic.* Boston, 1926.

————. *The Adams Family.* New York, 1932.

"The John Adams Library." *Bulletin of the Boston Public Library,* V (1923), 1ff.

Adams, J. Q. *Writings.* Edited by W. C. Ford. 7 vols. New York, 1913–17.

————. *Memoirs Comprising Portions of His Diary From 1795 to 1848.* Edited by C. F. Adams. 12 vols. Philadelphia, 1874–77.

Adams, R. G. *Political Ideas of the American Revolution.* Durham, N.C., 1922.

Adams, S. *Writings.* Edited by H. A. Cushing. 4 vols. New York, 1904–1908.

Adams, T. R. *American Independence: The Growth of an Idea. A Bibliographical Study of the American Political Pamphlets Printed Between 1764 and 1776.* Providence, 1965.

Adams, W. P. "Republikanismus und die ersten amerikanischen Einzelstaatsverfassungen." Ph.D. dissertation, Berlin, 1968.

————. "Republicanism in Political Rhetoric Before 1776." *Political Science Quarterly,* LXXXV (1970), 397–421.

————. *Republikanische Verfassung und bürgerliche Freiheit.* Darmstadt, 1973.

————, ed. *Die Vereinigten Staaten von Amerika.* Frankfurt, 1977.

Adorno, T. W. *Jargon der Eigentlichkeit zur deutschen Ideologie.* Frankfurt, 1964.

Agahd, R. *De Varronis rerum divinarum.* Leipzig, 1896.

Agresto, J. T. "Liberty, Virtue, and Republicanism, 1776–1787." *Review of Politics,* XXXIX (1977), 473–504.

Albanese, C. L. *Sons of the Fathers: The Civil Religion of the American Revolution.* Philadelphia, 1976.

Alden, J. R. *The American Revolution, 1775–1783.* New York, 1954.

Alföldi, A. *Der Vater des Vaterlandes im römischen Denken.* Darmstadt, 1971.

Allen, W. B., ed. *Works of Fisher Ames as Published by Seth Ames.* 2 vols. Indianapolis, 1983.

Allison, J. M. *Adams and Jefferson: The Story of a Friendship.* Norman, Okla., 1966.

Almond, G. A., *et al. Comparative Politics.* Boston, 1966.

Almond, G. A., and S. Verba. *The Civic Culture.* Boston, 1965.

Altizer, T. J. J., ed. *Toward a New Christianity.* New York, 1967.

Altizer, T. J. J., *et al.*, eds. *Truth, Myth, and Symbol.* Englewood Cliffs, N.J., 1962.

Anderson, Q. *The Imperial Self.* New York, 1971.

Andrews, C. M. "The Boston Merchants and the Non-Importation Movement." *Publications of the Colonial Society of Massachusetts,* XIX (1916–17), 380–90.

———. "The American Revolution: An Interpretation." *American Historical Review,* XXXI (1926), 218–32.

———. *The Colonial Background of the American Revolution.* New Haven, Conn., 1931.

———. *The Colonial Period of American History.* 4 vols. New Haven, Conn., 1934–38.

Angermann, E. "Ständische Rechtstraditionen in der amerikanischen Unabhängigkeitserklärung." *Historische Zeitschrift,* CC (1965), 61–91.

Angerman, E., *et al. The New Wine in Old Skins: A Comparative View of Socio-Political Structures and Values Affecting the American Revolution.* Stuttgart, 1976.

Appleby, J. O. "The Jefferson-Adams Rupture and the First French Translation of John Adams' Defence." *American Historical Review,* LXXIII (1968), 1084–91.

———. "The New Republican Synthesis and the Changing Political Ideas of John Adams." *American Quarterly,* XXV (1973), 578–95.

———. "Liberalism and the American Revolution." *New England Quarterly,* XLIX (1976), 3–26.

———. "The Social Origins of the American Revolutionary Ideology." *Journal of American History,* XLIII (1978), 935–58.

———. *Capitalism and a New Social Order.* New York, 1984.

———. "Republicanism and Ideology." *American Quarterly,* XXXVII (1985), 461–73.

Apter, D. E., ed. *Ideology and Discontent.* Glencoe, Ill., 1964.

Arendt, H. *The Human Condition.* Chicago, 1950.

———. "Action and the 'Pursuit of Happiness.'" In *Politische Ordnung und menschliche Existenz,* edited by A. Dempf *et al.* Munich, 1962, 1–16.

———. *Between Past and Future.* Cleveland, 1963.

———. *On Revolution.* New York, 1963.

Arieli, Y. *Individualism and Naturalism in American Ideology.* Cambridge, Mass., 1964.

Aristotle. *The Categories, On Interpretation, Prior Analytics.* Edited by H. P. Cook and H. Tredennik. London, 1962.

———. *Politics.* Edited by H. Rackham. London, 1959.

———. *The Nichomachean Ethics.* Edited by R. McKeon. New York, 1947.

Arnold, T. W. *The Symbols of Government.* New Haven, Conn., 1935.

———. *The Folklore of Capitalism.* London, 1937.

Augustinus, Aurelius. *De Civitate Dei.* 7 vols. London, 1957–72.

Baas, L. R. "The Constitution of Symbol Patterns of Meaning." *American Politics Quarterly,* VIII (1980), 237–56.

———. "The Constitution as Symbol: Interpersonal Sources of Meaning of a Secondary Symbol." *American Journal of Political Science,* XXIII (1979), 101–20.

Bacon, F. *Works.* Edited by J. Spedding *et al.* London, 1857–74.

Bailyn, B. "Butterfield's Adams: Notes for a Sketch." *William and Mary Quarterly,* XIX (1962), 238–56.

———. "Political Experience and Enlightenment Ideas in Eighteenth Century America." *American Historical Review,* LXVII (1962), 339–51.

———, ed. *Pamphlets of the American Revolution.* Vol. I: *1750–1765.* Cambridge, Mass., 1965.

———. *The Ideological Origins of the American Revolution.* Cambridge, Mass., 1967.

———. *The Origins of American Politics.* New York, 1968.

Bakunin, M. *Philosophie der Tat.* Cologne, 1968.

Baldwin, A. M. *The New England Clergy and the American Revolution.* Durham, N.C., 1928.

Baldwin, L. D. *The Stream of American History.* New York, 1952.

Ballestrem, K. "Graf, Die schottische Aufklärung." In *Festabge für Heinz Hürken,* edited by H. Dickerhof. Frankfurt, 1988.

Balthasar, H. U. V. *Prometheus.* Heidelberg, 1947.

Bancroft, G. *History of the United States.* 10 vols. Boston, 1934–74.

———. *Literary and Historical Miscellanies.* New York, 1855.

Banning, L. "Republican Ideology and the Triumph of the Constitution, 1789 to 1793." *William and Mary Quarterly,* XXXI (1974), 167–88.

———. *The Jefferson Persuasion: Evolution of a Party Ideology.* Ithaca, N.Y., 1978.

Baran, P. *The Political Economy of Growth.* New York, 1951.

Baran, P., and P. M. Sweezy. *Monopoly Capitalism.* New York, 1966.

Baritz, L. "The Idea of the West." *American Historical Review,* LXVI (1961), 618–40.

———. *City on a Hill.* New York, 1964.

Barrow, T. C. "Colonial Customs Service, 1660–1775." Ph.D. dissertation, Harvard University, 1961.

————. *Trade and Empire: The British Customs Service in Colonial America, 1660–1775.* Cambridge, Mass., 1967.

Barth, H. *Wahrheit und Ideologie.* Erlenbach, 1961.

Bassett, J. S. *The Life of Andrew Jackson.* New York, 1931.

Basye, A. H. "The Secretary of State for the Colonies, 1768–1782." *American Historical Review,* XXVIII (1922), 13–24.

Bates, J. L. *The United States, 1898–1928: Progressivism and the Society in Transition.* New York, 1976.

Bauer, J. R. "James Madison and the Revision of Republicanism in Post-Revolutionary America (Federalist)." Ph.D. dissertation, Duke University, 1984.

Baumgarten, E. *Die geistigen Grundlagen des amerikanischen Gemeinwesens.* 2 vols. Frankfurt, 1936–38.

Beard, C. A. *An Economic Interpretation of the Constitution of the United States.* New York, 1913.

————. *Economic Origins of Jeffersonian Democracy.* New York, 1915.

————, ed. *The Enduring Federalist.* Garden City, N.Y., 1948.

Beard, C. A., and M. R. Beard. *The American Spirit.* New York, 1943.

Beardslee, W. A., ed. *America and the Future of Theology.* Philadelphia, 1967.

Becelaere, E. G. L. von. *La Philosophie en Amérique depuis les origines jusqu'a nos jours (1607–1900).* New York, 1904.

Becker, C. L. *The Declaration of Independence.* New York, 1922.

————. *The Heavenly City of Eighteenth Century Philosophers.* New Haven, Conn., 1932.

Beeman, R., et al. *Beyond Confederation.* Chapel Hill, N.C., 1987.

Beer, G. L. *British Colonial Policy, 1754–1765.* New York, 1907.

————. *The Old Colonial System, 1660–1754.* 2 vols. New York, 1912.

Bein, A. *Die Staatsidee Alexander Hamilton.* Munich, 1927.

Bell, D. *The End of Ideology.* New York, 1960.

————. *The Coming of the Postindustrial Society.* New York, 1972.

Bell, R. M. *Party and Faction in American Politics: The House of Representatives, 1789–1809.* Westport, Conn., 1973.

Bellah, R. N. "Civil Religion in America." *Daedalus,* XCVI (1967), 1–21.

Bemis, S. F. *John Quincy Adams.* 2 vols. New York, 1949–1956.

————. *Pinckney's Treaty.* New Haven, Conn., 1960.

————. *The Diplomacy of the American Revolution.* Bloomington, Ind., 1957.

————. *Jay's Treaty.* New Haven, Conn., 1962.

Berens, J. T. *Providence and Patriotism.* Charlottesville, Va., 1978.

Berelson, Bernard, P. F. Lazarsfeld, and W. N. McPhee. *Voting: A Study of Opinion Formation in a Presidential Campaign.* Chicago, 1954.

Berg-Schlosser, D. "Die Erforschung 'politischer Kultur.'" Ph.D. dissertation, Munich, 1971.

Berger, P. L. *The Sacred Canopy.* Garden City, N.Y., 1967.

————. *Auf den Spuren der Engel.* Frankfurt, 1970.

Berger, P. L., *et al. The Homeless Mind.* Harmondsworth, Eng., 1974.

Berger, P. L., and T. Luckmann. *The Social Construction of Reality.* New York, 1966.

Berle, A. A. *The Twentieth Century Capitalist Revolution.* New York, 1954.

————. *The American Economic Republic.* New York, 1963.

Bernard, J. S.-B. "Luther Lee, Origins of American Sociology." *Social Science Movement in the U.S.* New York, 1943.

Bernhard, W. E. A. *Fisher Ames: Federalist and Statesman, 1758–1808.* Chapel Hill, N.C., 1965.

Berry, R. B. "John Adams: Two Further Contributions to the Boston Gazette, 1766–1768." *New England Quarterly,* XXXI (1958), 90–99.

Billias, G. A. *Elbridge Gerry: Founding Father and Republican Statesman.* New York, 1976.

————, ed. *The American Revolution.* New York, 1965.

Billington, R. A., ed. *The Reinterpretation of Early American History.* San Marino, Calif., 1966.

Binkley, W. E. *American Political Parties.* New York, 1963.

Bishop, C. F. *History of Elections in the American Colonies.* New York, 1893.

Blackstone, W. *Commentaries on the Laws of England.* Oxford, 1770.

Blau, J. L., ed. *Social Theories of Jacksonian Democracy.* New York, 1954.

Blitzer, C., ed. *The Commonwealth of England, 1641–1660.* New York, 1963.

Bloch, R. H. *Visionary Republic: Millennial Themes in American Thought, 1756–1800.* Cambridge, Eng., 1985.

Blum, J. M. *The Republican Roosevelt.* Cambridge, Mass., 1954.

Boas, R., and L. S. Boas. *Cotton Mather.* New York, 1928.

Boller, P. F. "George Washington and Religious Liberty." *William and Mary Quarterly,* XVII (1960), 486–506.

Boorstin, D. J. *The Genius of American Politics.* Chicago, 1953.

————. *The Mysterious Science of the Law.* Boston, 1958.

————. *The Americans.* 3 vols. New York, 1958–73.

————. *America and the Image of Europe.* New York, 1960.

————. *The Lost World of Thomas Jefferson.* Boston, 1960.

Borch, H. von. *Amerika—Die unfertige Gesellschaft.* Munich, 1964.

————. "Leiden am Imperium." *Süddeutsche Zeitung,* no. 120 (May 18–19, 1968).

Borden, M., ed. *The Antifederalist Papers.* N.p., 1965.

Bosl, K. "Die germanische Kontinuität im deutschen Mittelalter." In Bosl, *Frühformen der Gesellschaft im mittelalterlichen Europa.* Munich, 1964.

Boudin, L. B. "Government by Judiciary." *Political Science Quarterly* (1911), 238ff.

BIBLIOGRAPHY

Bowen, L. D. *John Adams and the American Revolution*. Boston, 1950.

Bowers, C. G. *The Party Battles of the Jackson Period*. Boston, 1922.

Boyd, J. P. *Anglo-American Union: Joseph Galloway's Plans to Preserve the British Empire, 1774–1788*. Philadelphia, 1941.

———. *The Declaration of Independence*. Princeton, N.J., 1945.

Boyd, R. S. *The Politics of Opposition: Antifederalists and the Acceptance of the Constitution*. Millwood, N.Y., 1979.

Bradford, A., ed. *The Speeches of the Governors of Massachusetts from 1765 to 1775*. Boston, 1818.

Brant, I. *James Madison*. 6 vols. Indianapolis, 1941–61.

Brasch, F. E. "The Newtonian Epoch in the American Colonies, 1680–1783." *Proceedings of the American Antiquarian Society*, XLIX (1939), 314–22.

Breen, T. H. "John Adams' Fight Against Innovation in the New England Constitution 1776." *New England Quarterly*, XL (1967), 301–320.

Brennan, E. E. "James Otis: Recreant and Patriot." *New England Quarterly*, XII (1939), 691–725.

———. *Plural Office Holding in Massachusetts, 1760–1780*. Chapel Hill, N.C., 1945.

Bridenbaugh, C. *Mitre and Sceptre: Transatlantic Faiths, Ideas, Personalities, and Politics, 1689–1775*. New York, 1962.

Brooke, J. *The Chatham Administration, 1766–1768*. London, 1956.

Brown, R. E. "Economic Democracy Before the Constitution." *American Quarterly*, VII (1955), 257–74.

———. *Middle-Class Democracy and the Revolution in Massachusetts, 1691–1780*. Ithaca, N.Y., 1955.

———. *Charles Beard and the Constitution*. Princeton, 1956.

———. *Reinterpretation of the Formation of the American Constitution*. Boston, 1963.

———. *Revolutionary Politics in Massachusetts: The Boston Committee of Correspondence and the Towns, 1772–1774*. Cambridge, Mass., 1970.

Brown, R., and K. A. Brown. *Virginia, 1705–1786: Democracy or Aristocracy?* East Lansing, Mich., 1964.

Bruchey, S. "The Forces Behind the Constitution: A Critical Review of the Framework of E. J. Ferguson's 'The Power of the Purse!' with a Rebuttal by E. J. Ferguson." *William and Mary Quarterly*, XIX (1962), 429–58.

Bryan, W. A. "The Genesis of Weem's Life of Washington." *Americana*, XXXVI (1942), 147–65.

———. *George Washington in the American Literature*. New York, 1952.

Bryce, J. *The American Commonwealth*. 2 vols. New York, 1959.

Bryson, L., *et al.*, eds. *Symbols and Society*. New York, 1955.

Buel, R. Jr. "Democracy and the American Revolution: A Frame of Reference." *William and Mary Quarterly*, XXI (1964), 165–90.

———. *Securing the Revolution: Ideology in American Politics, 1789–1815.* New York, 1972.

Bugg, J., ed. *Jacksonian Democracy, Myth or Reality.* New York, 1967.

Bulloch, J. M. *Thomas Gordon: The "Independent Whig."* Aberdeen, 1918.

Bullock, C. J. *Finances of the United States from 1775 to 1789.* Madison, Wis., 1895.

Buranelli, V. "Colonial Philosophy." *William and Mary Quarterly,* XVI (1959), 343–62.

Burckhardt, J. C. *Gesammelte Werke.* 10 vols. Berlin, 1955–57.

———. *Weltgeschichtliche Betrachtungen.* Stuttgart, 1955.

Burnett, E. .C. *The Continental Congress.* New York, 1964.

———, ed. *Letters of the Members of the Continental Congress.* 8 vols. Washington, D.C., 1921–36.

Burns, E. M. *The American Idea of Mission.* New Brunswick, N.J., 1957.

Burns, J. M. *Roosevelt: The Lion and the Fox.* New York, 1956.

———. *The Deadlock of Democracy.* Englewood Cliffs, N.J., 1963.

———. *Uncommon Sense.* New York, 1972.

Bury, J. B. *The Idea of Progress.* New York, 1955.

Bush, C. *The Dream of Reason: American Consciousness and Cultural Achievement from Independence to the Civil War.* N.p., 1977.

Bushman, R. L. *From Puritan to Yankee: Character and the Social Order in Connecticut, 1690–1765.* Cambridge, Mass., 1967.

———. "Corruption and Power in Provincial America." In *The Development of a Revolutionary Mentality.* Washington, D.C., 1972, 63–91.

Butterfield, L. H. *George III, Lord North and the People, 1779–1780.* London, 1949.

———. *George III and the Historians.* London, 1957.

———. "The Dream of Benjamin Rush: The Reconciliation of John Adams and Thomas Jefferson." *Yale Review,* XL (1950–51), 297–319.

———. "The Jubilee of Independence, July 4, 1826." *Virginia Magazine of History and Biography,* LXI (1953), 119–40.

———. "The Adams Papers. 'What Ever You Write Preserve.'" *American Heritage,* X (1959), 26–33, 88–93.

———. "The Papers of the Adams Family: Some Account to Their History." *Proceedings of the Massachusetts Historical Society,* LXXI (1959), 328–56.

———. "John Adams' Correspondence with Hezekiah Niles: Some Notes and a Query." *Maryland Historical Magazine,* LVII (1962), 150–54.

Caldera, G. H. "Neither the Purse nor the Sword: Dynamic of Public Confidence in the Supreme Court." *American Political Science Review,* LXXX (1986), 1209–26.

Calhoun, J. *The Papers of John C. Calhoun.* Edited by R. L. Meriwether. 16 vols. Columbia, 1959–.

——. *The Works of John C. Calhoun.* Edited by R. K. Cralle. 6 vols. New York, 1851–56.

Calkin, H. "Pamphlets and Public Opinion During the American Revolution." *Pennsylvania Magazine of History and Biography,* LXIV (1940), 22–42.

Campbell, A., *et al. The American Voter.* New York, 1960.

——. *The Voter Decides.* Evanston, Ill., 1954.

Campbell, Joseph. *The Hero with a Thousand Faces.* New York, 1953.

Camus, A. *The Rebel.* Translated by Anthony Bower. New York, 1956.

Carlyle, T. *Carlyle on Heroes, Hero-Worship, and the Heroic in History.* Edited by A. MacMechan. Boston, 1901.

Carman, H., H. C. Syrett, and B. W. Wishy. *A History of the American People.* 2 vols. 2nd ed. New York, 1960–61.

Carmichael, S., and C. V. Hamilton. *Black Power.* New York, 1967.

Carpenter, W. S. "The Separation of Powers in the Eighteenth Century." *American Political Science Review,* XXII (1928), 32–44.

——. *The Development of American Political Thought.* Princeton, N.J., 1930.

Carroll, W. H. "John Adams. Puritan Revolutionist." Ph.D. dissertation, Columbia University, 1939.

Carse, J. P. "Mr. Locke's Magic Onions and an Unboxed Beetle for Young Jonathan." *Journal of Religion,* XLVII (1967), 331–39.

Cash, W. J. *The Mind of the South.* New York, 1969.

Cassirer, E. *An Essay on Man.* New Haven, Conn., 1944.

——. *Vom Mythos des Staates.* Zurich, 1949.

Cattelain, F. *Etude sur l'influence de Montesquieu dans les constitutions Américaines.* Besançon, France, 1927.

Chaffee, Z. "Colonial Courts and the Common Law." *Proceedings of the Massachusetts Historical Society,* LXVIII (1952), 132–59.

Chambers, W. N. *Political Parties in a New Nation.* New York, 1963.

Charles, J. *The Origins of the American Party System.* New York, 1961.

Chinard, G. *Jefferson et les Idéologues.* Baltimore, 1925.

——. *Thomas Jefferson: The Apostle of Americanism.* Boston, 1929.

——. "Notes de John Adams sur Voltaire et Rousseau." *Modern Language Notes,* XLVI (1931), 26–31.

——. *Honest John Adams.* Boston, 1933.

——. "Polybios and the American Constitution." *The Journal of the History of Ideas,* I (1940), 38–58.

——. "Adventures in a Library." *Newberry Library Bulletin,* VIII (1952), 223–38.

Christoffel, T., *et al. Up Against the American Myth.* New York, 1970.

Cicero, *De Republica.* Zurich, 1960.

Clark, D. M. *British Opinion and the American Revolution.* New Haven, Conn., 1930.

———. *The Rise of the British Treasury: Colonial Administration in the Eighteenth Century.* New Haven, Conn., 1960.

Clark, G., ed. *The New Cambridge Modern History.* 14 vols. Cambridge, Eng., 1957–.

Clay, H. *Papers.* Edited by J. F. Hopkins. 10 vols. Lexington, Ky., 1959–.

Clebsh, W.-A. "Christian Interpretations of the Civil War." *Church History,* XXX (June, 1961), 212–22.

Clough, W. O., ed. *Intellectual Origins of American National Thought: Pages from the Books Our Founding Fathers Read.* 2nd rev. ed. Secaucus, N.J., 1961.

Cohen, I. B. *Franklin and Newton.* Philadelphia, 1950.

———. *Benjamin Franklin: His Contribution to the American Tradition.* Indianapolis, 1953.

Cohen, L. H. "Explaining the Revolution: Ideology and Ethics in Mercy Otis Warren's Historical Theory." *William and Mary Quarterly,* XXXVII (1980), 218.

Cohen, M. R. *American Thought: A Critical Sketch.* Glencoe, Ill., 1954.

Coit, M. L. *John C. Calhoun.* Boston, 1950.

Colbourn, H. T. *The Lamp of Experience.* Chapel Hill, N.C., 1965.

Cole, M. L. "The Rise of the Legislative Assembly in Provincial Massachusetts." Ph.D. dissertation, Iowa State University, 1939.

Coleman, F. M. *Hobbes and America: Exploring the Constitutional Foundings.* Toronto, 1977.

Collins, E. D. "Committees of Correspondence in the American Revolution." *American Historical Association Annual Report* (1901), 243–71.

Commager, H. S. *The American Mind.* New Haven, Conn., 1959.

———. *The Empire of Reason: How Europe Imagined and America Realized the Enlightenment.* New York, 1977.

Commager, H. S., and R. B. Morris. *The Spirit of "Seventy-Six": The Story of the American Revolution as Told by Participants.* 2 vols. Indianapolis, 1958.

Committee on Political Parties of the American Political Science Association. *Toward a More Responsible Two-Party System: A Report.* New York, 1950.

Conkin, P. K. *The New Deal.* New York, 1967.

Conrad, A. H., and J. R. Meyer. "The Economics of Slavery in the Ante-Bellum South." *Journal of Political Economy,* LXVI (1958), 95–130.

Converse, P. E. "The Nature of Belief Systems in Mass Publics." In *Ideology and Discontent,* edited by D. E. Apter. New York, 1964.

Cook, G. A. *John Wise.* New York, 1952.

Cooke, J. E., ed. *The Federalist.* Cleveland, 1961.

Coolidge, A. C. *Theoretical and Foreign Elements in the Formation of the American Constitution.* Freiburg, 1892.

Corwin, E. S. "The Progress of Constitutional Theory Between the Declaration of Independence and the Meeting of the Philadelphia Convention." *American Historical Review,* XXX (1925), 511–36.

———. "The Constitution as Instrument and Symbol." *American Political Science Review,* XXX (1936), 1071–75.

———. *Court over Constitution.* Princeton, 1938.

———. *The Constitution and What it Means Today.* Princeton, 1948.

———. *The "Higher Law" Background of American Constitutional Law.* Ithaca, N.Y., 1955.

Counts, M. L. "The Political Views of the Eighteenth Century New England Clergy as Expressed in Their Election Sermons." Ph.D. dissertation, Columbia University, 1956.

Cowing, C. B. *The Great Awakening and the American Revolution: Colonial Thought in the 18th Century.* Chicago, 1971.

Cragg, G. R. *Reason and Authority in the Eighteenth Century.* Cambridge, 1964.

Crane, V. W. *Benjamin Franklin and a Rising People.* Boston, 1954.

Craven, A. O. *The Coming of the Civil War.* 2nd ed. Chicago, 1957.

Craven, W. F. *The Legend of the Founding Fathers.* New York, 1956.

Cresson, W. F. *Francis Dana: A Puritan Diplomat at the Court of Catharine the Great.* New York, 1930.

———. *James Monroe.* Chapel Hill, N.C., 1946.

Crick, B. *The American Science of Politics.* Berkeley, Calif., 1959.

Croly, H. *The Promise of American Life.* Cambridge, Mass., 1965.

Crosskey, W. W. *Politics and the Constitution in the History of the United States.* 2 vols. Chicago, 1953.

Crosskey, W. W., and W. Jeffrey, Jr. *The Political Background of the Federal Convention.* Chicago, 1980. Vol. III of *Politics and the Constitution in the History of the United States.* 3 vols.

Cunliffe, M. *George Washington, Man and Monument.* New York, 1958.

———. *The Nation Takes Shape, 1789–1837.* Chicago, 1959.

Cunningham, N. E., ed. *The Making of the American Party System, 1789 to 1809.* Englewood Cliffs, N.J., 1965.

Current, R. *Daniel Webster.* Boston, 1955.

Curti, M. E. *The Growth of American Thought.* New York, 1943.

Curti, M. E., *et al. An American History.* New York, 1950.

Cushing, A. "Political Activity of Massachusetts Towns During the Revolution." *Annual Report of the American Historical Association.* Washington, D.C., 1896.

Dahl, R. *A Preface to Democratic Theory.* Chicago, 1956.

———. *Modern Political Analysis.* Englewood Cliffs, N.J., 1963.

———. *Democracy in the United States.* Chicago, 1972.

Dahrendorf, R. *Die angewandte Aufklärung.* Frankfurt, 1968.

Dangerfield, G. *The Era of Good Feeling*. New York, 1952.

Dauer, M. J. "The Political Economy of John Adams." *Political Science Quarterly*, LVI (1941), 545–72.

———. *The Adams Federalists*. Baltimore, 1953.

David, H., *et al.*, eds. *The Economic History of the United States*. 9 vols. New York, 1945–62.

Davidson, J. W. *The Logic of the Millennial Thought*. New Haven, Conn., 1977.

Davidson, P. *Propaganda and the American Revolution, 1763–1783*. Chapel Hill, N.C., 1941.

Davies, J. C. "Theorie der Revolution." In *Theorien des sozialen Wandels*, edited by W. Zapf. Cologne, 1968.

Davies, W. E. *Patriotism on Parade*. Cambridge, Mass., 1955.

D'Ella, D. J. *Banjamin Rush: Philosopher of the American Revolution*. Philadelphia, 1974.

Delmage, R. E. "The American Idea of Progress, 1780–1800." *Proceedings of the American Philosophical Society*, XCI (1947), 307–14.

DePauw, L. G., ed. *Documentary History of the First Federal Congress of the United States of America, March 4, 1789–March 3, 1791*. 9 vols. Baltimore, 1972–.

Detweiler, P. "Congressional Debate on Slavery and the Declaration of Independence, 1819–1821." *American Historical Review*, LXIII (1958), 598–616.

———. "The Changing Reputation of the Declaration of Independence: The First Fifty Years." *William and Mary Quarterly*, XIX (1962), 557–74.

Deutsch, K. W. *The Nerves of Government*. Glencoe, Ill., 1966.

———. *The Development of Revolutionary Mentality*. Washington, D.C., 1972.

Devine, D. J. *The Political Culture of the United States*. Boston, 1972.

Dickerson, O. M. *American Colonial Government 1696–1765*. Cleveland, 1912.

Dickinson, J. *Writings*. Edited by P. L. Ford. Philadelphia, 1895.

Dodd, E. M. *American Business Corporations Until 1860: With Special Reference to Massachusetts*. Cambridge, Mass., 1954.

Donnelly, L. M. "The Celebrated Mrs. Macauly." *William and Mary Quarterly*, VII (1949), 173–207.

Dorfman, J. *The Economic Mind in the American Civilization*. 5 vols. New York, 1946–59.

Douglas, D. C. *English Scholars, 1660–1730*. London, 1951.

Douglass, E. P. *Rebels and Democrats*. Chapel Hill, N.C., 1955.

Down, R. B., ed. *Three Presidents and Their Books*. Urbana, Ill., 1955.

Draper, T. "Hume and Madison." *Encounter*, LVIII (1982), 34–47.

Drexter, H. "Honos." In *Römische Wertbegriffe*, edited by H. Opperman. Darmstadt, 1967.

Duberman, M. B., ed. *The Anti-Slavery Vanguard*. Princeton, 1965.

Dumbauld, E. *The Bill of Rights and What It Means Today.* Norman, Okla., 1957.

Dummer, J. A. *Defence of the New England Charters.* Boston, 1721.

Dunbar, L. B. *A Study of "Monarchical" Tendencies in the United States from 1776 to 1801.* Urbana, Ill., 1922.

Dunn, R. N. "Social History of Early New England." *American Quarterly,* XXIV (1972), 661–79.

Dunne, J. S. *The City of Gods.* New York, 1965.

East, R. A. "The Massachusetts Conservatives in the Critical Period." In *The Era of the American Revolution,* edited by R. B. Morris. New York, 1939.

———. *Business Enterprise in the American Revolutionary Era.* New York, 1938.

Easton, D. *The Political System: An Inquiry into the State of Political Science.* New York, 1964.

Echeverria, D. *Mirage in the West: A History of the French Image of American Society to 1815.* Princeton, 1957.

Eckardt, U. M. von. *The Pursuit of Happiness in the Democratic Creed.* New York, 1959.

Edes, P., ed. *Orations Delivered at the Request of Inhabitants. . . .* Boston, 1785.

Edwards, J. *Works.* Edited by E. D. Sereno. 10 vols. New York, 1829–39.

———. *Representative Selections.* Edited by C. F. Faust and T. H. Johnson. New York, 1935.

Egnal, M. "The Origins of the Revolution in Virginia: A Reinterpretation." *William and Mary Quarterly,* XXXVII (1980), 404–28.

Egnal, M., and J. A. Ernst. "An Economic Interpretation of the American Revolution." *William and Mary Quarterly,* XXIX (1972), 3–32.

Eitrem. "Heroes." In *Paulys Realenzyklopädie der klassischen Altertumswissenschaften.* Vol. XV. Stuttgart, 1912.

Ekirch, A. A. *The Idea of Progress in America, 1815–1860.* New York, 1944.

———. *The Decline of American Liberalism.* New York, 1955.

Eliade, M. "Paradis et Utopie: Géographie Mythique et Eschatologie." In *Vom Sinn der Utopie.* Zurich, 1964.

———. *Myth and Reality.* New York, 1963.

Elkins, S., and E. McKitrick. "The Founding Fathers: Young Men of the Revolution." *Political Science Quarterly,* LXXVI (1961), 181–216.

Elliot, W. T. "The Constitution as the American Social Myth." In *The Constitution Reconsidered,* edited by Conyers Read. New York, 1938.

Elliott, J., ed. *The Debates in the Several State Conventions, on the Adoption of the Federal Constitution.* 5 vols. Washington, D.C., 1836.

Ellis, G. E. *The Puritan Age and Rule in the Colony of Massachusetts Bay, 1629–1685.* Boston, 1888.

Ellis, R. "The Political Economy of Thomas Jefferson." In *Thomas Jefferson: The Man, His World, His Influence*. Edited by L. Weymouth. London, 1973.

Emerson, Ralph Waldo. *The Complete Works of Ralph Waldo Emerson*. 12 vols. Boston, 1903–1904.

Erdmann, C. *Forschungen zur politischen Ideengeschichte des Frühmittelalters*. Berlin, 1951.

Erikson, R. S., and N. R. Luttbeg. *American Public Opinion: Its Origins, Content, and Impact*. New York, 1973.

Evans, C. *American Bibliography: A Chronological Dictionary of All Books, Pamphlets and Periodical Publications Printed in the United States of America . . . 1639 . . . to 1820. . . .* 14 vols. Chicago, 1903–59.

Everett, E. *Orations and Speeches on Various Occasions*. 4 vols. Boston, 1868.

Farrand, M., ed. *The Records of the Federal Convention*. 4 vols. New Haven, Conn., 1937.

Fay, B. *The Revolutionary Spirit in France and America*. New York, 1927.

Fenton, J. F. *The Theory of the Social Compact and Its Influence upon the American Revolution*. N.p., 1891.

Ferguson, E. J. *The Power of the Purse*. Chapel Hill, N.C., 1961.

Fielding, H. I. "John Adams: Puritan, Deist, Humanist." *Journal of Religion*, XX (1940), 33–46.

Fink, Z. S. *The Classical Republicans*. Evanston, Ill., 1945.

Fischer, D. H. *The Revolution of American Conservatism: The Federalist Party in the Era of Jeffersonian Democracy*. New York, 1965.

Fisher, S. G. *True History of the American Revolution*. Philadelphia, 1902.

———. "The Legendary and Myth-Making Process in Histories of the American Revolution." *Proceedings of the American Philosophical Society*, XL (1912).

Fishwick, M. W. *A Bibliography of the American Hero*. Charlottesville, N.C., 1950.

Flaumenhaft, H. "Hamilton on the Foundation of Good Government." *Political Science Reviewer*, IV (1976), 143–214.

Fletcher, F. T. H. *Montesquieu and English Politics, 1750–1800*. London, 1939.

Fliegelman, J. *Prodigals and Pilgrims: The American Revolution Against Patriarchal Authority, 1750–1800*. Cambridge, Eng., 1982.

Fogel, R. W., and S. L. Engerman. *Time on the Cross: The Economics of American Negro Slavery*. Boston, 1974.

Foner, E. *Free Soil, Free Labor, Free Men: The Ideology of the Republican Party Before the Civil War*. New York, 1970.

Foote, H. W. *The Religion of Thomas Jefferson*. Boston, 1960.

Ford, P. L. *The True George Washington*. Philadelphia, 1897.

———, ed. *Pamphlets on the Constitution of the United States*. Brooklyn, N.Y., 1888.

————, ed. *Essays on the Constitution*. Brooklyn, N.Y., 1892.

Ford, W. C., ed. *Journals of the Continental Congress 1774–1789*. 34 vols. Washington, D.C., 1904–37.

Formisano, R. P. "Deferential-Participant Politics: The Early Republic's Culture, 1789–1840." *American Political Science Review*, LVIII (1974), 473–87.

Forster, F. H. "The Eschatology of the New England Divines." *Bibliotheca Sacra*, XLIII (1886), 6–19.

Forsythe, D. W. *Taxation and Political Change in the Young Nation, 1781–1833*. New York, 1977.

Franklin, B. *Writings*. Edited by A. H. Smyth. 10 vols. New York, 1905–1907.

————. *Papers*. Edited by L. W. Larabee. 28 vols. New Haven, Conn., 1959–.

Free, L. A., and H. Cantril. *The Political Beliefs of Americans: A Study of Public Opinion*. New York, 1968.

Freeman, D. S. *George Washington*. 7 vols. New York, 1948–57.

Frese, J. R. "James Otis and the Writs of Assistance." *New England Quarterly*, XXX (1957), 496–508.

Freud, S. *Abriß der Psychoanalyse—Das Unbehagen in der Kultur*. Frankfurt, 1953.

Freund, P. A., *et al.*, eds. *Constitutional Law*. 2 vols. Boston, 1961.

Fried, A., ed. *Socialism in America*. New York, 1970.

Friedrich, C. J. *The New Belief in the Common Man*. Boston, 1942.

————. *Man and His Government*. New York, 1963.

————. *Christliche Gerechtigkeit und Verfassungsstaat*. Cologne, 1967.

————, ed. *Community*. New York, 1959.

Frings, M. *Henry Clay's American System*. Frankfurt, 1979.

Fuess, C. M. *Daniel Webster*. 2 vols. Boston, 1930.

Funke, G. *Gewohnheit*. Bonn, 1961.

Furtwangler, A. *The Authority of Publius—A Reading of the Federalist Papers*. Ithaca, N.Y., 1984.

Fussner, F. S. *The Historical Revolution: English Historical Writing and Thought, 1580–1640*. New York, 1962.

Gabriel, R. H. *The Course of American Democratic Thought*. New York, 1956.

Galbraith, J. K. *American Capitalism*. Boston, 1952.

————. *The New Industrial State*. New York, 1967.

Garrett, W. "John Adams and the Limited Role of the Arts." *Winterthur Portfolio*, I (1964), 243–55.

Gaustad, E. S. *The Great Awakening in New England*. New York, 1957.

Gay, P. *The Party of Humanity*. New York, 1963.

————. *The Enlightenment: An Interpretation. The Rise of Modern Paganism*. New York, 1968.

Gebhardt, J. "The Federalist." In *Klassiker des politischen Denkens 2*, edited by H. Maier *et al.* Munich, 1968.

———. "James Harrington." In *Zwischen Revolution und Restauration*, edited by Eric Voegelin. Munich, 1968.

———. "Die Republik eines Humanisten." In *James Harrington: Politische Schriften*, edited by J. Gebhardt. Munich, 1973.

Geertz, C. "Ideology as a Cultural System." In *Ideology and Discontent*, edited by D. E. Apter. London, 1964.

Germino, D. *Beyond Ideology. The Revival of Political Theory*. New York, 1967.

Gilbert, F. *To the Farewell Address: Ideas of Early American Foreign Policy*. Princeton, N.J., 1961.

Gipson, L. H. *The British Empire Before the American Revolution*. 13 vols. New York, 1936–67.

———. *The Coming of the Revolution, 1763–1775*. New York, 1954.

———. "Aspects of the Beginning of the American Revolution in Massachusetts Bay, 1760–1762." *Proceedings of the American Antiquarian Society*, LXVII (1957), 11–32.

Goen, C. C. *Revivalism and Separatism in New England, 1740–1800*. New Haven, Conn., 1962.

Goldsmith, S. S. "'That Means That Republican Government Will Admit': The Political Thought of the Founding." Ph.D. dissertation, Brandeis University, 1984.

Goodman, P. *The Democratic-Republicans of Massachusetts: Politics in a Young Republic*. Cambridge, Mass., 1964.

Goodwyn, L. *The Populist Movement*. 1979.

———. *Democratic Promise: The Populist Moment in America*. New York, 1978.

Gottschalk, L. R. *The Place of the American Revolution in the Causal Pattern of the French Revolution*. Easton, Pa., 1948.

Gough, J. W. *Fundamental Law in English Constitutional History*. Oxford, 1955.

Granger, B. I. *Political Satire in the American Revolution, 1763–1783*. Ithaca, N.Y., 1960.

Green, C. *Eli Whitney and the Birth of American Technology*. Boston, 1956.

Greene, E. B. *The Foundation of American Nationality*. New York, 1935.

———. *The Revolutionary Generation*. New York, 1943.

Greene, J. P. "The Flight from Determinism: A Review of Recent Literature on the Coming of the American Revolution." *South Atlantic Quarterly*, LXI (1962), 235–59.

———. *The Quest for Power*. Chapel Hill, N.C., 1963.

———. *The Reinterpretation of the American Revolution*. New York, 1968.

———. "The Plunge of Lemmings: A Consideration of Recent Writings on British Politics and the American Revolution." *South Atlantic Quarterly* (1968), 1941–75.

————. "The Preconditions for American Republicanism." In *The Development of a Revolutionary Mentality.* Washington, D.C., 1972.

————. "The Social Origins of the American Revolution." *Political Science Quarterly,* LXXXVIII (1973), 1–22.

————. *All Men are Created Equal: Some Reflections on the Character of the American Revolution.* Oxford, 1976.

Greene, J. P., and J. R. Pole, eds. *Colonial British America: Essays in the New History of the Early Modern Era.* Baltimore, 1984.

Greene, L. J. *The Negro in Colonial New England, 1620–1776.* New York, 1942.

Greenough, C. N. "Algernon Sidney and the Motto of the Commonwealth of Massachusetts." *Proceedings of the Massachusetts Historical Society,* LI (1918), 259–82.

Greven, P. J. "Historical Demography and Colonial America." *William and Mary Quarterly,* XXIV (1967), 438–54.

Grey, L. "John Adams and John Trumball in the Boston Cycle." *New England Quarterly,* IV (1931), 509–14.

Grimes, A. P. *American Political Thought.* New York, 1955.

Grinnell, F. W. "Mussolini, Machiavelli and John Adams." *Massachusetts Law Quarterly,* IX (1924), 32 ff.

————. "John Winthrop and the Constitutional Thinking of John Adams." *Proceedings of the Massachusetts Historical Society,* LXIII (1930), 91 ff.

Gummere, R. M. "The Classical Politics of John Adams." *Boston Public Library Quarterly,* IX (1957), 167–82.

————. "Thomas Hutchinson and Samuel Adams: A Controversy in the Classical Tradition." *Boston Public Library Quarterly,* X (1958), 203–12.

————. *The American Colonial Mind and the Classical Tradition.* Cambridge, Mass., 1963.

Guttridge, G. H. *English Whiggism and the American Revolution.* Berkeley, Calif., 1942.

Gwyn, W. B. *The Meaning of the Separation of Powers.* New Orleans, 1965.

Habermas, J. *Legitimationsprobleme im Spätkapitalismus.* Frankfurt, 1973.

Hacker, L. M. "The American Revolution: Economic Aspects." *Marxist Quarterly,* I (1937), 46–67.

————. *Alexander Hamilton and the American Tradition.* New York, 1957.

Haddon, A. C., *et al.* "Heroes and Hero-Gods." In *Encyclopedia of Religion and Ethics.* Vol. VI. New York, 1955.

Haddow, A. *Political Science in American Colleges and Universities, 1636–1900.* New York, 1939.

Haines, C. G. *The Revival of Natural Law Concepts.* Cambridge, Mass., 1930.

————. *The American Doctrine of Judicial Supremacy.* Berkeley, Calif., 1932.

Hall, M. G., *et al.*, eds. *The Glorious Revolution in America*. Chapel Hill, N.C., 1964.

Hamby, A. L., ed. and comp. *The New Deal: Analysis and Interpretation*. New York, 1981.

Hamilton, A. *Works*. Edited by H. C. Lodge. 12 vols. New York, 1903.

———. *Papers*. Edited by H. C. Syrett and J. E. Cooke. 27 vols. New York, 1961–.

Hamilton, W. H., and D. Adair. *The Power to Govern*. New York, 1937.

Hammond, B. *Banks and Politics in America*. Princeton, 1957.

Handler, E. *America and Europe in the Political Thought of John Adams*. Cambridge, Mass., 1964.

Handlin, O., and M. Handlin. "Radicals and Conservatives in Massachusetts After Independence." *New England Quarterly*, XVII (1944), 343–55.

———. *Commonwealth: A Study of the Role of Government in the American Economy, Massachusetts, 1774–1861*. New York, 1947.

———. "James Burgh and the American Revolutionary Theory." *Proceedings of the Massachusetts Historical Society*, LXXIII (1961), 38–57.

———, eds. *The Popular Sources of Political Authority: Documents on the Massachusetts Constitution of 1780*. Cambridge, Mass., 1966.

Handley, T. O. "Young Mr. Carrol and Montesquieu." *Maryland Historical Magazine*, LXII (1967), 394–418.

Hanson, R. L. *The Democratic Imagination in America*. Princeton, 1985.

Haraszti, Z. "Madame de Stael. The Vain Woman. John Adams of Her and Her Books." *More Books*, I (1926), 101–105.

———. "The Golden Verses of Pythagoras. More Marginal Notes by John Adams." *More Books*, I (1926), 106–10.

———. "More Books from the Adams Library." *Library Quarterly*, VIII (1951), 109–26.

———. *John Adams and the Prophets of Progress*. Cambridge, Mass., 1952.

———. "The 32nd Discourse on Davila." *William and Mary Quarterly*, XI (1954), 89–92.

Harding, S. B. *The Contest over the Ratification of the Federal Constitution in the State of Massachusetts*. New York, 1896.

Harlow, V. T. *The Founding of the Second English Empire, 1763–1793*. London, 1952.

Haroutunian, J. *Piety versus Moralism: The Passing of the New England Theology*. New York, 1932.

Harrison, J. F. C. *The Second Coming: Popular Millenarism, 1780–1850*. Brunswick, N.J., 1979.

Hart, A. B., ed. *Commonwealth History of Massachusetts*. 5 vols. New York, 1927–30.

BIBLIOGRAPHY

Hartz, L. *Economic Policy and Democratic Thought: Pennsylvania, 1776–1860.* Cambridge, Mass., 1948.

———. *The Liberal Tradition in America.* New York, 1955.

Hartz, L., et al. *The Founding of New Societies.* New York, 1964.

Harvey, R. F. *Jean Jacques Burlemaqui: A Liberal Tradition in American Constitutionalism.* Chapel Hill, N.C., 1937.

Haskins, G. L. *Law and Authority in Early Massachusetts.* New York, 1960.

Hatch, N. O. "The Origins of Civil Millennialism in America: New England Clergymen, War with France and the Revolution." *William and Mary Quarterly,* XXXI (1974), 407–30.

Hauriou, M. *Die Theorie der Institution.* Berlin, 1965.

Hawke, D. F. *A Transaction of Free Men: The Birth and Course of the Declaration of Independence.* New York, 1964.

———. *Benjamin Rush: Revolutionary Gadfly.* Indianapolis, 1971.

Hawley, E. W. "New Deal und 'organisierter Kapitalismus' in internationaler Sicht." In *Die große Krise in Amerika,* edited by H. A. Winkler. Göttingen, 1973.

Hazelton, J. H. *The Declaration of Independence: Its History.* New York, 1906.

Hazen, C. D. *Contemporary American Opinion of the French Revolution.* Baltimore, 1897.

Heath, M. S. *Constructive Liberalism.* Cambridge, Mass., 1954.

Heckscher, A. *The Public Happiness.* New York, 1962.

Hegel, G. W. F. *Politische Schriften.* Edited by J. Habermas. Frankfurt, 1966.

Heimann, E. *Soziale Theorie der Wirtschaftssysteme.* Tübingen, 1963.

Heimert, A. *Religion and the American Mind: From the Great Awakening to the Revolution.* Cambridge, Mass., 1966.

Heimert, A., and P. Miller, eds. *The Great Awakening.* Indianapolis, 1967.

Henningsen, M. *Der Fall Amerika.* Munich, 1974.

———. "Die Realität des Common Sense." *Politische Studien.* Munich, 1974.

Hereth, M. *Freiheit, Politik und Ökonomie.* Munich, 1974.

Herwig, H. *Therapie der Menschheit.* Munich, 1969.

Hicks, J. D. *Populist Revolt.* Lincoln, Nebr., 1967.

Higham, J., ed. *The Reconstruction of American History.* London, 1962.

Highet, G. *The Classical Tradition.* New York, 1957.

Hill, J. E. C. *Puritanism and Revolution.* New York, 1964.

Hinrich, C. *Ranke und die Geschichtstheologie der Goethezeit.* Göttingen, 1954.

Historical Statistics of the United States, Colonial to 1957. Washington, D.C., 1961.

Hobbes, T. *Leviathan.* Edited by M. Oakeshott. Oxford, 1960.

Hofmann, H. *Recht—Politik—Verfassung.* Frankfurt, 1986.

Hofstadter, R. *Social Darwinism.* Philadelphia, 1944.

————. *The Age of Reform.* New York, 1955.

————. *The American Political Tradition and the Men Who Made It.* New York, 1961.

————. *The Idea of a Party System: The Rise of Legitimate Opposition in the United States, 1780–1840.* Berkeley, Calif., 1969.

————. *America at 1750.* New York, 1972.

Hofstadter, R., and W. Smith, eds. *American Higher Education: A Documentary History.* 2 vols. Chicago, 1961.

Holbrook, C. A. "Edwards and the Ethical Question." *Harvard Theological Review,* LX (1967), 163–75.

Holcombe, A. N. *Our More Perfect Union: From Eighteenth Century Principles to Twentieth Century Practice.* Cambridge, Mass., 1950.

Holloway, M. *Heavens on Earth.* New York, 1966.

Holst, H. E. von. *Verfassung und Demokratie der Vereinigten Staaten von Amerika.* 2 vols. 1878; rpr. Berlin, 1884.

Hook, S. *Common Sense and the Fifth Amendment.* Chicago, 1957.

Hooker, R. *Of the Laws of Ecclesiastical Polity.* Edited by J. Keble. 3 vols. Oxford, 1888.

Hooker, T. "Application of Redemption." In *The Puritans,* edited by P. Miller and T. Johnson. New York, 1963.

Horwitz, M. *The Transformation of American Law, 1780–1860.* Cambridge, Mass., 1980.

Hotwitz, R., ed. *The Moral Foundations of the American Revolution.* Charlottesville, Va., 1977.

Howe, J. R. *The Changing Political Thought of John Adams.* Princeton, 1966.

Howe, D. W. "The Political Psychology of 'The Federalist.'" *William and Mary Quarterly,* XLIV (1987), 485–509.

Hughs, J. R. T. *Social Control in the Colonial Economy.* Charlottesville, Va., 1976.

Hume, D. *Philosophical Works.* Edited by T. H. Green and T. H. Grose. 4 vols. Aalen, 1964.

————. *Political Essays.* Edited by C. W. Hendel. New York, 1953.

Humphreys, R. H. "The Rule of Law and the American Revolution." *Law Quarterly Review,* LIII (1937), 80–98.

Hunt, G. *The History of the Seal of the United States.* Washington, D.C., 1909.

Huntington, S. P. "Postindustrial Politics: How Benign Will It Be?" *Comparative Politics,* VI (1973–74), 163–92.

————. *American Politics: The Promise of Disharmony.* Cambridge, Mass., 1981.

Hutchinson, T. *The History of the Colony and the Province of Massachusetts Bay.* Edited by L. S. Mayo. Cambridge, Mass., 1936.

Hutson, J. H. "John Adams' Title Campaign." *New England Quarterly,* XLI (1968), 30–39.

———. "Country, Court and Constitution: Antifederalism and the Historians." *William and Mary Quarterly,* XXXVIII (1981), 337–68.

Hutson, J. *John Adams and the Diplomacy of the American Revolution.* Lexington, Ky., 1980.

Hyneman, C. S., and G. W. Carey, eds. *A Second Federalist.* New York, 1967.

Hyneman, C. S., and D. S. Lutz, eds. *American Policy Writing During the Founding Era, 1760–1805.* 2 vols. Indianapolis, 1983.

Iacuzzi, A. *John Adams: Scholar.* New York, 1952.

Irelan, J. R. *History of the Life, Administration and Times of John Quincy Adams.* Chicago, 1886.

Isaac, R. "Preachers and Patriots: Popular Culture and the Revolution in Virginia." In *Explorations in the History of American Radicalism,* edited by A. F. Young. DeKalb, 1976.

Jackson, H. F. *Scholar in the Wilderness: Francis Adrian van der Kemp.* Syracuse, N.Y., 1963.

Jacob, M. C. *The Radical Enlightenment: Pantheists, Freemasons and Republicans.* London, 1981.

Jacobs, P., and S. Landau, eds. *The New Radicals.* New York, 1967.

Jaeger, W. W. *Theologie der frühen griechischen Denker.* Darmstadt, 1964.

Jameson, J. F. *The American Revolution Considered as a Social Movement.* Princeton, 1926.

Janowitz, M. *The Reconstruction of Patriotism.* Chicago, 1983.

Jaspers, K. *Philosophie.* 3 vols. Berlin, 1932.

Jay, J. *Correspondence and Public Papers of John Jay.* Edited by H. P. Johnston. 4 vols. New York, 1890–93.

Jefferson, T. *Writings.* Edited by P. L. Ford. 20 vols. New York, 1892–99.

———. *Papers.* Edited by J. P. Boyd. 24 vols. Princeton, 1950–.

———. *Political Writings.* Edited by E. Dumbauld, New York, 1955.

Jensen, M. "The Idea of a National Government During the Revolution." *Political Science Quarterly,* LVIII (1943), 356–79.

———. *The Articles of Confederation.* Madison, Wis., 1948.

———. *The New Nation.* New York, 1950.

———. "Democracy and the American Revolution." *Huntington Library Quarterly,* XX (1957), 321–41.

———. *The Founding of a Nation.* New York, 1968.

———, ed. *American Colonial Documents to 1776.* New York, 1955. Vol. IX of D. C. Douglas, ed., *English Historical Documents.* 12 vols.

Jensen, M., *et al.,* eds. *The Documentary History of the Ratification of the Constitution.* 16 vols. Madison, Wis., 1976–.

Johnson, E. A. *The Foundations of American Economic Freedom, Government and Enterprise with Age of Washington.* Minneapolis, 1973.

Jonas, H. *Gnosis und spätantiker Geist.* 2 vols. Göttingen, 1934–35.

———. *Zwischen Nichts und Ewigkeit.* Göttingen, 1963.

Jones, H. M. *America and French Culture, 1750–1848.* Chapel Hill, N.C., 1927.

———. *The Pursuit of Happiness.* Cambridge, Mass., 1953.

Jordan, W. D. *White Over Black.* Chapel Hill, N.C., 1968.

Journal of the Convention for Framing a Constitution of Government for the State of Massachusetts Bay. Boston, 1832.

Jouvenel, B. de. *Sovereignty.* Chicago, 1957.

———. *De la souveraineté.* Paris, 1955.

Kagle, S. "Instrument for Ambition: The Diaries of John Adams." Ph.D. dissertation, Michigan State University, 1968.

Kammen, M. G., ed. *Politics and Society in Colonial America.* New York, 1967.

———. *A Season of Youth.* New York, 1979.

———. *Spheres of Liberty: Changing Perceptions of Liberty in American Culture.* Madison, Wis., 1986.

———. *A Machine That Would Go.* New York, 1986.

Kant, I. *Werke in 10 Bänden.* Edited by W. Weischedel. Darmstadt, 1956–64.

Kaplan, L. S. "Jefferson's Foreign Policy and Napoleon's Idéologues." *William and Mary Quarterly,* XIX (1962), 344–59.

Katz, S. N., ed. *Colonial America: Essays in Politics and Social Development.* Boston, 1971.

Keller, H. G. *Die Wurzeln der amerikanischen Demokratie.* Bern, 1958.

Kelley, R. "Ideology and Political Culture From Jefferson to Nixon." In *American Historical Review,* LXXXII (1977), 531–62.

———. *The Cultural Pattern of American Politics.* New York, 1979.

Kendall, W., and G. W. Carey. *The Basic Symbols of the American Political Tradition.* Baton Rouge, 1970.

Kennedy, D. M., ed. *Progressivism.* Boston, 1971.

Kenyon, C. M. "Alexander Hamilton: Rousseau of the Right." *Political Science Quarterly,* LXXIII (1958), 161–78.

———. "Republicanism and Radicalism in the American Revolution: An Old-Fashioned Interpretation." *William and Mary Quarterly,* XIX (1962), 153–82.

———. "Men of Little Faith: The Antifederalists on the Nature of Representative Government." *William and Mary Quarterly,* XII (1965), 3–43.

———, ed. *The Antifederalists.* Indianapolis, 1966.

Kenyon, J. P., ed. *The Stuart Constitution.* Cambridge, Mass., 1966.

Kerber, L. K. *Federalists in Dissent.* Ithaca, N.Y., 1970.

———. "The Republican Ideology of the Revolutionary Generation." *American Quarterly,* XXXVII (1985), 474–95.

Kern, F. *Gottesgnadentum und Widerstandsrecht im frühen Mittelalter.* Darmstadt, 1973.

Kesler, C. R., ed. *Saving the Revolution: The Federalist Papers and the American Founding.* New York, 1987.

Key, V. O., Jr. *Public Opinion and American Democracy.* New York, 1961.

———. *The Responsible Electorate.* Cambridge, Mass., 1966.

Kilian, H. *Das enteignete Bewußtsein.* Neuwied, 1971.

Kirk, R. *The Conservative Mind.* Chicago, 1960.

Kirschner, D. S. "The Ambiguous Legacy: Social Justice and Social Control in the Progressive Era." *Historical Reflections,* II (1975), 69–88.

Kliger, S. *The Goths in England: A Study in Seventeenth and Eighteenth Century Thought.* Cambridge, Mass., 1952.

Klimowsky, E. *Die englische Gewaltenteilungslehre bis zu Montesquieu.* Berlin, 1927.

Kluckhohn, C. "The Evaluations of Contemporary American Values." *Daedalus,* LXXXVII (1938), 78–109.

Knoche, U. "Der römische Ruhmesgedanke." In *Römische Wertbegriffe,* edited by H. Oppermann. Darmstadt, 1967.

Knollenberg, B. *Origins of the American Revolution, 1759–1766.* New York, 1960.

———. "John Dickinson vs. John Adams 1774–1776." *Proceedings of the American Philosophical Society,* CVII (1963), 138–44.

———, ed. "The Revolutionary Correspondence of Nathanael Green and John Adams." *Rhode Island History,* I (1942), 45–55, 73–83.

Kobylka, J. F., and B. K. Carter. "Madison, The Federalist, and the Constitutional Order: Human Nature and Institutional Structure." *Polity,* XX (1987), 190–208.

Koch, A. G. *Republican Religion: The American Revolution and the Cult of Reason.* New York, 1933.

Koch, A. *The Philosophie of Thomas Jefferson.* New York, 1943.

———. *Jefferson and Madison.* New York, 1950.

———. *Power, Morals, and the Founding Fathers.* Ithaca, N.Y., 1961.

———. *Madison's "Advice to my Country."* Princeton, 1966.

Koebner, R. *Empire.* Cambridge, Eng., 1961.

Kohn, H. *American Nationalism.* New York, 1957.

Korchin, P., ed. *The American Revolution and Eighteenth Century Culture.* New York, 1982.

Kornhauser, W. *The Politics of Mass Society.* Glencoe, Ill., 1959.

Kramer, E. F. "John Adams, Elbridge Gerry, and the Origins of the XYZ Affair." *Essex Institute Historical Collections,* XCIV (1958), 57–68.

Kramnick, I. "Republican Revisionism Revisited." *American Historical Review,* LXXXVII (1982), 628–69.

——. "The 'Great National Discussion': The Discourses of Politics in 1787." *William and Mary Quarterly,* XLV (1988), 3–32.

Kraus, M. *The Writing of the American History.* Norman, Okla., 1953.

Krippendorf, E. "Amerikas verlorene Ziele." *Die Neue Gesellschaft,* IX (1962), 295–305.

Kristol, I. *On the Democratic Idea in America.* New York, 1972.

Kurtz, S. G. *The Presidency of John Adams.* Philadelphia, 1957.

——. "The French Mission of 1799–1800: Concluding Chapter in the Statecraft of John Adams." *Political Science Quarterly,* LXXX (1965), 543–57.

——. "The Political Science of John Adams: A Guide to his Statecraft." *William and Mary Quarterly,* XXV (1968), 605–13.

Kurtz, S. G., and J. H. Hutson. *Essays on the American Revolution.* Chapel Hill, N.C., 1973.

Labaree, L. W. *Royal Government in America.* New Haven, Conn., 1930.

La Feber, W. *The New Empire: An Interpretation of American Expansion, 1860–1898.* Ithaca, N.Y., 1963.

Landes, D. S. *The Unbound Prometheus: Technological Change and Industrial Development in Western Europe from 1750 to the Present.* Cambridge, Eng., 1969.

Landi, A. "Madison's Political Theory." *The Political Science Review,* VI (1976), 73–111.

Lane, R. E. *Political Life.* Glencoe, Ill., 1959.

——. *Political Ideology.* New York, 1962.

Langdon, G. D. *Pilgrim Colony: A History of New Plymouth 1620–1691.* New Haven, Conn., 1966.

La Palombara, J. "Decline of Ideology: A Dissent and an Interpretation." *American Political Science Review,* LX (1966), 5–16.

Larkin, P. *Property in the Eighteenth Century.* Dublin, 1930.

Laslett, J. H. M., and S. M. Lipset, eds. *Failure of a Dream: Essays in the History of American Socialism.* Garden City, N.Y., 1974.

——. *The People's Choice.* New York, 1968.

Leavelle, A. B. "James Wilson and the Relation of the Scottish Metaphysics to American Political Thought." *Political Science Quarterly,* LVII (1942), 394–410.

Lehmann, K. *Thomas Jefferson: American Humanist.* New York, 1947.

Lenk, K., ed. *Ideologie.* 2nd ed. Neuwied, 1964.

328

Lerner, M. "Constitution and Court as Symbols." *Yale Law Journal,* XLVI (1937), 1290–1319.

Leuchtenburg, W. E. *Franklin D. Roosevelt and the New Deal, 1932–1940.* New York, 1963.

Levinson, S. V. "'The Constitution' in American Civil Religion." *Supreme Court Review* (1979), 123 51.

Levy, L. W. *The Law of the Commonwealth and Chief Justice Shaw.* Cambridge, Mass., 1957.

Linares, F. *Der Held.* Bonn, 1967.

Lincoln, A. *Collected Works.* Edited by R. P. Basler. 9 vols. New Brunswick, N.J., 1953–55.

Lindsay, A. D. *The Modern Democratic State.* London, 1955.

Link, E. P. *Democratic-Republican Societies, 1790–1800.* New York, 1942.

Lippmann, W. *The Public Philosophy.* London, 1955.

Lipset, S. M. *Political Man.* Garden City, N.Y., 1959.

———. *The First New Nation.* New York, 1963.

———. "Some Further Comments on 'The End of Ideology.'" *American Political Science Review,* LX (1966), 17–18.

Livermore, S. *The Twilight of Federalism: The Disintegration of the Federalist Party, 1815–1830.* Princeton, 1962.

Livingstone, W., *et al. The Independent Reflector, New York, 1752–1753.* Edited by M. M. Klein. Cambridge, Mass., 1963.

Locke, J. *An Essay Concerning Human Understanding.* Edited by A. C. Fraser. 2 vols. New York, 1959.

Lockridge, K. A. "Land, Population and the Evolution of New England Society, 1630–1790." *Past and Present,* XXXIX (1968), 62–80.

———. "Social Change and the Meaning of the American Revolution." *Journal of Social History,* VI (1973), 403–39.

Lokken, R. N. "The Concept of Democracy in Colonial Political Thought." *William and Mary Quarterly,* XVI (1959), 568–80.

Lonergan, B. J. *Insight.* London, 1963.

Longeley, R. S. "Mob Activities in Revolutionary Massachusetts." *New England Quarterly,* VI (1933), 98–130.

Loring, J., ed. *The Hundred Boston Orations Appointed by the Municipal Authorities.* Boston, 1852.

Love, W. D. *The Fast and Thanksgiving Days of New England.* Boston, 1895.

Lovejoy, A. O. *The Great Chain of Being.* New York, 1960.

Lovejoy, D. S. "Rights Imply Equality: The Case Against Admiralty Jurisdiction in America, 1764–1776." *William and Mary Quarterly,* XVI (1959), 459–84.

Lowi, T. J. *The End of Liberalism.* New York, 1969.

————. *The Politics of Disorder.* New York, 1971.

Lubell, S. *The Future of American Politics.* New York, 1955.

Luckmann, T. *The Invisible Religion.* New York, 1967.

Lüthy, H. "Tugend und Menschenrechte." *Merkur,* CCCVIII (1974), 23–36; CCCIX (1974), 117–35.

Lutz, D. S. "The Relative Influence of European Writers on Late Eighteenth Century American Political Thought." *American Political Science Review,* LXXVII (1984), 189–97.

————. *Popular Consent and Popular Control: Whig Political Theory in the Early State Constitutions.* Baton Rouge, 1980.

Lynd, S. *Intellectual Origins of American Radicalism.* New York, 1968.

Lynn, K. S. *The Comic Tradition in America.* Garden City, 1958.

McCarthy, D. J. "James Wilson and American Republicanism." Ph.D. dissertation, University of Notre Dame, 1983.

McCoy, D. R. *The Elusive Republic: Political Economy in Jeffersonian America.* Chapel Hill, N.C., 1980.

McDonald, F. *The Presidency of Thomas Jefferson.* Lawrence, Kan., 1976.

Machiavelli, N. *Discourses.* New York, 1940.

McKeon, R. "The Development of the Concept of Property in Political Philosophy: A Study of the Background of the Constitution." *Ethics,* XLVIII (1938), 297–366.

McKitrick, E. L., ed. *Slavery Defended.* Englewood Cliffs, N.J., 1963.

McLaughlin, A. C. "Social Compact and Constitutional Construction." *American Historical Review,* V (1900), 467–90.

————. *The Confederation and the Constitution, 1783–1789.* New York, 1905.

————. *The Foundations of American Constitutionalism.* New York, 1932.

————. *A Constitutional History of the United States.* New York, 1936.

Maclear, J. F. "'The True American Union' of Church and State: The Reconstruction of the Theoretic Tradition." *Church History,* XXIX (1959), 1, 41–62.

MacLeod, D. J. *Slavery, Race and the American Revolution.* London, 1974.

McLoughlin, W. G. *Revivals, Awakening and Reform: An Essay on Religious and Social Change in America, 1607–1977.* Chicago, 1980.

————. "The American Revolution as a Religious Revival. The Millennium in a Country." *New England Quarterly,* XL (1967), 99–110.

Macridis, R. C., and B. B. Brown. *Comparative Politics.* 3rd ed. Homewood, Ill., 1968.

McWilliams, W. *The Idea of Fraternity in America.* Berkeley, Calif., 1973.

Madison, J., and A. Hamilton, and J. Jay. *The Federalist Papers.*

Maier, P. "The Beginnings of American Republicanism, 1763–1776." In *The Development of Revolutionary Mentality.* Washington, D.C., 1972.

————. *From Resistance to Revolution: Colonial Radicals and the Development of American Opposition to Britain 1765–1776.* New York, 1972.

Mailer, N. *Armies of the Night.* New York, 1968.

Main, J. T. *The Social Structure of Revolutionary America.* Princeton, 1965.

Manion, C. "The Natural Law Philosophy on the Founding Fathers." Notre Dame, Ind., 1949.

Mann, T. *Lotte in Weimar.* Frankfurt, 1959.

————. "Freud und die Zukunft." In S. Freud, *Abriß der Psychoanalyse,* Frankfurt, 1953.

Manuel, F. E. *The Eighteenth Century Confronts the Gods.* Cambridge, Mass., 1959.

Marcuse, H. *Counterrevolution and Revolt.* Boston, 1972.

Marmon, S. M. "Sword of Damocles: The Federalist, the Antifederalists, and the American Experiment With the Good Republic." Ph.D. dissertation, University of Texas, 1983.

Marshall, J. *The Life of George Washington.* 5 vols. Philadelphia, 1804–1807.

Marshall, P. "Radicals, Conservatives and the American Revolution." *Past and Present,* XXIII (1962), 44–56.

Martin, J. W. *Public Space: Congress and the Republican Political Tradition.* Amherst, Mass., 1984.

Marx, K. *Die deutsche Ideologie.* Berlin, 1953.

————. *Werke.* Edited by H. J. Lieber. 2 vols. Darmstadt, 1962–.

Marx, K., and F. Engels. *The Civil War in the United States.* New York, 1961.

Mathews, A. "Celebrations of Washington's Birthday." *Colonial Society of Massachusetts Publication* (1906), 252–58.

Matson, C., and P. Onuf. "Toward a Republican Empire: Interest and Ideology in Revolutionary America." *American Quarterly,* XXXVII (1985), 486–531.

Maurer, R. *Platons "Staat" und die Demokratie.* Berlin, 1970.

May, E. R. *American Imperialism.* New York, 1968.

————. *Imperial Democracy.* New York, 1961.

Mead, S. E. "The Nation with the Soul of a Church." *Church History,* XXXVI (1967), 262–83.

Mellen, C. *John Adams: The Statesman of the American Revolution.* Boston, 1898.

Mellou, M. T. *Early American Views on Negro Slavery.* Boston, 1934.

Merk, F. *Manifest Destiny and Mission in American History.* New York, 1963.

Merle, C. *Human Nature in American Thought: A History.* Madison, Wis., 1980.

Meyers, M. *The Jacksonian Persuasion: Politics and Belief.* Stanford, Calif., 1957.

Michels, R. *Der Patriotismus*. Munich, 1929.

Middlekauff, R. *Ancients and Axioms: Secondary Education in Eighteenth Century New England*. New Haven, Conn., 1963.

———. "Piety and Intellect in Puritanism." *William and Mary Quarterly*, XXII (1965), 435–56.

———. *The Glorious Cause: The American Revolution, 1763–1789.*

Middleton, C. *Miscellaneous Works*. 2nd ed. London, 1755.

Miller, H. D. *George Mason, Constitutionalist*. Cambridge, Mass., 1938.

Miller, J. C. *Origins of the American Revolution*. Boston, 1943.

———. *Triumph of Freedom, 1775–1783*. Boston, 1948.

———. *Alexander Hamilton*. New York, 1959.

———. *The Federalist Era, 1789–1801*. New York, 1960.

———. *Sam Adams*. Stanford, Calif., 1960.

Miller, P. *Jonathan Edwards*. New York, 1949.

———. *Roger Williams: His Contribution to the American Tradition*. 1953; rpr. New York, 1970.

———. *Errand into the Wilderness*. Cambridge, Mass., 1956.

———. "The Great Awakening from 1740–1750." *Encounter* (1956), 5ff.

———. *The New England Mind*. 2 vols. Boston, 1961.

———. "From Covenant to the Revival." In *The Shaping of American Religion*. Princeton, 1961. Vol. I of J. W. Smith and A. L. Jamison, eds., *Religion in American Life*. 4 vols.

———. *The Life of the Mind in America*. New York, 1965.

———. *Nature's Nation*. Cambridge, Mass., 1967.

———, ed. "Jonathan Edwards' Sociology of the Great Awakening." *New England Quarterly*, XXI (1948), 50–77.

Miller, P., and T. Johnson, eds. *The Puritans*. 2 vols. New York, 1963.

Miller, W., ed. *Men in Business: Essays on the History of Entrepreneurship*. Cambridge, Mass., 1952.

Mills, C. W. *The Sociological Imagination*. New York, 1959.

Mitchell, B. *Alexander Hamilton*. 2 vols. New York, 1957–62.

Mommsen, T. *Römisches Staatsrecht*. Darmstadt, 1971.

Monaghan, F. *John Jay*. New York, 1955.

Monsen, R. J. *Modern American Capitalism*. Boston, 1963.

"Monuments and Memorials." In *Encyclopedia Britannica*. 15th ed.

Moore, B. *Social Origins of Dictatorship and Democracy*. New York, 1963.

Moorhead, J. D. *American Apocalypse: Yankee Protestants and the Civil War, 1860–1896*. New Haven, Conn., 1978.

Morais, H. M. *Deism in Eighteenth Century America*. New York, 1934.

Morey, W. C. "The Genesis of a Written Constitution." *Annals of the American*

Academy of Political and Social Science, I (1891), 529–57.

———. "The First State Constitutions." *Annals of the American Academy of Political and Social Science,* IV (1893), 201–32.

Morgan, E. S. "Colonial Ideas of Parliamentary Power, 1764–1766." *William and Mary Quarterly,* 5 (1948), 311–41.

———. "Thomas Hutchinson and the Stamp Act." *New England Quarterly,* XXI (1948), 478ff.

———. *The Birth of the Republic, 1763–1789.* Chicago, 1956.

———. "The American Revolution: Revisions in Need of Revising." *William and Mary Quarterly,* XIV (1957), 3–15.

———. *The American Revolution: A Review of Changing Interpretations.* Washington, D.C., 1958.

———. "John Adams and the Puritan Tradition." *William and Mary Quarterly,* XXXIV (1961), 518–29.

———. "New England Puritanism: Another Approach." *William and Mary Quarterly,* XVIII (1961), 236–42.

———. *The Gentle Puritan.* New Haven, Conn., 1962.

———. "The American Revolution Considered as an Intellectual Movement." In *Paths of American Thought,* edited by A. M. Schlesinger and M. White. Boston, 1963.

———. *The Founding of Massachusetts.* Indianapolis, 1964.

———. *Visible Saints.* Ithaca, N.Y., 1965.

———. "The Puritan Ethic and the American Revolution." *William and Mary Quarterly,* XXIV (1967), 3–43.

———, ed. *Prologue to Revolution: Sources and Documents on the Stamp Act Crisis, 1764 to 1766.* Chapel Hill, N.C., 1959.

Morgan, E. S., and H. M. Morgan. *The Stamp Act Crisis: Prologue to Revolution.* Chapel Hill, N.C., 1953.

Morgan, R. J. "Madison's Analysis of the Sources of Political Authority." *American Political Science Review,* LXXV (1981), 613–25.

Morgan, S. E. "The American Revolution: Who Were the 'People'?" *New York Review of Books,* 1976, 29–33.

Morgan, W. *Memoirs of the Life of the Revolutionary Richard Price.* London, 1815.

Morison, S. E. *A History of the Constitutions of Massachusetts.* Boston, 1917.

———. "The Struggle over the Adoption of the Constitution of Massachusetts, 1780." *Proceedings of the Massachusetts Historical Society,* L (1917), 353–411.

———. "Elbridge Gerry: Gentleman-Democrat." *New England Quarterly,* II (1929), 6–33.

———. *The Intellectual Life of Colonial New England.* Ithaca, N.Y., 1960.

———. "John Adams and the Puritan Tradition." *New England Quarterly,* XXXIV (1961), 518–29.

———, ed. *Sources and Documents Illustrating the American Revolution, 1764–1788.* New York, 1965.

———. *The Oxford History of the American People.* New York, 1965.

Morison, S. E., and H. S. Commager. *The Growth of the American Republic.* 2 vols. New York, 1960.

Morris, B. F. *Christian Life and Character of the Civil Institutions of the United States.* Philadelphia, 1864.

Morris, R. B. "The Confederation Period and the American Historian." *William and Mary Quarterly,* XIII (1956), 139–56.

———. "Class Struggle and the American Revolution." *William and Mary Quarterly,* XIX (1962), 3–29.

———, ed. *The Era of the American Revolution.* New York, 1939.

Morse, A. D. "The Politics of John Adams." *American Historical Review,* IV (1899), 292–312.

———. *The Federalist Party in Massachusetts to the Year 1800.* Princeton, 1909.

Morse, J. T., Jr. *John Adams.* Boston, 1884.

Morton, R. L. *Colonial Virginia.* Chapel Hill, N.C., 1960.

Mullett, C. F. "Coke and the American Revolution." *Economica,* XII (1932), 457–71.

———. *Fundamental Law and the American Revolution, 1760–1776.* New York, 1933.

———. "Classical Influences on the American Revolution." *Classical Journal,* XXXV (1939), 92–104.

Murdock, K. B. *Increase Mather.* Cambridge, Mass., 1925.

———. *Literature and Theology in Colonial New England.* New York, 1963.

Murray, J. C. *We Hold These Truths.* New York, 1960.

Murrin, J. M. "The Legal Transformation: The Bench and Bar of Eighteenth Century Massachusetts." In *Colonial America,* edited by S. N. Katz. Boston, 1971.

———. Review Essay. *History and Theory.* XI (1972), 226–75.

Myrdal, G. *An American Dilemma.* New York, 1944.

Nagel, P. C. *This Sacred Trust: American Nationality, 1798–1898.* New York, 1971.

Namier, L. B. *The Structure of Politics at the Accession of George III.* London, 1957.

———. *Charles Townshend: His Character and Career.* Cambridge, Eng., 1959.

———. *England in the Age of the American Revolution.* London, 1961.

Nash, G. B., ed. *Class and Society in Early America*. Englewood Cliffs, N.J., 1970.

Natch, N. O. *The Sacred Cause of Liberty*. New Haven, Conn., 1977.

Nedham, M. *The Excellencie of a Free State*. Edited by R. Baron. London, 1767.

Nelson, W. H. "The Revolutionary Character of the American Revolution." *American Historical Review*, LXX (1964–65), 998–1014.

Nettles, C. P. *The Roots of American Civilization*. New York, 1938.

Neumann, F. *Introduction to Montesquieu: The Spirit of the Laws*. New York, 1949.

Nevins, A. *The American States During and After the Revolution, 1775–1789*. New York, 1924.

————. *Ordeal of the Union*. 8 vols. New York, 1947–71.

Newcomer, L. N. *The Embattled Farmers: A Massachusetts Countryside in the American Revolution*. New York, 1953.

Newfield, J. A. *Prophetic Minority*. New York, 1967.

Nicholas, H. "Franklin, Jefferson and the English Radicals at the End of the Eighteenth Century." *Proceedings of the American Philosophical Society*, XCVIII (1954), 406–26.

Niebuhr, H. R. *The Kingdom of God in America*. New York, 1959.

Niebuhr, R. *The Irony of American History*. New York, 1952.

————. *The Godly and the Ungodly*. London, 1958.

————. *The Children of the Light and the Children of the Darkness*. New York, 1960.

Nietzsche, F. *Werke*. Edited by K. Schlechta. 3 vols. Darmstadt, 1966.

Niles, H. *Niles' Weekly Register*. 75 vols. Baltimore, 1811–49.

North, D. C. *The Economic Growth of the United States*. Englewood Cliffs, N.J., 1961.

Nye, R. B. *The Almost Chosen People*. East Lansing, Mich., 1966.

Olson, A. G. "The British Government and Colonial Union, 1754." *William and Mary Quarterly*, XVII (1960), 22–34.

Opie, J., ed. *Jonathan Edwards and the Enlightenment*. Lexington, Ky., 1969.

Orwell, G., and R. Reynolds, eds. *British Pamphleteers*. 2 vols. London, 1948–51.

Osgood, H. L. *The American Colonies in the Eighteenth Century*. 3 vols. New York, 1924.

————. *The American Colonies in the Seventeenth Century*. 3 vols. New York, 1930.

Ostrom, V. *The Political Theory of a Compound Republic: Designing the American Experiment*. Bloomington, 1969.

Paine, T. *The Complete Writings*. Edited by P. S. Foner. 2 vols. New York, 1945.

Palmer, R. R. "Notes on the Use of the Word 'Democracy' 1789–1799." *Political Science Quarterly,* LXVIII, pp. 203–26.

———. "The Dubious Democrat: Thomas Jefferson in Bourbon France." *Political Science Quarterly,* LXXII (1957), 388–404.

———. *The Age of the Democratic Revolution: A Political History of Europe and America, 1760–1880.* 2 vols. Princeton, 1959–64.

Pares, R. *King George III and the Politicians.* Oxford, 1953.

Pargellis, S. "The Theory of Balanced Government." In *The Constitution Reconsidered,* edited by Conyers Read. New York, 1938.

Parish, P. J. *The American Civil War.* New York, 1973.

Parrington, V. L. *Main Currents in American Thought.* 2 vols. New York, 1954.

Parsons, T. *The Social System.* Glencoe, Ill., 1951.

Pascal, B. *Pensées.* Classiques Garnier. Paris, n.d.

———. *Pensées.* Edited by Chevalier. Paris, n.d.

Paul, R. S. "Hooker, Puritanism, and Democracy." *Hartford Quarterly,* VII (1967), 60–80.

Paynes, J. "John Adams: On the Principles of the Political Science." *Political Science Reviewer* (1976), 35–72.

Peckham, H. H. *The War of Independence.* Chicago, 1958.

Peele, G. *Revival and Reaction: The Right in Contemporary America.* Oxford, 1984.

Pells, R. H. *Radical Visions and American Dreams.* New York, 1973.

Perkins, B. *Prologue to War: England and the United States, 1805–1812.* Berkeley, Calif., 1961.

Perry, R. B. *Puritanism and Democracy.* New York, 1964.

Persons, S. "The Cyclical Theory of History in the 18th Century America." *American Quarterly,* VI (1954), 147–63.

Pessen, E. *Jacksonian America.* Homewood, Ill., 1969.

Peterson, M. D. *The Jefferson Image in the American Mind.* New York, 1960.

———, ed. *Democracy, Liberty and Property.* Indianapolis, 1966.

———. *Adams and Jefferson: A Revolutionary Dialogue.* Athens, Ga., 1976.

Plamenatz, J. R. *Ideology.* London, 1970.

Plato. *The Republic.* London, 1969–70.

Plucknett, T. F. T. "Bonham's Case and Judicial Review." *Harvard Law Review,* XL (1926–27), 30–70.

Plumb, J. H. "The Fascination of Republican Virtue Amongst the Known and the Unknown." In *The Development of Revolutionary Mentality.* Washington, D.C., 1972.

Pocock, J. G. A. *The Ancient Constitution and the Feudal Law: A Study of English Historical Thought in the Seventeenth Century.* Cambridge, Eng., 1957.

BIBLIOGRAPHY

————. *Politics, Language and Time.* New York, 1971.

————. "Virtue and Commerce in the Eighteenth Century." *Journal of Interdisciplinary History,* III (1972).

————. *The Machiavellian Moment.* Princeton, 1975.

————. *Virtue, Commerce, and History: Essays on Political Thought and History, Chiefly in the Eighteenth Century.* Cambridge, Eng., 1985.

Pole, J. R. "Suffrage and Representation in Massachusetts: A Statistical Note." *William and Mary Quarterly,* XVIV (1957), 560–92.

————. "Historians and the Problem of Early American Democracy." *American Historical Review,* LXVII (1961–62), 626–46.

————. *Political Representation in England and the Origins of the American Republic.* New York, 1966.

————. *The Seventeenth Century.* Charlottesville, Va., 1969.

————. *Paths to the American Past.* New York, 1979.

————. *Pursuit of Equality in American History.* Berkeley, 1978.

————. *American Individualism and the Promise of Progress.* Oxford, 1980.

Porter, B. *Critics of Empire.* New York, 1968.

Pound, R. *The Spirit of the Common Law.* Boston, 1963.

Powell, J. H., ed. "Calendar of the Letters from John Adams to Francis van der Kemp 1783–1825 in the Historical Society of Pennsylvania." *Pennsylvania Magazine of History and Biography,* LXVI (1942), 334–50.

Powell, S. C. *Puritan Village: The Formation of a New England Town.* Middletown, Conn., 1963.

Primm, J. N. *Economic Policy in the Development of a Western State: Missouri 1820 to 1860.* Cambridge, Mass., 1954.

Puhle, H.-J. "Der übergang zum organisierten Kapitalismus in den USA." In *Organisierter Kapitalismus,* edited by H. A. Winkler. Göttingen, 1974.

Pye, L. W. "Culture and Political Science." *Social Science Quarterly,* LII (1972), 285–96.

Pye, L. W., and S. Verba, eds. *Political Culture and Political Development.* Princeton, 1965.

Quarles, B. *The Negro in the American Revolution.* Chapel Hill, N.C., 1961.

Quincy, J., ed. *Reports of Cases Argued and Adjudged in the Superior Court . . . 1761 to 1772.* Boston, 1865.

Raglan, F. R. R. S. *The Hero: A Study in Tradition, Myth, and Drama.* London, 1936.

Ramsay, D. *History of the American Revolution.* Philadelphia, 1789.

Rank, O. *Der Mythos von der Geburt des Helden.* Leipzig, 1922.

Ranney, J. C. "The Bases of American Federalism." *William and Mary Quarterly,* III (1946), 1–35.

Rea, R. R. *The English Press in Politics, 1760–1774.* Lincoln, Nebr., 1963.

Read, C., ed. *The Constitution Reconsidered*. New York, 1938.

Rehm, W. *Experimentum Medietatis*. Munich, 1947.

Reich, C. *The Greening of America*. New York, 1970.

Reid, T. *Works*. Edited by W. Hamilton. 3 vols. Edinburgh, 1895.

Reitan, E. A., ed. *George III: Tyrant or Constitutional Monarch*. Boston, 1964.

Revel, J.-F. *Without Marx and Jesus*. Garden City, N.Y., 1970.

Rezneck, S. "The Rise and Early Development of Industrial Consciousness in the United States, 1760–1830." *Journal of Economic and Business History*, IV (1931–32), 784–811.

Rice, H. C. *The Adams Family in Auteuil, 1784–1785*. Boston, 1956.

Richardson, J. M., ed. *A Compilation of the Messages and Papers of the Presidents, 1789–1897*. Washington, D.C., 1896–99. 10 vols.

Richey, R., and D. G. Jones. *American Civil Religion*. New York, 1974.

Riemer, M. *American Political Theory V. 1 The Democratic Experiment*. New York, 1967.

Riley, I. W. *American Philosophy: The Early Schools*. New York, 1907.

Ritcheson, C. R. *British Politics and the American Revolution*. Norman, Okla., 1954.

Robathan, D. M. "John Adams and the Classics." *New England Quarterly*, XIX (1946), 91–98.

Robbins, C. "'When It Is That Colonies May Turn Independent': An Analysis of the Environment and Politics of Francis Hutcheson (1694–1746)." *William and Mary Quarterly*, XI (1954), 214–51.

———. *The Eighteenth-Century Commonwealth Man: Studies in the Transmission, Development, and Circumstance of English Liberal Thought From the Restoration of Charles II Until the War with the Thirteen Colonies*. Cambridge, Mass., 1959.

———. "European Republicanism in the Century and a Half Before 1776." In *The Development of a Revolutionary Mentality*. Washington, 1972.

Robinson, D. L. *Slavery in the Structure of American Politics, 1765–1820*. New York, 1971.

Robinson, W. A. *Jeffersonian Democracy in New England*. New Haven, Conn., 1916.

Robson, E. *The American Revolution in its Political and Military Aspects, 1763–1783*. London, 1955.

Roosevelt, F. D. *The Public Papers and Addresses of Franklin Delano Roosevelt*. 13 vols. New York, 1938–50.

Rose, J. H., *et al.*, eds. *The Cambridge History of the British Empire*. Vol. I of 8 vols. Cambridge, Eng., 1929–.

Rossiter, C. L. *Seedtime of the Republic*. New York, 1953.

———. *Conservatism in America*. New York, 1955.

————. "The Legacy of John Adams." *Yale Review*, XLVI (1957), 528–50.

————. *Alexander Hamilton and the Constitution*. New York, 1964.

Roszak, T. *The Making of the Counter Culture*. New York, 1969.

————. *Where the Wasteland Ends*. New York, 1973.

Rozwenc, E. C., ed. *The Meaning of Jacksonian Democracy*. Boston, 1963.

————, ed. *The New Deal*. Boston, 1968.

Rush, B. *Selected Writings*. Edited by D. Runes. New York, 1947.

————. *Letters*. Edited by L. H. Butterfield. 2 vols. Princeton, 1951.

Rustow, D. A. "Philosophers and Kings: Studies in Leadership." *Daedalus*, XCVII (1968), 683–94.

Rutland, R. A. *The Birth of the Bill of Rights, 1776–1791*. Chapel Hill, N.C., 1955.

Rutmann, D. B. "God's Bridge Falling Down: 'Another Approach' to New England Puritanism Assayed." *William and Mary Quarterly*, XIX (1962), 408–21.

The Sacral Kingship. Studies in History of Religion, IV. London, 1959.

Salomon, D., ed. *LSD*. New York, 1966.

Salomon, G. "Heroworship." In *Encyclopedia of the Social Sciences*. Vol. 7. New York, 1955.

Sandburg, C. *Abraham Lincoln: The Prairie Years and the War Years*. New York, 1954.

Sanders, J. B. *Evolution of Executive Departments of the Continental Congress, 1774–1789*. Chapel Hill, N.C., 1935.

Sandoz, E. "The Civil Theology of Liberal Democracy: Locke and His Predecessors." *Journal of Politics*, XXXIV (1972), 2–36.

Sanford, C. I. *The Quest for Paradise*. Urbana, Ill., 1961.

Saveth, E. N., ed. *Understanding the American Past*. Boston, 1954.

Schattschneider, E. E. *The Semisovereign People*. New York, 1960.

Schechter. "The Early History of the Tradition of the Constitution." *American Political Science Review*, XXIX (1915), 707ff.

Scheler, M. "Vorbilder und Führer." *Schriften aus dem Nachlaß*, Vol. 1. Bern, 1957.

Schlesinger, A. M., Jr. *The Age of Jackson*. Boston, 1945.

————. *The Age of Roosevelt*. 3 vols. Boston, 1957–60.

————. "On Heroic Leadership: The Decline of Greatness." In *The Politics of Hope*. Boston, 1963.

————. "The Lost Meaning of 'The Pursuit of Happiness.'" *William and Mary Quarterly*, XXI (1964), 325–27.

————. *The Crisis of Confidence*. Boston, 1969.

————. *The Imperial Presidency*. Boston, 1973.

————. *The Cycles of American History*. Boston, 1986.

Schlesinger, A. M., Sr. "The American Revolution Reconsidered." *Political Science Quarterly*, XXXIV (1919), 63–75.

―――. *The Colonial Merchants and the American Revolution, 1763–1776.* New York, 1939.

―――. "Political Mobs and the American Revolution, 1767–1776." *Proceedings of the American Philosophical Society*, XCIX (1955), 244–50.

―――. *Prelude to Independence.* New York, 1958.

―――. *The Birth of the Nation.* London, 1969.

Schmitt, G. J., and R. K. Webking. "Revolutionaries, Antifederalists, and Federalists. Comments on Gordon Woods' Understanding of the American Founding." *Political Science Reviewer*, IX (1979), 195–229.

Schouler, J. *History of the United States of America Under the Constitution.* 7 vols. New York, 1894–1913.

Schramm, P. E. *Kaiser, Rom und Renovatio.* Darmstadt, 1957.

Schröder, H.-C. "Das Eigentumsproblem in den Auseinandersetzungen um die Verfassung von Massachusetts, 1775–1787." In *Eigentum und Verfassung: Zur Eigentumsdiskussion im ausgehenden 18. Jh.*, edited by R. Vierhaus. Göttingen, 1972.

Schumpeter, J. *Kapitalismus, Sozialismus und Demokratie.* 1940; rpr. Munich, 1950.

Schütz, A. *Collected Papers.* 3 vols. The Hague, 1962–66.

―――. *Der Sinnhafte Aufbau der sozialen Welt.* 2nd ed. Vienna, 1960.

Schuyler, R. L. *The Constitution of the United States.* New York, 1923.

―――. *Parliament and the British Empire.* New York, 1929.

Scott, W. R. *Francis Hutcheson.* Cambridge, Mass., 1900.

Sears, L. M. *George Washington and the French Revolution.* Detroit, 1960.

A Selection of Eulogies Pronounced in the Several States, in Honor of those Illustrious Patriots and Statesmen, John Adams and Thomas Jefferson. Hartford, Conn., 1826.

Sensabaugh, G. *Milton in Early America.* Princeton, 1964.

Sewell, R. H. *Ballots for Freedom: Antislavery Politics in the United States, 1837–60.* New York, 1976.

Shackleton, R. "Montesquieu, Bolingbroke, and the Separation of Powers." *French Studies*, III (1949), 25–38.

Shalope, R. E. "Toward a Republican Synthesis." *William and Mary Quarterly*, XXIX (1972), 49–80.

―――. "Thomas Jefferson's Republicanism and Antebellum Southern Thought." *Journal of Southern History*, XLII (1976), 537–45.

―――. "Republicanism and Early American Historiography." *William and Mary Quarterly*, XXXIX (1982), 334–56.

―――. *John Taylor of Caroline: Pastoral Republicanism.* Columbia, 1980.

Shattuck, C. G. "The True Meaning of the Term 'Liberty' in those Clauses in the Federal and State Constitutions Which Protect 'Life, Liberty and Property.'" *Harvard Law Review,* IV (1890–91), 365–92.

Shaw, P. *American Patriots and the Rituals of Revolution.* Cambridge, Mass., 1981.

———. *The Character of John Adams.* Chapel Hill, N.C., 1976.

Sheldon, G. W. *The Political Philosophy of Thomas Jefferson.* Baltimore, 1991.

Shils, E. "The End of Iedology?" *Encounter,* V (1955), 52–58.

Shoemaker, R. W. "'Democracy' and 'Republic' as Understood in Late Eighteenth Century America." *American Speech,* XLI (1966), 83–95.

Shonfield, A. *Geplanter Kapitalismus.* Cologne, 1969.

Shortreed, A. "The Antislavery Radicals: From Crusade to Revolution, 1840–1868." *Past and Present,* XVI (1959), 65–87.

Simpson, A. *Puritanism in Old and New England.* Chicago, 1955.

Skotheim, R. A. *American Intellectual Histories and Historians.* Princeton, 1966.

Slater, P. *The Pursuit of Loneliness.* Boston, 1970.

Smith, A. *Works.* 5 vols. Aalen, 1963.

Smith, E. A., ed. *The Religion of the Republic.* Philadelphia, 1971.

Smith, J. A. *The Spirit of American Government.* New York, 1907.

Smith, J. M. "President John Adams, Thomas Cooper and Sedition: A Case Study in Suppression." *Mississippi Valley Historical Review,* XLII (1955), 438–65.

———. "John Adams Pardons William Durrel: A Note on Sedition Proceedings, 1798–1800." *New York Historical Society Quarterly,* XL (1956), 176–81.

———. *Freedom's Fetters: The Alien and Sedition Laws and American Civil Liberties.* Ithaca, N.Y., 1956.

———, ed. *Seventeenth Century America.* Chapel Hill, N.C., 1959.

Smith, J. W., and A. L. Jamison, eds. *Religion in American Life.* Princeton, 1961.

Smith, P. *James Wilson.* Chapel Hill, N.C., 1956.

———. *John Adams.* 2 vols. Garden City, N.Y., 1962.

———. *A City Upon a Hill.* New York, 1966.

Smith, W. C. *The Meaning and End of Religion.* New York, 1965.

Somkin, F. *Unquiet Eagle: Memory and Desire in the Idea of American Freedom, 1815 to 1860.* New York, 1967.

Sonnemann, U. *Negative Anthropologie.* Hamburg, 1969.

Sparks, J. *Life of George Washington.* Boston, 1839.

Spector, M. M. *The American Department of the British Government, 1768–1782.* New York, 1940.

Spencer, H. R. *Constitutional Conflict in Provincial Massachusetts.* Columbus, Ohio, 1905.

Spengler, J. J. "Political Economy of Jefferson, Madison and Adams." In *American Studies in Honor of William Kenneth Boyd*, edited by D. K. Jackson. Durham, N.C., 1940.

Spurlin, P. M. *Montesquieu in America, 1760–1801*. Baton Rouge, 1940.

Stampp, K. M., ed. *Causes of the Civil War*. Englewood Cliffs, N.J., 1959.

Starobin, R. S. *Industrial Slavery in the Old South*. New York, 1970.

Stenzel, K. "Pascals Theorie des Divertissement." Ph.D. dissertation, Munich, 1966.

Stephen, L. *History of English Thought in the Eighteenth Century*. 2 vols. New York, 1962.

Stevens, J. *Observations on Government, Including some Animadversions on Mr. Adams' Defence of the Constitutions of Government.* . . . New York, 1787.

Stewart, D. H., and G. P. Clark. "Misanthrope or Humanitarian? John Adams in Retirement." *New England Quarterly*, XXVIII (1955), 216–36.

Storing, H. J. "The 'Other' Federalist Papers." *Political Science Reviewer*, VI (1976), 215–47.

———. *The Complete Anti-Federalist*. 7 vols. Chicago, 1977.

———. *What the Anti-Federalists Were For*. Chicago, 1981.

Stourzh, G. *Benjamin Franklin*. Chicago, 1954.

———. "Die tugendhafte Republik." In *Österreich und Europa*, edited by H. Hantsch. Graz, 1965.

———. *Alexander Hamilton and the Idea of Republican Government*. Stanford, Calif., 1970.

———. "Staatsformenlehre und Fundamentalgesetze in England und Nordamerika im 17. und 18. Jahrhundert." In *Herrschaftsverträge, Wahlkapitulationen, Fundamentalgesetze*, edited by R. Vierhaus. Göttingen, 1977.

Strout, C. *The New Heavens and New Earth: Political Religion in America*. New York, 1974.

Sumner, W. G. *The Financier and Finances of the American Revolution*. New York, 1892.

Swift, L. "Literary Work of John Adams." *Book Buyer*, XX (1900), 287–88.

Swisher, C. B. *The Growth of Constitutional Power in the United States*. Chicago, 1946.

———. *American Constitutional Development*. Boston, 1954.

Syrett, H. C. *Andrew Jackson*. Indianapolis, 1953.

Taeger, F. *Charisma*. 2 vols. Stuttgart, 1957–60.

Tate, T. W. *The Social Contract in America, 1774–1787*.

———. "Revolutionary Theory as a Conservative Instrument." *William and Mary Quarterly*, XX (1965), 375–91.

Taylor, R. J. *Western Massachusetts in the Revolution*. Providence, R.I., 1954.

———, ed. *Massachusetts: Colony to Commonwealth*. Chapel Hill, N.C., 1961.

Thorne, S. E. "Dr. Bonham's Case." *Law Quarterly Review,* LIV (1938), 545ff.

Thornton, W. J., ed. *The Pulpit of the American Revolution.* Boston, 1860.

Thorpe, F. N. "The Political Ideas of John Adams." *Pennsylvania Magazine,* LIV (1920), 1–46.

———. "Adams and Jefferson, 1826–1926." *North American Review,* CCXXIII (1926).

———. *The Federal and State Constitutions, Colonial Charters.* Washington, 1909.

Tipple, J., comp. *Crisis of the American Dream: A History of American Social Thought, 1920–1940.* New York, 1968.

Tocqueville, A. de. *Democracy in America.* Edited by P. Bradley. 2 vols. New York, 1945.

Tolles, F. B. "The American Revolution Considered as a Social Movement: A Re-Evaluation." *American Historical Review,* LX (1954), 1–12.

Tonsor, St. J., ed. *America's Continuing Revolution.* Garden City, N.Y., 1976.

Townsend, C. R. "The Thoughts of Samuel Adams." Ph.D. dissertation, University of Wisconsin, 1968.

Toynbee, A. J. *A Study of History.* 12 vols. London, 1934–61.

Trent, W. P., *et al.,* eds. *The Cambridge History of American Literature.* New York, 1917.

Trousson, R. *Le Théme de Promethée dans la litterature européenne.* Geneva, 1964.

Turner, F. J. *The Significance of the Frontier in American History.* Madison, Wis., 1894.

———. *The United States, 1830–1850: The Nation and Its Sections.* Englewood Cliffs, N.J., 1961.

Tuveson, E. L. *Redeemer Nation.* Chicago, 1968.

Tyler, M. C. *The Literary History of the American Revolution, 1763–1783.* 2 vols. New York, 1897.

Ubbelohde, C. *The Vice-Admiralty Courts and the American Revolution.* Chapel Hill, N.C., 1960.

Upton, R. F. *Revolutionary New Hampshire.* Hanover, N.H., 1936.

Vail, R. W. G. "A Check List of New England Election Sermons." *Proceedings of the American Antiquarian Society,* XLV (1935), 233–66.

Van Alstyne, R. W. *The Rising American Empire.* New York, 1960.

———. "Parliamentary Supremacy vs. Independence: Notes and Documents." *Huntington Library Quarterly,* XXVI (1963), 201–33.

Van Doren, C. C. *Secret History of the American Revolution.* New York, 1941.

———. *The Great Rehearsal: The Story of the Making and Ratifying of the Constitution of the United States.* New York, 1948.

Van Tassel, D. D. *Recording America's Past: An Interpretation of the Development of Historical Studies in America, 1607–1884.* Chicago, 1960.

Van Tyne, C. H. *The Loyalists in the American Revolution.* New York, 1929.

———. *A History of the Founding of the American Republic.* 2 vols. Boston, 1922–29.

Van Zandt, R. *The Metaphysical Foundations of American History.* The Hague, 1959.

Ver Steeg, C. L. "The American Revolution Considered as an Economic Movement." *Huntington Library Quarterly,* XX (1957), 361–72.

Vico, G. *Opere.* Milan, n.d.

Vile, M. J. C. *Constitutionalism and the Separation of Powers.* Oxford, 1967.

Voegelin, E. *Über die Form des amerikanischen Geistes.* Tübingen, 1928.

———. "Machiavelli's Prince: Background and Formation." *Review of Politics,* XIII (1951), 142–68.

———. *Order and History.* 4 vols. Baton Rouge, 1956–74.

———. *Die Neue Wissenschaft der Politik.* Munich, 1959.

———. *Anamnesis.* Munich, 1966.

———. "The Eclipse of Reality." In *Phenomenology and Social Reality,* edited by M. Natanson. The Hague, 1970.

———. "Equivalences of Experience and Symbolization in History." In *Eternita e Storia.* Florence, 1970.

Vossler, O. *Die amerikanischen Revolutionsideale in ihrem Verhältnis zu den europäischen.* Munich, 1929.

Wahlke, J. C., ed. *The Causes of the American Revolution.* Boston, 1962.

Walett, F. G. "The Massachusetts Council, 1766–1774: The Transformation of a Conservative Institution." *William and Mary Quarterly,* VI (1949), 605ff.

Walsh, C. M. *The Political Science of John Adams.* New York, 1915.

Walton, G. M., and J. F. Sheperd. *The Economic Rise of Early America.* Cambridge, Eng., 1979.

Walzel, O. *Das Prometheussymbol von Shaftesbury zu Goethe.* Leipzig, 1910.

Warner, W. L. *The Living and the Dead: A Study of the Symbolic Life of Americans.* New Haven, Conn., 1959.

Warren, C. *A History of the American Bar.* Boston, 1911.

———. "John Adams and the American Constitutions." *George Washington University Bulletin,* XXVI (1926).

———. *The Making of the Constitution.* Boston, 1928.

———. "Elbridge Gerry, James Warren, Mercy Warren, and the Ratification of the Federal Constitution in Massachusetts." *Proceedings of the Massachusetts Historical Society,* LXIV (1931), 143–64.

———. "How Politics Intruded into the Washington Centenary of 1832." *Proceedings of the Massachusetts Historical Society,* LXV (1932), 37–62.

———. *Congress, the Constitution, and the Supreme Court.* Boston, 1935.

BIBLIOGRAPHY

————. "Fourth of July Myths." *William and Mary Quarterly,* II (1945), 237–72.

————. "The Doctored Letters of John Adams." *Proceedings of the Massachusetts Historical Society,* LXVIII (1952), 160–70.

Warren, M. *The History of the Rise, Progress, and Termination of the American Revolution.* 3 vols. Boston, 1805.

Washington, G. *Writings.* Edited by J. C. Fitzpatrick. 39 vols. Washington, D.C., 1931–44.

Waters, J. J., and J. A. Schutz. "Patterns of Massachusetts Colonial Politics." *William and Mary Quarterly,* XXIV (1967), 543–67.

We, the People: The Story of the United States Capitol. Washington, D.C., 1963.

Weber, M. *Wirtschaft und Gesellschaft.* 2 vols. Cologne, 1964.

Weber-Schäfer, P. *Der Edle und der Weise.* Munich, 1963.

————. *Oikumene und Imperium.* Munich, 1968.

————. "'Sozial' und 'Rational.'" *Staat,* VII (1968), 17–40.

Webster, D. *Writings and Speeches.* 18 vols. Boston, 1903.

Webster, W. C. "Comparative Study of the State Constitutions of the American Revolution." *Annals of the American Academy of Political and Social Science,* IX (1897), 380–420.

Wector, Dixon. *The Hero in America: A Chronicle of Hero Worship.* New York, 1942.

Weems, M. L. *The Life of Washington.* Edited by M. Cunliffe. Cambridge, Mass., 1962.

Wehler, H.-U. "Der amerikanische Imperialismus vor 1914." In *Der moderne Imperialismus,* edited by W. J. Mommsen. Stuttgart, 1971.

————. *Aufstieg des amerikanischen Imperialismus.* Göttingen, 1974.

Weinberg, A. K. *Manifest Destiny.* Baltimore, 1935.

Weinstein, J. *The Corporate Ideal in the Liberal State, 1900–1918.* Boton, 1968.

Welch, S., and J. Comer, eds. *Public Opinion: Its Formation, Measurement, and Impact.* Palo Alto, Calif., 1975.

Wertenbaker, T. J. *The Puritan Oligarchy: The Founding of American Civilization.* New York, 1947.

————. *The Golden Age of Colonial Culture.* Ithaca, N.Y., 1959.

Wharton, F., ed. *The Revolutionary Diplomatic Correspondence of the United States.* 6 vols. Washington, D.C., 1889.

Wheeler, H. "Calvin's Case (1608) and the McIlwain-Schuyler Debate." *American Historical Review,* LXI (1956), 587–98.

White, L. D. *The Federalists.* New York, 1965.

————. *The Jeffersonians.* New York, 1965.

White, M. *The Philosophy of the American Revolution: A Historical and Analytic Study.* New York, 1978.

Whitehead, A. N. *Symbolism: Its Meaning and Effect.* New York, 1927.
———. *Science and the Modern World.* New York, 1967.
Widukind v. Korvey, *Rerum gestarum saxonicarum.* Hannoverae, 1882.
Wiebe, R. H. *The Search for Order.* New York, 1967.
Wilcox, A. R., ed. *Public Opinion and Political Attitudes.* New York, 1974.
Willey, B. *The Eighteenth Century Background.* Boston, 1961.
Williams, R[aymond]. *Culture and Society, 1780–1950.* 1958; rpr. New York, 1983.
Williams, R[oger]. *Works.* 3 vols. Providence, R.I., 1866–74.
Williams, W. A. *The Contours of American History.* Cleveland, 1961.
———. *The Roots of the Modern American Empire.* New York, 1969.
Williamson, C. *American Suffrage from Property to Democracy, 1760–1860.* Princeton, 1960.
Williamson, J. "The Professional Tours of John Adams in Maine." *Collections and Proceedings of the Maine Historical Society Portland,* I (1890), 301–308.
Williston, E. P., ed. *Eloquence of the United States.* 5 vols. Middletown, Conn., 1827.
Wills, G. *Inventing America: Jefferson's Declaration of Independence.* 1980.
———. *Explaining America: The Federalists.* Garden City, 1981.
———. *Cincinnatus: George Washington and the Enlightenment.* Garden City, N.Y., 1984.
Wilson, E. *Patriotic Gore: Studies in the Literature of the American Civil War.* New York, 1966.
Wilson, J. *Lectures on Law.* Philadelphia, 1804. Vol. I of *Works,* edited by B. Wilson.
———. *Works.* Edited by R. G. McGloskey. 2 vols. Cambridge, Mass., 1967.
Wilson, W. *The New Freedom.* Englewood Cliffs, N.J., 1961.
Wiltse, C. M. *John Calhoun.* 3 vols. Indianapolis, 1944–51.
———. *The Jeffersonian Tradition in American Democracy.* Chapel Hill, N.C., 1935.
Winkler, H. A., ed. *Die große Krise in Amerika: Vergleichende Studien zur politischen Sozialgeschichte, 1929–1939.* Göttingen, 1973.
———, ed. *Organisierter Kapitalismus.* Göttingen, 1974.
Winslow, O. E. *Master Roger Williams.* New York, 1957.
Wish, H. *The American Historian.* New York, 1960.
———, ed. *Antebellum.* New York, 1960.
Wolf, W. J. *The Almost Chosen People: A Study of the Religion of Abraham Lincoln.* Garden City, N.Y., 1959.
———. *Lincoln's Religion.* Boston, 1970.
Wood, G. S. "Rhetoric and Reality in the American Revolution." *William and Mary Quarterly,* XXIII (1966), 3–23.

———. *The Creation of the American Republic, 1776–1787.* Chapel Hill, N.C., 1969.

———, ed. *The Rising Glory of America (1760–1820).* New York, 1971.

———. *Representation in the American Revolution.* Charlottesville, Va., 1969.

Wood, J. *The History of the Administration of John Adams, Late President of the United States.* New York, 1802.

———. *A Correct Statement of the Various Sources From Which the History of the Administration of John Adams Was Compiled and the Motives for its Suppression by Col. Burr.* New York, 1802.

Woodward, W. E. *George Washington.* New York, 1926.

Wormuth, F. D. *The Origins of Modern Constitutionalism.* New York, 1949.

Wright, B. F. *American Interpretations of Natural Law: A Study in the History of Political Thought.* 1931; rpr. New York, 1962.

———. "Origins of the Separations of Power in America." *Economia,* XIII (1935), 169ff.

———. "The Early History of Written Constitutions in America." In *Essays in History and Political Theory.* Cambridge, 1936.

———. *The Growth of American Constitutional Law.* Boston, 1942.

Wright, C. *The Beginnings of Unitarianism in America.* Boston, 1955.

Wright, E. *Fabric of Freedom, 1763–1800.* New York, 1968.

———, ed. *Causes and Consequences of the American Revolution.* Chicago, 1966.

Wright, L. B. *Religion and Empire.* Chapel Hill, N.C., 1943.

———. "Thomas Jefferson and the Classics." *Proceedings of the American Philosophical Society,* LXXXVIII (1943), 223–33.

———. *The Cultural Life of the American Colonies, 1607–1763.* New York, 1957.

———. *The Atlantic Frontier.* Ithaca, N.Y., 1959.

Young, A. F., ed. *The Debate Over the Constitution.* Chicago, 1965.

———. *The American Revolution.* DeKalb, Ill., 1976.

Young, J. P. *The Politics of Affluence.* San Francisco, 1968.

Zuckerman, M. "The Social Context of Democracy in Massachusetts." *William and Mary Quarterly,* XXV (1968), 523–44.

Index

INDEX

INDEX